PARTICIPATORY DEMOCRACY, CIVIL SOCIETY AND SOCIAL EUROPE

PARTICIPATORY DEMOCRACY, CIVIL SOCIETY AND SOCIAL EUROPE

A Legal and Political Perspective

Gautier Busschaert

intersentia
Cambridge – Antwerp – Portland

Intersentia Ltd
Sheraton House | Castle Park
Cambridge | CB3 0AX | United Kingdom
Tel.: +44 1223 370 170 | Fax: +44 1223 370 169
Email: mail@intersentia.co.uk
www.intersentia.com | www.intersentia.co.uk

Distribution for the UK and Ireland:
NBN International
Airport Business Centre, 10 Thornbury Road
Plymouth, PL6 7 PP
United Kingdom
Tel.: +44 1752 202 301 | Fax: +44 1752 202 331
Email: orders@nbninternational.com

Distribution for Europe and all other countries:
Intersentia Publishing nv
Groenstraat 31
2640 Mortsel
Belgium
Tel.: +32 3 680 15 50 | Fax: +32 3 658 71 21
Email: mail@intersentia.be

Distribution for the USA and Canada:
International Specialized Book Services
920 NE 58th Ave. Suite 300
Portland, OR 97213
USA
Tel.: +1 800 944 6190 (toll free) | Fax: +1 503 280 8832
Email: info@isbs.com

Participatory Democracy, Civil Society and Social Europe. A Legal and Political Perspective

Artwork on cover: Rythme n° 3, décoration pour le Salon des Tuileries, Delaunay Robert (1885-1941), Paris, musée d'Art moderne de la Ville de Paris, Photo © RMN-Grand Palais / Agence Bulloz

ISBN 978-1-78068-395-9
D/2016/7849/69
NUR 828

GPRC Guaranteed Peer Reviewed Content

British Library Cataloguing in Publication Data. A catalogue record for this book is available from the British Library.

ACKNOWLEDGEMENTS

This book originates from a doctoral thesis completed in September 2013. It could not have been written without the support of my beloved wife, Christina. I thank her for our endless discussions, for her proof-reading skills and for reminding me that there is a life worth living outside PhD research.

I also thank my friends and family for being there in times of doubt. One of them, Sébastien, made a decisive contribution to my thesis but unfortunately passed away just before I could thank him. I bid him farewell.

I am grateful to the scholars I met during the UACES conferences. I have also greatly benefited from a workshop on post-national rulemaking organised by the University of Amsterdam. I particularly wish to thank Alex Warleigh, Deirdre Curtin and Dawid Friedrich for their input.

I am also thankful to the Catholic University of Louvain for entrusting me with a job of teaching assistant during the last two years of my PhD. My participation in the activities of its Centre for European law have greatly contributed to my research. I particularly wish to thank Stéphanie Francq and Jean-Yves Carlier in that respect.

Of course, thank you to Adam Cygan, my PhD supervisor, for his patience and guidance. I could not have hoped for better support at the University of Leicester. Likewise, I am grateful to Michael Dougan and Oxana Golynker for their encouraging comments during the viva voce examination.

Last but not least, thank you to the editorial staff and the two anonymous reviewers at *Intersentia*, without whom you could not possibly hold this book in your hands today.

CONTENTS

ABBREVIATIONS

APA	Administrative Procedure Act
CJEL	*Columbia Journal of European Law*
Can J L & Jurisprudence	*Canadian Journal of Law and Jurisprudence*
CLR	*Columbia Law Review*
CM	Community Method
CML Rev	*Common Market Law Review*
CoR	Committee of the Regions
CSCC	Civil Society Contact Group
CSO	Civil Society Organisation
CUP	Cambridge University Press
CYELS	*Cambridge Yearbook of European Legal Studies*
DDP	Directly-Deliberative Polyarchy
DG	Directorate-General
EAPN	European Anti-Poverty Network
EBLR	*European Business Law Review*
EBOR	*European Business Organization Law Review*
ECI	European Citizen Initiative
ECJ	European Court of Justice
ECJ	*European Competition Journal*
ECLR	*European Competition Law Review*
EC Tax Rev	*EC Tax Review*
EESC	European Economic and Social Committee
EIoP	*European Integration online Papers*
EJIL	*European Journal of International Law*
EJSL	*European Journal of Social Law*
EJSS	*European Journal of Social Security*
ELJ	*European Law Journal*
EL Rev	*European Law Review*
EMU	Economic and Monetary Union
EPL	*European Public Law*
EPP	European Platform against Poverty
ESM	European Stability Mechanism
EStAL	*European State Aid Law Quarterly*
EU	European Union

FEANTSA	European Federation of National Organisations working with the Homeless
Fordham Int'l LJ	*Fordham International Law Journal*
GC	General Court
IA	Impact Assessment
ICLQ	*International & Comparative Law Quarterly*
IGC	Intergovernmental Conference
ISG	Inter Service Group
IJNFPL	*International Journal of Not-for-Profit Law*
JCER	*Journal of Contemporary European Research*
JCMS	*Journal of Common Market Studies*
JDE	*Journal de Droit Européen*
JECL&P	*Journal of European Competition Law & Practice*
JEPP	*Journal of European Public Policy*
JESP	*Journal of European Social Policy*
JHPPL	*Journal of Health Politics, Policy and Law*
Jnl Soc Pol	*Journal of Social Policy*
LIEI	*Legal Issues of European Integration*
Living Rev Dem	*Living Reviews in Democracy*
Living Rev Eur Gov	*Living Reviews in European Governance*
MJ	*Maastricht Journal of European & Comparative Law*
ML Rev	*Modern Law Review*
MTBO	Medium-Term Budgetary Objective
NCAs	National Competition Authorities
NRPs	National Reform Progammes
NSRs	National Social Reports
OMC	Open Method of Coordination
OUP	Oxford University Press
PSCs	Public Service Compensations
RDUE	*Revue du Droit de l'Union Européenne*
RMUE	*Revue du Marché Unique Européen*
SGEI	Services of General Economic Interest
SMEs	Small and Medium-sized Enterprises
Social Platform	European Platform of social NGOs
SPC	Social Protection Committee
TFEU	Treaty on the Functioning of the European Union
TEU	Treaty on European Union
U Chic Legal Forum	*University of Chicago Legal Forum*
Voluntas	*Voluntas: International Journal of Voluntary and Nonprofit Organizations*
White Paper	White Paper on European Governance
YEL	*Yearbook of European Law*

CHAPTER 1

DEMOCRATIC EU: FROM REPRESENTATION TO PARTICIPATION

1.1. INTRODUCTION

The crisis surrounding the ratification of the Maastricht Treaty signalled the end of the permissive consensus of the public in favour of deeper European integration.[1] After the Danish 'no' and the French 'petit oui', the governing elite came to realise that the passive approval of the masses for the European project could no longer be taken for granted.[2] These events were interpreted as the signs of a growing crisis of legitimacy.[3] European public opinion had voiced its discontent as to the current state of European integration: something was definitely wrong with the EU.[4] European studies took a normative turn,[5] with scholars expressing diverse, and sometimes conflicting, opinions as to the symptoms, diagnoses and cures they found most appropriate for the sick EU patient.[6]

1.2. REPRESENTATIVE DEMOCRACY AND THE COMMUNITY METHOD

The perception which prevailed at the time of Maastricht was that the EU suffers from a democratic deficit. This deficit may be variously defined, depending on

---

1 A Follesdal, 'Legitimacy Theories of the European Union' (2004) ARENA Working Paper no. 15/2004, 3–4.

2 See P Norris, 'Representation and the Democratic Deficit' (1997) 32 European Journal of Political Research 273, 276.

3 R Dehousse, 'Constitutional Reform in the European Community: Are There Alternatives to the Majoritarian Avenue?' (1995) 18 West European Politics 118, 119–121.

4 This expression draws from S Hix, *What's Wrong with the European Union and How to Fix it* (Polity Press 2008).

5 See R Bellamy and D Castiglione, 'Legitimizing the Euro-"Polity" and its "Regime": The Normative Turn in EU Studies' (2003) 2 European Journal of Political Theory 7, 7–8.

6 Follesdal, 'Legitimacy Theories of the European Union' (n 1) 4–6.

the democratic ideal chosen.[7] The standard view was that this is caused by 'the absence or underdevelopment of the institutions and processes of parliamentary democracy at the European level'.[8] The democratic deficit literature was dominated by 'the parliamentary model': government should emanate from and be responsible before an elected parliament.[9] The EU's original sin, therefore, laid in the gradual transfer of powers to the EU which had empowered executives at the expense of national parliaments.[10] With the disease identified as 'deparliamentarisation' at the national level,[11] the cure seemed plain and simple: constitutional mimetism, as if turning the EU into a parliamentary democracy modelled upon those of its Member States would solve its democratic deficit.[12]

Since then, the parliamentarisation of the EU has been associated with the rise of the Community Method (CM) seen as the joint exercise of legislative power by the Council and Parliament on a proposal of the Commission.[13] Treaty after Treaty, the co-decision procedure has been extended to an increasing range of fields. With the Lisbon Treaty, it has become the 'ordinary legislative procedure' applicable in all cases where the Treaties do not provide otherwise.[14] National parliaments have also emerged as proper actors in the EU law-making process, with a right to receive information directly from European institutions and a direct role in checking that the latter respect the principle of subsidiarity.[15] Yet, securing ministerial accountability in the Council remains their overwhelming priority with subsidiarity monitoring seen a useful but weak adjunct to scrutinise the effectiveness of European legislative activities.[16]

---

7 T Jensen, 'The Democratic Deficit of the European Union' (2009) 1 Living Rev Dem 2 <www.livingreviews.org/lrd-2009-2> accessed 1 September 2015. For an overview, see B Kohler-Koch and B Rittberger, 'Charting Crowded Territory: Debating the Democratic Legitimacy of the European Union' in B Kohler-Koch and B Rittberger (eds), *Debating the Democratic Legitimacy of the European Union* (Rowman & Littlefield 2007).

8 G Majone, 'The Common Sense of European Integration' (2006) 13 JEPP 607, 608.

9 S Smismans, *Law, Legitimacy, and European Governance: Functional Participation in Social Regulation* (OUP 2004) 3. See also JHH Weiler, *The Constitution of Europe: "Do the New Clothes Have an Emperor?" and Other Essays on European Integration* (CUP 1999) 77.

10 UR Haltern, FC Mayer and JHH Weiler, 'European Democracy and its Critique' (1995) 18 West European Politics 4, 6–9.

11 See A Cygan, 'The Parliamentarisation of EU Decision-Making? The Impact of the Treaty of Lisbon on National Parliaments' (2011) 36 EL Rev 478, 479–481.

12 See P Magnette, 'Democracy in the European Union: Why and How to Combine Representation and Participation?' in S Smismans (ed), *Civil Society and Legitimate European Governance* (Edward Elgar 2006) 37.

13 P Craig and G De Búrca, *EU Law: Text, Cases, and Materials* (5th edn, OUP 2011) 160.

14 Articles 289 and 294 TFEU.

15 JC Piris, *The Lisbon Treaty: A Legal and Political Analysis* (CUP 2010) 122–133. The powers attributed by the Treaties to national parliaments are listed in Article 12 TEU, with reference to Protocol no. 1 on the role of national parliaments in the European Union [2012] OJ C326/203 and Protocol no. 2 on the application of the principles of subsidiarity and proportionality [2012] OJ C326/206.

16 See Cygan, 'The Parliamentarisation of EU Decision-Making?' (n 11) 497.

As things stand, therefore, the democratic legitimacy of EU law-making would seem to rest on a two-fold basis where, as stipulated in Article 10(2) TEU,

> [c]itizens are directly represented at Union level in the European Parliament [while] Member States are represented (...) in the Council by their governments, themselves democratically accountable either to their national Parliaments, or to their citizens.

The CM has received praise for its democratic achievements from none other than Moravcsik:

> [c]onstitutional checks and balances, indirect democratic control via national governments, and the increasing powers of the European Parliament are sufficient to ensure that EU policy-making is, in nearly all cases, clean, transparent, effective and politically responsive to the demands of European citizens.[17]

This links up with the argument made by Lord and Beetham that already 'the EU has developed its own means of adjusting representative politics to a post-national and post-state polity (...)'[18] by acquiring consensual features akin to those found in heterogeneous polities such as Belgium or Switzerland.[19] They argue that the search for consensus which characterises the CM produces pathologies that could be addressed if the EU opted for a majoritarian system of government.[20] However, consensualists agree that majoritarian politics is an unsavoury prospect for a polity so deeply fragmented as the EU; they remain confident that the democratic shortcomings of the CM may be handled within the boundaries of the current institutional framework.[21]

More sceptical, Majone criticises the CM for being undemocratic. He takes issue with the Commission's monopoly of initiative which 'represents a violation of fundamental democratic principles that is unique in modern constitutional history (...)'.[22] At the same time, he guards against the idea of giving more powers to the Parliament which 'rests on a fallacious analogy with

17 A Moravcsik, 'In Defence of the "Democratic Deficit": Reassessing Legitimacy in the European Union' (2002) 40 JCMS 603, 605. See also A Moravcsik, 'The Myth of Europe's "Democratic Deficit"' (2008) 43 Intereconomics 331.

18 C Lord and D Beetham, 'Legitimizing the EU: Is there a "Post-Parliamentary Basis" for its Legitimation?' (2001) 39 JCMS 443, 456.

19 See Y Papadopoulos, 'Implementing (and Radicalizing) Art. I-47.4 of the Constitution: Is the Addition of some (Semi-) Direct Democracy to the Nascent Consociational European Federation just Swiss Folklore?' (2005) 12 JEPP 448; Y Papadopoulos and P Magnette, 'On the Politicisation of the European Union: Lessons from Consociational National Polities' (2010) 33 West European Politics 711.

20 D Beetham and C Lord, *Legitimacy and the EU* (Longman 1998) 93.

21 See Papadopoulos and Magnette, 'On the Politicisation of the European Union' (n 19) 721–723.

22 G Majone, *Europe as the Would-Be World Power: the EU at Fifty* (CUP 2009) 30.

the institutions of parliamentary democracy at the state level'.[23] This mimetic strategy is bound to fail, he says, for turning the EU into a fully-fledged federal state is exactly what national governments and the people they represent do not want.[24] Nevertheless, the democratic deficit did not appear problematic to Majone as long as the EU was a 'regulatory state' whose effectiveness precisely rested on its insulation from redistributive politics.[25] The democratic deficit has become a cause for concern with the increase of EU powers beyond the regulatory field, most clearly exemplified by the set up of a strict regime of budgetary and economic surveillance in the wake of the euro crisis.[26] Majone's faith in the welfare-enhancing capacity of the CM has also been shaken off. He now argues that a return to the primacy of negative integration combined with the use of more flexible integration methods would improve the effectiveness of European regulation under conditions of diversity.[27]

From a socio-democratic standpoint, the limits of the CM have been highlighted by Scharpf who claims that 'the enthusiasts of European democracy tend to ignore the preconditions of legitimate *majority rule* (...)'.[28] European elections are second-order national elections, while European media and Europe-wide party competition are nowhere in sight. More importantly, the EU does not possess the 'thick' collective identity which protects minorities from the misdeeds of tyrannical majorities.[29] For all those reasons, Scharpf concludes that the CM had better give up on democracy and reinforce its legitimacy by delivering outputs that citizens demand.[30] As Majone, Scharpf has grown pessimistic about the problem-solving capacity of the CM and now sees differentiated integration as a better way to cope with the challenges of national welfare diversity.[31]

To summarise, the European integration process seems to be facing an insurmountable dilemma: *either* one accepts that the CM is democratic (Moravcsik) *or* one admits that the CM is far from democratic yet should not (Majone)/cannot (Scharpf) be democratised. In any case, we end up with

---

23 G Majone, 'Transaction-Cost Efficiency and the Democratic Deficit' (2010) 17 JEPP 150, 151.

24 Majone, *Europe as the Would-Be World Power* (n 22) 154.

25 G Majone, 'Regulatory Legitimacy' in G Majone and P Baake (eds), *Regulating Europe* (Routledge 1996) 287.

26 G Majone, *Rethinking the Union of Europe Post-Crisis: Has Integration Gone Too Far?* (CUP 2014, ebook) 4214.

27 Majone, *Europe as the Would-Be World Power* (n 22) 188–193.

28 FW Scharpf, 'Problem Solving Effectiveness and Democratic Accountability in the EU' (2006) Political Science Series no. 107, Institute for Advanced Studies, Vienna, 18.

29 FW Scharpf, *Governing Europe: Effective and Democratic?* (OUP 1999) 9. For a recent reformulation of the argument, see FW Scharpf, 'Legitimacy in the Multi-level European Polity' in P Dobner and M Loughlin (eds), *The Twilight of Constitutionalism?* (OUP 2010) 94–95.

30 Ibid 12.

31 FW Scharpf, 'The European Social Model: Coping with the Challenges of Diversity' (2002) 40 JCMS 645, 659–665.

the conservative view that the CM is as good as democracy will ever get for the EU. Both Scharpf and Majone had hoped that the CM would redeem its democratic deficit by delivering outputs valued by European citizens. They now seriously question its problem solving capacity so that more flexible governance arrangements are promoted as a way ahead for European integration. Because representative democracy as it was embedded in the CM may be reaching its limits, the EU has turned to participatory democracy.

The next two sections will show that the EU has been torn between a radical and a moderate version of participatory democracy. The *moderate* version maintains the CM as the leading tool for European integration but revitalises it by directly involving citizens in the political life of the EU while forging a dialogue between European institutions and organised civil society. The *radical* version celebrates the demise of the CM as an opportunity to decentralise EU decision-making, by bringing powers back to the Member States working in partnership with civil society within the framework of the Open Method of Coordination (OMC).

1.3. PARTICIPATORY DEMOCRACY AND THE COMMUNITY METHOD

Participatory democracy has permeated the institutional and, eventually, the constitutional discourse of the EU; to such an extent that the Lisbon Treaty elevates it to the status of a democratic principle which should guide the EU in its quest for legitimacy.[32] Article 11 TEU presents a two-dimensional picture of participatory democracy in the EU. It is, on the one hand, concerned with the direct participation of *citizens* in the political life of the EU, while it deals, on the other hand, with the dialogue of *organised civil society* with European institutions. In both cases, Article 11 TEU promotes a moderate version of the participatory turn where the legitimacy of the CM finds itself reinforced rather than seriously questioned.

1.3.1. CITIZENSHIP

Republicans have long argued that endowing European citizens with direct democratic rights, through referenda and popular initiatives, points the way

[32] Article 11 TEU, indeed, lies under title II which contains the 'Provisions on Democratic Principles'. Article 11 TEU reproduces Article I-47 of the Treaty establishing a Constitution for Europe ([2004] OJ C310/01) which was entitled 'The Principle of Participatory Democracy'. On participatory democracy as a democratic principle of the EU legal order, see J Mendes, 'Participation and the Role of Law after Lisbon: A Legal View on Article 11 TEU' (2011) 48 CML Rev 1849.

towards the kind of radical reforms which are needed to democratise a post-national polity such as the EU.[33] Yet, as Union citizenship was established by the Treaty of Maastricht, the political rights granted to EU citizens were, to say the least, minimal.[34] The right to vote and to stand as a candidate in elections to the European Parliament,[35] the right to petition the European Parliament and the right to apply to the European Ombudsman[36] were the only means for citizens to interact with the EU until the right to write to European institutions and advisory bodies in one of the official languages of the EU and to have a reply in the same language was added in Amsterdam.[37] This amounts to a thin model of republican citizenship, for neither the right to petition the European Parliament nor the right to apply to the European Ombudsman offers direct opportunities to gain political influence.[38]

After Lisbon, direct democracy remains 'the Achilles heel of EU citizenship'.[39] Existing rights were reaffirmed, while the European Citizen Initiative (ECI) was introduced in Article 11 TEU after intense lobbying by a couple of NGO activists.[40] This participatory instrument may well be the first transnational direct democratic tool in human history.[41] Nevertheless, it is still in line with a moderate version of the participatory turn, most obviously because citizens may only invite the Commission to submit a proposal which then needs to go through the usual law-making process.[42] It is therefore not surprising

---

33 See, eg, M Nentwich, 'Opportunity Structures for Citizens' Participation: The Case of the European Union' in A Weale and M Nentwich (eds), *Political Theory and the European Union* (Routledge 1998) 136–137; Y Mény, 'The "Democratic Principle" and the European Union: The Challenge of a Post-National Democracy' in C Moury and L de Sousa (eds), *Institutional Challenges in Post-Constitutional Europe: Governing Change* (Routledge 2009) 130–131; Papadopoulos and Magnette, 'On the Politicisation of the European Union' (n 19) 723–725.

34 See part II of the Treaty establishing the European Community (consolidated version 1992) [1992] OJ C224/01.

35 Article 8(b) (now Article 22 TFEU).

36 Article 8(d) (now Article 24(2) and (3) TFEU).

37 Article 21(3) of the Treaty establishing the European Community (consolidated version 1997) [1997] OJ C340/03 (now Article 24(4) TFEU).

38 Nentwich, 'Opportunity Structures for Citizens' Participation' (n 33) 128–129.

39 R Bellamy, D Castiglione and J Shaw, 'Introduction: From National to Transnational Citizenship' in R Bellamy, D Castiglione and J Shaw (eds), *Making European Citizens: Civic Inclusion in a Transnational Context* (Palgrave Macmillan 2006) 9.

40 See Article 11(4) TEU; Article 24(1) TFEU; M Efler and C Berg, 'Initiative for the European Citizens' Initiative: How the Convention got Convinced' (2003) <www.citizens-initiative.eu/?p=35> accessed 1st September 2015.

41 B Kaufmann, 'Citizen Power Beyond the Nation-State' in C Berg, P Carline, B Kaufmann, J Leinen and D Wallis (eds), *Initiative for Europe Handbook 2008 – the Guide to Transnational Democracy in Europe* (Initiative & Referendum Institute Europe 2007) 10 <www.iri-europe.org/publications/handbooks/european-citizens-initiative-handbook/> accessed 1st September 2015.

42 For a balanced appraisal of the pros and cons of the ECI, see A Warleigh, 'On the Path to Legitimacy? A Critical Deliberativist Perspective on the Right to the Citizens' Initiative' in C Ruzza and V Della Sala (eds), *Governance and Civil Society in the European Union: Normative Perspectives* (Manchester University Press 2007).

that the Lisbon Treaty has positioned the right for citizens to participate in the democratic life of the Union in Article 10 TEU specifically dedicated to representative democracy.[43] It is a timely reminder that 'apart from European elections every five years, there are no direct ways to participate in European politics'.[44] In between, as per Article 11 TEU, citizens can 'make known and publicly exchange their views in all areas of Union action'.[45] They can also, for the Union's actions which are of concern to them, participate in the broad consultations organised by the Commission.[46] These provisions of Article 11 TEU are, however, of limited significance to citizens. Given the necessary levels of skill, money and time they require, they are most likely to be exploited by organised interests.[47]

1.3.2. ORGANISED CIVIL SOCIETY

Article 11 TEU mostly fosters a dialogue between *organised civil society* and European institutions. Indeed, 'the Commission shall carry out broad consultations with parties concerned (...)',[48] most of which organise to express their voice, while 'the institutions shall, by appropriate means, give (...) representative associations the opportunity to make known and publicly exchange their views in all areas of Union action'.[49] In addition, 'the institutions shall maintain an open, transparent and regular dialogue with representative associations and civil society'.[50] These provisions may be seen as the constitutional endorsement of a participatory discourse which has developed within two institutional fora: the Commission and the European Economic and Social Committee (EESC). They, for different reasons, discovered organised civil society as a legitimating agent that could strengthen their institutional position within the CM at a time when it was threatened.[51]

---

43 See S Smismans, 'The Constitutional Labelling of "the Democratic Life of the EU": Representative and Participatory Democracy' in L Dobson and A Follesdal (eds), *Political Theory and the European Constitution* (Routledge 2004) 135; P Nieuwenburg, 'Democratic Life in Europolis' in A Kinneging (ed), *Rethinking Europe's Constitution* (Wolf Legal Publishers 2007) 165.

44 Nentwich, 'Opportunity Structures for Citizens' Participation' (n 33) 133.

45 Article 11(1) TEU.

46 Article 11(3) TEU.

47 See A Warleigh, 'Making Citizens from the Market? NGOs and the Representation of Interests' in R Bellamy, D Castiglione and J Shaw (eds), *Making European Citizens: Civic Inclusion in a Transnational Context* (Palgrave Macmillan 2006) 120; V Cuesta Lopez, 'The Lisbon Treaty's Provisions on Democratic Principles: A Legal Framework for Participatory Democracy' (2010) 16 EPL 123, 136.

48 Article 11(3) TEU.

49 Article 11(1) TEU.

50 Article 11(2) TEU.

51 S Smismans, 'European Civil Society: Shaped by Discourses and Institutional Interests' (2003) 9 ELJ 482, 493.

The Commission has a long tradition of consulting interest groups and deems it to be fundamental to the development of its policies.[52] Yet, it is only in March 1996, when DG Employment organised its first European Social Policy Forum in cooperation with the European Platform of social NGOs (Social Platform), that the concept of 'civil dialogue' was introduced.[53] DG Trade quickly followed suit by creating its own civil dialogue with NGOs.[54] Moving away from a narrow policy focus on trade and social policy,[55] the Commission issued in 2000 a Discussion Paper which throws the reasons for strengthening the relationship between the Commission and NGOs into sharp relief.[56] Beside their output-based contribution to policy-making, the Discussion Paper finds a democracy-enhancing rationale for involving NGOs in European governance. The latter foster participatory democracy in that:

> [t]he right of citizens to form associations to pursue a common purpose is a fundamental freedom in a democracy. Belonging to an association provides an opportunity for citizens to participate actively in new ways other than or in addition to involvement in political parties or trade unions.[57]

There is no doubt that the context in which the Discussion Paper was drafted – a far-reaching process of administrative reform launched with a view to regain public confidence after the fall of the Santer Commission – has contributed to the discovery that organised civil society could legitimise the EU through participatory means.[58]

This thinking went mainstream with the 2001 White Paper on European Governance.[59] With a view to reinvigorate the CM, the Commission proposes to structure the EU's relationship with organised civil society. In line with the Discussion Paper, the Commission finds two rationales for a reinforced culture of consultation and dialogue: involving organised civil society will improve the effectiveness of EU policies, while it will be a democratic chance 'to get citizens

52 Commission 'An Open and Structured Dialogue between the Commission and Special Interest Groups' (Communication) [1993] OJ C63/2, 2.

53 See Commission, 'Promoting the Role of Voluntary Organisations and Foundations in Europe' (Communication) COM (97) 241 final, 7.

54 R Goehring, 'Interest Representation and Legitimacy in the European Union' in A Warleigh and J Fairbrass (eds), *Influence and Interests in the European Union: The New Politics of Persuasion and Advocacy* (Europa Publications 2002) 130–132.

55 *Contra*, see K Armstrong, 'Rediscovering Civil Society: The European Union and the White Paper on Governance' (2002) 8 ELJ 102, 119.

56 Commission, 'The Commission and Non-Governmental Organisations: Building a Stronger Partnership' (Discussion Paper) COM (2000) 11 final.

57 Ibid 4.

58 Smismans, 'European Civil Society' (n 51) 488. See also Commission, 'The Commission and Non-Governmental Organisations' (n 56) 2.

59 Commission, 'European Governance: A White Paper' COM (2001) 428 final. See also J Greenwood, *Interest Representation in the European Union* (3rd edn, Palgrave Macmillan 2011) 143.

more actively involved in achieving the Union's objectives (...)'.[60] With a view to implement this commitment, the Commission has adopted a Communication setting out 'general principles and minimum standards for consultation of interested parties' in which the specific role of civil society organisations (CSOs) in modern democracies is once again acknowledged.[61]

Meanwhile, the EESC has reinvented itself as 'a bridge between Europe and organised civil society' by fear of its marginalisation in the institutional game.[62] As from 1999, its main role became to implement 'the participatory model of civil society; [enabling] civil society to participate in the decision-making process; and [helping] reduce a certain "democratic deficit" and so [underpinning] the legitimacy of democratic decision-making processes'.[63] In Nice, the EESC obtained mention of this role in Article 257 TEC: 'the Committee shall consist of representatives of the various economic and social components of organised civil society (...)'.[64]

After its discovery by the Commission and the EESC, participatory democracy came to be accepted by other institutions. It eventually found its way into the works of the Convention tasked with drafting the Constitution for Europe. From the very first draft, the Praesidium had suggested an article that would 'set out the principle of participatory democracy'.[65] After many amendments,[66] the final version of Article I-46 on 'the principle of participatory democracy' was adopted under the title 'The democratic life of the Union'.[67] As the Constitutional Treaty failed to win acceptance in the French and Dutch referenda, a new IGC was convened so as to adopt the Lisbon Treaty modifying the existing Treaty on the European Union and Treaty establishing the European Community.[68] Article I-46 became Article 11 TEU. The participatory provisions are kept as they were, although reference to the principle of participatory

60 Ibid 15.

61 Commission, 'Towards a Reinforced Culture of Consultation and Dialogue – General Principles and Minimum Standards for Consultation of Interested Parties by the Commission' (Communication) COM (2002) 704 final, 5-6.

62 <www.eesc.europa.eu/?i=portal.en.about-the-committee> accessed 1st September 2015. For more details, see Smismans, 'European Civil Society' (n 51) 490–493.

63 EESC, 'The Role and Contribution of Civil Society Organisations in the Building of Europe' (Opinion) [1999] OJ C329/10, point 10.3.1, cited in Smismans, 'European Civil Society' (n 51) 492.

64 Article 257 of the Treaty establishing the European Community (consolidated version 2002) [2002] OJ C325/01. Current Article 300 TFEU provides that the EESC 'shall consist of representatives of organisations of employers, of the employed, and of other parties representative of civil society, notably in socio-economic, civic, professional and cultural areas'.

65 Praesidium, 'Preliminary Draft Constitutional Treaty' (28 October 2002, CONV 2002, 369/02) Article 34.

66 These are analysed in Smismans, 'The Constitutional Labelling of "the Democratic Life of the EU"' (n 43) 132–137.

67 See Treaty establishing a Constitution for Europe [2004] C310/01.

68 [2007] OJ C306/01.

democracy has been dropped and the title under which they remained was renamed 'Provisions on democratic principles'.

Albeit in a *backward-looking* mode, Article 11 TEU provides formal recognition to existing participatory practices, having particular regard to the civil dialogue promoted by both the Commission and the EESC.[69] However, Article 11 TEU means more than business as usual since, in also a *forward-looking* mode, it requires the participation of organised civil society to be guaranteed by other European institutions which are often reluctant to involve it.[70] More importantly, Article 11 TEU demands a shift in the rationale for organising consultations. Civil society participation can therefore no longer be (solely) understood as a means of increasing the problem-solving capacity of the CM. European institutions are legally compelled to redirect participatory practices towards democratic ends.[71] And, although Article 11 TEU does not confer participatory rights upon organised civil society, it does impose duties on European institutions for which they enjoy wide discretionary powers.[72] In a nutshell, Article 11 TEU is a programmatic provision which, as the EESC noted, 'needs to be defined, fleshed out and put into practice with appropriate legal arrangements and it is up to the parties involved to bring it to life'.[73]

European institutions are already taking steps to implement Article 11 TEU.[74] Of particular interest is that the European Parliament, initially reluctant, now shares the Commission's view that participatory democracy can supplement representative democracy.[75] Since 2011, it is party to an agreement with the Commission establishing a common transparency register for interest representatives.[76] The latter was set up having regard to Article 11 TEU. The Council, relying on the flexibility clause, has also adopted a regulation

69 R Bieber and F Maiani, 'Bringing the Union Closer to its Citizens? "Participatory Democracy" and the Potential Contribution of the Lisbon Treaty' (2009) Annuaire Suisse de Droit Européen 229, 235.

70 Mendes, 'Participation and the Role of Law after Lisbon' (n 32) 1868–1869.

71 Ibid 1858–1863.

72 Bieber and Maiani, 'Bringing the Union Closer to its Citizens?' (n 69) 233.

73 EESC, 'The Implementation of the Lisbon Treaty: Participatory Democracy and the Citizens' Initiative (Article 11)' (Opinion) [2010] OJ C354/59, point 3.4, cited in Bieber and Maiani, 'Bringing the Union Closer to its Citizens?' (n 69) 247.

74 See E Bernard, 'La Démocratie Participative sous l'Angle du Dialogue Civil et du Dialogue Social' in V Constantinesco, Y Gautier and V Michel (eds), *Le Traité établissant une Constitution pour l'Europe: Analyses & Commentaires* (Presses universitaires de Strasbourg 2005) 382.

75 European Parliament, 'Resolution of 24 March 2009 on Active Dialogue with Citizens on Europe' [2010] OJ C117E/27, para 9.

76 Agreement between the European Parliament and the European Commission of 23 June 2011 on the Establishment of a Transparency Register for Organisations and Self-employed Individuals Engaged in EU Policy- Making and Policy Implementation [2011] OJ L191/29, replaced by Agreement between the European Parliament and the European Commission of 16 April 2014 on the Transparency Register for Organisations and Self-Employed Individuals Engaged in EU Policy-Making and Policy Implementation [2014] OJ L277/11.

establishing for the period 2014–2020 a new 'Europe for Citizens' programme as a means to implement Article 11 TEU through greater civic participation.[77] Finally, the Commission has recently set up a framework for civil dialogue in matters covered by the common agricultural policy,[78] while obliging its commissioners and directors-general to publish information on meetings held with organisations and self-employed individuals.[79]

Despite all these implementation efforts, one should keep in mind that Article 11 TEU embodies a moderate version of the participatory turn. It does not go beyond the useful but limited agenda of reinforcing the dialogue of European institutions with civil society within the framework of the CM. Indeed, a combined reading of Articles 10 and 11 TEU reveals that the functioning of the Union is above all founded on representative democracy channelled through the Parliament and Council with participatory democracy as a mere add-on which compensates for the CM's democratic shortcomings. As the next section shows, participatory democracy has taken a more radical turn with the launch of the OMC by the Lisbon European Council.

1.4. PARTICIPATORY DEMOCRACY AND THE OPEN METHOD OF COORDINATION

In March 2000, the Lisbon European Council set out the details of its socio-economic strategy for the decade to come.[80] It proposed to apply a new Open Method of Coordination[81] (OMC) as 'a broadly applicable new governance instrument designed to assist the Union in achieving the ambitious goals of the Lisbon Strategy through iterative benchmarking of national progress towards common European objectives and organised mutual learning'.[82] The European Council defines the OMC as an ensemble of four interdependent procedural elements:

---

77 Council Regulation (EU) 390/2014 of 14 April 2014 Establishing the 'Europe for Citizens' Programme for the Period 2014–2020 [2014] OJ L115/3.

78 Commission Decision 2013/767/EU of 16 December 2013 Setting Up a Framework for Civil Dialogue in Matters Covered by the Common Agricultural Policy and Repealing Decision 2004/391/EC [2013] OJ L338/115.

79 Commission Decision 2014/838/EU of 25 November 2014 on the Publication of Information on Meetings Held Between Directors-General of the Commission and Organisations or Self-employed Individuals [2014] OJ L343/19; Commission Decision 2014/839/EU of 25 November 2014 on the Publication of Information on Meetings Held Between Members of the Commission and Organisations or Self-employed Individuals [2014] OJ L343/22.

80 European Council, 23–24 March 2000, Lisbon, presidency conclusions.

81 Ibid point 37.

82 J Zeitlin, 'Is the Open Method of Coordination an Alternative to the Community Method?' in R Dehousse (ed), *The "Community Method": Obstinate or Obsolete?* (Palgrave Macmillan 2011) 135.

- fixing guidelines for the Union combined with specific timetables for achieving the goals which they set in the short, medium and long terms;
- establishing, where appropriate, quantitative and qualitative indicators and benchmarks against the best in the world and tailored to the needs of different Member States and sectors as a means of comparing best practice;
- translating these European guidelines into national and regional policies by setting specific targets and adopting measures, taking into account national and regional differences;
- periodic monitoring, evaluation and peer review organised as mutual learning processes.[83]

Since then, specific OMCs which more or less depart from this template have been set up in a wide range of policy fields such as R&D, education, or immigration.[84] Social policy has been at the forefront of this development with the creation of a 'social' OMC dedicated to social inclusion, health and long-term care as well as pensions.[85]

The constitutional significance of the OMC could easily be discarded as yet another experiment in soft law which takes place in the shadow of the all-mighty CM. That would miss the point that the OMC is distinct from the old soft law procedures and contents which have so far accompanied the European integration process.[86] Proponents of the OMC claim that it is a fully-fledged alternative to the CM.[87] They advocate that it would represent a radical departure from hierarchical governing by the institutional actors (Commission, Council, Parliament) which dominate EU law-making.[88] The OMC's distinctive approach towards Europeanization would lie in the fact that it devolves powers back to Member States which are free to develop their own policies in accordance with political guidelines set by European institutions.

As the Lisbon conclusions stipulate, the OMC is meant to be '[a] fully decentralised approach (…) applied in line with the principle of subsidiarity in which the Union, the Member States, the regional and local levels, as well as the social partners and civil society, [are] actively involved, using variable forms of partnership'.[89] The OMC would therefore express the participatory turn in its

---

83 Lisbon European Council (n 80) point 37.

84 For a comprehensive mapping exercise, see B Laffan and C Shaw, 'Classifying and Mapping OMC in Different Policy Areas' (2009) NewGov Working Paper no. 02/D09, 13–14.

85 See Commission, 'Working Together, Working Better: A New Framework for the Open Coordination of Social Protection and Inclusion Policies in the European Union' (Communication) COM (2005) 706 final.

86 S Borrás and K Jacobsson, 'The Open Method of Co-Ordination and New Governance Patterns in the EU' (2004) 11 JEPP 185, 188–189.

87 J Scott and DM Trubek, 'Mind the Gap: Law and New Approaches to Governance in the European Union' (2002) 8 ELJ 1, 4.

88 Craig and De Búrca, *EU Law* (n 13) 166.

89 Lisbon European Council (n 80) point 38.

most drastic form, as it replaces top-down law-making by bottom-up learning through benchmarking, peer review and exchange of best practices. It is also expected to provide the EU with an effective policy tool to address the regulatory shortcomings of the CM and might become part of that quest for a more flexible Europe to which both Majone and Scharpf aspire.[90] Those are, at least, the theoretical promises that laid behind this new mode of governance when the Lisbon strategy was adopted.

Ten years later, the Lisbon strategy was widely regarded as a failure.[91] This has not prevented the European Council from launching, in March 2010, a new strategy for smart, sustainable and inclusive growth.[92] 'Europe 2020', as it is called, very much resembles its Lisbon predecessor in both form and content. Yet, enthusiasm for the OMC as a policy tool seems to be fading away. The strategic goals of Europe 2020 are to be delivered through a wide range of instruments among which European *legislation*, not the OMC, ranges foremost.[93] This does not seem to be the end of the OMC though, for governance of the overall strategic framework of Europe 2020 continues to build on the coordination mechanisms which underlay the Lisbon strategy for growth and jobs and subscribes to the same partnership approach where all stakeholders are to be fully involved, including civil society.[94]

1.5. ASSESSING THE PARTICIPATORY TURN: OUTLINE

Because representative democracy as it was embedded in the CM may be reaching its limits (*1.2*), the EU has turned to participatory democracy. The participatory turn is torn between a moderate and a radical version. The moderate version revitalises the CM by formalising the dialogue of European institutions with organised civil society (*1.3*), while the radical version celebrates its demise as a chance for national governments to coordinate their policies in partnership with civil society through the OMC (*1.4*). The prospect of democratising the EU through the participation of civil society in governance

90 See E Szyszczak, 'Experimental Governance: The Open Method of Coordination' (2006) 12 ELJ 486, 487.

91 P Copeland, 'Conclusion: The Lisbon Strategy - Evaluating Success and Understanding Failure' in P Copeland and D Papadimitriou (eds), *The EU's Lisbon Strategy: Evaluating Success, Understanding Failure* (Palgrave Macmillan 2012) 229.

92 European Council, 25–26 March 2010, presidency conclusions.

93 M Dawson and B De Witte, 'The EU Legal Framework of Social Inclusion and Social Protection: Between the Lisbon Strategy and the Lisbon Treaty' in B Cantillon, H Verschueren and P Ploscar (eds), *Social Inclusion and Social Protection in the EU: Interactions between Law and Policy* (Intersentia 2012) 50–51.

94 Commission, 'Europe 2020: A Strategy for Smart, Sustainable and Inclusive Growth' (Communication) COM (2010) 2020 final, 6, 27.

raises as many questions as it answers. The ultimate purpose of this book is to contribute to the on-going debate on the merits and demerits of the participatory turn by looking at both its moderate and radical versions, while questioning whether the latter really performs better than the former.

To that effect, *Chapter 2* will review existing literature and show that scholars are strongly divided over the participatory turn. Assessments vary according to the normative lenses through which participatory democracy in the EU is looked at. Scholars are fighting for the soul of European civil society. Does civil society equal state, market or something in between? They also disagree as to the manner civil society, however conceptualised, should contribute to democracy in the EU. Is it in a pluralist, deliberative or associative mode? Their assessment is often determined by different stances taken as to the nature of the beast.[95] Is the EU a state in the making, a political system or a system of participatory governance? Any scholar willing to contribute to the debate on the participatory turn is bound to take a stand on these issues and this book will do just that. The literature review will also show that current scholarship fails to go back to basics. It provides for a participatory ideal of bits and pieces that does not account for the core normative concerns that animate the traditional participatory theory of democracy: self-government through citizen's *participation* and fighting the inequality bias of *market* capitalism.

Chapter 3 will, and that is where the originality of this book lies, propose a normative framework which brings those critical elements into a coherent whole. It will be argued that civil society is a pluralist sphere of participation between state and market wherein deliberative democracy realises its full potential. From this perspective, democratisation proceeds whenever civil society manages to assert control over both state and market without falling prey to their colonising tendencies. This emancipatory process has so far taken place within the context of national welfare states. A fundamental question therefore arises from the participatory turn to civil society: will multilevel social Europe be able to continue this emancipatory process or, on the contrary, will it bring about its collapse under the colonising forces of power and money?

Therefrom flow three specific research questions which the remaining chapters of this book will explore in detail:

1) The investigation will start with an examination of the impact of European economic law on civil society. *Does European economic law, mainly free movement and competition law, stand for civil society's colonisation or for its empowerment?* This question provides the building block for the reasoning to follow, for a civil society colonised by markets would be in no position

95 This expression draws from T Risse-Kappen, 'Exploring the Nature of the Beast: International Relations Theory and Comparative Policy Analysis Meet the European Union' (1996) 34 JCMS 53.

to legitimise social Europe at a time where it more than ever needs its protection.

2) The second step will be to question the participatory-democratic credentials of European governance by analysing the involvement of civil society in the two methods, the CM and the OMC, on which multilevel social Europe is built. *Is social Europe democratic in the sense that it opens European governance to the democratic influence of civil society?* In that respect, does radical OMC really perform better than moderate CM?
3) Finally, having regard to previous findings regarding, first, the potentially colonising impact of European economic law and, second, democratic support available for protective social law and policy making through, respectively, the CM and the OMC, *is social Europe effective, that is, able to protect civil society from European economic integration?* Once again, it may be asked whether radical OMC really fares better than moderate CM.

CHAPTER 2

REVIEWING THE PARTICIPATORY IDEAL OF BITS AND PIECES

2.1. INTRODUCTION

Whereas the participatory theory of democracy, and the arguments contemporary theorists have made against it, sheds light on the EU's timid turn to *citizen-based* participatory democracy, it leaves us empty-handed when it comes to assessing the embrace of *civil-society-centric* participatory democracy (*2.2*). The latter understanding of participatory democracy has brought up many questions with which European integration literature is still struggling. Scholars are battling for the soul of (European) civil society. How can one define civil society, what are its conceptual boundaries and the function it performs in modern societies, particularly in the EU (*2.3*)? They also see civil society, however defined, through the lenses of different democratic theories which, they claim, are modern variants of the old participatory ideal. Different views on the nature of the EU-polity bring up a further layer of complexity to the debate on the merits and demerits of the participatory turn. Is the EU a state in the making, a political system or a system of participatory governance (*2.4*)? This chapter will take a stand on these issues so that the reader understands where this book positions itself in the theoretical debate on the participatory turn. This chapter will also identify a major shortcoming in the literature which the theoretical framework exposed in *Chapter 3* aims to overcome: by systematically neglecting the maximum *participation* of citizens in political life as well as the inequality bias of *market* capitalism, existing scholarship only incorporates bits and pieces of the ideal of participatory democracy (*2.5*).

2.2. THE PARTICIPATORY THEORY OF DEMOCRACY AND ITS LIMITS

The participatory theory of democracy seems like the most convenient starting point for finding normative benchmarks against which to assess the participatory turn. There is not one single participatory theory of democracy, but rather an elusive list of authors who have expressed a common weariness towards the contemporary theory of democracy for its neglect of participation.[1] Indeed, the contemporary theory of democracy, contrary to the classical democratic theory and its modern participatory proponents, advocates minimal participation:[2] too much participation would threaten the stability of the system, while no participation would quickly turn into tyranny. The main features of the participatory theory of democracy as well as the arguments contemporary theorists hold against it will be presented in this section with a view to assess the participatory turn.

Participatory democracy can roughly be defined as 'self-government by citizens rather than representative government in the name of citizens'.[3] This implies two things: maximum *participation*, as opposed to representation, and *political equality* in its widest sense. Regarding the former, participatory theorists admit the importance of leadership[4] and the necessity for some kind of representative institutions in modern societies.[5] They, however, contend that representative institutions at the state level do not satisfy the democratic ideal of maximum participation of the people, for voting at the national level merely registers voters' preferences without inducing any development of their capacities for self-rule.[6] As said by Mill, a political act to be done only once in a few years very much leaves citizens as it found them.[7] If self-development, taken to be the normative justification of participatory democracy, is to occur, citizens need to be prepared for this kind of political activity through participation in other governmental and non-governmental spheres of society.[8] Participatory opportunities are therefore to be extended all the way down to the local level of government,[9] while new technologies as well as innovative institutional designs

1 GDH Cole, *Social Theory* (Methuen & Co 1920); P Bachrach, *The Theory of Democratic Elitism* (Little, Brown and Company 1967); C Pateman, *Participation and Democratic Theory* (CUP 1970); CB Macpherson, *The Life and Times of Liberal Democracy* (OUP 1977); B Barber, *Strong Democracy: Participatory Politics for a New Age* (University of California Press 1984); JD Wolfe, 'A Defense of Participatory Democracy' (1985) 47 The Review of Politics 370; P Craig, *Public Law and Democracy in the United Kingdom and the United States of America* (Clarendon Press 1990) chaps 10–11; Y Sintomer, *La Démocratie Participative* (La Documentation Française 2009).

2 Pateman, *Participation and Democratic Theory* (n 1) 1–16.

3 Barber, *Strong Democracy* (n 1) 151.

4 See Cole, *Social Theory* (n 1) 112–114; Barber, *Strong Democracy* (n 1) 237–242; Wolfe, 'A Defense of Participatory Democracy' (n 1) 385.

5 See Cole, *Social Theory* (n 1) 103–116; Macpherson, *The Life and Times of Liberal Democracy* (n 1) 108; Wolfe, 'A Defense of Participatory Democracy' (n 1) 380. See, however, Barber, *Strong Democracy* (n 1) 145–148.

6 Pateman, *Participation and Democratic Theory* (n 1) 42; Macpherson, *The Life and Times of Liberal Democracy* (n 1) 78–79.

7 Pateman, *Participation and Democratic Theory* (n 1) 30, quoting JS Mill, *Essays on Politics and Culture* (Anchor Books 1963) 229.

8 Pateman, *Participation and Democratic Theory* (n 1) 42.

9 For the importance of local democracy, see T Zittel, 'Participatory Engineering: Promises and Pitfalls' in B Kohler-Koch, D De Bièvre and W Maloney (eds), *Opening EU-Governance to Civil Society – Gains and Challenges* (2008) CONNEX Report

of a decentralised nature ought to be harnessed towards breaking the barriers of size at higher levels.[10] Although industry is often cited as the primary target for reform, participatory theorists make the case for a more participatory society in general: 'democracy implies (...) for everybody at least the opportunity to be an active citizen, not only of the State, but of every association with which his personality or circumstances cause him to be concerned'.[11]

The other element constitutive of participatory democracy is *political equality* writ large: 'equality of power in determining the outcome of decisions (...)'.[12] Equality of power defies the elite-mass structure of our societies:[13] the power to make decisions which significantly affect the polity needs to be shared equally among all, not entrusted to a few leaders.[14] This holds for government but also for non-governmental organs which have power, that is, which allocate values for society in an authoritative manner.[15] Equality of power directs our attention to society in another way. There cannot be political equality without a fair degree of social and economic equality.[16] With the workplace often advanced as the primary target for democratisation,[17] participatory democracy prescribes a reform of the structures of corporate capitalism.[18] Ideally, wealth should be distributed in such a way that 'no citizen shall ever be wealthy enough to buy another, and none poor enough to be forced to sell himself'.[19] 'A society of economic equality and economic independence',[20] that is, 'a one-class society of working proprietors',[21] is therefore needed.

The main function assigned to participation is an educative one: by participating into the affairs of the republic, man transforms itself into an intelligent being, his faculties are stimulated and developed, his ideas extended, his feelings ennobled, and his whole soul uplifted.[22] Participatory democracy is animated by a normative ideal: the self-development of its citizens.[23] This is a virtuous circle, for participatory democracy provides citizens with exactly the

Series no. 5, 132 <www.mzes.uni-mannheim.de/projekte/typo3/site/index.php?id=596> accessed 1st September 2015.

10 Macpherson, *The Life and Times of Liberal Democracy* (n 1) 108; Barber, *Strong Democracy* (n 1) 245–251.

11 Cole, *Social Theory* (n 1) 113.

12 Pateman, *Participation and Democratic Theory* (n 1) 43.

13 Bachrach, *The Theory of Democratic Elitism* (n 1) 99.

14 Ibid 89.

15 Ibid 102.

16 Macpherson, *The Life and Times of Liberal Democracy* (n 1) 100.

17 See Bachrach, *The Theory of Democratic Elitism* (n 1) 103–105; Pateman, *Participation and Democratic Theory* (n 1) 67–84.

18 Barber, *Strong Democracy* (n 1) 251–257.

19 JJ Rousseau, *The Social Contract or Principles of Political Right* (first published 1762, GDH Cole tr, EP Dutton and Co 1913) book II, chap 11.

20 Pateman, *Participation and Democratic Theory* (n 1) 22.

21 Macpherson, *The Life and Times of Liberal Democracy* (n 1) 16–17.

22 Rousseau, *The Social Contract* (n 19) book I, chap 8.

23 Bachrach, *The Theory of Democratic Elitism* (n 1) 100.

skills and attitudes that it needs in order to be sustainable.[24] Another function of participation is that it facilitates acceptance of collective decisions since such decisions are expressed through laws to which individuals have themselves given their assent.[25] Finally, participation plays an integrative function by contributing to the emergence of a we-feeling of community among those that participate in collective decisions.[26]

On the contrary, the contemporary theory of democracy is above all a call for giving up the maximum participation of the people in political life as an ideal.[27] As opposed to the unrealistic assumptions of the participatory theory of democracy[28] and the drift towards totalitarianism to which it may give rise,[29] the contemporary theory of democracy claims that democracy is 'that institutional arrangement for arriving at political decisions in which individuals acquire the power to decide by means of a competitive struggle for the people's vote'.[30] The contrast with the participatory theory of democracy is striking.[31] Whereas the contemporary theory describes democracy as a method for selecting political leaders, participatory democracy prescribes a normative model 'where maximum input (participation) is required and where output includes not just policies (decisions) but also the development of the social and political capacities of each individual, so that there is a "feedback" from output to input'.[32] While contemporary democracy enables citizens to choose leaders which will represent them through periodic, free and fair elections, participatory democracy stresses citizens' equal participation in the decisions which affect them. Finally, political equality is given a wider definition in the participatory theory: equality of political power rather than the equal opportunity to exercise power.[33]

To what extent does the participatory turn fit into the participatory theory of democracy exposed above? The debate on the pros and cons of the *citizen* dimension of participatory democracy clearly follows the thread of the participatory/contemporary divide. The proponents of direct democracy in the EU rely on the virtues of participation so dear to participatory theorists: direct democratic devices such as referenda and popular initiatives would educate citizens to European affairs, be conductive towards a European *demos*, and

---

24 Pateman, *Participation and Democratic Theory* (n 1) 42–43.

25 Ibid 27.

26 Ibid 27.

27 Ibid 1–16. See also JA Schumpeter, *Capitalism, Socialism and Democracy* (5th edn, Allen and Unwin 1976) 250–268.

28 See Pateman, *Participation and Democratic Theory* (n 1) 2–3.

29 See Bachrach, *The Theory of Democratic Elitism* (n 1) 8, 26–46.

30 Schumpeter, *Capitalism, Socialism and Democracy* (n 27) 269.

31 For a comparison, see Bachrach, *The Theory of Democratic Elitism* (n 1) 100; Pateman, *Participation and Democratic Theory* (n 1) 43.

32 Pateman, *Participation and Democratic Theory* (n 1) 43.

33 For a comparison between the two concepts, see Bachrach, *The Theory of Democratic Elitism* (n 1) 83–92.

further acceptance of EU decisions; meanwhile its opponents share with the contemporary theory of democracy a concern for the stability of the EU were such mechanisms to be adopted.[34]

Much more challenging is the view that participatory democracy comes down to opening EU governance to civil society.[35] We have already seen that this civil-society-centric vision of participatory democracy is largely a 'fiction'[36] which has been engineered top-down by a small circle of self-interested actors.[37] It attests to an epistemological sliding occurring in political debates but also in European integration literature:[38] participatory democracy no more as self-legislation by free and equal citizens but as involvement of civil society in governance.[39] This sliding is problematic, for it 'creates the illusion that such functional representation automatically implies direct citizen participation from the base upwards'.[40] It leaves scholars wondering about which normative standards are appropriate for assessing the participatory turn to civil society. We will see here below that this is a complex question on which views diverge widely depending on respective stands taken as to the civil society/democratic theory/EU-polity questions.

2.3. BATTLING FOR THE SOUL OF (EUROPEAN) CIVIL SOCIETY

The concept of civil society has given rise to an endless flow of contradictory and irreconcilable statements to the point that the usefulness of the concept for

34 On the pros and cons of direct democracy in the EU, see A Auer and JF Flauss (eds), *Le Référendum Européen* (Bruylant 1997); LP Feld and G Kirchgassner, 'The Role of Direct Democracy in the European Union' in CB Blankart and DC Mueller (eds), *A Constitution for the European Union* (MIT Press 2004); I Pernice, 'Référendum sur la Constitution pour l'Europe: Conditions, Risques et Implications' in C Kaddous and A Auer (eds), *Les Principes Fondamentaux de la Constitution Européenne* (Bruylant 2006); 'Direct Democracy and the European Union… Is that a Threat or a Promise?' (2008) 45 CML Rev 929.

35 See B Kohler-Koch, 'Chapter 17: Does Participatory Governance Hold its Promises?' in B Kohler-Koch and F Larat (eds), *Efficient and Democratic Governance in the European Union* (2008) CONNEX Report Series no. 9, 267 <www.mzes.uni-mannheim.de/projekte/typo3/site/index.php?id=596> accessed 1st September 2015. For more detail, see Sec 1.3 and 1.4.

36 L Cram, 'Civil Society, Participatory Democracy and the Governance of the Union: The Institutionalisation of a Fiction' (2006) paper delivered at the 2–4 November 2006 Osnabrück conference on governance and policy-making in the EU <http://web.uvic.ca/jmtrg/Papers_files/cram_paper_1.pdf> accessed 1st September 2015.

37 S Smismans, 'European Civil Society: Shaped by Discourses and Institutional Interests' (2003) 9 ELJ 482, 493; B Kohler-Koch, 'The Organization of Interests and Democracy in the European Union' in B Kohler-Koch and B Rittberger (eds), *Debating the Democratic Legitimacy of the European Union* (Rowman & Littlefield 2007) 255.

38 See, eg, O De Schutter, 'Europe in Search of its Civil Society' (2002) 8 ELJ 198, 202.

39 S Smismans, 'The Constitutional Labelling of "the Democratic Life of the EU": Representative and Participatory Democracy' in L Dobson and A Follesdal (eds), *Political Theory and the European Constitution* (Routledge 2004) 129.

40 Ibid 129.

research has even been questioned.[41] Invoking the contribution of civil society to democratic EU remains then an empty shell so long as light is not shed on the exact meaning conferred to civil society and the precise function one expects it to perform in modern societies. This section will show where this book positions itself in the civil society debate and explain how it intends to bring it further.

For the sake of brevity, one may say that three conceptual positions have chronologically made their appearance.[42] Civil society originally figured in the writings of Aristotle under the heading of *politike koinonia*, meaning political society/community. Civil society was thus seen as a political community of free and equal citizens who administer their *polis* according to a common vision of the good life.[43] This Aristotelian notion of political community, which brings under the same roof state and civil society, contrasts with the notion of civil society which materialised during the Enlightenment period.

From that time on, civil society came to be defined in economic terms, either positively as a self-regulating economic society subject to the civilising force of commerce (Smith), or more negatively as a system of needs (Hegel) or a bourgeois society which had to be overcome by a proletarian revolution (Marx).[44] Another strand of modern thought, largely inspired by de Tocqueville, came to hold that civil society was 'an intermediate sphere of voluntary association and activity standing between the individual and the state'.[45] In such a scheme, a strong society made of a multitude of voluntary organisations is to act as a check upon state power, while, at the same time, socialising citizens and teaching them the civic virtues and the political skills that make democracy work.[46] This liberal strand of thought, still very influential today, has been criticised for being impervious to the impact of the market on the associational life it praises. If the equality of conditions which impressed de Tocqueville at the time of his travel to America may have justified shielding market liberalism from democratic critique,[47] such a stance cannot be validly taken today when 'the problem of inequality of capitalism'[48] has become more salient than ever.[49]

This critical stance towards the market came to fruition with the contemporary tripartite model of civil society/economy/state relations.[50]

---

41 See MN Jensen, 'Concepts and Conceptions of Civil Society' (2006) 2 Journal of Civil Society 39, 39.

42 This chronological overview draws from JL Cohen and A Arato, *Civil Society and Political Theory* (MIT Press 1992); J Ehrenberg, *Civil Society: The Critical History of an Idea* (New York University Press 1999).

43 Cohen and Arato, *Civil Society and Political Theory* (n 42) 84–86.

44 Ehrenberg, *Civil Society* (n 42) 83–143.

45 Ibid 144.

46 Ibid 144–169. See also RD Putnam, R Leonardi and R Nanetti, *Making Democracy Work: Civic Traditions in Modern Italy* (Princeton University Press 1993).

47 Ibid 169.

48 Barber, *Strong Democracy* (n 1) 251.

49 Ehrenberg, *Civil Society* (n 42) 234.

50 Cohen and Arato, *Civil Society and Political Theory* (n 42) 425.

According to this model, 'civil society delineates a sphere that is formally distinct from the body politic and state authority on one hand, and from the immediate pursuit of self-interest and the imperatives of the market on the other'.[51] Such a model, which finds support in some major research projects,[52] describes civil society as an autonomous sphere of society between state and market, while recognising that it constitutes and is constituted by both.[53] Proponents of this contemporary conception differ as to the function they assign to civil society. According to the deliberative-democratic view defended by Habermas, civil society provides the institutional anchor of the public sphere into the lifeworld.[54] For communitarians like Barber, civil society incarnates a civic sphere of voluntary associations devoted to public goods.[55] According to the third, sociological, reading proposed by Cohen and Arato,[56] modern civil society refers to the social institutions through which society governs and reproduces itself.[57]

The intermediary and tripartite conceptions of civil society are fighting each other and, to some extent, overlapping in the academic debate on who can claim to represent civil society in the EU.[58] From the first conception's perspective, European civil society is an intermediary sphere of representation: it comprises all those voluntary, non-profit organisations which articulate and represent the interests of a constituency.[59] This image of civil society corresponds to that

---

51 Ehrenberg, *Civil Society* (n 42) 235.

52 See LM Salamon, SW Sokolowski and R List, *Global Civil Society: An Overview* (Johns Hopkins Center for Civil Society Studies 2003); A Evers and JL Laville (eds), *The Third Sector in Europe* (Edward Elgar 2004); VF Heinrich, 'Assessing and Strengthening Civil Society Worldwide: A Project Description of the CIVICUS Civil Society Index' (2003) CIVICUS Civil Society Index Paper Series vol 2, issue 1.

53 Ehrenberg, *Civil Society* (n 42) 235.

54 J Habermas, *Between Facts and Norms: Contributions to a Discourse Theory of Law and Democracy* (Polity Press 1996) 366–367.

55 B Barber, 'Three Challenges to Reinventing Democracy' in PQ Hirst and S Khilnani (eds), *Reinventing Democracy* (Blackwell 1996); B Barber, 'How to Make Society Civil and Democracy Strong' in A Giddens (ed), *The Global Third Way Debate* (Polity Press 2001).

56 Cohen and Arato, *Civil Society and Political Theory* (n 42).

57 B Kohler-Koch and C Quittkat, 'What is Civil Society and Who Represents Civil Society in the EU? – Results of an Online Survey among Civil Society Experts' (2009) 28 Policy and Society 11, 14–15.

58 For an overview, see Kohler-Koch and Quittkat, 'What is Civil Society and Who Represents Civil Society in the EU?' (n 57).

59 Ibid 21. See MP van Schendelen, *Machiavelli in Brussels: The Art of Lobbying the EU* (Amsterdam University Press 2002) 344; K Karr, *Democracy and Lobbying in the European Union* (Campus Verlag 2007); T Hüller and B Kohler-Koch, 'Assessing the Democratic Value of Civil Society Engagement in the European Union' in B Kohler-Koch, D De Bièvre and W Maloney (eds), *Opening EU-Governance to Civil Society – Gains and Challenges* (2008) CONNEX Report Series no. 5 <www.mzes.uni-mannheim.de/projekte/typo3/site/index.php?id=596> accessed 1st September 2015; J Steffek and P Nanz, 'Emergent Patterns of Civil Society Participation in Global and European Governance' in J Steffek, C Kissling and P Nanz (eds), *Civil Society Participation in European and Global Governance: a Cure for the Democratic Deficit?* (Palgrave Macmillan 2008) 7; T Hüller, 'Conceptualising Democratic

embraced by the main promoters of the participatory turn, the Commission[60] and the EESC for which civil society is the sum of all organisational structures who act as mediators between the public authorities and citizens.[61] This conception is all-encompassing in the sense that it covers all organisations which represent interests, no matter the type of interests represented. It is in line with the governance approach and in conformity with the principles of representative democracy.[62]

This book subscribes to the second, tripartite, conception. European civil society is therefore an autonomous sphere between state and market.[63] Business interests, trade unions, and professional interests will be excluded from civil society on the ground that they are too intermeshed with productive forces.[64] So will political parties and parliaments, for they are directly involved with state power.[65] Like the partisans of this conception, we see European governance as a potential threat to the autonomy of civil society seen as a non-governmental space. Instead of following Habermas' two-track model which expects that civil society will stand outside and, if need be, against the EU polity,[66] we accept that civil society may contribute to the construction of a transnational civic sphere sustained by the active engagement of European citizens, but on condition that deliberative spaces be created within European governance structures.[67]

Associational Involvement in EU Decision Making -Contributions from Contemporary Political Theory' (2010) 45 Acta Politica 298, 303; S Saurugger, 'Interest Groups and Democracy in the European Union' in J Beyers, R Eising and W Maloney (eds), *Interest Group Politics in Europe: Lessons from EU Studies and Comparative Politics* (Routledge 2010); J Greenwood, *Interest Representation in the European Union* (3rd edn, Palgrave Macmillan 2011); KO Lindgren and T Persson, *Participatory Governance in the EU: Enhancing or Endangering Democracy and Efficiency?* (Palgrave Macmillan 2011).

60 Commission, 'European Governance: A White Paper' COM (2001) 428 final, 14.

61 EESC, 'The Role and Contribution of Civil Society Organisations in the Building of Europe' (Opinion) [1999] OJ C329/10, 33–34.

62 Kohler-Koch and Quittkat, 'What is Civil Society and Who Represents Civil Society in the EU?' (n 57) 21.

63 Ibid 21.

64 Ibid 21.

65 Cohen and Arato, *Civil Society and Political Theory* (n 42) pref ix.

66 See EO Eriksen, 'Deliberative Supranationalism in the EU' in EO Eriksen and JE Fossum (eds), *Democracy in the European Union: Integration through Deliberation?* (Routledge 2000) 52–55; J Habermas, *The Postnational Constellation: Political Essays* (MIT Press 2001) 98–103; K Eder, 'The Construction of a Transnational Public: Prerequisites for Democratic Governance in a Transnationalising Society' in V Della Sala and C Ruzza (eds), *Governance and Civil Society in the European Union: Exploring Policy Issues* (vol 2, Manchester University Press 2007) 9–10, 24–26; HJ Trenz, 'A Transnational Space of Contention? Patterns of Europeanisation of Civil Society in Germany' in C Ruzza and V Della Sala (eds), *Governance and Civil Society in the European Union: Normative Perspectives* (vol 1, Manchester University Press 2007) 89–90.

67 See D Curtin, *'Civil Society' and the European Union: Opening Spaces for Deliberative Democracy?* (Collected courses of the Academy of European law 1996) 206–208. See also A Warleigh, '"Europeanizing" Civil Society: NGOs as Agents of Political Socialization' (2001)

In opposition to current contributions taking their cue from the tripartite model, we also see in European economic integration a potential threat to the autonomy of civil society seen as a non-economic sphere. This concern is in line with the tripartite model which protects civil society from market colonisation,[68] but it has been missing in scholarship on European civil society. The EU is a supranational organisation which has been driven by the functional need to regulate competitive markets. Isn't it possible that creating an internal market in which competition is free and undistorted could, in effect, colonise the civic space on which the EU has come to rely for its democratic renewal? The exclusively political focus of the debate on the democratic contribution of European civil society has so far left this risk unaccounted for whereas this book will give it centre stage.

2.4. DELIBERATIVE DEMOCRACY AND ITS LIMITS

Once the precise contours of civil society are settled, agreement needs to be found on the nature of its democratic contribution. As the old-fashioned participatory theory of democracy is silent on this issue, European integration scholars naturally turned to three democratic theories which, they claim, could provide a modern account of the participatory ideal: deliberative democracy, liberal pluralism and associative democracy.[69] These three theoretical strands share the same insight that it is mainly civil society, not citizens, which participate in the political process. Further specification of the democratic function assigned to civil society depends on the normative stand taken (associative/deliberative/pluralist) and respective views as to the nature of the European polity (state/political system/system of participatory governance).

This section will focus on the theoretical strand which is most relied upon regarding the democratic contribution of civil society in the EU: deliberative democracy,[70] and distinguish between various positions taken as to the

---

39 JCMS 619; K Armstrong, 'Rediscovering Civil Society The European Union and the White Paper on Governance' (2002) 8 ELJ 102.

68 See J Habermas, *The Theory of Communicative Action /Vol.2, Lifeworld and System: A Critique of Functionalist Reason* (Polity Press 1987) chap 8; Cohen and Arato, *Civil Society and Political Theory* (n 42) chap 9; Barber, 'How to Make Society Civil' (n 55).

69 See Curtin, *'Civil Society' and the European Union* (n 67) 202, 208; J Cohen and C Sabel, 'Directly-Deliberative Polyarchy' (1997) 3 ELJ 313, 31?; P Nieuwenburg, 'Democratic Life in Europolis' in A Kinneging (ed), *Rethinking Europe's Constitution* (Wolf Legal Publishers 2007) 165; Saurugger, 'Interest Groups and Democracy in the European Union' (n 59) 173–175.

70 Regarding the associative variant, see Saurugger, 'Interest Groups and Democracy in the European Union' (n 59); Lindgren and Persson, *Participatory Governance in the EU* (n 59). Regarding the pluralist variant, see van Schendelen, *Machiavelli in Brussels* (n 59); Karr, *Democracy and Lobbying in the European Union* (n 59); Greenwood, *Interest Representation in the European Union* (n 59).

nature of the Euro-polity. Throughout the section, it will be shown that current contributions on the EU participatory turn fail to account for the core normative concerns – maximum participation and political equality writ large – that animate the participatory theory of democracy.

Deliberative democracy has had a profound influence on the academic debate on civil society and its democratic contribution to the EU. Its appeal is largely found in the fact that it makes post-national democracy possible by decoupling democracy from the need of a pre-existing *demos* defined in substantive terms.[71] There are two dimensions to deliberative democracy: a *democratic* one since it 'includes collective decision-making with the participation of all who will be affected by the decision or their representatives',[72] and a *deliberative*, or rational, one since it 'includes decision making by means of arguments offered by and to participants who are committed to the values of rationality and impartiality'.[73]

As highlighted by Hendriks,[74] the role played by civil society in deliberative democracy is ambiguous. She identifies two emerging streams of thought which prescribe very different roles for civil society:

> *Micro* deliberative theorists concentrate on defining the ideal conditions of a deliberative procedure. This stream of theory provides only a limited discussion on who should deliberate and does not refer to civil society per se (...) Micro theories of deliberative democracy suggest that civil society actors should engage in deliberative politics to the extent that they are willing and capable of participating in structured deliberative fora. In this sense, civil society is implicitly called to take on communicative forms of action through collaborating with the state.[75]

Micro-theories find resonance with the conception of the EU as 'a system of participatory governance'.[76] On the contrary,

> *[M]acro* deliberative theorists emphasise informal discursive forms of deliberation, which take place in the public sphere. Their primary focus is on the unstructured and open conversations outside formal decision-making institutions (...) [M]acro theories of deliberative democracy emphasise the informal and unstructured nature

---

71 See EO Eriksen and JE Fossum, 'Post-National Integration' in EO Eriksen and JE Fossum (eds), *Democracy in the European Union: Integration through Deliberation?* (Routledge 2000) 18–19; R Schmalz-Bruns, 'The Euro-Polity in Perspective: Some Normative Lessons from Deliberative Democracy' in B Kohler-Koch and B Rittberger (eds), *Debating the Democratic Legitimacy of the European Union* (Rowman & Littlefield 2007) 287.

72 J Elster, 'Introduction' in J Elster (ed), *Deliberative democracy* (CUP 1998) 5.

73 Ibid 5.

74 CM Hendriks, 'Integrated Deliberation: Reconciling Civil Society's Dual Role in Deliberative Democracy' (2006) 54 Political Studies 486.

75 Ibid 486–487 (references omitted).

76 B Kohler-Koch, 'The Three Worlds of European Civil society – What Role for Civil Society for what Kind of Europe?' (2009) 28 Policy and Society 53, 53.

> of public discussion. Under this conception, civil society plays a role in informal political activities both outside and against the state.[77]

Macro-theories have inspired the depiction of the EU as 'an emergent polity with a social constituency in the making'.[78]

Finally, in addition to micro-and macro-theories, it is claimed that deliberative democracy has motivated a few middle-ground theories which conceive of the EU as 'a regulatory political system with civil society involvement'.[79]

Taking each of the above three models in turn, macro-deliberative theories have left their imprint into the conception that the EU is in a state of deep transformation: from 'a multi-level system of governance which relied mainly on the legitimacy of its constituent units, i.e., the Member States'[80] to 'a system of authoritative decisionmaking in its own right'.[81] This system of government cannot democratically rule without the support of a trans-national European public sphere.[82] The parliamentarisation of EU decision-making is depicted as its logical corollary.[83] This conception relies on the discursive theory of democracy formulated by Habermas.[84] For him, the public sphere is essential to democratic legitimacy: only laws which have been subject to a free and public debate are legitimate.[85] However, popular sovereignty is secured by a 'two-track' model: the public sphere generates political influence, but political influence is converted into political power after it passes through a parliamentary filter.[86]

The emergence of a European public sphere requires its prior anchoring into an organised civil society standing outside and, if need be, against the Euro-polity.[87] At the same time, proponents of the European public sphere readily admit that the EU governs through networks of public and civil actors.[88] These

77 Hendriks, 'Integrated Deliberation' (n 74) 487.

78 Kohler-Koch, 'The Three Worlds of European Civil Society' (n 76) 53.

79 Ibid 53.

80 Ibid 51.

81 Ibid 51.

82 See Hüller and Kohler-Koch, 'Assessing the Democratic Value of Civil Society Engagement in the European Union' (n 59) 162; Kohler-Koch, 'The Three Worlds of European Civil Society' (n 76) 51.

83 EO Eriksen, 'A Comment on Schmalz-Bruns' in B Kohler-Koch and B Rittberger (eds), *Debating the Democratic Legitimacy of the European Union* (Rowman & Littlefield 2007) 310.

84 Kohler-Koch, 'The Three Worlds of European Civil Society' (n 76) 51.

85 EO Eriksen and JE Fossum, 'Democracy through Strong Publics in the European Union?' (2002) 40 JCMS 401, 403–404.

86 J Habermas, *Between Facts and Norms* (n 54) 304–308, 371–372.

87 See Eriksen, 'Deliberative Supranationalism' (n 66) 52–55; Eder, 'The Construction of a Transnational Public' (n 66) 9–10, 24–26; Trenz, 'A Transnational Space of Contention?' (n 66) 89–90.

88 Eriksen and Fossum, 'Democracy through Strong Publics' (n 85) 416–420; HJ Trenz and K Eder, 'The Democratizing Dynamics of a European Public Sphere: Towards a Theory of Democratic Functionalism' (2004) 7 European Journal of Social Theory 5, 14–15; K Eder

normative and empirical insights are difficult to reconcile. How can a civil society which conforms to the demands of participatory democracy 'carr[y] with it the normative potential associated with a sphere of social action characterised by its autonomy, plurality, and communicative openness'?[89] Simply put, civil society cannot be expected to stand against the state and act within the state at the same time.[90] Not only Habermas' two-track model fails to fit into the participatory turn,[91] it also harbours federal ambitions for the EU which appear unrealistic, since 'the necessary conditions for the functioning of [his] normative model, such as the democratic constitutionalization, a European wide public sphere, and the spontaneous emergence of civil society have not yet materialised at EU level'.[92]

It is hard to see why Habermas' model has been called a modern version of the participatory theory of democracy in the first place. While participatory democracy emphasises the participation of citizens, Habermas 'shifts some of the burdens for securing democratic outcomes away from the individual virtues of an active citizenry onto the "anonymous network of communication" in civil society'.[93] Power no more emanates from the people, but rather from 'subjectless forms of communication'[94] within the public sphere. More importantly, contrary to the need for self-legislation highlighted by participatory theorists, the communicative structures of the public sphere do not 'rule' since, according to the two-track model, decisions are left to the parliamentary complexes.[95]

---

and HJ Trenz, 'Prerequisites of Transnational Democracy and Mechanisms for Sustaining it: The Case of the European Union' in B Kohler-Koch and B Rittberger (eds), *Debating the Democratic Legitimacy of the European Union* (Rowman & Littlefield 2007) 171–173; K Eder, 'The Making of a European Civil Society: "Imagined", "Practised" and "Staged"' (2009) 28 Policy and Society 23, 25; HJ Trenz, 'European Civil Society: Between Participation, Representation and Discourse' (2009) 28 Policy and Society 35, 36.

89 Armstrong, 'Rediscovering Civil Society'(n 67) 127.

90 See JS Dryzek, *Deliberative Democracy and Beyond* (OUP 2002) 81–114; C Hunold, 'Green Political Theory and the European Union: The Case for a Non-Integrated Civil Society' (2005) 14 Environmental Politics 324; M Tsakatika, 'Governance Vs. Politics: The European Union's Constitutive "Democratic Deficit"' (2007) 14 JEPP 867, 875; D Della Porta and M Caiani, *Social Movements & Europeanization* (OUP 2009) 180–181. For a diverging view, see Curtin, *'Civil Society' and the European Union* (n 67) 206–208; B Kohler-Koch and B Finke, 'The Institutional Shaping of EU-Society Relations: A Contribution to Democracy via Participation?' (2007) 3 Journal of Civil Society 205, 214–215.

91 P Nanz, 'Les Voix Multiples de l'Europe. Une Idée Interdiscursive de la Sphère Publique' (2003) 2 Raisons Politiques, paras 8–11; K Armstrong, 'Inclusive Governance? Civil Society and the Open Method of Co-Ordination' in S Smismans (ed), *Civil Society and Legitimate European Governance* (Edward Elgar 2006) 46–54.

92 Hüller and Kohler-Koch, 'Assessing the Democratic Value of Civil Society Engagement in the European Union' (n 59) 163. Cf J Habermas, *The Crisis of the European Union: A Response* (Polity Press 2012) 1–53.

93 K Baynes, 'A Critical Theory Perspective on Civil Society and the State' in NL Rosenblum and RC Post (eds), *Civil Society and Government* (Princeton University Press 2002) 134.

94 Habermas, *Between Facts and Norms* (n 54) 301.

95 Ibid 359.

The micro-theories of deliberative democracy don't fare much better. At first sight, micro-theories may seem more appropriate because they embrace the participatory turn in both its moderate and radical versions. Micro-theorists are confident that the participatory turn possesses deliberative qualities which will enhance the problem-solving capacity of the EU.[96] When procedural rules orient stakeholders towards a deliberative style of politics,[97] participatory arrangements are endowed with procedural legitimacy.[98] The latter arises from the fact that decisions are adopted according to a fair procedure[99] abiding by principles of transparency, openness and participation.[100] It is hoped that procedural legitimacy will complement and beneficially interact with democratic legitimacy provided through normal parliamentary channels.[101]

Still, at the same time, micro-theories of deliberative democracy are unable to capture the democratic relevance of the participatory turn. For, they are essentially concerned with collective actors, while participatory democracy was meant to empower citizens.[102] As a result, these theories lose sight of the democratic commitment to self-determination and would easily leave citizens 'represented' by unelected and unaccountable elites. Their emphasis on collective actors is largely a consequence of another change, from the self-developmental

---

96 See Cohen and Sabel, 'Directly-Deliberative Polyarchy' (n 69) 313; S Hix, 'The Study of the European Union II: The "New Governance" Agenda and its Rival' (1998) 5 JEPP 38, 39–41; MA Pollack, 'Theorizing EU Policy-Making' in H Wallace, W Wallace and MA Pollack (eds), *Policy-Making in the European Union* (5th edn, OUP 2005) 36–45; PC Schmitter, 'Governance in the European Union: A Viable Mechanism for Future Legitimation?' in Y Papadopoulos and A Benz (eds), *Governance and Democracy: Comparing National, European and International Experiences* (Routledge 2006) 161–163.

97 C Joerges, 'Reconceptualizing the Supremacy of European Law: A Plea for a Supranational Conflict of Laws' in B Kohler-Koch and B Rittberger (eds), *Debating the Democratic Legitimacy of the European Union* (Rowman & Littlefield 2007) 317. See also O Gerstenberg and CF Sabel, 'Directly-Deliberative Polyarchy: An Institutional Ideal for Europe?' in C Joerges and R Dehousse (eds), *Good Governance in Europe's Integrated Market* (OUP 2002) 337–341.

98 See G Majone, 'Regulatory Legitimacy' in G Majone and P Baake (eds), *Regulating Europe* (Routledge 1996) 291–294.

99 R Dehousse, 'European Governance in Search of Legitimacy: The Need for a Process-Based Approach' in O De Schutter, N Lebessis and J Paterson (eds), *Governance in the European Union* (Office for Official Publications of the European Communities 2001) 177.

100 Ibid 182. See also C Joerges, '"Good Governance" through Comitology?' in C Joerges and E Vos (eds), *EU Committees: Social Regulation, Law and Politics* (Hart 1999) 332–338.

101 See A Héritier, 'Elements of Democratic Legitimation in Europe: An Alternative Perspective' (1999) 6 JEPP 269, 271–273; Dehousse, 'European Governance in Search of Legitimacy' (n 99) 186–187; C Lord and D Beetham, 'Legitimizing the EU: Is there a "Post-Parliamentary Basis" for its Legitimation?' (2001) 39 JCMS 443, 452–453; C Lord and P Magnette, 'E Pluribus Unum? Creative Disagreement about Legitimacy in the EU' (2004) 42 JCMS 183, 187; C Lord, 'Parliamentary Representation in a Decentered Polity' in B Kohler-Koch and B Rittberger (eds), *Debating the Democratic Legitimacy of the European Union* (Rowman & Littlefield 2007) 146–150.

102 MT Greven, 'Some Considerations on Participation in Participatory Governance' in B Kohler-Koch and B Rittberger (eds), *Debating the Democratic Legitimacy of the European Union* (Rowman & Littlefield 2007) 234–237.

effect of participation emphasised by participatory democrats to its instrumental value as a means for improved problem-solving in complex governance arrangements.[103] Now that participation has become instrumental to the quality of deliberative problem-solving, what matters is no more the citizen with his opinions and preferences but the participation of functional holders,[104] those collective actors which possess the necessary quality or resources relevant to the problem at hand.[105] Micro-theorists also fail to see that, as a result of their elite politics, the democratic counterpart of self-determination, political equality, might be under threat.[106]

Half way between micro-deliberative theorists' focus on functional problem-solving and macro-deliberative theorists' concern for the emergence of a European public sphere, lie quite a few contributions which hold that, no more a mere system of participatory governance, not yet a state, the EU is a political system in need of direct legitimacy for the increasing range of policies it delivers.[107] These contributions identify the problem as follows: when compared and evaluated in accordance with the tools that political science has previously applied to the nation-state, the EU appears as suffering from a deep crisis of legitimacy rooted in a lack of democratic credentials, the absence of a European demos and a record of underperformance.[108] Whether the participatory turn, in either its moderate or radical version, can remedy this malaise will depend on the extent to which European governance itself, and civil society as an actor thereof, can meet democratic norms of public control and political equality.[109]

The middle-ground theories mostly assess the democratising potential inherent in the participation of civil society in European governance according to the ideal of public deliberation.[110] It is expected that organised civil society

103 Ibid 239.

104 Schmitter, 'Governance in the European Union' (n 96) 167–169.

105 Greven, 'Some Considerations on Participation in Participatory Governance' (n 102) 241.

106 Ibid 241. See also P Magnette, 'Democracy in the European Union: Why and how to Combine Representation and Participation?' in S Smismans (ed), *Civil Society and Legitimate European Governance* (Edward Elgar 2006) 23; Lord and Beetham, 'Legitimizing the EU' (n 101) 453–455.

107 Kohler-Koch, 'The Three Worlds of European Civil Society' (n 76) 50. See also D Beetham and C Lord, *Legitimacy and the EU* (Longman 1998) 22–23; Hix, 'The Study of the European Union' (n 96) 41.

108 Ibid 50. See also Beetham and Lord, *Legitimacy and the EU* (n 107).

109 Lord and Beetham, 'Legitimizing the EU' (n 101) 453–455. On European governance and the challenges it raises for democracy, see A Benz and Y Papadopoulos (eds), *Governance and Democracy: Comparing National, European and International Experiences* (Routledge 2006); D Curtin, P Mair, and Y Papadopoulos (eds), *Accountability and European Governance* (2010) 33 West European Politics 929; A Héritier and M Rhodes (eds), *New Modes of Governance in Europe: Governing in the Shadow of Hierarchy* (Palgrave Macmillan 2011).

110 Steffek and Nanz, 'Emergent Patterns of Civil Society Participation' (n 59) 7. See also De Schutter, 'Europe in Search of its Civil Society' (n 38); Hüller and Kohler-Koch, 'Assessing the Democratic Value of Civil Society Engagement in the European Union' (n 59); Hüller, 'Conceptualising Democratic Associational Involvement in EU Decision Making'

will function as a transmission belt between European citizens and the EU.[111] Vertically, CSOs gather citizens' concerns and bring them to bear on European institutions, while collecting information from those institutions and communicating them to citizens. Horizontally, CSOs contribute to the emergence of a European public sphere by informing the wider public about EU politics.[112] Seen from the upper half of the transmission belt, European governance will be democratic to the extent that it brings about free, informed and inclusive deliberation.[113] Looking at the lower half of the transmission belt, CSOs are expected to mediate a relation of accountability between European institutions and their constituencies. Or to put it a different way, they are to represent the interests of their members and the wider public *vis-à-vis* European institutions.[114]

The middle-ground theories are more attractive than their micro- and macro-counterparts. Contrary to the two-track model of Habermas, they reinstate the participatory moment of deliberation.[115] They do at the same time look beyond functional holders by addressing the citizen as the ultimate stakeholder of governance.[116] Yet, they are still unsatisfactory from a participatory-democratic perspective, for they bind organised civil society to the same norms of representation and accountability which have been devised for modern representative government. Without going as far as considering that representation is antithetical to participation,[117] this book holds the view that the concepts of representation and accountability insufficiently convey the ideal of maximum participation which has motivated the turn to participatory democracy. They offer no guarantee that citizens will participate *actively* in European governance in new ways other than voting for European elections every five years.

(n 59); I Tanasescu, *The European Commission and Interest Groups: Towards a Deliberative Interpretation of Stakeholder Involvement in EU Policy-Making* (VUB Press 2009); K Heard-Lauréote, *European Union Governance: Effectiveness and Legitimacy in European Commission Committees* (Routledge 2010); D Friedrich, *Democratic Participation and Civil Society in the European Union* (Manchester University Press 2011); B Kohler-Koch and C Quittkat with V Buth and C Altides, *De-Mystification of Participatory Democracy: EU Governance and Civil Society* (OUP 2013).

111 Ibid 8.

112 Ibid 8.

113 Ibid 9.

114 Hüller and Kohler-Koch, 'Assessing the Democratic Value of Civil Society Engagement in the European Union' (n 59) 167. See also B Kohler-Koch, 'Civil Society and EU Democracy: "Astroturf" Representation?' (2010) 17 JEPP 100; B Kohler-Koch, 'How to Put Matters Right? Assessing the Role of Civil Society in EU Accountability' (2010) 33 West European Politics 1117.

115 Steffek and Nanz, 'Emergent Patterns of Civil Society Participation' (n 59) 6–9; D Friedrich, 'Actual and Potential Contributions of Civil Society Organisations to Democratic EU Governance' in M Freise (ed), *European Civil Society on the Road to Success?* (Nomos 2008) 71.

116 Steffek and Nanz, 'Emergent Patterns of Civil Society Participation' (n 59) 6.

117 See Rousseau, *The Social Contract* (n 19) book III, chap 15.

By contrast, this book builds on a discrete strand of the literature[118] which holds that deliberative democracy implies wide public participation in decision-making processes.[119] A specific contribution to public deliberation is expected from civil society seen as a civic space between state and market.[120] We will claim that bringing civil society into European governance holds the promise to bridge the gap between the EU and its citizens on condition that this 'participation from the bottom takes place within and through the framework of a governance structure which facilitates such a discursive process'.[121] In the absence of discursive structures, civil society would become governmentalized as it gets closer to the European governance arrangements it tries to influence.[122] This book will attempt to reconcile European governance with active citizenship. Unlike other middle-ground theories, we do not accept that the participatory turn, in either its moderate or radical version, should sacrifice active citizenship for the more elitist position of a representative civil society accountable to European citizens. Rather, we believe that a public of active citizens may participate in European governance provided that the structures of the latter are democratised with a view to meet deliberative norms of publicity, pluralism and participation.

The belief that civil society acts as a school of democracy in which citizens 'gain the spirit, the experience, and the skills that elevate them to critical and active political citizens',[123] will fare high in our assessment of the participatory turn. But, is such a view realistic considering that the school of democracy thesis already faces quite staggering evidence as to the difficulty for CSOs to activate European citizens?[124] We claim that this does not justify abandoning civic engagement within civil society as a normative ideal for the EU. While the

118 See Curtin, *'Civil Society' and the European Union* (n 67); Armstrong, 'Rediscovering Civil Society' (n 67); A Warleigh, 'Civil Society and Legitimate Governance in a Flexible Europe: Critical Deliberativism as a Way Forward' in S Smismans (ed), *Civil Society and Legitimate European Governance* (Edward Elgar 2006) 71.

119 Curtin, *'Civil Society' and the European Union* (n 67) 279.

120 Ibid 206–207.

121 Ibid 208.

122 See Armstrong, 'Rediscovering Civil Society' (n 67) 130.

123 Kohler-Koch, 'The Organization of Interests and Democracy in the European Union' (n 37) 263.

124 See Warleigh, '"Europeanizing" Civil Society' (n 67) 635; I Sudbery, 'Bridging the Legitimacy Gap in the EU: Can Civil Society Help to Bring the Union Closer to its Citizens?' (2003) 26 Collegium 75, 93–94; S Saurugger, 'The Professionalisation of Interest Representation: a Legitimacy Problem for Civil Society in the EU?' in S Smismans (ed), *Civil Society and Legitimate European Governance* (Edward Elgar 2006); A Warleigh, 'Making Citizens from the Market? NGOs and the Representation of Interests' in R Bellamy, D Castiglione and J Shaw (eds), *Making European Citizens: Civic Inclusion in a Transnational Context* (Palgrave Macmillan 2006) 128; G Jordan and W Maloney, *Democracy and Interest Groups: Enhancing Participation?* (Palgrave Macmillan 2007) 191; E Monaghan, '"Communicating Europe": The Role of Organised Civil Society' (2008) 4 JCER 18, 26–27; JW van Deth, 'The "Good European Citizen": Congruence and Consequences of Different Points of View' (2009) 8 European Political Science 175, 183–186; B Kohler-Koch, 'Post-Maastricht Civil Society and Participatory Democracy' (2012) 34 Journal of European Integration 809, 820;.

black box of CSOs is left largely unexplored,[125] the empirical evidence currently opposed to the 'school of democracy' thesis seems, according to a recent study, rather overblown.[126] Moreover, the ideal of participatory democracy is exactly meant to 'confront the elite-mass structure characteristic of modern societies'[127] in whichever organisations citizens are led to participate. If empirical evidence came to confirm that the participatory turn boils down to elite activism by a few representative leaders, one should, rather than discarding the participatory virtues of European civil society *en bloc*, address the extent to which the bureaucratic structures of European governance contribute to this state of affairs and whether their democratisation might further wider participation. Particular attention could be paid to the radical version of participatory democracy embodied by the OMC. For the latter institutional innovation supposedly offers the opportunity to address local CSOs where one would expect active citizenship to be much stronger than at the national or European level.[128]

In addition, this book will distinguish itself most clearly from the literature reviewed by integrating a market variable into its assessment of the participatory turn. Participatory theorists wanted to reform the capitalistic structures of our societies. Modern theories of participatory democracy have also explicitly addressed the need to reform such structures or, at least, to protect civil society from their invasive tendencies. Habermas has paid a great deal of attention to the need to protect the lifeworld against the colonising tendencies of the economic subsystem,[129] while Hirst has put forth associative democracy as a means for citizens to reassert control over corporate capitalism, pleading for an extension of associative principles to the corporate sector.[130] Finally, Dahl, an important proponent of pluralism, has pointed out that market capitalism, even though it is far more favourable to democratic institutions than any nonmarket economy, harms democracy in a number ways.[131] Nevertheless, the market variable has not been taken into consideration when those democratic theories were uploaded

---

125 Saurugger, 'Interest Groups and Democracy in the European Union' (n 59) 184.

126 M Piewitt, M Rodekamp and J Steffek, 'Civil Society in World Politics: How Accountable are Transnational CSOs?' (2010) 6 Journal of Civil Society 237, 255. See also H Johansson, 'Whom Do They Represent? Mixed Modes of Representation in EU-Based CSOs' in S Kröger and D Friedrich (eds), *The Challenge of Democratic Representation in the European Union* (Palgrave Macmillan 2012) 90; M Rodekamp, 'Representing their Members? Civil Society Organizations and the EU's External Dimension' in S Kröger and D Friedrich (eds), *The Challenge of Democratic Representation in the European Union* (Palgrave Macmillan 2012) 107.

127 Bachrach, *The Theory of Democratic Elitism* (n 1) 99.

128 See A Fung, 'Associations and Democracy: Between Theories, Hopes, and Realities' (2003) 29 Annual Review of Sociology 515, 521.

129 J Habermas, *The Theory of Communicative Action /Vol. 2, Lifeworld and System: A Critique of Functionalist Reason* (Polity Press 1987) chap 8.

130 PQ Hirst, 'Can Associationalism Come Back?' (2001) 4 Critical Review of International Social and Political Philosophy 15, 25–26.

131 R Dahl, *On Democracy* (Yale University Press 1998) 166–179.

to the European stage. It is curious, to say the least, because the EU is heir to the European *Economic* Community, a supranational organisation born out of the functional need to regulate markets effectively. This book will, therefore, contend that European economic integration will hinder democratisation if it does not properly constrain its tendency to colonise the civil society on which the EU has come to rely for its democratic renewal.

2.5. CONCLUSIONS

This literature review illustrates the complexity which surrounds the debate on participatory democracy in the EU. Any scholar willing to contribute to the discussion in a meaningful way is bound to take a stand as to the civil society/ democratic theory/EU-polity questions. The purpose of the next chapter will be to devise a normative framework which answers, precisely, these three questions. Its originality will lie in its attempt at overcoming the participatory ideal of bits and pieces which afflicts current scholarship. In this respect, the challenge will be to recast the core normative concerns that have animated the traditional participatory theory of democracy – self-government through citizen's *participation* and fighting the inequality bias of *market* capitalism – in a modern setting where civil society's contribution to the democratisation of the EU-polity is given centre stage.

Another original aspect of this framework will be to give *law* its proper place. While the EU's participatory turn has become a subject of research for social scientists from all backgrounds, the contribution of lawyers to this interdisciplinary debate has so far remained minimal. As to the role that law ought to play in implementing Article 11 TEU, they have called for European institutions to enact procedural rules and to confer participatory rights with a view to strengthen participation in their activities,[132] but the legal community has yet to engage into a deeper reflection as to the function that EU law could perform in a participatory society.[133] The next chapter will propose to fill this gap by applying to EU law the notion of reflexivity, characteristic of a legal order that ensures the peaceful coexistence of civil society with, respectively, European governance and the internal market.

---

132 See R Bieber and F Maiani, 'Bringing the Union Closer to its Citizens? "Participatory Democracy" and the Potential Contribution of the Lisbon Treaty' [2009] Annuaire Suisse de Droit Européen 229; V Cuesta Lopez, 'The Lisbon Treaty's Provisions on Democratic Principles: A Legal Framework for Participatory Democracy' (2010) 16 EPL 123; J Mendes, 'Participation and the Role of Law after Lisbon: A Legal View on Article 11 TEU' (2011) 48 CML Rev 1849.

133 See, however, Armstrong, 'Rediscovering Civil Society' (n 67) 112–113; Joerges, 'Reconceptualizing the Supremacy of European Law' (n 97).

CHAPTER 3

OVERCOMING THE PARTICIPATORY IDEAL OF BITS AND PIECES

3.1. INTRODUCTION

This chapter endeavours to present normative benchmarks for assessing in a coherent and systematic manner the EU participatory turn. As mentioned in the previous chapter, this requires taking a stand on three highly contested issues. As to the conception of *civil society* and the nature of its *democratic* contribution, the theoretical framework developed by Cohen and Arato in 'Civil Society and Political Theory'[1] will support the view that civil society is a pluralist sphere of participation between state and market wherein deliberative ethics realises its full potential. Democratisation proceeds whenever civil society manages to assert influence over the state and market subsystems without falling prey to their colonising tendencies. This emancipatory process has so far taken place within the context of national welfare states. This begs the question: how will it play out in the EU which is not a state (*3.2*)?

A proper answer entails agreement to be reached as to the *nature* of the EU-polity. It will be argued that the EU is a multilevel political system with a social policy in the making. Multilevel social Europe turned to civil society's involvement in European governance in the hope that it would democratise its representative system of government. The crucial issue raised by the participatory turn is whether multilevel social Europe will be able to continue the emancipatory process engaged by national welfare states. In others words, will social Europe contribute to civil society's empowerment or to its collapse under the colonising forces of power and money (*3.3*)?

This brings up three sets of questions an affirmative answer to which appears necessary if civil society is to democratise social Europe. Firstly, is European economic law colonising or sufficiently reflexive to limit the impact of negative integration on civil society (*3.4*)? Secondly, is social Europe democratic in the sense that it opens European governance to the democratic influence of civil society (*3.5*)? Lastly, is social Europe effective, that is, able to protect civil society from the market imperative of European economic integration (*3.6*)? A cursory

1 JL Cohen and A Arato, *Civil Society and Political Theory* (MIT Press1992).

glance will be given to these questions and the specific case studies chosen to test them will be introduced. The remaining chapters will be dedicated to their in-depth analysis.

3.2. CIVIL SOCIETY: A SPHERE OF PARTICIPATION BETWEEN STATE AND MARKET

Among the many conceptions of civil society,[2] Cohen and Arato's is one of the most relied upon by scholars with regard to the EU.[3] According to their tripartite framework to which this book has already subscribed, civil society is 'a sphere of social interaction between economy and state, composed above all of the intimate sphere (especially the family), the sphere of associations (especially voluntary associations), social movements, and forms of public communication'.[4] This sphere is distinguished 'from both a political society of parties, political organizations, and political publics (in particular, parliaments) and an economic society composed of organizations of production and distribution'.[5] 'Political and economic society generally arise from civil society'; they however do not belong in civil society, for they 'are directly involved with state power and economic production, which they seek to control and manage'.[6]

With civil society so defined, one can turn to the nature of its democratic contribution. Cohen and Arato ground democratic legitimacy in Habermas' discourse ethics which holds that 'just those norms deserve to be valid that could meet with the approval of those potentially affected, insofar as the latter participate in rational discourses'.[7] Rational discussion presupposes that participants recognise each other as equals, that is, 'as autonomous, rational subjects whose claims will be acknowledged if supported by valid arguments'.[8] The dialogue between participants must, moreover, be public, that is, unconstrained by political and economic factors and open to the participation of all interested parties.[9] With a view to prevent exclusionary effects attached

---

2 For an overview, see MN Jensen, 'Concepts and Conceptions of Civil Society' (2006) 2 Journal of Civil Society 39.

3 B Kohler-Koch and C Quittkat, 'What is Civil Society and Who Represents Civil Society in the EU? – Results of an Online Survey among Civil Society Experts' (2009) 28 Policy and Society 11, 16.

4 Cohen and Arato, *Civil Society and Political Theory* (n 1) pref ix.

5 Ibid pref ix.

6 Ibid pref ix-x.

7 J Habermas, *Between Facts and Norms: Contributions to a Discourse Theory of Law and Democracy* (Polity Press 1996) 127. See also Cohen and Arato, *Civil Society and Political Theory* (n 1) 347–348.

8 Cohen and Arato, *Civil Society and Political Theory* (n 1) 348.

9 Ibid 348.

to any kind of democratic organisation (representative, participative, or others), the discourse-ethical principle of legitimacy demands the institutionalisation of a plurality of democracies: what matters is that existing forms of democracy be democratised further according to the requirements of discourse ethics and be supplemented, completed, but never replaced, by other forms of democracy.[10]

While democratisation of the economic and administrative sphere is very much constrained by the coordinating mechanisms of money and power which prevail in those spheres, it can be argued that deliberative democracy finds its fullest expression in civil society. Not only civil society refers to the institutional anchoring of a communicatively-coordinated *public* sphere into the lifeworld,[11] it is also described as a *pluralist* sphere conductive to small-scale *participation* in a wide array of social institutions.[12] The foundations are then already laid in civil society for a democratisation of wider society according to the norms of *publicity*, *plurality* and *participation* which underpin discourse ethics.[13]

This political theory chimes with the democratic aspirations which have motivated the turn to civil society in the EU, for it too locates 'the normative necessity and empirical possibility of democratization in civil society'.[14] The next question is: how does democratisation proceed from civil society to the administrative and economic sphere? It was a question of crucial importance for the development of national welfare states. It becomes even the more so for the EU which is not a state with a proper welfare policy. Answering it requires that prior explanation be given as to the social theory which underpins the tripartite framework within which civil society is located.

The tripartite model is grounded on the conceptual framework elaborated by Habermas in its 'critique of functionalist reason'[15] wherein the economic and administrative subsystems are distinguished from each other and from the lifeworld.[16] While the state and the economy are steered by the media of power and money respectively, the lifeworld reproduces itself through the forces of communication.[17] For Cohen and Arato, the lifeworld is a double-headed concept. On the one hand, it refers to 'the linguistically structured stock of

10 Ibid 412.

11 Habermas, *Between Facts and Norms* (n 7) 366–367.

12 See B Barber, 'How to Make Society Civil and Democracy Strong' in A Giddens (ed), *The Global Third Way Debate* (Polity Press 2001).

13 Cohen and Arato, *Civil Society and Political Theory* (n 1) 346, 419. See also Habermas, *Between Facts and Norms* (n 7) 368; EESC, 'The Role and Contribution of Civil Society Organisations in the Building of Europe' (Opinion) [1999] OJ C329/10, 32–33.

14 Ibid 411.

15 Ibid 426. See also J Habermas, *The Theory of Communicative Action /Vol.2, Lifeworld and System: A Critique of Functionalist Reason* (Polity Press 1987).

16 On the lifeworld/system distinction, see S Chambers, 'A Critical Theory of Civil Society' in S Chambers and W Kymlicka (eds), *Alternative Conceptions of Civil Society* (Princeton University Press 2001) 92–96; L Goode, *Jürgen Habermas: Democracy and the Public Sphere* (Pluto Press 2005) 62–71.

17 Cohen and Arato, *Civil Society and Political Theory* (n 1) 426–427.

knowledge, the reservoir of unshaken convictions, and the forms of solidarity and competence' on which social actors rely without question.[18] On the other hand, it encompasses the institutions specialised in the reproduction of those very resources. It is on this last level that Cohen and Arato locate civil society as a distinctly modern construct referring to all those social institutions which specialise in the reproduction of solidarity, this scarce and precarious resource which needs to be constantly renewed through the life of associations.[19]

Civil society belongs to a lifeworld where deference to traditions has been replaced by 'a new and reflexive relation, *a nontraditional relation to tradition*'.[20] This rationalisation of the lifeworld would not have been possible without the development of the economic and administrative subsystems because they have unburdened the lifeworld from strategic concerns related to money and power.[21] The paradox of modernity is, however, that 'the same processes that are among the constitutive conditions of a modern lifeworld also represent the greatest potential threats to that lifeworld'.[22] Indeed, the expansion of the economic and administrative subsystems, which has relieved the lifeworld from the strategic concerns which stifled its communicative potential, now comes to threaten the lifeworld it has set free; to such an extent, say Cohen and Arato, that a primordial task is for the lifeworld to protect itself against the dark side of modernity, that is, its colonisation by the media of power and money.[23]

Democratisation implies then a two-pronged strategy: erecting barriers against colonisation by and establishing sensors of influence over the administrative and economic subsystems.[24] The two steps presuppose one another and are inherently linked since 'only an adequately defended, differentiated, and organized civil society can monitor and influence the outcomes of steering processes, but only a civil society capable of influencing the state and economy can help to restrain or redirect the expansive tendencies of the media'.[25] It is for fundamental rights, seen as 'the *organizing principle* of a modern civil society',[26] to stabilise social differentiation and strengthen the barriers defending the lifeworld against both media.[27] The correlated need to influence the economic and administrative subsystems while protecting itself from them seems to present civil society with the Michelsian dilemma between

18 Ibid 428.
19 Ibid 429, 472.
20 Ibid 435–436.
21 Ibid 439.
22 Ibid 440.
23 Ibid 448–449. On the concept of 'colonisation', see Chambers, 'A Critical Theory of Civil Society' (n 16) 94; W Outhwaite, *Habermas: A Critical Introduction* (2nd edn, Polity Press 2009) 80–105.
24 Ibid 489, 471.
25 Ibid 471–472.
26 Ibid 442.
27 Ibid 477–478.

democracy and organisation,[28] for, the moment that civil society actors step over the boundaries of the lifeworld, they reproduce the organisational structures determined by power and money, thereby giving up their communicative rationality.[29]

However, it is contended that there is no 'iron law of oligarchy' attached to a politics of influence by civil society aimed at those in political society and economic society or at the publics which exist at their level.[30] For, rather than seeking inclusion within the organisational structures of the state or the market, such a politics aims at altering 'the universe of political discourse to accommodate new need-interpretations, new identities, and new norms'.[31] It does not imply instrumentalisation because it is discursive, rather than power or market-driven. For a politics of influence to be successful, the state and the economy need to be provided with sensors able to make them receptive to the discursive influence generated in civil society.

From a lifeworld perspective, it is proposed to introduce, within the economic and administrative subsystems, institutionalised forms of communicative action. These publics, economic and political societies as it were, can democratise the subsystems and act, from within them, as receptors for the influence of civil society.[32] This necessarily entails a project of limited democratisation since the communicative potential of these institutions must remain subordinated to the need to maintain the proper rationality of the systems to which they belong if the foundations of modernity are to be preserved.[33]

From a systemic point of view, the strategic rationality of the administrative and economic subsystems needs to be tamed by some kind of reflexive law. According to Teubner, 'reflexion within social subsystems is possible only insofar as processes of democratization create discursive structures within these subsystems'.[34] Here too, reflexive law only calls for limited democratisation since 'the primary function of the democratization of subsystems lies neither in increasing individual participation nor in neutralizing power structures but in the internal reflexion of social identity'.[35] Reflexive law, unlike formal and substantive law, intends to achieve its aims through procedural means: it establishes 'norms of procedure, organization, membership, and competence that can alter decision making, change the weight of different parties and

28 R Michels, *Political Parties: A Sociological Study of the Oligarchical Tendencies of Modern Democracy* (Free Press 1949).

29 Cohen and Arato, *Civil Society and Political Theory* (n 1) 473–474, 560–561.

30 Ibid 561.

31 Ibid 526.

32 Ibid 479–480.

33 Ibid 479.

34 G Teubner, 'Substantive and Reflexive Elements in Modern Law' (1983) 17 Law & Society Review 239, 273.

35 Ibid 273.

members, and make overall processes of decision sensitive to side effects and externalities'.[36]

This self-conservation strategy, through which democratic civil society asserts its autonomy by establishing sensors of influence over state and market while erecting barriers against them, is essentially bound up with the historical transformations of the modern state. To put it schematically, civil society first asserted its freedom from the absolutist state by claiming civil rights.[37] It then took control of the constitutional state by obtaining the political right to participate in the exercise of political power.[38] It, finally, fought against the inequalities of market capitalism by making the democratic state the guarantor of its social rights.[39] The democratic welfare state is therefore the endpoint of a process through which civil society has progressively emancipated itself from both bureaucratic and market forces. The crucial question raised by the participatory turn to civil society is whether the EU will continue this emancipatory process or, on the contrary, contribute to its defeat.

3.3. ORGANISED CIVIL SOCIETY IN MULTILEVEL SOCIAL EUROPE

Answering that question requires taking a stand as to the nature of the EU-polity. The EU is certainly not a democratic welfare state. Nor is it a mere international organisation born out of an economic agreement between sovereign welfare states. It lies somewhere in between. The EU has emerged as the central (albeit weak) level of a multi-tiered political system, with positive integration resulting from social policy initiatives taken at the centre, and negative integration occurring through ECJ's enforcement of the market compatibility requirements of European economic law.[40]

Multilevel social Europe has been democratised according to a strategy which perfectly fits the pluralist credo so dear to Cohen and Arato.[41] This strategy has involved, on the one hand, developing a political society at the EU level with, at its centre, a strong European Parliament empowered to keep the European executive in check, and, on the other, reinforcing the grip of national

36 Cohen and Arato, *Civil Society and Political Theory* (n 1) 482.

37 Habermas, *The Theory of Communicative Action* (n 15) 358–360.

38 Ibid 360–361.

39 Ibid 361. For a similar view, see TH Marshall, 'Citizenship and Social Class' in J Manza and M Sauder (eds), *Inequality and Society* (W.W. Norton and Co. 2009).

40 P Pierson and S Leibfried, 'Multitiered Institutions and the Making of Social Policy' in S Leibfried and P Pierson (eds), *European Social Policy: Between Fragmentation and Integration* (The Brookings Institution 1995) 3, 5–6; S Leibfried, 'Social Policy: Left to the Judges and the Markets?' in H Wallace, M Pollack and A Young (eds), *Policy-Making in the European Union* (6th edn, OUP 2010) 254–256.

41 This paragraph reformulates the points made in Sec 1.2.

parliaments over their own executive in the Council. Territorial representation has even been extended down to regional and local interests since the creation of the Committee of the Regions (CoR), while functional interests are represented in the EESC. Yet, this is not enough: while national parliaments' scrutiny of their executive in the Council is inevitably limited, the European political society has not yet fully taken off.

This democratic deficit has contributed to the creation of a legitimacy gap between EU power-holders and their constituencies. So as to overcome the limits of representative democracy, the EU naturally turned to participatory democracy.[42] Beside timid inroads into direct, citizen-based democracy, participatory democracy is mainly understood from a civil-society-centric perspective as the participation of organised civil society in European governance, with the confidence that this will represent 'a chance to get citizens more actively involved in achieving the Union's objectives'.[43]

As the previous section illustrates, merely eulogising the democratic virtues of civil society on paper will not do. In order to take advantage of them, multilevel social Europe has to confront the paradoxes of its participatory discourse. This bottom-up participation for which it praises civil society's involvement in European governance crucially hinges on the autonomy civil society has gained from both the administrative and economic subsystems as a result of national welfare state building. Multilevel social Europe can only continue this emancipatory process if it manages to tame the *bureaucratic* logic of European governance on the one hand and the *market* imperative of European economic integration on the other. Therefrom flow three sets of challenges which the EU would be well advised to take seriously if it wants its institutional practice to fall into line with the democratic aspirations underlying the participatory turn.

Firstly, with a view to build an internal market where competition is free and undistorted, the original EEC Treaty contained provisions aiming at the removal of barriers to the free movement of factors of production, as well as provisions prohibiting anti-competitive practices.[44] Both sets of provisions, reinforced by the subsequent case law of the ECJ consecrating their primacy and direct applicability in the European legal order,[45] have been elevated to a constitutional status.[46] This raises the question: has European economic law

42 This paragraph reformulates the points made in Sec 1.3 and 1.4.

43 Commission, 'European Governance: A White Paper' COM (2001) 428 final, 15.

44 See Articles 2–3 of the Treaty establishing the European Economic Community, signed in Rome, 25 March 1957.

45 JHH Weiler, *The Constitution of Europe: "Do the New Clothes Have an Emperor?" and Other Essays on European Integration* (CUP 1999) 19–22.

46 See J Baquero Cruz, *Between Competition and Free Movement: The Economic Constitutional Law of the European Community* (Hart 2002); D Schiek, 'Re-Embedding Economic and Social Constitutionalism: Normative Perspectives for the EU' in D Schiek, U Liebert and H Schneider, *European Economic and Social Constitutionalism after the Treaty of Lisbon* (CUP 2011) 24–29.

become a carte blanche given to the functional need of expanding competitive markets in fields traditionally occupied by civil society? Or, has European economic law incorporated elements of reflexivity so as to confine the expansive tendencies of the economic subsystem to a well-circumscribed, self-limited market sphere? This provides the building block for the reasoning to follow, for a civil society inadequately protected against markets would be in no position to legitimise the governance of social Europe at a time where, paradoxically, it is more in need of protective European social policy than ever.

Logically, the *second* step would be to question the participatory-democratic credentials of European governance. This book will do so by analysing the involvement of civil society in the two main methods, the Community Method (CM) and the Open Method of Coordination (OMC), through which the EU builds social Europe.[47] Is the governance of social Europe merely driven by bureaucratic power, or has it institutionalised reflexive structures which open EU bureaucracy to the democratic influence of civil society? Is this civil dialogue legally guaranteed or softly promoted, and with what consequences for civil society's autonomy? Does it fruitfully interact with the political societies of parties and parliaments active at the national and European level? How does that reflect upon the European constitutional structure?

Finally, the effectiveness of EU social law and policy making ought to be assessed. Is multilevel social Europe able to protect civil society adequately from the market imperative of European economic integration? Or, does it merely subordinate EU social law and policy making to the satisfaction of market needs? This requires detailed analysis of the social achievements of, respectively, the *hard* CM and the *soft* OMC, having regard to previous findings on the colonising impact of European economic law and democratic support available for a truly protective social Europe.

In the remaining part of this book, these three sets of questions will be examined with particular attention being paid to *voluntary associations* which represent the most *organised* part of civil society compared to social movements and other forms of public communication. Voluntary associations, sometimes called CSOs, NGOs or third sector organisations, share the following characteristics:

- They are non-profit-distributing;
- They are voluntary;
- They have some degree of formal or institutional existence;

47 The CM and the OMC are not the only instruments through which the EU develops its social dimension. The social dialogue, EU funding, and soft law are relevant tools as well. For more detail, see Commission, 'Renewed Social Agenda: Opportunities, Access and Solidarity in 21st Century Europe' (Communication) COM (2008) 412 final, 15–17. See also C Barnard, *EU Employment Law* (4th edn, OUP 2012) chaps 2–3.

- They are independent from state and market; and finally,
- They are not self-serving in aims and related values, their aim is to act in the public arena at large.[48]

For reasons of convenience, these associations will be referred to as 'CSOs' in the rest of the book as it is the abbreviation most often relied on in EU institutional discourse. However, 'civil society' will be preferred when speaking of the sphere of social interaction between state and market to which Cohen and Arato more generally refer.

This being said, CSOs are often singled out for their contribution to democracy.[49] This holds particularly true for *social* CSOs. Social CSOs represent a sizeable share of organised civil society and volunteering is more present there than in any other part of the voluntary sector.[50] Social CSOs also offer the promise to reach to the poor, the excluded, and the unemployed, that is, exactly those persons who have the least benefited from European integration and who show the greatest resentment towards it.[51] Finally, as became clear from *Chapter 1*, social CSOs have been at the forefront of the debate on participatory democracy in the EU with the Social Platform being one of the main advocates for the establishment of the civil dialogue.[52] For all these reasons, social CSOs will provide the primary focus of this book.

It is important to keep in mind that social CSOs are two-dimensional organisations.[53] They provide social services, while, at the same time, advocating social change, although 'the move to political advocacy work in almost all those organisations can historically be traced as a secondary move once it became clear that the political circumstances relating to their work needed to be changed'.[54] This two-dimensionality should not be overlooked

---

48 Commission, 'The Commission and Non-Governmental Organisations: Building a Stronger Partnership' (Discussion Paper) COM (2000) 11 final, 3–4. See also Commission, 'Promoting the Role of Voluntary Organisations and Foundations in Europe' (Communication) COM (1997) 241 final, 1–2.

49 See D Curtin, *'Civil Society' and the European Union: Opening Spaces for Deliberative Democracy?* (Collected courses of the Academy of European law 1996) 206–207; B Kohler-Koch, 'Post-Maastricht Civil Society and Participatory Democracy' (2012) 34 Journal of European Integration 809, 813.

50 LM Salamon, SW Sokolowski, and R List, *Global Civil Society: An Overview* (Johns Hopkins Center for Civil Society Studies 2003) 23–24.

51 See O Costa and P Magnette, 'Introduction. L'Europe des Élites, Anatomie d'un Mythe' in O Costa and P Magnette (eds), *Une Europe des Élites? Réflexions sur la Fracture Démocratique de l'Union Européenne* (Editions de l'Université de Bruxelles 2007) 2.

52 See Sec 1.3.

53 A Evers, 'Part of the Welfare Mix: The Third Sector as an Intermediate Area' (1995) 6 Voluntas 159, 171, 177–178. See also Commission, 'Promoting the Role of Voluntary Organisations and Foundations in Europe' (n 48) 2–3.

54 N Berger, 'Participatory Democracy: Organised Civil Society and the "New" Dialogue' (2004) Online Paper 09/04, the Federal Trust, 3. See also E Fazi and J Smith, 'Civil Dialogue: Making it Work Better' (2006) Study commissioned by the Civil Society Contact

when studying social CSOs in the multilevel context of the EU. European civil society is the result of a process by which social CSOs active at the local level have mobilised so as to advocate social reform at the national level first, and now increasingly direct their advocacy to Brussels in the hope of adducing a social dimension to the European economic project; yet, they still have strong roots to local activity, and they claim to represent a civil society in which 'advocacy and the provision of practical resources or services are two sides of the same coin'.[55]

Multilevel social Europe entails specific challenges for social CSOs: a) while delivering social services at the local level, CSOs risk marketization through the process of negative integration if European economic law does not learn to limit the reach of its market imperative; and b) while advocating social Europe, CSOs are threatened by bureaucratisation if they participate in European governance arrangements which have not been democratised. Considering the two sides of European civil society, both processes, bureaucratisation by European governance and marketization by negative integration, may threaten the autonomy which is necessary for social CSOs to realise their participatory potential in the EU.

3.4. EUROPEAN ECONOMIC LAW: COLONISING?

Many would argue that social policy is threatened by the legal force of negative integration,[56] a process by which the Commission and the ECJ, with the complicity of market-minded claimants, would impose on recalcitrant Member States the market compatibility requirements of European economic law.[57] The case law of the ECJ is indeed quite interventionist.[58] Many times, it has considered that 'whilst EU law does not detract from the power of the Member States to organise their social security systems (...) the fact nevertheless remains that, when exercising that power, Member States must comply with EU law (...)',[59] in particular with European economic law. However, the extent to which this case law erodes, under the combined forces of the four freedoms and European competition law, the social sovereignty of Member States may at times be

Group, 17 <http://act4europe.horus.be/module/FileLib/Civil%20dialogue,%20making%20it%20work%20better.pdf> accessed 1st September 2015.

55 Ibid 3.

56 FW Scharpf, *Governing in Europe: Effective and Democratic?* (OUP 1999) chap 2.

57 See Leibfried, 'Social Policy: Left to the Judges and the Markets?' (n 40) 264–274.

58 See, eg, Case C-341/05 *Laval un Partneri Ltd v Svenska Byggnadsarbetareförbundet, Svenska Byggnadsarbetareförbundets avdelning 1, Byggettan and Svenska Elektrikerförbundet* [2007] ECR I-11767; Case C-438/05 *International Transport Workers' Federation and Finnish Seamen's Union v Viking Line ABP and OÜ Viking Line Eesti* [2007] ECR I-10779.

59 See Case C-562/10 *Commission v Germany* (ECJ, 12 July 2012) para 49, and the cases referred therein.

exaggerated.[60] The general impression one gets by reading the case law is that the ECJ hesitates to qualify as 'economic' social activities which are financed through solidary means,[61] and that, when it does, a balanced, rather than a strictly pro-market, stance is taken as a result of the proportionality test.[62] In this regard, one can expect that the new social provisions of the Lisbon Treaty will promote the further embedment of social values within the European economic constitution.[63]

The same reassuring tone is found in the political declarations of the Commission. The latter identifies, in addition to health and education services, two main categories of social services: 1) statutory and complementary social security schemes covering the main risks of life, and 2) other essential services provided directly to the person.[64] Social services are all engaged in a modernisation process as a result of which the state abandons its role of direct provider of services for that of the regulator/guarantor of social services provided by the private sector. This more competitive environment, the Commission says, creates a climate favourable to the development of a 'social economy' characterised by the importance of not-for-profit providers.[65] The indirect consequence of modernisation is however that an increasing proportion of social services now fall within the remit of European economic law insofar as they can be considered economic activities.[66]

The question which inevitably arises from these developments is whether European economic law acknowledges the specific nature of social services as pillars of the European society. For the Commission, difficulties with European economic law 'appear to be mainly due to a lack of awareness or misinterpretation of the rules rather than to the rules themselves'.[67] The

60 See KA Armstrong, *Governing Social Inclusion: Europeanization through Policy Coordination* (OUP 2010) chap 6; L Nistor, *Public Services and the European Union: Healthcare, Health Insurance and Education Services* (TMC Asser Press 2011) 401–403.

61 See, eg, Case 263/86 *Belgian State v René Humbel and Marie-Thérèse Edel* (Humbel) [1988] ECR 5365; Joined Cases C-159/91 and C-160/91 *Christian Poucet v Assurances Générales de France (AGF) and Caisse Mutuelle Régionale du Languedoc-Roussillon (Camulrac) and Daniel Pistre v Caisse Autonome Nationale de Compensation de l'Assurance Vieillesse des Artisans (Cancava)* (Poucet and Pistre) [1993] ECR I-637; Case C-70/95 *Sodemare SA, Anni Azzurri Holding SpA and Anni Azzurri Rezzato Srl v Regione Lombardia* (Sodemare) [1997] ECR I-3395; Case T-319/99 *Federación Nacional De Empresas De Instrumentación Científica, Médica, Técnica y Dental (FENIN) v Commission* (FENIN) [2003] ECR II-357.

62 On the centrality of the proportionality test in cases pertaining to welfare services, see Nistor, *Public Services and the European Union* (n 60) 403–404.

63 For a collection of essays on the subject, see N Bruun, K Lörcher and I Schömann (eds), *The Lisbon Treaty and Social Europe* (Hart 2012).

64 Commission, 'Implementing the Community Lisbon Programme: Social Services of General Interest in the European Union' (Communication) COM (2006) 177 final, 4.

65 Ibid 5.

66 Ibid 6. See also Commission, 'Services of General Interest, Including Social Services of General Interest: a New European Commitment' (Communication) COM (2007) 725 final, 8.

67 Commission, 'Second Biennial Report on Social Services of General Interest' (Staff Working Document) SEC (2010) 1284 final, 71. See also Commission, 'Biennial Report on Social Services of General Interest' (Staff Working Document) COM (2008) 418 final, 70.

Commission has therefore undertaken to clarify existing rules through the setting up of an interactive information service and the elaboration of FAQs. The latter have been updated with the enactment of a guide on Services of General Economic Interest (SGEI).[68] The Commission has also published in 2005 a SGEI package aiming at clarifying and simplifying the circumstances in which the grant of state aid with a view to finance SGEI is deemed compatible with EU law.[69] It has now been replaced by a new state aid package,[70] while a reform of public procurement rules has been adopted.[71] Both intend to better account for the specificity of social services.[72]

This optimistic assessment cannot stand on firm grounds as long as a closer examination of European economic law, with an eye to specific issues of social policy, is not conducted. Lawyers have already provided very detailed accounts of the way EU law impacts the content, process and timeframe within which social services are delivered by the state to citizens.[73] But, these accounts

68 Commission, 'Guide to the Application of the European Union Rules on State Aid, Public Procurement and the Internal Market to Services of General Economic Interest, and in particular to Social Services of General Interest' (Staff Working Document) SWD (2013) 53 final/2.

69 For more detail, see <http://ec.europa.eu/competition/state_aid/legislation/sgei_archive_en.html> accessed 1st September 2015.

70 See Commission Decision 2012/21/EU of 20 December 2011 on the application of Article 106(2) of the Treaty on the Functioning of the European Union to State aid in the form of public service compensation granted to certain undertakings entrusted with the operation of services of general economic interest [2012] OJ L7/3; Commission Regulation (EU) 360/2012 of 25 April 2012 on the application of Articles 107 and 108 of the Treaty on the Functioning of the European Union to de minimis aid granted to undertakings providing services of general economic interest [2012] OJ L114/8; Commission, 'The Application of the European Union State Aid Rules to Compensation Granted for the Provision of Services of General Economic Interest' (Communication) [2012] OJ C8/4; Commission, 'European Union Framework for State Aid in the Form of Public Service Compensation' (Communication) [2012] OJ C8/15.

71 Directive 2014/24/EU of the European Parliament and of the Council of 26 February 2014 on public procurement and repealing Directive 2004/18/EC [2014] OJ L94/65.

72 See Commission, 'A Quality Framework for Services of General Interest in Europe' (Communication) COM (2011) 900 final, 6–8; Commission, '3rd Biennal Report on Social Services of General Interest' SWD (2013) 40 final, 33–34.

73 See J Shaw (ed), *Social Law and Policy in an Evolving European Union* (Hart 2000); G De Búrca (ed), *EU Law and the Welfare State: In Search of Solidarity* (OUP 2005); E Spaventa and M Dougan (eds), *Social Welfare and EU Law* (Hart 2005); U Neergaard, R Nielsen and L Roseberry (eds), *The Services Directive – Consequences for the Welfare State and the European Social Model* (DJOF Publishing 2008); M Krajewski, U Neergaard and JW van de Gronden (eds), *The Changing Legal Framework for Services of General Interest in Europe: Between Competition and Solidarity* (TMC Asser Press 2009); U Neergaard, R Nielsen and L Roseberry (eds), *Integrating Welfare Functions into EU Law: From Rome to Lisbon* (DJOF Publishing 2009); Schiek, Liebert and Schneider, *European Economic and Social Constitutionalism after the Treaty of Lisbon* (n 46); Bruun, Lörcher and Schömann, *The Lisbon Treaty and Social Europe* (n 63); B Cantillon, H Verschueren and P Ploscar (eds), *Social Inclusion and Social Protection in the EU: Interactions between Law and Policy* (Intersentia 2012); U Neergaard, E Szyszczak, JW van de Gronden and M Krajewski (eds), *Social Services of General Interest in the EU* (TMC Asser Press 2013).

have remained focused on social citizenship as passive entitlement to social services and benefits provided by the state. The legal possibility that negative integration might hinder wider civil society empowerment in the sense of active citizens coming together with a view to provide welfare outside state or market structures, has so far attracted little academic scrutiny.[74]

Why is it so? A plausible explanation might be that European economic law traditionally defines its material scope with regard to a functional divide between non-economic and economic activities which ascribes social services to, respectively, state or market without paying attention to the existence of a third sector between state and market.[75] This is problematic, for, as the Commission explains, 'non-profit providers often play an important role in the delivery of social services (…)'.[76] The SPC makes the same observation and calls for further attention to be paid to exactly this theme,[77] while Declaration no. 23 annexed to the Maastricht Treaty also insists on the importance of 'charitable associations and foundations as institutions responsible for social welfare establishments and services'.[78]

Another explanation might be that existing scholarship embraces the traditional notion that social policy pertains to state provision of individual welfare services through redistribution of resources.[79] This conception of

74 See, however, 6 Perri, 'European Competition Law and the Non-Profit Sector' (1992) 3 Voluntas 215; F Coursin, 'La Politique Européenne de Concurrence et les Entreprises de l'Économie Sociale' (1995) 1 Transnational Associations 26; K Eicker, 'Do the Basic Freedoms of the EC Treaty also Require an Amendment to the National Tax Laws on Charities and Non-Profit Organisations?' (2005) 14 EC Tax Rev 140; C Cicoria, 'European Competition Law and Nonprofit Organizations: A Law and Economics Analysis' (2006) 6 Global Jurist Topics <www.degruyter.com/view/j/gj.2006.6.1/issue-files/gj.2006.6.issue-1.xml> accessed 1 September 2015; M Helios, 'Taxation of Non-Profit Organizations and EC Law' (2007) 16 EC Tax Rev 65; OB Breen, 'EU Regulation of Charitable Organizations: The Politics of Legally Enabling Civil Society' (2008) 10 IJNFPL 50; S Stevens, 'Tax Aid and Non-profit Organizations' (2010) 19 EC Tax Rev 156; I Wendt and A Gideon, 'Services of General Interest Provision through the Third Sector under EU Competition Law Constraints: The Example of Organising Healthcare in England, Wales and the Netherlands' in D Schiek, U Liebert and H Schneider, *European Economic and Social Constitutionalism after the Treaty of Lisbon* (CUP 2011).

75 On the state/market distinction, see O Odudu, 'Economic Activity as a Limit to Community Law' in C Barnard and O Odudu (eds), *The Outer Limits of European Law* (Hart 2009).

76 Commission, 'Services of General Interest, including Social Services of General Interest' (n 66) 8. See also Commission, 'Towards Social Investment for Growth and Cohesion – including implementing the European Social Fund 2014–2020' (Communication) COM (2013) 83 final, 5; European Parliament, 'Resolution of 5 July 2011 on the Future of Social Services of General Interest' [2013] OJ C33E/65, para 22.

77 SPC, 'Operational Conclusions on the Application of Community Rules to SSGI' SPC (2008) 17 final, 21. See also EESC, 'Private Not-For-Profit Social Services in the Context of Services of General Interest in Europe' (Opinion) [2001] OJ C311/08.

78 [1992] OJ C191/01.

79 T Hervey, *European Social Law and Policy* (Longman 1998) 4. See also S Leibfried and P Pierson, 'Semisovereign Welfare States: Social Policy in a Multitiered Europe' in S Leibfried and P Pierson (eds), *European Social Policy: Between Fragmentation and Integration* (The Brookings Institution 1995) 43.

social policy seems unduly narrow, for it sets political power against market inequalities in a way that overlooks that organised civil society will very often step in where the state is unable or unwilling to deliver welfare. It also fails to account for the steps that welfare states take to empower organised civil society in welfare delivery.[80] With variations as to the family to which they belong,[81] welfare states confer CSOs legal recognition through appropriate statutes, fund, through tax exemption and grants, their activities, shield their conduct from the rigour of competitive markets and commission social services from them. These measures share a common purpose: nurturing a civic space between state and market where citizens may take welfare in their own hands.[82]

Revisiting the fundamentals of European economic law with a focus on civil society empowerment is a particularly timely endeavour for this book, considering that the EU has recently turned to participatory democracy. This book will fill a gap in scholarship which is difficult to explain since cases involving social CSOs have already come before the ECJ.[83] *Chapter 4* will examine, from the perspective of the freedom of establishment and freedom to provide services, how internal market law impacts on laws and administrative measures which favour the provision of social services by CSOs as opposed to market operators, while *Chapter 5* will ask whether European competition law, with its commitment towards competitive markets, puts social CSOs under threat of assimilation to the market sphere, or, on the contrary, whether it may integrate their distinctiveness into its workings. Put together, the two chapters will provide a preliminary picture of the constraints European economic law imposes on CSOs' empowerment as a third sector between state and market.

These chapters will put to the test the reflexive approach which already seems to characterise the case law of the ECJ regarding social policy more narrowly considered. They will investigate European economic law from the vantage point of organised civil society, while drawing more general conclusions as to

---

80 On social policy as civil society empowerment, see J Habermas, *The Postnational Constellation: Political Essays* (MIT Press 2001) 77. See also Habermas, *The Theory of Communicative Action* (n 15) 347; A Bartholomew, 'Democratic Citizenship, Social Rights and the "Reflexive Continuation" of the Welfare State' (1993) 42 Studies in Political Economy 141, 142; K Baynes, 'A Critical Theory Perspective on Civil Society and the State' in NL Rosenblum and RC Post (eds), *Civil Society and Government* (Princeton University Press 2002) 133; Marshall, 'Citizenship and Social Class' (n 39) 149.

81 See LM Salamon and HK Anheier, 'Social Origins of Civil Society: Explaining the Nonprofit Sector Cross-Nationally' (1998) 9 Voluntas 213, which identifies four models of state/society relationship (liberal, social democratic, corporatist and statist).

82 See Evers, 'Part of the Welfare Mix' (n 53) 178.

83 See *Sodemare* (n 61); Case C-475/99 *Firma Ambulanz Glöckner v Landkreis Südwestpfalz* [2001] ECR I-8089; Case C-113/13 *Azienda sanitaria locale n. 5 "Spezzino" and Others v San Lorenzo Soc. coop. sociale and Croce Verde Cogema cooperativa sociale Onlus* (ECJ, 11 December 2014).

its capacity to integrate social concerns. As previously explained, one will expect reflexity to arise from i) the exclusion of activities financed by social solidarity from the economic sphere and ii) a balanced integration of social and market concerns through the proportionality test.

The positive conclusions to which this investigation might lead ought to still be taken with cautious optimism, for, in addition to legal constraints, there are further indirect *de facto* pressures that the European process of economic integration imposes on national social policy.[84] Beside fears of Member States engaging in 'a race to the bottom',[85] another concern comes from the strict fiscal discipline associated with the move towards the Economic and Monetary Union (EMU). The imperative of budgetary austerity prompted by the current euro crisis seems to reinforce existing trends towards welfare retrenchment.[86] As will be discussed in *Chapter 8*, there is growing concern that social policy might become the main casualty of the economic reforms undertaken with a view to save the common currency. For, the latter have so far mainly been about regaining competitiveness through social levelling-down,[87] this in the wider context of a globalised economic order where Member States are increasingly keen to renounce their social commitments.[88]

Does that mean the irreversible subordination of civil society to the economic imperative of globalised markets?[89] Not necessarily so. It is sometimes claimed that positive, interventionist social policy can still 'catch up' with globalised markets provided that nation-states summon the necessary strength to impose redistributive duties on market participants at a higher, European, level.[90] The argument goes that, so long as the European economy is enjoying a relatively strong independence from global competition, a European welfare state could reassert control over the market.[91]

84 See Leibfried, 'Social Policy: Left to the Judges and the Markets?' (n 40) 274–277.

85 See Barnard, *EU Employment Law* (n 47) 38–41.

86 S Klosse, 'Balancing Europe's Economic and Social Goals: Fighting a Losing Battle?' [2012] EJSL 176, 176. On the deregulatory impact of the euro crisis on social law, see Barnard, *EU Employment Law* (n 47) 133–139; S Laulom, E Mazuyer, C Teissier, C E Triomphe and P Vielle, 'How Has the Crisis Affected Social Legislation in Europe?' (2012) ETUI Policy Brief no. 2/2012.

87 A Hemerijck, 'The Euro-Crisis – Welfare State Conundrum' in MJ Rodrigues and E Xiarchogiannopoulou (eds), *The Eurozone Crisis and the Transformation of EU Governance: Internal and External Implications* (Ashgate 2014, ebook) loc 3173.

88 See Scharpf, *Governing in Europe: Effective and Democratic?* (n 56) 38–42; Habermas, *The Postnational Constellation* (n 80) 68–80. For the opposite view that the welfare state might be a key source of competitiveness, see C Hay and D Wincott, *The Political Economy of European Welfare Capitalism* (Palgrave Macmillan 2012) chap 3.

89 See J Habermas, *Une Époque de Transition: Écrits Politiques (1998–2003)* (Fayard 2005) 137–140.

90 Habermas, *The Postnational Constellation* (n 80) 84, 98.

91 Ibid 98–99. See also FW Scharpf, 'The European Social Model: Coping with the Challenges of Diversity' (2002) 40 JCMS 645, 649–650.

Has the EU come any close to meet this expectation? A European social dimension has been slowly emerging,[92] with some important harmonising victories to account for, notably in the fields of non-discrimination and health and security at work.[93] Yet, even the most ardent proponent of single social Europe would agree that 'European social policy will for a long time, and for all practical purposes forever, be made simultaneously at two levels, a supranational and a national one',[94] positive integration being left with the narrow social function of regulating the internal market with a view to correct market failures,[95] while supporting, coordinating or supplementing social policies essentially defined, funded and implemented at the national level.[96] Will that be enough to protect civil society effectively from the economic imperative of negative integration? Answering that question requires first to be clear about the legal constraints imposed by negative integration itself. This is the task to which *Chapters 4 and 5* hope to contribute. What social Europe can effectively achieve against markets will also depend on the democratic support on which it can count. This is the issue to which we now turn.

3.5. SOCIAL EUROPE: DEMOCRATIC?

There is a sense that social Europe cannot (or should not) grow strong because it does not possess the democratic legitimacy to do so.[97] At the current stage of the integration process, it is not possible to identify a political community which could legitimate Europe's transition towards a proper welfare state.[98] The European Parliament is a keen supporter of social Europe but European elections are still fought over national issues by national parties, while Member States zealously defend their social prerogatives in an institutional context where it is much easier to block EU reforms than to enact them.[99] Yet, social, not political,

---

92 See Leibfried, 'Social Policy: Left to the Judges and the Markets?' (n 40) 256–264; P Watson, *EU Social and Employment Law: Policy and Practice in an Enlarged Europe* (OUP 2009) 43–64.

93 Those are the two areas of encapsulated federalism described in W Streeck, 'Neo-Voluntarism: A New European Social Policy Regime?' in G Marks, FW Scharpf, PC Schmitter and W Streeck (eds), *Governance in the European Union* (Sage Publications 1996) 76–77.

94 Ibid 65. See also Pierson and Leibfried, 'Multitiered Institutions and the Making of Social Policy' (n 40) 5–6; R Geyer, *Exploring European Social Policy* (Polity Press 2000) 56–57, 207–213; Leibfried, 'Social Policy: Left to the Judges and the Markets?' (n 40) 278–279.

95 G Majone, 'The European Community between Social Policy and Social Regulation' (1993) 31 JCMS 153.

96 See Articles 5(3), 6, 153, 165, 168 TFEU.

97 Streeck, 'Neo-Voluntarism: A New European Social Policy Regime?' (n 93) 67–68; G Majone, 'Transaction-Cost Efficiency and the Democratic Deficit' (2010) 17 JEPP 150, 172–174; FW Scharpf, 'Legitimacy in the Multi-level European Polity' in P Dobner and M Loughlin (eds), *The Twilight of Constitutionalism?* (OUP 2010) 92–95.

98 T Hervey, *European Social Law and Policy* (Longman 1998) 201.

99 Leibfried, 'Social Policy: Left to the Judges and the Markets?' (n 40) 257.

fragmentation might be the main obstacle on the road to single social Europe. Indeed, the euro crisis time and again illustrates that there is no EU-wide civic solidarity to the point that EU citizens would accept to endorse redistributive policies directed towards citizens from other European countries.[100]

Multilevel social Europe has very much developed as a response to these legitimacy constraints. They explain why the EU has successfully managed to regulate markets while leaving the core business of traditional social policy to Member States.[101] Yet, even regulatory politics came to be seen as requiring a democratic legitimacy which the European Parliament seemed unable to provide. Social Europe therefore turned to participatory democracy.[102] Has the participatory turn been successful? Success depends on the extent to which civil society was given the opportunity to participate in the governance of social Europe without succumbing to its bureaucratising tendencies. As such, it is difficult to assess, for EU social law and policy covers various types of decision-making processes involving different institutions at different stages in decision-making.[103]

Detailed analysis will be restricted to the two main methods according to which the EU develops its social dimension:[104] the CM, on the one hand, with the Commission consulting organised civil society prior to exercising its exclusive right to propose social legislation to the Council and the Parliament, and the social OMC, on the other hand, more particularly the process through which Member States coordinate their social inclusion policies in partnership with civil society.[105] It is argued that the *Commission's consultation regime* and the *social OMC* are pertinent case studies for assessing the participatory-democratic merits of social Europe. They allow comparative insights to be drawn from two governance arrangements which differ regarding the decision-making process under scrutiny (CM/OMC), the institutions concerned (Commission/ Member States), and the stages in decision-making involved (agenda setting/ implementation).

The CM can be defined as

> the exercise of legislative power by the EU following the Commission's exercise of its almost exclusive right of initiative, leading to the adoption of legislation by the Council and Parliament, resulting in a binding uniform rule which is subject to the jurisdiction of the Court of Justice.[106]

---

100 See J Habermas, *The Crisis of the European Union: A Response* (Polity Press 2012) 44–53; G Majone *Rethinking the Union of Europe Post-Crisis: Has Integration Gone Too Far?* (CUP 2014, ebook) loc 4558.

101 See Majone, 'The European Community between Social Policy and Social Regulation' (n 95).

102 For further detail, see Sec 1.3 and 1.4.

103 See Watson, *EU Social and Employment Law* (n 92) chap 4.

104 See above, n 47.

105 For a comparison, see J Scott and DM Trubek, 'Mind the Gap: Law and New Approaches to Governance in the European Union' (2002) 8 ELJ 1, 1–5.

106 P Craig and G De Búrca, *EU Law: Text, Cases, and Materials* (5th edn, OUP 2011) 160.

Although it would be more appropriate to speak of the 'ordinary legislative procedure' since the entry into force of the Treaty of Lisbon, the term 'Community Method' will still be relied on as it provides a useful ideal-type against which the OMC can be compared. Formally, the CM stands as the prototype of hierarchical governing as laws are adopted at the top by the Commission, the Parliament and the Council.[107] Although centralised decision-making of this kind seems hardly amenable to wide bottom-up participation, interest group literature often points to the fragmented nature of the EU law-making process and highlights the many points of access it provides to non-state actors, be it through the national or supranational route.[108]

The primary target of interest groups has always been the European Commission because of its exclusive power to initiate legislation.[109] Consulting widely is particularly important for 'weak' DGs like DG Employment. Involving networks of social CSOs allows DG Employment to collect information and expertise, to legitimise its initiatives on the ground that they are supported by a wide range of actors, to reinforce its institutional position *vis-à-vis* other, especially market-friendly, DGs and to carry demands for further social integration to the door of Member States.[110] Together with small-scale action programmes, research projects and soft law production, consultations are one of those 'weapons of the weak' used by DG Employment so as to keep social Europe alive on the agenda and prepare the ground for a further extension of EU social competences should a window of opportunity arise.[111] DG Employment has recently hailed its partnership with social CSOs as the prototype of a new kind of participatory democracy through which a dialogue is engaged with organised civil society. This participatory discourse has quickly spread to the whole Commission and finally found its way into the Treaty of Lisbon.[112]

But, are the normative expectations which underpin it supported by institutional practice? DG Employment may well claim it is building social Europe bottom-up, in partnership with a civil society of active citizens. The Commission, more generally, may well assert that it has departed from the bureaucratic, top-down, governance which characterises the CM. All this would be nothing more than a cover for the pursuit of bureaucratic governance as usual if the Commission's consultation regime failed to institutionalise reflexive

---

107 Ibid 160.

108 See J Greenwood, *Interest Representation in the European Union* (3rd edn, Palgrave Macmillan 2011) chap 2.

109 Ibid 24.

110 L Cram, 'Civil Society, Participatory Democracy and the Governance of the Union: The Institutionalisation of a Fiction' (2006) paper delivered at the 2–4 November 2006 Osnabrück conference on governance and policy-making in the EU, 6 <http://web.uvic.ca/jmtrg/Papers_files/cram_paper_1.pdf> accessed 1 September 2015. See also Greenwood, *Interest Representation in the European Union* (n 108) 164–171.

111 Ibid 5.

112 See Sec 1.3.

structures opening EU governance to the democratic influence of civil society. It is with these considerations in mind that *Chapter 6* will analyse the consultations the Commission holds prior to proposing social legislation as a structure of opportunities. Particular attention will be paid to the nature and function of the rules which govern consultations. Are they soft or hard rules, and with what effect for civil society's autonomy? Their interaction with representative democracy provided by the Parliament and their compliance with the new Treaty article on participatory democracy will be other issues of concern.

Contrasting the CM with the OMC might be interesting at this point. The OMC was officially endorsed by the Lisbon European Council in March 2000, as a new and widely applicable tool of governance launched with a view to make the EU 'the most competitive and dynamic knowledge-based economy in the world capable of sustainable economic growth with more and better jobs and greater social cohesion'.[113] It can succinctly be defined as

> a flexible means of working towards shared European objectives via national plans, which are assessed in accordance with common criteria (indicators), following (in some but not all cases) guidelines and/or targets decided jointly by national ministers at European level.[114]

The OMC has become 'the central tool of EU social policy-making in the new millennium',[115] with the instauration of separate coordination processes for social inclusion, pensions, and healthcare and long-term care, followed by their merging into a single social OMC in 2005. Coordination under the social OMC is currently taking place within the framework of the Europe 2020 strategy for smart, sustainable and inclusive growth.[116]

The OMC is often described as a *new* mode of governance departing from the top-down, bureaucratic logic of the *old* CM.[117] Much of this newness arises from the fact that, according to its proponents, the OMC would further the wide participation of civil society into European governance.[118] This thinking is reflected in the Lisbon Conclusions which describe the OMC as a

---

113 European Council, 23–24 March 2000, Lisbon, presidency conclusions (italics omitted).

114 P Pochet, 'The Open Method of Co-ordination and the Construction of Social Europe. A Historical Perspective' in J Zeitlin, P Pochet and L Magnusson (eds), *The Open Method of Co-ordination in Action: the European Employment and Social Inclusion Strategies* (PIE-Peter Lang 2005) 41.

115 J Zeitlin, 'The Open Method of Co-Ordination in Question' in J Zeitlin, P Pochet and L Magnusson (eds), *The Open Method of Co-Ordination in Action: The European Employment and Social Inclusion Strategies* (PIE-Peter Lang 2005) 19.

116 See Commission, 'Europe 2020: A Strategy for Smart, Sustainable and Inclusive Growth' (Communication) COM (2010) 2020 final; SPC, 'Reinvigorating the Social OMC in the Context of the Europe 2020 Strategy' (Opinion) (2011) Doc 10405/11.

117 See Scott and Trubek, 'Mind the Gap: Law and New Approaches to Governance in the European Union' (n 105) 4–5.

118 See Zeitlin, 'The Open Method of Co-Ordination in Question' (n 115) 22–23.

fully decentralised approach in which civil society will be actively involved.[119] *Chapter 7* will test these democratic aspirations with a focus on the social OMC. The objective of mobilising all the relevant bodies was one of the four major objectives pursued by the social inclusion process at the time of its official launch in 2000[120] and, since it was merged into the social OMC, the social inclusion process has attracted the greatest share of CSOs' participation.[121] If the OMC embodies anything close to a radical alternative to the CM, one may hope that the social inclusion process in action would provide empirical support for such a claim. The nature of the social OMC as a *soft* tool will be central to our inquiry as well as its *reflexivity* in terms of procedural rules guaranteeing civil society's influence therein. Does the social OMC deliver the goods in the absence of legal rules ensuring compliance with its democratic promises? And if it does not, what kind of legal, political and constitutional reforms might be suggested with a view to bring institutional practice into line with theoretical expectations?

3.6. SOCIAL EUROPE: EFFECTIVE?

The question of whether multilevel social Europe stands for civil society's colonisation or for its empowerment could not be fully answered without addressing the effectiveness of EU social law and policy making. Assessing the effectiveness of social Europe comes down to asking whether it is strong enough to protect civil society against the colonising tendencies of European economic integration. This issue will necessarily come at the end of our inquiry. What social Europe *must* achieve in order to provide effective protection against markets will very much depend on the constraints negative integration imposes on civil society in the first place. What social Europe *can* legitimately hope to achieve will very much depend on its ability to draw democratic support from its dialogue with civil society. The final chapter will therefore be an opportunity to bring the threads of this book together. Previous findings as to the colonising tendencies of European economic law and democratic support available for social law and policy making will be summarised. The limits of these findings will be exposed as well as their relevance for the issue of effective social law and policy making.

The effectiveness of social Europe will be appraised through a preliminary assessment of the achievements of, respectively, the *hard* CM and the *soft* OMC. The examination of two important pieces of legislation pertaining to

119 Lisbon European Council (n 113) para 38.

120 Council, 'Fight against Poverty and Social Exclusion' (2000) Doc 14110/00.

121 B Vanhercke, 'Delivering the Goods for Europe 2020? The Social OMC's Adequacy and Impact Re-Assessed' in E Marlier and D Natali (eds), *Europe 2020: Towards a More Social EU?* (PIE – Peter Lang 2010) 131.

social services[122] will reveal that the hard CM suffers from an economic bias. When social services are harmonised or coordinated by EU legislation, it is as a precondition for the proper functioning of the internal market or as part of the internal market project itself. This raises the question: is the social Europe that is emerging from EU law-making able to protect civil society from European economic integration? Central to that inquiry will be the new social provisions of the Lisbon Treaty which many see as a chance to rebalance the economic constitution of the EU.[123] Should a social deficit emerge from EU law-making, increasing social competences would not change much to the state of affairs, for the diversity of European welfare states, in economic, institutional and ideological terms, has increased to such an extent that it would be unfeasible, and even democratically dangerous, to agree on common legislative solutions.[124]

This explains why the *hard* CM has progressively been complemented by the *soft* OMC as a tool for making social Europe more effective. Instead of striving for legislative uniformity, the social OMC takes the diversity of Europe as an opportunity to start a deliberative, learning process by which Member States can discover and experiment with new political solutions to the intractable problems their welfare systems are collectively facing.[125] Has the social OMC delivered on these promises? The softness of the social OMC will provide the main reason for concern as it seems too weak for securing social policy's influence over the budgetary and economic pillars of the Europe 2020 strategy as it unfolds in the context of the euro crisis, so that the social Europe that is emerging from current coordination processes is increasingly one that is subordinated to market-making.

122 Directive 2006/123/EC of the European Parliament and of the Council of 12 December 2006 on services in the internal market [2006] OJ L376/36; Directive 2011/24/EU of the European Parliament and of the Council of 9 March 2011 on the application of patients' rights in cross-border healthcare [2011] OJ L88/45.

123 For a collection of essays on the subject, see Schiek, Liebert and Schneider, *European Economic and Social Constitutionalism after the Treaty of Lisbon* (n 46).

124 Scharpf, *Governing in Europe* (n 56) 82; Scharpf, 'The European Social Model' (n 91) 650–652.

125 DM Trubek and LG Trubek, 'The Open Method of Co-Ordination and the Debate Over "Hard" and "Soft" Law' in J Zeitlin, P Pochet and L Magnusson (eds), *The Open Method of Co-Ordination in Action: The European Employment and Social Inclusion Strategies* (PIE – Peter Lang 2005) 87.

CHAPTER 4

REVISITING THE FUNDAMENTALS OF INTERNAL MARKET LAW

4.1. INTRODUCTION

As exemplified by a handful of cases decided by the ECJ in the fields of education,[1] healthcare[2] and social welfare,[3] the free market orientation of the European economic constitution[4] sometimes comes into conflict with Member States' core sovereign power to organise their welfare systems.[5] These clashes are to be seen through the lens of a state/market divide.[6] Activities are allocated to either sphere according to their economic nature. Non-economic activities escape the application of internal market law, while economic activities benefit from the four freedoms and cannot be restricted by Member States beyond what public interest requires.[7]

---

1 See the cases cited below, n 45.

2 See the cases cited below, n 48.

3 Case C-70/95 *Sodemare SA, Anni Azzurri Holding SpA and Anni Azzurri Rezzato Srl v Regione Lombardia* (Sodemare) [1997] ECR I-3395; Case C-355/00 *Freskot AE v Elliniko Dimosio* (Freskot) [2003] ECR I-05263; Case C-350/07 *Kattner Stahlbau GmbH v Maschinenbau- und Metall- Berufsgenossenschaft* (Kattner) [2009] ECR I-01513; C-113/13 *Azienda sanitaria locale n. 5 "Spezzino" and Others v San Lorenzo Soc. coop. sociale and Croce Verde Cogema cooperativa sociale Onlus* (Spezzino) (ECJ, 11 December 2014).

4 See Article 3 (3) TEU; Articles 3 (1) (b), 4 (2) (a), 26, 119 and 120 TFEU. The latter two articles refer to 'the principle of an open market economy with free competition'. Protocol no. 27 on the internal market and competition [2012] OJ C326/309, attached to the Lisbon Treaty, adds that 'the internal market (…) includes a system insuring that competition is not distorted'. See also J Baquero Cruz, *Between Competition and Free Movement: the Economic Constitutional Law of the European Community* (Hart 2002) 76–80.

5 This chapter is a revised version of an article published by the author with the following reference: G Busschaert, 'Revisiting the Fundamentals of Internal Market Law: Civil Society as a Third Sector between the State and the Market' (2011) 22 EBLR 725.

6 This divide is used here to demarcate between activities that are subject to internal market law and those that are not. It is to be distinguished from the conceptual use of the state/market divide as a device for defining the respective scopes of free movement and competition law. For the latter, see Baquero Cruz, *Between Competition and Free Movement* (n 4); W Sauter and H Schepel, *State and Market in European Union Law: The Public and Private Spheres of the Internal Market before the EU Courts* (CUP 2009).

7 On the distinction between economic and non-economic activities, see J Baquero Cruz, 'Beyond Competition: Services of General Interest and European Community Law' in G De Búrca (ed), *EU Law and the Welfare State: In Search of Solidarity* (OUP 2005) 179;

This chapter is an invitation to confront this legal dichotomy with the reality we live in, where one finds organised civil society lying between the state and the market.[8] It will be argued that the conflict mentioned hereinabove should not be merely stated as a case of state versus market, public versus private. One should go beyond this seemingly obvious legal divide and ask *how internal market law impacts on state policies that favour the provision of social services by organised civil society as opposed to market operators*.[9] This is not a rhetorical question. Such policies, although increasingly called into question by Member States, do exist in some European countries.[10] They may even come back in favour with the near-collapse of the Washington consensus and growing interest in third way policies.[11] This issue goes to the heart of what has been described in *Chapter 3* as a need for social policy to defend civil society against the colonising forces of markets.[12] It is asked whether resistance can take the shape of policies expressing the democratic will of a political community to keep profit-making at bay in a sector of fundamental importance: welfare delivery.

The main analytical tool used for the purpose of answering the above question will be the notion of solidarity,[13] defined here as 'a willingness to share the fate

---

Commission, 'Services of General Interest, Including Social Services of General Interest: A New European Commitment' (Communication) COM (2007) 725 final, 4–6; M Freedland, P Craig, C Jacqueson and N Kountouris, *Public Employment Services and European Law* (OUP 2007) 21–26; E Szyszczak, *The Regulation of the State in Competitive Markets in the EU* (Hart 2007) 8–13; O Odudu, 'Economic Activity as a Limit to Community Law' in C Barnard and O Odudu (eds), *The Outer Limits of European Law* (Hart 2009) 225; Commission, 'Guide to the Application of the European Union Rules on State Aid, Public Procurement and the Internal Market to Services of General Economic Interest, and in particular to Social Services of General Interest' (Staff Working Document) SWD (2013) 53 final/2, 103–104.

8 See JL Cohen and A Arato, *Civil Society and Political Theory* (MIT Press 1992), preface ix, where civil society is defined as 'a sphere of social interaction between economy and state (…)'. For more detail on the definition of civil society to which this book subscribes, see Sec 3.2.

9 This kind of policies is actively supported by the proponents of associative and civil democracy. In this respect, see V Pestoff, *Beyond the Market and State: Social Enterprises and Civil Democracy in a Welfare Society* (Ashgate 1998); PQ Hirst and VM Bader (eds), *Associative Democracy: The Real Third Way* (Frank Cass 2001).

10 See SPC, 'Operational Conclusions on the Application of Community Rules to SSGI' SPC (2008) 17 final, 14.

11 For a forceful critique of the Washington consensus, see JE Stiglitz, *Globalization and its Discontents* (Penguin 2002). For examples of third way proposals, see Pestoff, *Beyond the Market and State* (n 9); Hirst and Bader, *Associative Democracy* (n 9).

12 Cohen and Arato, *Civil Society and Political Theory* (n 8) 421–491, address the need to protect civil society against the colonising tendencies of the market economy. See also J Habermas, *The Theory of Communicative Action / Vol.2, Lifeworld and System: a Critique of Functionalist Reason* (Polity Press 1987) 332–373.

13 Solidarity has already been the focus of much scholarly attention in European law. See T Hervey, '*Social Solidarity*: A Buttress against Internal Market Law?' in J Shaw (ed), *Social Law and Policy in an Evolving European Union* (Hart 2000); C Barnard, 'EU Citizenship and the Principle of Solidarity' in E Spaventa and M Dougan (eds), *Social Welfare and EU Law* (Hart 2005); C Barnard, 'Solidarity and New Governance in Social Policy' in G De Búrca

of the other'.[14] Two dimensions of this multifarious notion will be considered, which together reflect the conception of solidarity as a non-economic resource rooted in civil society.[15] In its first, non-economic, dimension, solidarity may take the shape of a decision by which a political community transfers resources from one social group to another (thereafter referred to as 'social solidarity').[16] Social solidarity thereby understood as redistribution, represents the focus of welfare states. It is central to the financing of many social services which are often provided free of charge or at a below-cost price to beneficiaries and which therefore need some amount of solidary financing.

In its second, civil, dimension, solidarity may refer more specifically to the actors with whom a political community decides to entrust welfare delivery. It thereby expresses the will to prefer CSOs to corporate companies for providing social services, in view of the public-spiritedness those actors embody. The promotion of this second type of solidarity (thereafter referred to as 'civil solidarity') may, therefore, take the form of measures which prohibit profit-making in welfare delivery ('non-profit requirements'). While measures favouring civil solidarity reflect the belief that CSOs are the *locus* where solidarity, a scarce and vulnerable resource, is best nurtured and preserved,[17] social solidarity emphasises that solidarity is non-economic, in the sense that it is instituted in response to and against the inequalities generated by free markets.[18]

With this analytical frame in mind, internal market law will be scrutinised against its impact on policies favouring civil solidarity enacted in a welfare context. With a focus on, respectively, the freedom of establishment *(4.2)*

---

and J Scott (eds), *Law and New Governance in the EU and the US* (Hart 2006); C Newdick, 'Citizenship, Free Movement and Health Care: Cementing Individual Rights by Corroding Social Solidarity' (2006) 43 CML Rev 1645; N Boeger, 'Solidarity and EC Competition Law' (2007) 32 EL Rev 319; M Ross, 'Promoting Solidarity: From Public Services to a European Model of Competition?' (2007) 44 CML Rev 1057; M Ross and Y Borgmann-Prebil (eds), *Promoting Solidarity in the European Union* (OUP 2010); T Kotkas, 'Who Needs Social Rights when We've got Solidarity: Juridification of Solidarity and the Depoliticisation of EU Social Policy' [2012] EJSL 84; I Domurath, 'The Three Dimensions of Solidarity in the EU Legal Order: Limits of the Judicial and Legal Approach' (2013) 35 Journal of European Integration 459.

14 Cohen and Arato, *Civil Society and Political Theory* (n 8) 472.

15 See Pestoff, *Beyond the Market and State* (n 9) 62–65; Boeger, 'Solidarity and EC Competition Law' (n 13) 321.

16 See Opinion of AG Fennelly in *Sodemare* (n 3), para 29: 'Social solidarity envisages the inherently uncommercial act of involuntary subsidisation of one social group by another.'

17 Cohen and Arato, *Civil Society and Political Theory* (n 8) 473. See also W Outhwaite, 'Who Needs Solidarity?' in N Karagiannis (ed), *European Solidarity* (Liverpool University Press 2007) 90: 'Civil society, despite its lack of institutional clout, has a kind of spontaneity and flexibility that may, in favourable circumstances, become a vital source of solidarity.'

18 T Hervey, *European Social Law and Policy* (Longman 1998) 3; V Hatzopoulos, 'Health Law and Policy: The Impact of the EU' in G De Búrca (ed), *EU Law and the Welfare State: In Search of Solidarity* (OUP 2005) 157.

and the freedom to provide services (*4.3*), it will be asked whether and under what circumstances, social solidarity, owing to its non-economic nature, is instrumental to define on which side of the state/market divide policies favouring civil solidarity stand. A synthesis on this question will be provided by bringing together both freedoms (*4.4*). It will then be assessed to what extent these two freedoms may be relied on by for-profit companies to challenge measures favouring civil solidarity instituted in an economic, as opposed to social solidarity, context (*4.5*). In conclusion, some final thoughts will be put forward, particularly linking up the findings of this chapter with previous research as to the capacity of internal market law to integrate social concerns (*4.6*).

4.2. FREEDOM OF ESTABLISHMENT

The freedom of establishment allows EU companies 'to participate, on a stable and continuous basis, in the economic life of a Member State other than [their] State of origin and to profit therefrom'.[19] This includes their right to establish in another Member State with a view to provide social services. Yet, by virtue of its sovereign power to organise its social welfare system, the host Member State may decide that public funding, reflecting a community's solidary commitment towards each of its constituents, should only be devoted to private entities that have the pursuit of the social good as their primary purpose. By so doing, a state imposes on the commercial companies established in its jurisdiction restrictions entailed by the need to compete with the third sector on what is considered to be unfair terms. This is exactly the crux of the matter in *Sodemare*,[20] a case dealing with a piece of legislation in the region of Lombardy that made reimbursement for social welfare services of a health-care nature conditional upon the requirement for the providing institution to be non-profit making.[21] This law was challenged before the ECJ by Sodemare, a Luxemburg company established

---

19 Case C-55/94 *Reinhard Gebhard v Consiglio dell'Ordine degli Avvocati e Procuratori di Milano* (Gebhard) [1995] ECR I-4165, para 25.

20 *Sodemare* (n 3). On this case, see Hervey, '*Social Solidarity*: a Buttress against Internal Market Law' (n 13) 35–36; Hatzopoulos, 'Health Law and Policy: The Impact of the EU' (n 18) 137–138; K Stoger, 'The Freedom of Establishment and the Market Access of Hospital Operators' (2006) 17 EBLR 1545; L Hancher and W Sauter, 'One Step Beyond? From Sodemare to Docmorris: The EU's Freedom of Establishment Case Law concerning Healthcare' (2010) 47 CML Rev 117; L Nistor, *Public Services and the European Union Healthcare, Health Insurance and Education Services* (TMC Asser Press 2011) 72; JW van de Gronden, 'Social Services of General Interest and EU Law' in E Szyszczak, J Davies, M Andenæs and T Bekkedal (eds), *Developments in Services of General Interest* (TMC Asser Press 2011) 130–131; JW van de Gronden, 'Free Movement of Services and the Right of Establishment: Does EU Internal Market Law Transform the Provision of SSGI?' in U Neergaard, E Szyszczak, JW van de Gronden and M Krajewski (eds), *Social Services of General Interest in the EU* (TMC Asser Press 2013) 145.

21 Ibid paras 3–10.

in Italy. For, it had the effect of reserving the provision of social services of a health-care nature to non-profit organisations, by obliging users of the services provided by commercial operators to bear a financial burden to which they would not have been subject had they sought the same service from a non-profit-making company.[22]

On the compatibility of the non-profit requirement with the freedom of establishment, the ECJ first stated that internal market law does not detract from the powers of the Member States to organise their social security systems.[23] The ECJ then took note that the non-profit requirement was forming part of a social welfare system based on the principle of solidarity (i.e. 'social solidarity' for the purpose of this chapter).[24] The ECJ finally accepted that, as internal market law stands at present, a Member State may, in the exercise of the powers it retains to organise its social security system, consider that such a requirement is necessary for the social security system at hand to attain its objectives.[25] Thereby, the ECJ gave reason to the Italian government's argument that the non-profit requirement represented the most logical approach, on the grounds that non-profit-making private operators are not influenced by the need to derive profit from the provision of services, which enables them to pursue social aims as a matter of priority.[26] Before concluding that the non-profit requirement cannot be viewed as contrary to the right of establishment, the ECJ said that the latter is not liable to place profit-making companies from other Member States in a less favourable factual or legal situation than profit-making companies from the Member State in which they are established.[27]

It appears from the above that the ECJ adopts in *Sodemare* a position deferential to Member States' powers to deliver welfare to their citizens through non-market means. Indeed, in paragraph 32 of the Judgment, the ECJ approaches the necessity of the non-profit requirement very leniently, without even questioning whether the social objectives of the welfare system at hand may be attained by less restrictive means; moreover, in paragraph 33, in order to conclude that the non-profit requirement is not discriminatory, the ECJ chooses profit-making companies established in another Member State as a comparator.[28] This interpretation of the principle of non-discrimination contrasts starkly with the opinion that the Advocate General Fennelly filed in that case,[29] wherein he argued that non-profit requirements are inherently discriminatory.[30] As the

22 Ibid para 15.
23 Ibid para 27.
24 Ibid para 29.
25 Ibid para 32.
26 Ibid para 31.
27 Ibid paras 33–34.
28 See Hervey, '*Social Solidarity*: a Buttress against Internal Market Law' (n 13) 36.
29 Opinion of AG Fennelly in *Sodemare* (n 3).
30 Ibid paras 32–35.

Advocate General rightly said, 'charity begins at home'.[31] In this sense, non-profit requirements are indirectly discriminatory on the grounds that they favour local entities over foreign ones.[32] It could also be added that the mere fact that the ECJ relied on the principle of non-discrimination in itself bears witness to its deference.[33] Indeed, the ECJ could easily have ruled, on the basis of *Gebhard*,[34] that the non-profit requirement was restrictive, that is, liable to hamper or to render less attractive the exercise by foreign companies of their economic freedoms, and then proceed with a full blown proportionality test.[35]

It is striking that the Judgment hinges on both types of solidarity mentioned in the introduction of this chapter albeit, *stricto sensu*, it is only the second type of solidarity (civil solidarity) that is challenged by the Sodemare company.[36] It could be argued that the reference to social solidarity is far from accidental. Rather, it invites us to look back on earlier cases where free movement law was invoked against social solidarity. In this respect, it could be said that *Humbel*,[37] albeit not mentioned in *Sodemare*,[38] is central to understand the ECJ's deference. For, in that case regarding public education, the ECJ had already ruled that a service financed essentially by the state was not economic and therefore made clear that public funding is what defines the non-economic sphere.[39]

Hence, with *Humbel* in mind, it can be argued that the Sodemare company requires access to a monetary resource of a specific kind, that is, money provided by the state for redistributive purposes. The reference to social solidarity is therefore essential because it gives the non-profit requirement a non-economic context which, it is argued, justifies its protection by the ECJ.[40] Allowing the plaintiff to challenge the non-profit requirement would, in this case, legally amount to the use of internal market law for the purpose of colonising the non-market sphere of social solidarity. Had the ECJ taken a stricter stand, it would have substituted its own judgment on the institutional limits within

31 Ibid para 35.

32 See Case C-3/88 *Commission v Italy* [1989] ECR 4035, para 9.

33 See Hatzopoulos, 'Health Law and Policy: The Impact of the EU' (n 18) 137.

34 *Gebhard* (n 19).

35 Ibid para 37. See Hancher and Sauter, 'One Step Beyond?' (n 20) 133–134.

36 See Hervey, '*Social Solidarity*: A Buttress against Internal Market Law?' (n 13) 35–36; Barnard, 'EU Citizenship and the Principle of Solidarity' (n 13) 163–164; Boeger, 'Solidarity and EC Competition Law' (n 13) 325 and 335–338.

37 Case 263/86 *Belgian State v René Humbel and Marie-Thérèse Edel* (Humbel) [1988] ECR 5365. Contrary to this chapter which claims that *Humbel* is an important statement as to the content of the notion of solidarity in European law, most authors do not usually give centre stage to the latter as a case of internal market versus solidarity. See, eg, Hervey, '*Social Solidarity*: A Buttress against Internal Market Law?' (n 13); Barnard, 'EU Citizenship and the Principle of Solidarity' (n 13).

38 *Sodemare* (n 3).

39 *Humbel* (n 37) paras 17–18.

40 See Boeger, 'Solidarity and EC Competition Law' (n 13) 335, 338; Opinion of AG Fennelly in *Sodemare* (n 3), paras 29–30, 41.

which welfare services financed by social solidarity should be delivered for the democratic will of a political community.

4.3. FREEDOM TO PROVIDE SERVICES

It is common place that, in order to enter the remit of internal market law, a service needs to be 'normally provided for remuneration'[41] and that 'the essential characteristic of remuneration (...) lies in the fact that it constitutes consideration for the service in question, and is normally agreed upon between the provider and the recipient of the service'.[42] Welfare provides the battleground where the interpretation to be given to this requirement has been fought the hardest.[43] Since *Humbel*,[44] the acid test for remuneration comes down to asking whether the service is financed *entirely* or *mainly* by the public purse.[45] If yes, the latter belongs to the non-economic sphere. This conveys the idea that, since nothing comes for free, what matters is cost allocation. If the service recipient pays, the transaction is strictly guided by private interest and should come under the purview of internal market

---

41 Article 57 TFEU.

42 *Humbel* (n 37) para 17.

43 See S O'Leary, *The Evolving Concept of Community Citizenship: From the Free Movement of Persons to Union Citizenship* (Kluwer Law International 1996) 67–78; G Davies, 'Welfare as a Service' (2002) 29 LIEI 27; E Spaventa, 'Public Services and European Law: Looking for Boundaries' (2003) 6 CYELS 271; D Damjanovic and B De Witte, 'Welfare Integration through EU Law: The overall Picture in the Light of the Lisbon Treaty' in U Neergaard, R Nielsen and L Roseberry (eds), *Integrating Welfare Functions into EU Law: from Rome to Lisbon* (DJOF Publishing 2009); C Barnard, *The Substantive Law of the EU: The Four Freedoms* (4th edn, OUP 2013) 377; P Craig and G De Búrca, *EU Law: Text, Cases, and Materials* (5th edn, OUP 2011) 793–797; Nistor, *Public Services and the European Union* (n 20) 31–59; S O'Leary, 'Free Movement of Persons and Services' in P Craig and G De Búrca, *The Evolution of EU Law* (2nd edn, OUP 2011) 529–533; van de Gronden, 'Social Services of General Interest and EU Law' (n 20) 126–131; van de Gronden, 'Free Movement of Services and the Right of Establishment' (n 20) 125–129.

44 *Humbel* (n 37).

45 Ibid paras 18–19. See also Case C-109/92 *Stephan Max Wirth* v *Landeshauptstadt Hannover* (Wirth) [1993] ECR I-6447, paras 15–17; *Freskot* (n 3) paras 54–59; Case C-76/05 *Herbert Schwarz and Marga Gootjes-Schwarz v Finanzamt Bergisch Gladbach* (Schwarz) [2007] ECR I-6849, paras 38–40; Case C-318/05 *Commission v Germany* [2007] ECR I-6957, paras 67–69; Case C-281/06 *Hans-Dieter Jundt and Hedwig Jundt v Finanzamt Offenburg* (Jundt) [2007] ECR I-12231, paras 29–30; C-56/09 *Emiliano Zanotti v Agenzia delle Entrate – Ufficio Roma 2* (Zanotti) [2010] ECR I-04517, paras 30–32. It has been argued that an essential factor for the freedom to provide services to apply is the for-profit objective of the service provider (see O'Leary, 'The Evolving Concept of Community Citizenship' (n 43) 399). However, the ECJ has now made clear that 'the decisive factor which brings an activity within the ambit of the Treaty provisions on the freedom to provide services is its economic character, that is to say, the activity must not be provided for nothing. By contrast (...), there is no need in that regard for the person providing the service to be seeking to make a profit.' (references omitted) (*Jundt* (n 45) paras 32–33).

principles. However, as soon as a service is paid *essentially* by public monies, it embodies the democratic will of a polity to maintain social solidarity among its members and this solidarity should be allowed to act as a 'buttress against internal market law'.[46] In sum, this case law clearly endorses the view that social solidarity, expressed through public funding, is what defines the non-economic sphere and therefore guards state or civil society-based welfare delivery against market encroachment.[47]

However, a brief account of the cases on the right of EU citizens to receive medical treatment abroad[48] suffices to inform us that social solidarity does not rest on grounds as safe as the above case law might lead one to believe. Confronted with the issue of EU citizens challenging Member States' health authorities' refusal to cover the costs of medical treatment received in another Member State, the ECJ, giving full force to the ruling that 'the freedom to provide services includes the freedom for the recipients of services, including persons in need of medical treatment, to go to another Member State in order to receive those services there',[49] has repeatedly stated that Article 56 TFEU applies as soon as medical services are provided for consideration in

46 Hervey, '*Social Solidarity*: A Buttress against Internal Market Law?' (n 13). However, Hervey does not mention *Humbel* as a case where solidarity acts as a buttress against internal market law.

47 Spaventa, 'Public Services and European Law' (n 43) 275, refers to *Humbel* as one of those cases where 'public services which are an expression of social solidarity were excluded from the scope of the Treaty'.

48 Joined Cases 286/82 and 26/83 *Graziana Luisi and Giuseppe Carbone v Ministero del Tesoro* [1984] ECR 377; Case C-120/95 *Nicolas Decker v Caisse de maladie des employés privés* [1998] ECR I-1831; Case C-158/96 *Raymond Kohll v Union des caisses de maladie* [1998] I-1931; Case C-368/98 *Abdon Vanbraekel and Others v Alliance nationale des mutualités chrétiennes (ANMC)* (Vanbraekel) [2001] ECR I-5363; Case C-157/99 *B.S.M. Geraets-Smits v Stichting Ziekenfonds VGZ and H.T.M. Peerbooms v Stichting CZ Groep Zorgverzekeringen* (Smits and Peerbooms) [2001] ECR I-5473; Case C-385/99 *V.G. Müller-Fauré v Onderlinge Waarborgmaatschappij OZ Zorgverzekeringen UA and E.E.M. van Riet v Onderlinge Waarborgmaatschappij ZAO Zorgverzekeringen* (Müller-Fauré) [2003] ECR I-4509; Case C-372/04 *The Queen, on the application of Yvonne Watts v Bedford Primary Care Trust and Secretary of State for Health* (Watts) [2006] ECR I-4325; Case C-444/05 *Aikaterini Stamatelaki v NPDD Organismos Asfaliseos Eleftheron Epangelmation (OAEE)* (Stamatelaki) [2007] ECR I-3185; Case C-208/07 *Petra von Chamier-Glisczinski v Deutsche Angestellten-Krankenkasse* [2009] ECR I-6095; Case C-211/08 *Commission* v *Spain* [2010] ECR I-05267; Case C-512/08 *Commission* v *France* [2010] ECR I-08833; Case C-173/09 *Georgi Ivanov Elchinov v Natsionalna zdravnoosiguritelna kasa* [2010] ECR I-08889; Case C-255/09 *Commission v Portugal* (ECJ, 27 October 2011); Case C-490/09 *Commission v Luxemburg* [2011] ECR I-00247; Case C-562/10 *Commission v Germany* (ECJ, 12 July 2012). For an overview of the case law, see T Hervey, 'The Current Legal Framework on the Right to Seek Health Care Abroad in the European Union' (2007) 9 CYELS 261; J Baquero Cruz, 'The Case Law of the European Court of Justice on the Mobility of Patients: an Assessment' in JW van de Gronden, E Szyszczak, U Neergaard and M Krajewski (eds), *Health Care and EU Law* (TMC Asser Press 2011). This case law has now been codified in Directive 2011/24/EU of the European Parliament and of the Council of 9 March 2011 on the application of patients' rights in cross-border healthcare [2011] OJ L88/45. For more details on the Directive, see Sec 8.4.

49 *Watts* (n 48) para 87.

the host state, regardless of the way in which the national system with which the patient is registered and from which reimbursement of the cost of those services is subsequently sought, operates.[50] The ECJ has also made clear that a health system which subjects to prior authorisation reimbursement of the costs incurred by insured patients abroad or which forbids its patients to rely on the private healthcare market of another Member State, constitutes, both for insured patients and service providers, a barrier to the freedom to provide services.[51] Albeit internal market law does not preclude a system of prior authorisation at least as regards intramural care[52] and treatment in a non-hospital setting involving the use of major medical equipment,[53] it requires the conditions attached thereto to be justified with regard to the overriding considerations of general interest accepted by the ECJ and to satisfy the requirement of proportionality.[54] As regards the absolute refusal to reimburse costs incurred on the private health care market abroad, the ECJ ruled in *Stamatelaki*[55] that such a refusal is not proportionate to the objective of maintaining a balanced social security system, since measures which are less restrictive and more in keeping with the freedom to provide services could be adopted, such as a prior authorisation scheme.[56]

As the case law illustrates, patients may rely on the freedom to receive commercial services in order to get reimbursement for healthcare services received abroad, no matter whether they were provided by publicly-funded or purely private hospitals. This a major difference with the regime instituted by Articles 19 and 20 of Regulation 883/2004[57] which only cover EU citizens' access to medical services provided within the framework of the public health system of the host Member State.[58] Although this opening to private operators does not directly endanger the public structure of the welfare system with which patients travelling abroad are insured, it may, however, come to threaten the latter indirectly, once applied to those public health systems which do not recognise the right for their patients to be treated by commercial operators outside a

50 *Smits and Peerbooms* (n 48) para 55; *Müller-Fauré* (n 48) para 103; *Watts* (n 48) para 90; *Stamatelaki* (n 48) para 21.

51 *Smits and Peerbooms* (n 48) para 69; *Müller-Fauré* (n 48) para 44, 103; *Watts* (n 48) paras 94–98; *Stamatelaki* (n 48) paras 25–28.

52 *Müller-Fauré* (n 48) paras 93–98.

53 *Commission v France* (n 48) para 42.

54 *Smits and Peerbooms* (n 48) paras 80–82; *Müller-Fauré* (n 48) para 83; *Watts* (n 48) paras 113–114.

55 *Stamatelaki* (n 48).

56 Ibid para 35.

57 Regulation (EC) 883/2004 of the European Parliament and of the Council of 29 April 2004 on the coordination of social security systems [2004] OJ L166/1.

58 For more detail on the difference between the two regimes, see F Pennings, 'The Draft Patient Mobility Directive and the Coordination Regulations of Social Security' in JW van de Gronden, E Szyszczak, U Neergaard and M Krajewski (eds), *Health Care and EU Law* (TMC Asser Press 2011).

pre-organised non-profit structure.[59] Since the mere reliance of publicly-insured patients on the private health care market of another Member State suffices to bring into play the free movement of services,[60] it is inevitable that any refusal to cover the costs of medical services received abroad could be challenged under the free movement of services, even if this refusal is justified by the absence of recognition by the welfare structure at home of any right to receive commercial services.

This would not be problematic if the ECJ showed deference towards Member States' powers to organise their social security system, when examining the existence of a restriction on the freedom to receive private health care abroad. This is however not the case. The absence of any right to be treated by commercial operators, and even the recognition of such a right subject to prior authorisation, is, according to the ECJ, a restriction.[61] Should a patient challenge a Member State's refusal to reimburse medical services provided abroad by a commercial operator on a for-profit basis, it would therefore fall on the ECJ, substituting its own judgment for the democratic will of a political community, to determine, according to a proportionality test, whether there are means less restrictive than the organisation of a welfare system along strictly non-profit lines, which would allow such a system to meet the social objectives it has been assigned. The serious issue of legitimacy this raises[62] is all the more pronounced now that this case law has been transposed to other welfare services such as education and social insurance, where the right to receive services outside non-profit structures is not as firmly embedded as in health care.[63]

A contrario, this book advocates that, instead of the *unrestricted* notion of restriction used by the ECJ,[64] room should be made for a more respectful

---

59 See Stoger, 'The Freedom of Establishment and the Market Access of Hospital Operators' (n 20) 1551.

60 Craig and De Búrca, *EU Law: Text, Cases, and Materials* (n 43) 796.

61 *Smits and Peerbooms* (n 48) para 69; *Müller-Fauré* (n 48) para 44, 103; *Watts* (n 48) paras 94–98; *Stamatelaki* (n 48) paras 25–28.

62 See J Snell and M Andenas, 'Exploring the Outer Limits: Restrictions on the Free Movement of Goods and Services' in M Andenas and W Roth (eds), *Services and Free Movement in EU Law* (OUP 2002) 96–100.

63 Spaventa, 'Public Services and European Law: Looking for Boundaries' (n 43) 282–284. The same concern is expressed in M Dougan, 'Cross-Border Educational Mobility and the Exportation of Student Financial Assistance' (2008) 33 EL Rev 723, 732–733. For a transposition of the case law on the right to seek healthcare abroad to *education*, see *Schwarz* (n 45) paras 36–47, 64–82; *Commission v Germany* (n 45) paras 65–100. On the latter cases, see Dougan, 'Cross-Border Educational Mobility' (n 63). For a transposition of the case law on the right to seek healthcare abroad to *social insurance*, see *Freskot* (n 3) paras 61–74; *Kattner* (n 3) paras 71–92. On the latter cases, see van de Gronden, 'Social Services of General Interest and EU Law' (n 20) 126–129.

64 The ECJ has consistently held in healthcare cases (see, eg, *Watts* (n 48) para 94; *Stamatelaki* (n 48) para 25), that the freedom to provide services 'precludes the application of any national legislation which has the effect of making the provision of services between Member States more difficult than the provision of services purely within one Member State'. When assessing

approach towards the state/market divide.[65] Rather than affirming that some degree of closure in the welfare system is restrictive of trade, the ECJ, building upon the wisdom of *Sodemare*,[66] could confine itself to assure that the right to be reimbursed for social services received outside the welfare system, only *once* and *if* it is granted, does not discriminate between commercial operators according to their location.[67]

The case law on the right to receive healthcare abroad is all the more worrying if one takes into account the unjustified interventionism of one specific case, *Smits and Peerbooms*,[68] where the ECJ was asked whether the specific features of the health system from which reimbursement for medical treatment received abroad was sought could dispel the existence of remuneration.[69] In response to objections raised against the economic character of an insurance-based health system delivering benefits in kind and free of charge, the ECJ ruled that such system is to be considered as economic on the grounds that, since *Bond*,[70] there is no need for a service to be paid by those for whom it is performed.[71]

It could be argued that this reasoning was unnecessary. The conclusion that the medical service had been paid for directly by the patient in the host Member State was sufficient to justify the application of the freedom to provide services. The validity of this claim is confirmed in *Watts*,[72] where the ECJ declined to rule on whether NHS was providing services against remuneration.[73] Moreover, the extension of the *Bond* line of case law[74] to welfare seems to be in contradiction

whether the freedom to provide services has been restricted, the ECJ does not compare the situation of private operators in the home state with that of private operators in the host state but rather compare public operators in the home state with private operators in the host state (see, eg, *Smits and Peerbooms* (n 48) paras 61–69; *Watts* (n 48) paras 94–98; *Stamatelaki* (n 48) para 27). In this respect, in *Watts* (n 48), the ECJ made abundantly clear regarding the aforementioned case law that:

> [T]he conditions for the NHS's assuming the cost of hospital treatment to be obtained in another Member State should not be compared to the situation in national law of hospital treatment received by patients in private local hospitals. On the contrary, the comparison should be made with the conditions in which the NHS provides such services in its hospitals. (Para 100).

65 See the approach advocated by AG Colomer in his opinion in *Stamatelaki* (n 48) paras 41–49.

66 *Sodemare* (n 3) para 33.

67 Spaventa, 'Public Services and European Law: Looking for Boundaries' (n 43) 289. See also Opinion of AG Colomer in *Stamatelaki* (n 48), paras 41–49.

68 *Smits and Peerbooms* (n 48).

69 Ibid paras 48–51.

70 Case 352/85 *Bond van Adverteerders and others v The Netherlands State* [1988] ECR 2085, para 16.

71 *Smits and Peerbooms* (n 48) paras 56–58.

72 *Watts* (n 48).

73 Ibid para 91.

74 *Bond* (n 70) para 16: 'Article 60 does not require the service to be paid for by those for whom it is performed.' See also Joined Cases C-51/96 and C-191/97 *Christelle Deliège v Ligue francophone de judo et disciplines associées ASBL, Ligue belge de judo ASBL, Union européenne de judo (C-51/96) and François Pacquée (C- 191/97)* [2000] ECR I-2549, paras 56–57.

with the ECJ's ruling in *Humbel*[75] that public financing excludes the application of internal market rules.[76] Besides, the ECJ's motivation lacks in substance.[77] The ECJ does not explain why the ruling in *Bond*, which was given in a clearly commercial context, is transposable to welfare.[78] Nor does the ECJ explain why it finds it justifiable to depart from the opinions of two learned Advocate Generals arguing, on the basis of *Humbel*, that the specificity of national health systems should prevent the application of the TFEU.[79]

4.4. DELIVERING WELFARE SERVICES FINANCED BY SOCIAL SOLIDARITY: AN ECONOMIC ACTIVITY?

With a view to summarise the above developments, one can say that social solidarity has been approached in the case law regarding the freedom of establishment and the freedom to provide services from three different angles, with dramatically different consequences for measures favouring civil solidarity:

1) *Delivering services financed by social solidarity is not an economic activity.* By establishing financial solidarity among them, citizens erect a political buttress against markets.[80] This is clear since *Humbel*:[81] a service financed essentially through public funds is non-economic.[82] Similarly, in *Sodemare*,[83] the ECJ, based on a deferential reading of the principle of

75 *Humbel* (n 37).

76 Ibid para 18. For a defence of the notion of remuneration as construed by the ECJ in *Smits and Peerbooms*, see O'Leary, 'The Evolving Concept of Community Citizenship' (n 43) 75–78; P Koutrakos, 'Healthcare as an Economic Service' in E Spaventa and M Dougan (eds), *Social Welfare and EU Law* (Hart 2005) 112–115. For the opinion that *Humbel* might not be good law anymore, see Newdick, 'Citizenship, Free Movement and Health Care' (n 13) 1655–1656. For a restrictive reading of *Humbel* in order to accommodate *Smits and Peerbooms*, see Davies, 'Welfare as a Service' (n 43) 35–40; AP Van Der Mei, *Free Movement of Persons within the European Community: Cross-Border Access to Public Benefits* (Hart 2003) 313–315; Freedland et al, *Public Employment Services and European Law* (n 7) 23.

77 V Hatzopoulos, '*Killing* National Health and Insurance Systems but *Healing* Patients? The European Market for Health Care Services After the Judgments of the ECJ in *Vanbraekel* and *Peerbooms*' (2002) 39 CML Rev 683, 693–694.

78 *Bond* (n 70). For more detail on this case, see Barnard, *The Substantive Law of the EU* (n 43) 369. On its transposition to welfare, see O'Leary, 'The Evolving Concept of Community Citizenship' (n 43) 73–75.

79 Opinion of AG Colomer in *Smits and Peerbooms* (n 48) paras 20–33; Opinion of AG Saggio in *Vanbraekel* (n 48) para 21. For more details, see Hatzopoulos, '*Killing* National Health' (n 77) 690–694.

80 Hervey, '*Social Solidarity*: A Buttress against Internal Market Law?' (n 13).

81 *Humbel* (n 37).

82 Ibid para 18.

83 *Sodemare* (n 3).

necessity and equal treatment, decided that a state can legitimately entitle non-profits to participate in its welfare system to the exclusion of for-profit companies, without restricting markets. The ECJ, therefore, did not allow for-profit companies to use internal market law for the purpose of challenging the non-economic sphere, that is, the institutional limits within which it is decided to deliver welfare services financed by social solidarity, thereby adopting a hands-off approach towards the configuration of our welfare societies along civil solidarity lines.

2) *Delivering services financed by social solidarity is an economic activity* since services do not need to be paid for by those for whom they are performed. *Smits and Peerbooms*,[84] by transposing *Bond*[85] to welfare, reflects this approach. Therefore, as long as a service is paid for, this service is economic, whoever the financing operator might be (private, semi-public or public) and whatever redistributive purpose this type of financing might embody. This reading blurs the state/market divide to a point where one can legitimately ask which services still belong to the non-economic sphere. It gives commercial operators arguments to challenge civil society-based welfare delivery more successfully than in *Sodemare* since, in a strictly functional fashion, the principle of social solidarity cannot shield civil solidarity from the full application of internal market principles.
3) *Social solidarity at home does not matter*, according to *Watts*,[86] as long as the service has been provided against remuneration in another Member State. This approach, combined with an extensive definition of the notion of restriction, allows citizens, by invoking the freedom to receive commercial services abroad, to challenge in court the proportionality of welfare systems which do not recognise them the right to be reimbursed for services provided outside a pre-organised non-profit structure. Conversely, companies established in other Member States can also challenge such systems because they are deterred from providing services in the Member States concerned.[87] With this approach, the ECJ turns its back to the right of Member States to sovereignly decide who can deliver welfare services financed by social solidarity.

These three judicial approaches hardly make for a coherent answer to the question of the legal status of social solidarity. They reflect the casuistic approach of the ECJ which is bound to deal with the sensitive issues raised before it on a case-by-case basis. Although the conviction that services paid for by the state are performed against remuneration has already gained ground in

84 *Smits and Peerbooms* (n 48) paras 57–58.
85 *Bond* (n 70) para 16.
86 *Watts* (n 48).
87 See *Freskot* (n 3) para 63; *Kattner* (n 3) para 82.

the discourse of the European Commission[88] and in the comments of some legal practitioners,[89] the first approach still holds its ground today. Indeed, *Humbel*[90] has been recently reaffirmed by the ECJ[91] and politically construed in the 'services' Directive[92] as including activities performed by the state or *on behalf* of the state.[93] Moreover, the ECJ, in *Schwarz*,[94] gave a restrictive interpretation of the *Bond* ruling, by limiting its ambit to private financing.[95] This strongly suggests that services mainly financed by the state are not to be affected by the ruling that services do not need to be paid for by those for whom they are performed. This would leave within the non-economic sphere social solidarity and the way it is delivered, whether by the state or by civil society *on behalf of* the state.

The third approach has yet to be invoked by service recipients or providers in order to challenge refusals of reimbursement by welfare systems defined along strictly non-profit lines.[96] However, in view of the *unrestricted* notion of restriction already espoused in the case law,[97] it seems unlikely that the ECJ will, when faced with that kind of case, revert to the deferential position adopted

---

88 Commission, 'Services of General Interest, Including Social Services of General Interest: A New European Commitment' (Communication) COM (2007) 725 final, 5. See also Commission, 'Implementing the Community Lisbon Programme – Social Services of General Interest in the European Union' (Communication) COM (2006) 177 final, 6–7; Commission, 'Guide to the Application of the European Union Rules on State Aid, Public Procurement and the Internal Market to Services of General Economic Interest, and in particular to Social Services of General Interest' (n 7) 103–104. On the latter communications and the confusion to which they have contributed as to the respective scopes of the public and private spheres, see Damjanovic and De Witte, 'Welfare Integration through EU Law' (n 43) 73–77.

89 See Opinion of AG Maduro in Case C-205/03 P *Federación Española de Empresas de Tecnología Sanitaria (FENIN) v Commission* (FENIN) [2006] ECR I-6295, para 51. See also Freedland et al, *Public Employment Services and European Law* (n 7) 23.

90 *Humbel* (n 37).

91 See *Schwarz* (n 45) paras 38–40; *Commission v Germany* (n 45) paras 67–69; *Jundt* (n 45) paras 29–30; *Zanotti* (n 45) paras 30–32.

92 Directive 2006/123/EC of the European Parliament and of the Council of 12 December 2006 on services in the Internal Market [2006] OJ L376/36. The Services directive is not expected to have a profound impact on welfare in view of the exclusion of both healthcare services and most social services from its scope (art 2). For more detail, see U Neergaard, R Nielsen and L Roseberry (eds), *The Services Directive – Consequences for the Welfare State and the European Social Model* (DJOF Publishing 2008). This issue is further discussed in Sec 8.4.

93 See preamble, indent 34. Compare with the initial proposal of the Commission (COM (2004) 2 final) indent 16. See also Commission, 'Guide to the Application of the European Union Rules on State Aid, Public Procurement and the Internal Market to Services of General Economic Interest' (n 7) 104.

94 *Schwarz* (n 45).

95 Ibid para 41. See also *Commission v Germany* (n 45) para 70.

96 The closest one has come to this situation is *Stamatelaki* (n 48) where the Greek authorities' refusal to reimburse healthcare services received by private hospitals abroad was considered disproportionate by the ECJ (see above, n 55). However, this refusal was not grounded on the need for medical operators to be non-profit.

97 See above, n 64.

in *Sodemare*.[98] This being said, even the third approach has been tempered by *Humbel*.[99] Indeed, the ECJ has refused that the freedom to receive commercial services abroad be invoked regarding schools which are financed entirely or mainly by public funds.[100] This contrasts with the case law on the freedom to receive medical services which only requires that healthcare be provided for consideration in another Member State no matter whether the provider is financed essentially by private funds or not. Whether the third approach will be similarly constrained in future sensitive cases regarding welfare services other than education remains to be seen.[101]

4.5. CIVIL SOLIDARITY IN AN ECONOMIC CONTEXT

Those welfare services which are not financed by social solidarity, but rather rely on private financing, are, undeniably, considered as provided 'for remuneration' according to internal market law.[102] They enter the economic sphere, regardless of whether they are paid directly by their beneficiaries or indirectly by third parties.[103] Policies favouring civil solidarity enacted in such an economic context cannot hide behind the protective veil of social solidarity. They are inevitably subject to the full rigour of internal market law.

As a result, measures which would require pursuing an economic activity in the host state through a non-profit entity would indubitably be considered discriminatory, at least indirectly. Indeed, the ECJ ruled that Article 49 TFEU expressly leaves traders free to choose the appropriate legal form in which to pursue their activities in another Member State,[104] and, later, held that measures which favour local entities over foreign ones are indirectly discriminatory.[105] Nor can Member States enact provisions which prevent operators from accessing certain markets on the basis of their type of corporate form. Those measures, notwithstanding their non-discriminatory nature, would in any case constitute

98 *Sodemare* (n 3).

99 *Humbel* (n 37).

100 See *Schwarz* (n 45) paras 38–40; *Commission v Germany* (n 45) paras 67–69.

101 See Nistor, *Public Services and the European Union* (n 20) 51–53.

102 Article 57 TFEU. On the notion of remuneration, see above, Sec 4.3.

103 *Bond* (n 70) para 16; *Smits and Peerbooms* (n 48) paras 56–58; Case C-422/01 *Försäkringsaktiebolaget Skandia (publ) and Ola Ramstedt v Riksskatteverket* [2003] ECR I-6817, para 24.

104 Case 270/83 *Commission v France* [1986] ECR 0273, para 22.

105 Case C-3/88 *Commission v Italy* [1989] ECR 4035, para 9. See also Case C-272/91 *Commission v Italy* [1994] ECR I-1409; Case C-101/94 *Commission v Italy* [1996] ECR I-02691, para 31; Barnard, *The Substantive Law of the EU* (n 43) 331.

a restriction on the right of those operators to conduct business in the host Member State.[106] Non-profit requirements are no exception in that respect.[107]

Therefore, the extremely lenient approach adopted by the ECJ in *Sodemare*[108] towards measures that discriminate against for-profit operators should not be taken out of its 'social solidarity' context, where non-profits were delivering services financed by the public purse. Internal market law does not confer any blanket exemption on non-profit requirements once formulated in an economic context. Such measures are considered inherently discriminatory. Or they are at least restrictions, liable to hamper or to render less attractive the exercise by foreign companies of their economic freedoms.[109] In either case, this suffices to bring them within the remit of the TFEU. If challenged before the ECJ, those measures will therefore need, first, to be justified by an imperative requirement in the general interest[110] or one of the express derogations provided for in the TFEU[111] and second, to satisfy the proportionality test.[112]

In that regard, *DocMorris*,[113] a case on the freedom of establishment wherein the ECJ upheld a legislation preventing commercial companies from owning and operating pharmacies,[114] suggests that the ECJ, when applying the test of proportionality to measures favouring civil solidarity, will be particularly receptive to some of the arguments usually advanced to justify non-profit requirements. Indeed, it is the first time that the ECJ explicitly reasons by analogy with the point made in *Sodemare* that non-profits are able to pursue social aims as a matter of priority, by saying that only pharmacies operated by independent pharmacists sufficiently guarantee that the pursuit of profit will be tempered by

---

106 Case C-243/01 *Criminal proceedings against Piergiorgio Gambelli and Others* [2003] ECR I-13031, para 48; Joined Cases C-338/04, C-359/04 and C-360/04 *Criminal proceedings against Massimiliano Placanica (C-338/04), Christian Palazzese (C-359/04) and Angelo Sorricchio (C-360/04)* [2007] ECR I-1891, paras 59–62; Joined Cases C-171/07 and C-172/07 *Apothekerkammer des Saarlandes and Others (C-171/07) and Helga Neumann-Seiwert (C-172/07) v Saarland and Ministerium für Justiz, Gesundheit und Soziales* (DocMorris) [2009] ECR I-4171, para 23; C-84/11 *Marja-Liisa Susisalo, Olli Tuomaala and Merja Ritala* (ECJ, 21 June 2012) paras 31–35. See also Case C-169/07 *Hartlauer Handelsgesellschaft mbH v Wiener Landesregierung and Oberösterreichische Landesregierung* [2009] ECR I-1721, para 63.

107 Case C-288/89 *Stichting Collectieve Antennevoorziening Gouda and others v Commissariaat voor de Media* [1991] ECR I-4007, paras 19, 21–25; Case C-439/99 *Commission* v *Italy* [2002] ECR I-305, para 32; *Spezzino* (n 3) para 52. See also Case C-353/89 *Commission v The Netherlands* [1991] ECR I-4069.

108 *Sodemare* (n 3) para 33.

109 See *Gebhard* (n 19) para 37.

110 For an extensive list of imperative requirements which have been accepted by the ECJ, see Barnard, *The Substantive Law of the EU* (n 43) 529–533.

111 Article 52 TFEU.

112 See *Gebhard* (n 19) para 37.

113 *DocMorris* (n 106). For a detailed analysis of the case, see Hancher and Sauter, 'One Step Beyond?' (n 20). See also Case C-531/06 *Commission v Italy* [2009] ECR I-4103.

114 Ibid para 17. For an extension of this reasoning to the biomedical analysis sector, see Case C-89/09 *Commission v France* [2010] ECR I-12941, paras 65, 82.

the objective of protecting public health.[115] If the independence of pharmacists is thought to be an adequate means to temper the pursuit of profit, the *a fortiori* assertion can easily be made that a non-profit requirement would even more adequately meet the need to ensure that public interest prevails over profit making. It should be highlighted that the specificity of medicinal products plays a pivotal role in the ECJ's assessment.[116] In the words of the Advocate General, pharmaceutical activity is characterised by an asymmetrical distribution of information, which makes all the more important the trustworthiness of its provider.[117] Here too, the parallel could be easily made with trust-related economic theories which support the view that information problems, especially present in health and social services, are less likely to be exploited by non-profits.[118] Finally, as regards the criterion of necessity, the ECJ gives weight to the consideration that ownership structure matters when it comes to compliance.[119] This is particularly important for the advocates of civil solidarity who argue that CSOs internalise the public interest in a way that makes them more likely to comply with relevant legislation than for-profit companies.

The favourable impression left by *DocMorris* is confirmed by the recent *Spezzino* judgment in which the ECJ holds that Articles 49 and 56 TFEU must be interpreted as not precluding a national legislation which provides that urgent and emergency ambulance services must be entrusted on a preferential basis to CSOs.[120] Recalling the *Sodemare* judgment, the ECJ considers that a Member state may validly take the view that recourse to CSOs is consistent with the social purpose of the emergency ambulance services and may help to control costs relating to those services.[121] However, it will be for the national judge to verify that CSOs actually contribute to the social purpose and budgetary efficiency on which that preferential system is based. In that respect, it is essential that CSOs do not pursue objectives other than the social objectives assigned, that they do not make any profit and that they do not procure any profit for their members.[122]

4.6. CONCLUSIONS

What are the constraints imposed by internal market law on policies aimed at promoting civil solidarity enacted in a welfare context? While *Humbel*[123] and

115 Ibid para 39, citing *Sodemare* (n 3) para 32.
116 Ibid paras 31–32, 60.
117 Opinion of AG Bot in *DocMorris* (n 106), para 51.
118 HK Anheier, *Nonprofit Organizations: Theory, Management, Policy* (Routledge 2004) 124–126.
119 *DocMorris* (n 106) paras 52–57.
120 *Spezzino* (n 3) para 65.
121 *Spezzino* (n 3) para 59.
122 *Spezzino* (n 3) para 61.
123 *Humbel* (n 37).

Sodemare[124] clearly position social solidarity in the non-economic sphere so that services financed essentially by the state, regardless of whether they are delivered by CSOs on behalf of the state or by the state itself, escape internal market law, *Smits and Peerbooms*[125] casts doubt on public financing as a boundary marker on the grounds that remuneration identifies the economic sphere without regard to the identity of the payer. However, *Schwarz*[126] strongly suggests that the finding of *Smits and Peerbooms* is to be limited to private financing, so as to leave intact the non-economic sphere of social solidarity and, by the same token, the non-profit structure through which a political community may choose to deliver welfare services financed by social solidarity to its members (*4.4*).

Does that mean that internal market law gives Member States free reign to erect their welfare system along civil solidarity lines if they so wish? It seems not. Firstly, should the case arise where a citizen, invoking the freedom to receive commercial services abroad, challenges its welfare system for not granting the right to be reimbursed for services provided by commercial operators, it is claimed that the ECJ will prefer pushing the *Social solidarity does not matter* approach of *Watts*[127] to its limits, thereby subjecting the absence of such a right to a strict proportionality test, rather than reverting to the deferential position of *Sodemare*. For, the ECJ, by releasing the unrestricted notion of restriction from its Pandora's Box, has already paved the way for such an outcome (*4.4*).[128] Secondly, policies favouring civil solidarity enacted in an economic context, where social services are privately financed, would inevitably be considered as restrictions on the freedom of establishment of commercial operators or on their freedom to provide services. Both considerations therefore point to the increasing role the proportionality test will come to play in balancing free markets against civil solidarity. In this respect, *DocMorris*[129] and *Spezzino*[130] give ground to think that the ECJ would be willing to interpret proportionality in a light favourable to state measures favouring civil solidarity in welfare delivery provided that CSOs are able to prove that they actually contribute to the social objectives they claim to be promoting (*4.5*).

Linking up with wider debate as to the capacity of internal market law to integrate social concerns, this chapter illustrates that the case for a European economic constitution which systematically endangers national social policy has been exaggerated. European economic law contains reflexive elements that make the internal market receptive to the social values underlying national welfare policies. This reflexivity has been demonstrated from the perspective of state

124 *Sodemare* (n 3).
125 *Smits and Peerbooms* (n 48).
126 *Schwarz* (n 45).
127 *Watts* (n 48).
128 See above, n 64.
129 *DocMorris* (n 106).
130 *Spezzino* (n 3).

measures aiming at empowering CSOs against for-profit companies, a specific dimension of social policy which had barely been explored until now.

The findings of this chapter are in line with previous research focusing on traditional social policy defined as citizens' entitlement to social services provided by the state.[131] They confirm that the reflexive capacity of internal market law manifests itself through the following two mechanisms: on the one hand, the ECJ carefully draws the state/market boundary according to a 'social solidarity' benchmark which, in some cases, suffices to shield the delivery of non-economic social services from internal market rules, while, on the other, it condones an inventive use of the proportionality test as a means to balance the pursuit of social objectives with economic activities that cannot be restricted beyond what is deemed necessary.

The next chapter will revisit the fundamentals of European competition law with a view to measure their impact on organised civil society. A crucial question will be raised: does European competition law assimilate CSOs to for-profit companies, or does it allow them to express their distinctiveness as a third sector between state and market? More broadly, it is the reflexivity of European competition law assessed in terms of receptiveness to social values that will be put to the test.

---

131 See KA Armstrong, *Governing Social Inclusion: Europeanization through Policy Coordination* (OUP 2010) chap 6; L Nistor, *Public Services and the European Union: Healthcare, Health Insurance and Education Services* (TMC Asser Press 2011) 401–403.

CHAPTER 5
REVISITING THE FUNDAMENTALS OF EUROPEAN COMPETITION LAW

5.1. INTRODUCTION

CSOs evolve in an increasingly competitive environment where fighting for market shares against for-profit companies, but also against their non-profit counterparts, is very much the order of the day.[1] At the same time, CSOs have a long tradition of cooperation between themselves which sometimes conflicts with the discipline imposed by competitive markets.[2] They may conclude catchment area agreements[3] so as to avoid 'wasteful duplication'.[4] It is also quite common for CSOs to agree on common pricing strategies which reflect social concerns by subsidising below-cost services to needy clients with higher fees paid by better-off clients.[5] Yet, CSOs are *not-for-profit*: they restrict competition with a view to further the social goals by which they are statutory bound, whereas commercial companies are presumed to do so with a view to increase profit. This fundamental difference raises the question of whether European competition law integrates CSOs' distinctiveness as a third sector between state and market or, on the contrary, if it assimilates them to for-profit companies.[6]

---

1 C Cicoria, 'European Competition Law and Nonprofit Organizations: A Law and Economics Analysis' (2006) 6 Global Jurist Topics, 5–12 <www.degruyter.com/view/j/gj.2006.6.1/issue-files/gj.2006.6.issue-1.xml> accessed 1st September 2015. See also R Steinberg, 'Nonprofit Organizations and the Market' in WW Powell (ed), *The Nonprofit Sector: a Research Handbook* (Yale University Press 1987); BA Weisbrod, *The Nonprofit Economy* (Harvard University Press 1988) 107–129.

2 See 6 Perri, 'European Competition Law and the Non-Profit Sector' (1992) 3 Voluntas 215, 226.

3 Ibid 232–233.

4 J Kendall, *The Voluntary Sector: Comparative Perspectives in the UK* (Routledge 2003) 120.

5 F Coursin, 'La Politique Européenne de Concurrence et les Entreprises de l'Économie Sociale' (1995) 1 Transnational Associations 26, 32.

6 For this kind of questioning, see Perri, 'European Competition Law and the Non-Profit Sector' (n 2); Coursin, 'La Politique Européenne de Concurrence et les Entreprises de l'Économie Sociale' (n 5); Cicoria, 'European Competition Law and Nonprofit Organizations' (n 1).

This is reminiscent of an issue which has attracted the attention of many scholars before: can European competition law internalise public service values?[7] Although pertinent, this chapter does not address this question in detail. It mainly considers the possible reconciliation of European competition law with the social values promoted by civil society rather than with the public service values guaranteed by the state. This book argues that too much focus on the state-centred conception of the general interest underpinning the notion of SGEI found in Article 106(2) TFEU has lost sight of the fundamental contribution of civil society to the welfare of modern societies. CSOs have pioneered many social services which have subsequently been 'entrusted' to them by the state[8] and they are still intervening today in response to the failure of the state to answer society's most basic needs.[9] States are well aware of civil society's essential role in promoting welfare and direct significant amounts of subsidies towards it as a result.[10] For the above reasons, it seems important to analyse European competition law's ability to account for the distinctive features of CSOs.

With this thread running through the chapter, it will first be examined under what circumstances CSOs are considered as 'undertakings' and, therefore, enter the jurisdictional boundaries of European competition law (*5.2*). CSOs will then be confronted to the substance of European competition law. For reasons of limited space and available case law, the investigation will be limited to Article 101 TFEU which prohibits anti-competitive agreements, although our findings will be largely relevant for mergers and abuses of dominant position as well (*5.3*).[11] The circumstances under which Member States can finance CSOs' activities without this being deemed to constitute a state aid prohibited by Article 107 TFEU will finally be examined (*5.4*). In conclusion, some final thoughts will be put forward particularly linking up with wider debate as to the capacity of European economic law to integrate social concerns (*5.5*).

---

7 T Prosser, *The Limits of Competition Law: Markets and Public Services* (OUP 2005) 24. For a similar concern, see E Szyszczak, J Davies, M Andenæs and T Bekkedal (eds), *Developments in Services of General Interest* (TMC Asser Press 2011).

8 On the pioneering role of CSOs, see RM Kramer, *Voluntary Agencies in the Welfare State* (University of California Press 1981) chap 9.

9 See H Hansmann, 'Economic Theories of Nonprofit Organization' in WW Powell (ed), *The Nonprofit Sector: a Research Handbook* (Yale University Press 1987); Weisbrod, *The Nonprofit Economy* (n 1) chap 2; HK Anheier, *Nonprofit Organizations: Theory, Management, Policy* (Routledge 2004) 113–135.

10 For the respective shares of fees, philanthropy and government in CSOs' revenue, see LM Salamon, SW Sokolowski and R List, *Global Civil Society: An Overview* (Johns Hopkins Center for Civil Society Studies 2003) 27–33. See also Kendall, *The Voluntary Sector* (n 4) chap 2.

11 In this sense, see C Townley, *Article 81 EC and Public Policy* (Hart 2009) 8.

5.2. ARE CSOs UNDERTAKINGS?

The notion of 'undertaking' is central to defining the jurisdictional boundaries of European competition rules.[12] However, the term 'undertaking' is nowhere defined in the European Treaties. The EU Courts and the Commission, in keeping with the case law on the notion of 'service' discussed in *Chapter 4*, have assigned a functional meaning thereto[13] in that 'it focuses on the type of activity performed rather than on the characteristics of the actors which perform it, the social objectives associated with it, or the regulatory or funding arrangements to which it is subject in a particular Member State'.[14] Since *Höfner*,[15] any entity engaged in an economic activity, regardless of its legal status and the way in which it is financed, is an undertaking for the purposes of competition law.[16]

This functional definition entails that the specific institutional features of CSOs, especially their not-for-profit status, do not justify any preferential treatment, for, any entity, no matter its public or non-profit status, will incur the wrath of competition law as soon as it engages in an 'economic activity' which violates competition rules. Indeed, the ECJ has repeatedly ruled that an undertaking is any entity offering goods or services on the market,[17] while, as underscored by Advocate General Jacobs in *Banking Foundations*,[18] 'the non-profit making nature of the entity in question or the fact that it seeks non-commercial objectives is irrelevant for the purposes of qualifying it as an undertaking'.[19] Therefore, competition law enters into play as soon as a CSO

---

12 For a full discussion on the notion of 'undertaking', see V Louri, '"Undertaking" as a Jurisdictional Element for the Application of EC Competition Rules' (2002) 29 LIEI 143; O Odudu, 'The Meaning of Undertaking within 81 EC' (2005) 7 CYELS 209; O Odudu, 'Are State Owned Healthcare Providers that are Funded by General Taxation Undertakings Subject to Competition Law?' (2011) 32 ECLR 231; R Whish and D Bailey, *Competition Law* (7th edn, OUP 2012) 83–99.

13 Odudu, 'The Meaning of Undertaking' (n 12) 211.

14 Opinion of AG Jacobs in Joined Cases C-264/01, C-306/01, C-354/01 and C-355/01 *AOK Bundesverband and others* (AOK) [2004] ECR I-2493, para 25.

15 Case C-41/90 *Klaus Höfner and Fritz Elser v Macrotron GmbH* [1991] ECR I-1979.

16 Ibid para 21. See also Case C-350/07 *Kattner Stahlbau GmbH v Maschinenbau- Und Metall-Berufsgenossenschaft* (Kattner) [2009] ECR I-01513, para 34; Case C-437/09 *AG2R Prévoyance v Beaudout Père et Fils SARL* (AG2R) [2011] ECR I-00973, para 41.

17 Case 118/85 *Commission v Italy* [1987] ECR 2599, para 7; C-343/95 *Diego Calì & Figli Srl v Servizi Ecologici Porto Di Genova SpA (SEPG)* (Diego Calì) [1997] ECR I-1547, para 16.

18 Case C-222/04 *Ministero dell'Economia e delle Finanze v Cassa di Risparmio di Firenze SpA, Fondazione Cassa di Risparmio di San Miniato and Cassa di Risparmio di San Miniato SpA* [2006] ECR I-289.

19 Opinion of AG Jacobs in *Banking Foundations* (n 18) para 74. For relevant case law, see Case 78/76 *Steinike & Weinlig v Germany* [1977] ECR 0595, para 18; Joined Cases 209 to 215 and 218/78 *Heintz van Landewyck SARL and others v Commission* (FEDETAB) [1980] ECR 3125, para 88; Case C-244/94 *Fédération Française des Sociétés d'Assurance, Société Paternelle-Vie, Union des Assurances de Paris-Vie and Caisse d'Assurance et de Prévoyance Mutuelle des Agriculteurs v Ministère de l'Agriculture et de la Pêche* (FFSA) [1995] ECR I-4013, para 21; *Banking Foundations* (n 18) para 123; Case C-49/07 *Motosykletistiki Omospondia Ellados*

offers goods or services on the market in competition with other operators.[20] In that respect, the EU Courts are attuned to the fact that CSOs can restrict competitive markets to the detriment of for-profit companies but also of other CSOs.[21]

There are roughly two types of activities which should be distinguished so as to identify whether a CSO offers goods or services on the market in competition with other operators. On the one hand, CSOs, increasingly faced with a decline in state funding as well as in private donations, have come to sell goods and services on secondary markets so as to raise profits to be reinvested into their primary social purpose.[22] These purely commercial activities will indubitably be considered economic by the ECJ, notwithstanding the social purpose for which they may be undertaken.[23]

On the other hand, CSOs provide services through which they fulfil directly their social aims. Social services are often provided free of charge to their beneficiaries or at below-cost prices. By providing such services on a not-for-profit basis, CSOs break the direct link found in competitive markets between cost and price, contribution and benefit. From a functional perspective, the exclusively social purpose of those services is irrelevant. A service provided for a remuneration covering no more than its costs is still an economic service according to the ECJ so long as it is not provided for nothing.[24] Moreover, it is provided in a competitive market as soon as this service competes with other similar services offered by for-profit or other not-for-profit operators.[25] It does not even matter that similar services are not currently provided in the market. The ECJ would be satisfied to know that a service has been or could be provided by other operators for-profit.[26] To borrow the words of Advocate General Tesauro in the case of *Eurocontrol*, what matters is that an activity is 'capable

NPID (MOTOE) v Elliniko Dimosio (MOTOE) [2008] ECR I-4863, paras 27–28; Case C-1/12 *Ordem dos Técnicos Oficiais de Contas v Autoridade da Concorrência* (Chartered accountants) (ECJ, 28 February 2013) para 57; Case T-347/09 *Germany v Commission* (GC, 12 September 2013) para 43.

20 Case C-475/99 *Firma Ambulanz Glöckner v Landkreis Südwestpfalz* (Ambulanz Glöckner) [2001] ECR I-8089, paras 19–20; *Banking Foundations* (n 18) paras 107–108, 122–123; *MOTOE* (n 19) paras 22, 27–28; *Chartered accountants* (n 19) para 57; *Germany v Commission* (n 19) para 43.

21 *MOTOE* (n 19) para 28.

22 See Weisbrod, *The Nonprofit Economy* (n 1) 107–129; Cicoria, 'European Competition Law and Nonprofit Organizations' (n 1) 5–8.

23 See *Ambulanz Glöckner* (n 20); Cicoria, 'European Competition Law and Nonprofit Organizations' (n 1) 27. By analogy, see also *Germany v Commission* (n 19).

24 Case C-281/06 *Hans-Dieter Jundt and Hedwig Jundt v Finanzamt Offenburg* (Jundt) [2007] ECR I-12231, para 32. For further reference on the notion of 'service' in European law, see Sec 4.3.

25 *Ambulanz Glöckner* (n 20) paras 19–20; *Banking Foundations* (n 18) paras 107–108, 122–123; *MOTOE* (n 19) paras 22, 27–28; *Chartered accountants* (n 19) para 57; *Germany v Commission* (n 19) para 43.

26 *Höfner* (n 15) para 22; *Ambulanz Glöckner* (n 20) para 20.

of being carried on, at least in principle, by a private undertaking with a view to profit'.[27] Such a wide understanding of the notion of economic activity has the effect of bringing *all* social services performed by CSOs in the economic sphere. Conversely, it confines the non-economic sphere to those essential state functions which cannot be privatised.[28] Competition law only keeps clear of what economists call public goods such as national defence and police services.[29]

An important consequence of this functional approach is that CSOs' reliance on state redistribution for the purpose of financing the delivery of social services would not bring them outside the remit of competition law. The ECJ indeed considers that competition law applies to any entity involved in an economic activity, *regardless* of its method of financing.[30] This means that all social functions typically associated with the rise of the modern welfare state would fall within the remit of competition rules.[31]

However, in its case law on compulsory membership of social and health insurance funds, the ECJ has retreated from this all-encompassing definition by holding that activities wherein the principle of social solidarity is predominant, escape the reach of competition rules.[32] The following features have been identified by the ECJ as constitutive of the core of social solidarity:

---

27 Opinion of AG Tesauro in Case C-364/92 *SAT Fluggesellschaft mbH v Eurocontrol* (Eurocontrol) [1994] ECR I-00043, para 9. See also JL Buendia Sierra, *Exclusive Rights and State Monopolies under EC Law: Article 86 (Formerly Article 90) of the EC Treaty* (OUP 1999) 48; Odudu, 'The Meaning of Undertaking'(n 12) 223–231; W Sauter and H Schepel, *State and Market in European Union Law: The Public and Private Spheres of the Internal Market before the EU Courts* (CUP 2009) 81–83.

28 Buendia Sierra, *Exclusive Rights and State Monopolies under EC Law* (n 27) 57. However, the ECJ has a wide understanding of what pertains to the essential functions of the state. In this respect, see *Eurocontrol* (n 27) para 30; *Diego Calì* (n 17) paras 22–23; Case C-138/11 *Compass-Datenbank GmbH v Republik Österreich* (ECJ, 12 July 2012), paras 36–40.

29 Odudu, 'The Meaning of Undertaking' (n 12) 228–231.

30 *Höfner* (n 15) para 20; Case C-237/04 *Enirisorse SpA v Sotacarbo SpA* [2006] ECR I-2843, paras 28–33. See Buendia Sierra, *Exclusive Rights and State Monopolies under EC Law* (n 27) 47–48.

31 Buendia Sierra, *Exclusive Rights and State Monopolies under EC Law* (n 27) 57.

32 See Joined Cases C-159/91 and C-160/91 *Christian Poucet v Assurances Générales de France (AGF) and Caisse Mutuelle Régionale du Languedoc-Roussillon (Camulrac) and Daniel Pistre v Caisse Autonome Nationale de Compensation de l'Assurance Vieillesse des Artisans (Cancava)* (Poucet and Pistre) [1993] ECR I-637; *FFSA* (n 19); Case C-67/96 *Albany International BV v Stichting Bedrijfspensioenfonds Textielindustrie* (Albany) [1999] ECR I-5751; Joined Cases C-180/98 to C-184/98 *Pavel Pavlov and Others v Stichting Pensioenfonds Medische Specialisten* (Pavlov) [2000] ECR I-6451; Case C-218/00 *Cisal Di Battistello Venanzio & C. Sas v Istituto Nazionale Per l'Assicurazione Contro Gli Infortuni Sul Lavoro (INAIL)* (Cisal) [2002] ECR I-691; Case C-355/00 *Freskot AE v Elliniko Dimosio* (Freskot) [2003] ECR I-5263; *AOK* (n 14); *Kattner* (n 16); *AG2R* (n 16). On the principle of solidarity in competition law, see N Boeger, 'Solidarity and EC Competition Law' (2007) 32 EL Rev 319; M Ross, 'Promoting Solidarity: From Public Services to a European Model of Competition?' (2007) 44 CML Rev 1057.

1. *Compulsion*: The insurance scheme must be compulsory.[33]
2. *State supervision*: The intensity of state supervision, notably the fact that the insurance fund is not able to influence the amount of benefits and contributions, is a defining element.[34]
3. *Absence of direct link between benefits and contributions*: The absence of link between costs and price necessarily entails redistribution.[35, 36]

Beyond these three elements, the exclusively social aim pursued by the social insurance scheme as well as the non-profit nature of the entity which manages it have sometimes come to bear on the qualification of an undertaking.[37] However, these are incidental elements which can only confirm the conclusion already reached on the basis of the aforementioned criteria.[38]

In *FENIN*,[39] the GC transposed the principle of social solidarity unveiled in insurance cases to a public health system financed by social security contributions and other state funding and delivering free health care to its members on a universal basis.[40] This case provides grounds to argue that social solidarity may be instrumental to protect from competition law social services delivered free of charge and financed by redistributive means. That *FENIN* concerned health services delivered by public institutions should not prevent the application of this case law to CSOs, for the ECJ has already accepted that a private entity can escape competition law where it exercises public powers on behalf of the state.[41] A major limitation of this case law is, however, that it concerns social solidarity engineered or endorsed by the state. In other words,

33 *Poucet and Pistre* (n 32) para 13; *FFSA* (n 19) para 17; *AOK* (n 14) para 52.

34 *Poucet and Pistre* (n 32) paras 14–15, 18; *Albany* (n 32) paras 81–82; *Cisal* (n 32) para 44; *Freskot* (n 32) para 78; *Kattner* (n 32) para 62; *AG2R* (n 16) para 53.

35 *Poucet and Pistre* (n 32) paras 10–11; *Albany* (n 32) para 81; *Cisal* (n 32) para 42; *AOK* (n 14) 53; *Kattner* (n 32) para 59; *AG2R* (n 16) paras 47–52.

36 For an alternative formulation of those features, see V Hatzopoulos, 'Health Law and Policy: The Impact of the EU' in G De Búrca (ed), *EU Law and the Welfare State: in Search of Solidarity* (OUP 2005) 153–155; Odudu, 'The Meaning of Undertaking' (n 12) 224–228.

37 *Poucet and Pistre* (n 32) para 18; *AOK* (n 14) para 51; Case T-155/04 *SELEX Sistemi Integrati SpA v Commission* [2006] ECR II-04797, para 116.

38 *FFSA* (n 19) 21; *Albany* (n 32) para 85; *Pavlov* (n 32) para 117; *Cisal* (n 32) para 37; *Freskot* (n 32) 77; *Kattner* (n 16) para 42; *AG2R* (n 16) para 43–45.

39 Case T-319/99 *Federación Nacional de Empresas de Instrumentación Científica, Médica, Técnica y Dental (FENIN) v Commission* (FENIN) [2003] ECR II-357. See also *AOK* (n 14); M Krajewski and M Farley, 'Non-Economic Activities in Upstream and Downstream Markets and the Scope of Competition Law after FENIN' (2007) 32 EL Rev 111; A Cygan, 'Public Healthcare in the European Union: Still a Service of General Interest?' (2008) 57 ICLQ 529.

40 *FENIN* (n 39) para 39. In Commission Decision on State Aid NN 54/2006 – Czech Republic: Přerov logistics College C (2006) 5228, 8 November 2006, paras 14–18, the Commission ruled that a college part of the national education system was not an undertaking. In Case E-5/07 *Private Barnehagers Landsforbund v EFTA surveillance authority* [2008] EFTA CR 62, para 83, the EFTA Court also came to the conclusion that municipal kindergartens predominantly funded by the public purse were not undertakings.

41 See *Diego Calì* (n 17) para 17.

the principle of solidarity as it is conceived by the EU Courts does not offer a safe harbour for social services relying on civil initiatives so long as they are not made compulsory and strictly supervised by the state. This reflects the state-centrist notion of general interest promoted by European competition law which does not account for the pursuit of the public good outside state boundaries. Another limitation is slowly taking shape. The Commission, after *FENIN*, held in a Decision concerning state aids granted to Belgian public hospitals that hospital care is of an economic nature, even if it is financed partially or exclusively by the state.[42] In a recent judgment, the GC endorsed this view and implicitly condoned the restrictive reading of *FENIN* proposed by the Commission, as protecting from competition law's interference the management of a national health system but not the delivery of public healthcare as such.[43] If this reasoning proved to be confirmed,[44] this would mean that all social services provided by CSOs, even those that are provided free of charge and funded by the state, are potentially economic and therefore bound by competition rules.

5.3. CSOs AND ANTI-COMPETITIVE AGREEMENTS

Can the substantive provisions of European competition law balance the need for competitive markets with the social goals pursued by CSOs? This question is of the utmost importance now that *Section 5.2* has shown that almost all social services provided by CSOs are considered economic and therefore enter the jurisdiction of competition rules. The hierarchical structure of the Treaties makes

42 Commission Decision on State Aid NN 54/2009 (ex- CP 244/2005) – Belgique: Financement des hôpitaux publics du réseau IRIS de la Région Bruxelles-Capitale C (2009) 8120 final, 28 October 2009, para 110. Similarly, in its Decision 2006/225/EC of 2 March 2005 on the aid scheme implemented by Italy for the reform of the training institutions [2006] OJ L81/25, the Commission did not exclude that some activities carried out within the framework of the public education system might qualify as economic activities (para 55). See also Odudu, 'Are State Owned Healthcare Providers that are Funded by General Taxation Undertakings?' (n 12) 236.

43 Case T-137/10 *Coordination bruxelloise d'institutions sociales et de santé (CBI) v Commission* (CBI) (GC, 7 November 2012), paras 90–91.

44 In Commission, 'The Application of the European Union State Aid Rules to Compensation Granted for the Provision of Services of General Economic Interest' (Communication) [2012] OJ C8/4, the Commission backtracks on this wide understanding of the notion of economic activity by holding that public hospitals directly funded from social security contributions and other state resources and which provide their services free of charge to affiliated persons on the basis of universal coverage do not act as undertakings (para 22). The Commission adds that public education organised within the national educational system funded and supervised by the state may be considered as a non-economic activity (para 26). See also Commission Decision 2013/284/EU of 19 December 2012 on State Aid SA.20829 (C 26/2010, ex NN 43/2010 (ex CP 71/2006)) Scheme concerning the municipal real estate tax exemption granted to real estate used by non-commercial entities for specific purposes implemented by Italy [2013] OJ L166/24, which follows the guidelines set in the aforementioned Communication with reference to earlier case law (paras 164–176).

clear that competition law is not only a value in itself[45] but also an instrument to achieve the economic and social objectives of Article 3 TEU.[46] This view has received clear recognition in the case law of the EU Courts.[47] The need for a teleological interpretation of competition law respectful of the economic *and* social goals of the Treaties is reinforced by two policy-linking clauses found in the TFEU,[48] one related to the social field,[49] the other one ensuring consistency between EU policies.[50] Yet, the social and economic objectives of the Treaties inevitably come to collide in some circumstances. This section will show that, as regards Article 101 TFEU in particular, the EU Courts prefer to settle conflicts between competition and social goals through a balancing process.[51] This is in line with what the policy-linking clauses require[52] and with the balancing logic which governs the Treaties as a whole.[53] The economic *rationale* which dominates competition law sometimes undermines this balancing process, to such an extent that this section will also ask whether, as an alternative, the

45 Article 3 (1) g) of the EC treaty entailed as one of the activities of the European community the achievement of 'a system ensuring that competition in the internal market is not distorted'. Since Lisbon, the Union shall, as one of its objectives, establish an internal market (Article 3 (3) TEU) which, according to Protocol no. 27 on the internal market and competition ([2012] OJ C326/309), 'includes a system insuring that competition is not distorted'. This downgrading of competition objectives in the EU legal hierarchy does not seem to influence the ECJ which refers to Article 3 (3) TEU and Protocol no. 27 as if there were no difference from Article 3 (1) g) TEC (Whish and Bailey, *Competition Law* (n 12) 50 citing Case C-52/09 *Konkurrensverket v TeliaSonera Sverige AB* (Konkurrensverket) [2011] ECR I-00527, paras 20–22).

46 Article 3 (3) TEU: 'The Union (...) shall work for the sustainable development of Europe based on (...) a highly competitive social market economy (...)'. See also Articles 3 (6) and 5 (2) TEU; Articles 2 (6) and 3 (1) TFEU. On the teleological approach adopted by the EU Courts, see W Sauter, *Competition Law and Industrial Policy in the EU* (Clarendon Press 1997) 120; R Wesseling, *The Modernisation of EC Antitrust Law* (Hart 2000) 48–49; O Odudu, *The Boundaries of EC Competition Law: the Scope of Article 81* (OUP 2006)160; C Semmelmann, *Social Policy Goals in the Interpretation of Article 81 EC* (Nomos 2008) 49–51; C Townley, 'Which Goals Count in Article 101 TFEU? Public Policy and its Discontents: the OFT's Roundtable Discussion on Article 101 (3) of the Treaty on the Functioning of the European Union' (2011) 32 ECLR 441, 442; L Nistor, *Public Services and the European Union: Healthcare, Health Insurance and Education Services* (TMC Asser Press 2011) 201; Whish and Bailey, *Competition Law* (n 12) 50–51.

47 Case 32/65 *Italy v Council and Commission* [1966] ECR 389, para 405; Case 14/68 *Walt Wilhelm and Others v Bundeskartellamt* [1969] ECR 1, para 5; Case 6/72 *Europemballage Corporation and Continental can Company Inc. v Commission* [1973] ECR 215, paras 22–25; Case 26/76 *Metro SB-Großmärkte GmbH & Co. KG v Commission* (Metro) [1977] ECR 1875, para 20; Case T-168/01 *GlaxoSmithKline Services Unlimited v Commission* (Glaxo) [2006] ECR II-02969, para 109; *Konkurrensverket* (n 45) paras 20–22.

48 Townley, *Article 81 EC and Public Policy* (n 11) 54.

49 Article 9 TFEU.

50 Article 7 TFEU.

51 Townley, *Article 81 EC and Public Policy* (n 11) 55–70.

52 See Articles 7 and 9 TFEU.

53 See Articles 36, 45 (3), 52 (1) TFEU and the reference in Article 3 (3) TEU to the objective of 'balanced economic growth'.

distinctiveness of CSOs has any chance to be integrated into a pure economic approach to competition law.

5.3.1. BALANCING COMPETITION AGAINST SOCIAL GOALS UNDER ARTICLE 101(1) TFEU

The ECJ has hardly ever made exception to the rule that all agreements restrictive of competition fall within the scope of competition law, save where derogation is expressly provided for in the Treaties.[54] However, in *Albany*, the ECJ brought outside the scope of competition law agreements concluded in the context of collective negotiations between management and labour adopted with a view to improve conditions of work and employment, based on a teleological interpretation of the TFEU taken as a whole.[55] Yet, *Albany* represents an 'anomalous',[56] 'exceptional'[57] case, the repercussions of which the ECJ seems willing to limit to the collective agreements expressly aimed at in that decision.[58]

The *Wouters*[59] case offers a much more promising way for settling conflicts between competition and social goals. Therein, the ECJ upheld a regulation issued by the Bar of the Netherlands prohibiting multi-disciplinary partnerships between lawyers and accountants on the grounds that such rule does not go beyond what is necessary in order to ensure the proper practice of the legal profession.[60] In *Meca-Medina*,[61] the ECJ, transposing *Wouters* to the area of sports, considered that the anti-doping rules of the International Olympic Committee (IOC) were justified by the objective of ensuring a healthy rivalry between athletes.[62] Therefore, an agreement between undertakings or a decision of an association of undertakings limiting the parties' freedom of action does not fall within the prohibition of Article 101 TFEU where it is justified by a legitimate objective, provided that the restrictions of competition inherent in the

---

54 See, eg, Articles 42 and 346 (1) b) TFEU.

55 *Albany* (n 32) paras 59–60. See also Joined Cases C-115/97 to C-117/97 *Brentjens' Handelsonderneming BV v Stichting Bedrijfspensioenfonds voor de Handel in Bouwmaterialen* [1999] ECR I-6025, para 61; Case C-219/97 *Maatschappij Drijvende Bokken BV v Stichting Pensioenfonds voor de Vervoer* [1999] ECR I-6121, para 51; Case C-222/98 *Hendrik van der Woude v Stichting Beatrixoord* [2000] ECR I-7111, paras 23–27; *AG2R* (n 16) paras 28–36.

56 Townley, *Article 81 EC and Public Policy* (n 11) 61.

57 Semmelmann, *Social Policy Goals in the Interpretation of Article 81 EC* (n 46) 95.

58 *Pavlov* (n 32) paras 67–70; Case C-413/13 *FNV Kunsten Informatie en Media v Staat der Nederlanden* (ECJ, 4 December 2014) para 42.

59 C-309/99 *J. C. J. Wouters, J. W. Savelbergh and Price Waterhouse Belastingadviseurs BV v Algemene Raad Van De Nederlandse Orde Van Advocaten* (Wouters) [2002] ECR I-1577.

60 Ibid paras 107, 109–110.

61 Case C-519/04 P *David Meca-Medina and Igor Majcen v Commission of the European Communities* (Meca-Medina) [2006] ECR I-6991.

62 Ibid para 45.

pursuit of the said objective do not go beyond what is necessary to attain it.[63] It is argued that *Wouters* imports into competition law the *Cassis*-jurisprudence by conferring the right to invoke public interest objectives as justifications against restrictions of competition as long as these restrictions are necessary for the pursuit of the said objectives.[64] If this wide interpretation is accepted, *Wouters* could allow CSOs to derogate from competition law whenever it is necessary to ensure the pursuit of their social objectives.

However, there are two issues to be settled before reaching such a conclusion. Firstly, can social objectives be invoked absent state tutorship?[65] *Wouters*[66] and *Meca-Medina*[67] represent cases of self-regulation by *semi-public* organisations. Yet, in neither case was this fact deemed relevant for determining whether a public interest justification could be raised.[68] Nor is state involvement relevant when determining whether an agreement can be exempted under Article 101(3) TFEU.[69] The case law regarding objective justifications invoked by undertakings with a view to excuse their presumably abusive behaviour under Article 102 TFEU confirms that public policy reasons may justify purely

---

63 *Wouters* (n 59) paras 97, 109–110; *Meca-Medina* (n 61) para 42. See also *Chartered accountants* (n 19) paras 93 and 96; Case C-136/12 *Consiglio nazionale dei geologi v Autorità garante della concorrenza e del mercato and Autorità garante della concorrenza e del mercato v Consiglio nazionale dei geologiparas* (ECJ, 18 July 2013) paras 53–54; Joined Cases C-184/13 to C-187/13, C-194/13, C-195/13 and C-208/13 *API – Anonima Petroli Italiana SpA v Ministero delle Infrastrutture e dei Trasporti and Ministero dello Sviluppo economico and others* (ECJ, 4 September 2014) paras 47–48; Case T-90/11 *Ordre national des pharmaciens (ONP) and Others v Commission* (GC, 10 December 2014) paras 37–38, 343–348.

64 G Monti, 'Article 81 EC and Public Policy' (2002) 39 CML Rev 1057, 1086–1088. On *Wouters*, see R Nazzini, 'Article 81 EC between Time Present and Time Past: A Normative Critique of Restriction of Competition in EU Law' (2006) 43 CML Rev 487, 526–527; G Monti, *EC Competition Law* (CUP 2007) 111–112; P Komninos, 'Non-Competition Concerns: Resolution of Conflicts in the Integrated Article 81 EC' (2008) Working Paper (L) 08/05, Oxford Centre for Competition Law and Policy, 9–13 <www.eui.eu/RSCAS/Research/Competition/2004/200409-compet-Komninos.pdf> accessed 1st September 2015; Semmelmann, *Social Policy Goals in the Interpretation of Article 81 EC* (n 46) 101–108; G Davies, 'Article 86 EC, the EC's Economic Approach to Competition Law, and the General Interest' (2009) 5 ECJ 549, 567–570; Nistor, *Public Services and the European Union* (n 46) 187–189; Whish and Bailey, *Competition Law* (n 12) 130–133.

65 Davies, 'Article 86 EC' (n 64) 570; Townley, *Article 81 EC and Public Policy* (n 11) 134, fn 156. Cf H Schweitzer, 'Competition Law and Public Policy: Reconsidering an Uneasy Relationship: The Example of Art. 81' (2007) EUI Working Papers LAW 2007/30, 3–4 <http://papers.ssrn.com/sol3/papers.cfm?abstract_id=1092883> accessed 1st September 2015; Whish and Bailey, *Competition Law* (n 12) 129.

66 *Wouters* (n 59) paras 56–64, 100.

67 For Whish and Bailey, *Competition Law* (n 12) 132, the IOC concerned in *Meca-Medina* (n 61) is 'a creature of public international law'. According to Article 15 of the Olympic charter, 'the IOC is an international non-governmental not-for-profit organization (...) recognized by the Swiss Federal Council in accordance with an agreement entered into on 1 November 2000'. See also Case T-193/02 *Laurent Piau v Commission* (Piau) [2005] ECR II-00209, paras 76–79, 105.

68 Davies, 'Article 86 EC' (n 64) 570.

69 See below, nn 100–102.

private restrictions, although the EU Courts will remain suspicious of steps taken by undertakings to promote the public interest on their own initiative.[70] Conversely, Article 101 TFEU does not apply where 'anti-competitive conduct is required of undertakings by national legislation [as] in such a situation, the restriction of competition is not attributable (...) to the autonomous conduct of the undertakings'.[71]

Secondly, since neither *Wouters* nor its followers have gone beyond the regulatory sphere, can legitimate objectives justify restrictions on competition caused by economic, as opposed to, regulatory activities? Odudu argues that the regulatory activities of an association of undertakings are non-economic and, therefore, should be subject to the public law of free movement rules.[72] This is why public interest claims were exceptionally admitted in *Wouters*,[73] while they should not be made available for economic activities.[74] This distinction seems superficial, since the reason Article 101 TFEU also applies to associations of undertakings is precisely to avoid that undertakings be allowed to produce the results which competition law aims to suppress by merely creating a non-economic association competent for regulating their activities.[75] Moreover, neither in *Wouters* nor in *Meca-Medina*, did the ECJ pay attention to the fact that the activities at stake were regulatory.[76] Rather, the emphasis was on the agreement's objectives.[77] It could be added that the ECJ has already challenged economic, as opposed to regulatory, activities under the public law of free movement,[78] thereby casting doubt on the relevance of a public/private divide in EU law.

---

70 Case T-30/89 *Hilti AG v Commission* [1991] ECR II-1439, para 118; Case T-83/91 *Tetra Pak International SA v Commission* [1994] ECR II-755, para 138. For more detail, see Davies, 'Article 86 EC' (n 64) 563–565.

71 Case C-280/08 P *Deutsche Telekom AG v Commission* [2010] ECR I-09555, para 80. Whish and Bailey, *Competition Law* (n 12) 137, refers thereto as the 'state compulsion' defence. See also Commission, 'Guidelines on the Applicability of Article 101 of the Treaty on the Functioning of the European Union to Horizontal Co-operation Agreements' [2011] OJ C11/1, para 22.

72 Odudu, 'The Meaning of Undertakings' (n 12) 218–221.

73 Odudu, *The Boundaries of EC Competition Law* (n 46) 166.

74 See Nazzini, 'Article 81 EC between Time Present and Time Past' (n 64) 527; Schweitzer, 'Competition Law and Public Policy' (n 65) 2–4; AC Witt, 'Public Policy Goals under EU Competition Law–Now is the Time to Set the House in Order' (2012) 8 ECJ 443, 467–468.

75 *Van Landewyck* (n 19) para 88.

76 The regulatory aspect of the case was discussed in *Wouters* (n 59) paras 54–64. Yet, this was only to determine whether the Bar was an association of undertakings for the purposes of competition law.

77 Townley, *Article 81 EC and Public Policy* (n 11) 134. See *Wouters* (n 59) para 97 and *Meca-Medina* (n 61) paras 40–55.

78 See Case 43/75 *Gabrielle Defrenne v Société Anonyme Belge De Navigation Aérienne Sabena* [1976] ECR 0455, para 39; C-281/98 *Roman Angonese v Cassa Di Risparmio Di Bolzano SpA* [2000] ECR I-04139, paras 30–36; Case C-94/07 *Andrea Raccanelli v Max-Planck-Gesellschaft zur Förderung der Wissenschaften eV* [2008] ECR I-5939, paras 40–46. See also Case 36/74 *B.N.O. Walrave and L.J.N. Koch v Association Union Cycliste Internationale, Koninklijke Nederlandsche Wielren Unie Et Federación Española Ciclismo* [1974] ECR 1405, para 19; Case C-415/93 *Union royale belge des sociétés de football association ASBL v Jean-Marc Bosman,*

5.3.2. INTEGRATING SOCIAL GOALS WITHIN COMPETITION UNDER ARTICLE 101(1) TFEU

Uncertainty as to the fate of *Wouters* naturally brings us to ask whether there is any chance that the social values which drive CSOs could be integrated into an autonomous approach to competition law, where balancing competition against external values is rejected. Article 101(1) TFEU prohibits agreements which have as their object or effect to restrict competition.[79] In that respect, the ECJ ruled in *Consten and Grundig*[80] that 'there is no need to take account of the concrete effects of an agreement once it appears that it has as its object the prevention, restriction or distortion of competition'.[81] The object and effect tests are therefore read disjunctively.[82]

Agreements which have as their object the restriction of competition, such as price fixing agreements or market sharing agreements, are considered so pernicious that they are presumed to be illegal under Article 101(1) TFEU without any investigation of their effect on competition.[83] The presumptions of illegality entailed by the object test ought to be handled with care where agreements concluded by CSOs are considered.[84] These presumptions have been devised for for-profit companies from which it can reasonably be expected that market power acquired through an agreement will be exercised in a way detrimental to consumer welfare by raising prices or restricting output. The assertion that non-profit entities exploit market power when given the opportunity is much more controversial among economists. Greaney, summarising the literature on non-profit behaviour, argues that 'ownership matters at least in certain circumstances',[85] so that even an agreement as

---

Royal club liégeois SA v Jean-Marc Bosman and others and Union des associations européennes de football (UEFA) v Jean-Marc Bosman (Bosman) [1995] ECR I-4921, paras 84–86.

79 According to Townley, *Article 81 EC and Public Policy* (n 11) 209, there is a fundamental disagreement as the notion of 'restriction of competition'. For an *economic freedom* approach, see Monti, 'Article 81 EC and Public Policy' (n 64) 1059–1069; Monti, *EC Competition Law* (n 64) 48–50. For a *consumer welfare* approach, see R Wesseling, 'The Commission White Paper on Modernisation of E.C. Antitrust Law: Unspoken Consequences and Incomplete Treatment of Alternative Options' (1999) 20 ECLR 420, 421–424; Nazzini, 'Article 81 EC between Time Present and Time Past' (n 64) 530; Townley, *Article 81 EC and Public Policy* (n 11) 231–249. For an overview, see Townley, *Article 81 EC and Public Policy* (n 11) 205–241.

80 Joined Cases 56 and 58/64 *Établissements Consten S.à.R.L. and Grundig-Verkaufs-GmbH v Commission,* [1966] ECR 0299.

81 Ibid p 342.

82 Whish and Bailey, *Competition Law* (n 12) 118. See also Case 56/65 *Société Technique Minière (L.T.M.) v Maschinenbau Ulm GmbH (M.B.U.)* [1966] ECR 235, p 249; Joined Cases C-501/06 P, C-513/06 P, C-515/06 P and C-519/06 P *GlaxoSmithKline Services Unlimited and others v Commission* (Glaxo (on appeal)) [2009] ECR I-09291, para 55.

83 See Whish and Bailey, *Competition Law* (n 12) 118.

84 Cicoria, 'European Competition Law and Nonprofit Organizations' (n 1) 32.

85 TL Greaney, 'Antitrust and Hospital Mergers: Does the Nonprofit Form Affect Competitive Substance?' (2006) 31 JHPPL 511, 523.

plainly anti-competitive as horizontal price fixing might deserve differential treatment.[86] For, CSOs often collude on price with a redistributive, rather than profit-maximising, concern in mind and redistribution is, from an economic point of view, efficiency-neutral.[87] An example that comes to mind, and with which both the Office of Fair Trading in the UK[88] and American Courts[89] have had to deal, is the conclusion of agreements by universities and schools whereby it is agreed to prevent or limit competition on the grant of scholarships based on academic merit so as to concentrate financial assistance on needy students, thereby redistributing resources from meritorious non-needy students to other, poor students.

It is not to say that CSOs never collude on price in order to raise their revenue. Our point is rather that they cannot be *presumed* to do so. If such an accusation is made against them, it should be backed by economic analysis demonstrating how the price-fixing collusion will or has created inefficiencies. In *Glaxo*, the GC reversed the *per se* stance usually taken as regards agreements which prevent parallel imports, holding that, in view of the legal and economic context in which the agreement at hand was applied, negative effects on consumer welfare could not be presumed.[90] This reasoning could have been applied to reverse *per se* presumptions affecting agreements concluded by CSOs, had the ECJ not overruled this approach on appeal.[91] Now that it did, it will surely become more difficult to reconsider *per se* presumptions in view of the economic context specific to agreements concluded by CSOs.

European competition law also prohibits agreements which have as their effect, potential or actual, the restriction of competition. Central to the economic approach adopted by the Commission[92] is the use of a market power screen[93]

---

86 DW Carlton, GE Bamberger and RJ Epstein, 'Antitrust and Higher Education' (1994) Working Paper no. 107, Center for the Study of the Economy and the State, University of Chicago, 10 <http://research.chicagobooth.edu/economy/research/articles/107.pdf> accessed 1st September 2015.

87 Ibid 28–29.

88 Office of Fair Trading, 'Exchange of Information on Future Fees by Certain Independent Fee-Paying Schools' (2006) <www.oft.gov.uk/shared_oft/ca98_public_register/decisions/schools.pdf> accessed 1st September 2015.

89 See *US v Brown University* 805 F Supp 288 (ED Pa 1992); *US v Brown University* 5 F 3d 658 (3rd Cir 1993).

90 *Glaxo* (n 47) paras 114–147.

91 *Glaxo (on appeal)* (n 82) paras 62–64.

92 See Commission, 'White Paper on Modernisation of the Rules Implementing Articles 85 and 86 of the EC Treaty' [1999] OJ C132/1, para 57; Commission, 'Guidelines on the Applicability of Article 81 of the EC Treaty to Horizontal Cooperation Agreements' [2001] OJ C3/2, paras 6–7, replaced by Commission, 'Guidelines on the Applicability of Article 101 of the Treaty on the Functioning of the European Union to Horizontal Co-operation Agreements' (n 71) para 5; Commission, 'Guidelines on the Application of Article 81(3) of the Treaty' [2004] OJ C101/97, paras 5, 24, 33.

93 Monti, *EC Competition Law* (n 64) 48–50.

as a tool to predict the likely anti-competitive effects of an agreement.[94] The concept of market power is problematic from the perspective of CSOs, for it postulates that 'those *able* to profitably contrive scarcity *will* contrive scarcity'.[95] This economic prediction ought to be used with caution. Although CSOs may exercise market power when they acquire it through an agreement, the extent to which they are likely to do so in a manner detrimental to consumer welfare is not sufficiently known to economists. In any case, the incentives inherent in CSOs' non-profit structure ought to be taken into consideration when undertaking such an assessment.[96]

5.3.3. INTEGRATING SOCIAL GOALS WITHIN COMPETITION UNDER ARTICLE 101(3) TFEU

One may wonder whether *Wouters* remains useful at all considering that Article 101(3) TFEU has become directly applicable by national competition authorities (NCAs) and tribunals.[97] Absent notification to the Commission, some have claimed that balancing competition against external values within Article 101(1) TFEU was the only way for the ECJ to save the agreements at issue in *Wouters* and *Meca-Medina*, while Article 101(3) TFEU would now do the trick.[98] We do not agree, for it will be shown below that, contrary to *Wouters*, Article 101(3) TFEU cannot save agreements that promote public policy objectives to the detriment of competition.

An agreement which restricts competition may be exempted under Article 101(3) TFEU where there is evidence that it 'contributes to improving the production or distribution of goods or to promoting technical or economic progress'. The other three conditions are that the agreement allows consumers a fair share of the resulting benefit, is indispensable and does not eliminate competition in respect of a substantial part of the products in question. The EU

94 Commission, 'Guidelines on the Application of Article 81(3) of the Treaty' (n 92) para 25. See also Commission, 'Guidelines on the Applicability of Article 101 of the Treaty on the Functioning of the European Union to Horizontal Co-operation Agreements' (n 71) paras 28, 39–44.

95 Odudu, *The Boundaries of EC Competition Law* (n 46) 108.

96 See Greaney, 'Antitrust and Hospital Mergers' (n 85) 524.

97 See Commission, 'White Paper on Modernisation of the Rules Implementing Articles 85 and 86 of the EC Treaty' (n 92); Council Regulation (EC) 1/2003 of 16 December 2002 on the implementation of the rules on competition laid down in Articles 81 and 82 of the Treaty [2003] OJ L1/1. In this respect, Case C-209/07 *Competition Authority v Beef Industry Development Society Ltd and Barry Brothers (Carrigmore) Meats Ltd* [2008] ECR I-08637, para 21, suggests that restrictions of competition pursuing a legitimate objective should be considered under paragraph 3, not paragraph 1.

98 Whish and Bailey, *Competition Law* (n 12) 133.

Courts have construed this provision generously.[99] The GC even went further than the letter of Article 101(3) TFEU by holding that 'the Commission is entitled to base itself on considerations connected with the pursuit of the public interest in order to grant exemption under Article 85(3) [now Article 101(3)]'.[100] The Commission, making use of its wide margin of appreciation, has, under this provision, balanced the anti-competitive effects of agreements against various public policy objectives.[101]

Nevertheless, Article 101(3) TFEU is and has always been an efficiency defence.[102] One cannot find any anti-competitive agreement which has been exempted under Article 101(3) TFEU by relying on the exclusive weight of public policy considerations. They were necessarily combined with some pro-competitive effects or translated into efficiencies.[103] Besides, in its 2004 Guidelines on the application of Article 81(3) of the Treaty, the Commission

---

99 Townley, *Article 81 EC and Public Policy* (n 11) 67. As regards *social policy* grounds, see Case 42/84 *Remia BV and Others v Commission* [1985] ECR 2545, para 42; *Metro* (n 47) para 43; *FEDETAB* (n 19) para 182. For the relevance of *industrial policy* grounds, see Case T-17/93 *Matra Hachette SA v Commission* [1994] ECR II-00595, paras 108–111. As regards *sports*, see *Piau* (n 67) paras 100–104.

100 Joined Cases T-528/93, T-542/93, T-543/93 and T-546/93 *Metropole télévision SA and Reti Televisive Italiane SpA and Gestevisión Telecinco SA and Antena 3 de Televisión v Commission of the European Communities* (Metropole) [1996] ECR II-649, para 118. See also Joined Cases 46/87 and 227/88 *Hoechst AG v Commission* [1989] ECR 2859, para 25; Case 85/87 *Dow Benelux NV v Commission* [1989] ECR 3137, para 36; Joined Cases 97/87, 98/87 and 99/87 *Dow Chemical Ibérica, SA, and Others v Commission* [1989] ECR 3165, para 22; Case 374/87 *Orkem v Commission* [1989] ECR 3283, para 19; *Glaxo* (n 47) para 244.

101 See Monti, 'Article 81 EC and Public Policy' (n 64) 1057–1099; Monti, *EC Competition Law* (n 64) chap 2; Semmelmann, *Social Policy Goals in the Interpretation of Article 81 EC* (n 46) 114–141; Townley, *Article 81 EC and Public Policy* (n 11) 70–86; Whish and Bailey, *Competition Law* (n 12) 157–159. As regards *environmental policy*, see *CECED* (Case IV.F.1/36.718) Commission Decision 2000/475/EC [2000] OJ L187/47. As regards *crisis cartels*, see *BPCL / ICI* (Case IV / 30.863) Commission Decision 84/387/EEC [1984] OJ L212/1; *ENI / Montedison* (Case IV / 31.055) Commission Decision 87/3/EC [1987] OJ L5/13; *Stichting Baksteen* (Case IV / 34.456) Commission Decision 94/296/EC [1994] OJ L131/15. As regards *consumer protection*, see *Grundig's EC Distribution System* (Case IV / 29.420) Commission Decision 94/29/EC [1994] OJ L20/15. As regards *social and economic cohesion*, see *Ford Volkswagen* (Case IV / 33.814) Commission Decision 93/49/EEC [1993] OJ L20/14, para 23. As regards *sport*, see *Joint Selling of the Commercial Rights of the UEFA Champions League* (Case COMP / C.2-37.398) Commission Decision 2003/778/EC [2003] OJ L291/25, paras 164–167.

102 Komninos, 'Non-Competition Concerns' (n 64) 6–8; Semmelmann, *Social Policy Goals in the Interpretation of Article 81 EC* (n 46) 140. See also Monti, 'Article 81 EC and Public Policy' (n 64) 1078; Odudu, *The Boundaries of EC Competition Law* (n 46) chap 7; P Craig and G De Búrca, *EU Law: Text, Cases, and Materials* (5th edn, OUP 2011) 988–989; Whish and Bailey, *Competition Law* (n 12) 160.

103 Monti, 'Article 81 EC and Public Policy' (n 64) 1077–1078. See also Komninos, 'Non-Competition Concerns' (n 64) 6–8; Semmelmann, *Social Policy Goals in the Interpretation of Article 81 EC* (n 46) 139–140. *Contra*, see Schweitzer, 'Competition Law and Public Policy' (n 64) 11; Townley, *Article 81 EC and Public Policy* (n 11) 168–175.

decided that, from now on, Article 81(3) should focus on efficiency only,[104] while 'goals pursued by other Treaty provisions [could] be taken into account to the extent that they can be subsumed under the four conditions of Article 81(3) [now 101(3) TFEU]'.[105]

This pure economic approach to competition law is open to criticism on many grounds. It goes against the structure of the Treaties and their policy-linking clauses.[106] It contradicts the teleological interpretation of competition law by the EU Courts and the Commission's previous practice.[107] It, moreover, relies on an erroneous perception of the public/private divide.[108] More importantly, purifying Article 101(3) TFEU from public interest considerations so as to make that provision directly effective and justiciable before national courts and NCAs,[109] is not within the powers of the Commission; primary law cannot be fixed by way of secondary law and soft law initiatives.[110]

As the pure economic approach advocated by the Commission is nevertheless there to stay, it is crucial to know whether Article 101(3) TFEU, as an efficiency-only defence, can be 'massaged' so as to include the social goals pursued by CSOs, and particularly the redistribution they often operate between profitable and charitable activities. According to the Guidelines on the application of Article 101(3) TFEU, there are two sorts of economic efficiencies which can exempt anti-competitive agreements: cost efficiencies and 'efficiencies of a qualitative nature'.[111] The Guidelines' fairly wide conception of efficiency gains should facilitate the translation of social goals into economic benefits.[112]

To come back to an example given earlier, it could be argued that the transfer of income from wealthy students to needy ones actually improves the quality of education by bringing about an educational system diverse and open to all.[113] It could more generally be claimed that social justifications

---

104 Commission, 'Guidelines on the Application of Article 81(3) of the Treaty' (n 92) paras 5, 11, 32–33, 50, 59.

105 Ibid para 42. See also Commission, 'White Paper on Modernisation of the Rules Implementing Articles 85 and 86 of the EC Treaty' (n 92) para 57; Commission, 'Guidelines on the Applicability of Article 101 of the Treaty on the Functioning of the European Union to Horizontal Co-operation Agreements' (n 71) paras 48–49.

106 Townley, *Article 81 EC and Public Policy* (n 11) 54.

107 Ibid 55–86.

108 Ibid 87–93.

109 See Odudu, 'The Meaning of Undertaking' (n 12) 170–173; Komninos, 'Non-Competition Concerns' (n 64) 4; Craig and De Búrca, *EU Law: Text, Cases, and Materials* (n 102) 988–989; Whish and Bailey, *Competition Law* (n 12) 159–160.

110 Schweitzer, 'Competition Law and Public Policy' (n 64) 9–10; Townley, *Article 81 EC and Public Policy* (n 11) 97–98.

111 Commission, 'Guidelines on the Application of Article 81(3) of the Treaty' (n 92) para 59.

112 See Monti, *EC Competition Law* (n 64) 120.

113 This argument is discussed favourably in *US v Brown University* (1993) (n 89) paras 65–67, 82–85. See also Carlton et al, 'Antitrust and Higher Education' (n 86) ft 36.

meet the 'efficiency' condition as long as they correct market failures.[114] In the aforementioned case, a 'competitive' education market would fail to bring about diversity in education, although this qualitative aspect is valued by many students.[115]

An inventive use of the efficiency defence seems therefore possible and will bring exemption if the other three conditions of Article 101(3) TFEU are fulfilled. If not, the agreement can still be saved by Article 106(2) TFEU provided that the CSOs party to the agreement prove they are entrusted with a SGEI and that the said agreement is necessary in order to enable them to perform their task of general interest.[116]

5.4. CSOs AND STATE AIDS

CSOs benefit from significant public support.[117] In many countries, this takes the form of grants[118] and preferential tax treatment.[119] One may wonder whether financial subsidies of that kind are compatible with the prohibition of state aids contained in Article 107 TFEU. This article provides that:

> Save as otherwise provided in the Treaties, any aid granted by a Member State or through State resources in any form whatsoever which distorts or threatens to distort competition by favouring certain undertakings or the production of certain goods shall, in so far as it affects trade between Member States, be incompatible with the internal market.

The ECJ has consistently held that 'Article 87(1) EC [now Article 107(1) TFEU] does not distinguish between measures of State intervention by reference to their causes or their aims but defines them in relation to their effects',[120] so that 'the

114 P Areeda, *The "Rule of Reason" in Antitrust Analysis: General Issues* (Federal Judicial Center 1981) 8. See also TL Greaney, 'Quality of Care and Market Failure Defenses in Antitrust Health Care Litigation' (1989) 21 Connecticut Law Review 605.

115 The same argument was made for cultural diversity by Areeda, *The "Rule of Reason" in Antitrust Analysis* (n 114) 8 and Monti, *EC Competition Law* (n 64) 122.

116 According to Buendia Sierra, *Exclusive Rights and State Monopolies under EC Law* (n 27) 190, invoking Article 101 TFEU in combination with Article 106 (2) TFEU is theoretically possible, although, in practice, there are few cases where the two provisions are applied together. See, however, *Chartered accountants* (n 19) paras 104–107.

117 Salamon et al, *Global Civil Society: An Overview* (n 10) 28.

118 According to NCVO (UK), grants accounted for £3 billion of Voluntary and Community Sector (VCS) income from the public sector in 2009/10. For more details, see <http://data.ncvo-vol.org.uk/almanac/voluntary-sector/income-in-focus/what-are-the-main-trends-in-statutory-funding/> accessed 1st September 2015.

119 S Stevens, 'Tax Aid and Non-profit Organizations' (2010) 19 EC Tax Rev 156, 157.

120 Case C-124/10 P *Commission v Électricité de France* (EDF) (ECJ, 5 June 2012) para 77. See also Case C-487/06 P *British Aggregates Association v Commission* [2008] ECR I-10515, para 85, and the case law cited therein.

social character of (…) State measures is not sufficient to exclude them outright from classification as aid for the purposes of Article 92 [now Article 107] of the Treaty'.[121] Since the social purpose underlying civil society support is irrelevant from a state aid perspective, grants and preferential taxation constitute state aid as soon as they confer CSOs an *economic advantage* they would not have obtained under normal market conditions.[122] Preferential taxation, in particular, will be considered a state aid if it mitigates the charges which are normally included in the budget of a CSO. For, without being subsidies in the strict sense of the word, it is of the same character and has the same effect.[123]

According to Article 107 TFEU, the recipient of an economic advantage must also be an *undertaking*. As seen in *Section 5.2*, the ECJ has opted for a functional approach. An undertaking is any entity which carries on an economic activity, regardless of its legal status or the way in which it is financed.[124] The non-profit-making status of CSOs is therefore irrelevant.[125] At the same time, we have seen that the social services CSOs provide may escape state aid law if they are delivered free of charge and financed by redistributive means.[126]

State aid must, moreover, favour *certain* undertakings.[127] Selectivity would not be difficult to prove regarding grants, which are often provided on a discretionary basis to one or some CSOs.[128] Preferential taxation for CSOs may also be deemed selective to the extent that it is provided on account of an undertaking's legal form and of the sectors in which that undertaking carries on its activities.[129] A selective measure may still be 'justified by the nature or general scheme of the system of which it is part'.[130] In that regard, the Commission

121 Case C-75/97 *Belgium v Commission* [1999] ECR I-03671, para 25. See also Case 173/73 *Italy v Commission* [1974] ECR 0709, para 13; Case C-172/03 *Wolfgang Heiser v Finanzamt Innsbruck* [2005] ECR I-0162, para 46. For further detail on the impact of state aid law on social policy, see A Biondi and L Rubini, 'Aims, Effects and Justifications: EC State Aid Law and its Impact on National Social Policies' in E Spaventa and M Dougan (eds), *Social Welfare and EU Law* (Hart 2005).

122 See Case C-39/94 *Syndicat français de l'Express international (SFEI) and others v La Poste and others* [1996] ECR I-3547, para 60; *Germany v Commission* (n 19) paras 60–73. On the notion of state aid, see C Quigley, *European State Aid Law and Policy* (2nd edn, Hart 2009) 1–12.

123 *Banking Foundations* (n 18) paras 131–132. See also Case C-126/01 *Ministère de l'Économie, des Finances et de l'Industrie v GEMO SA* [2003] ECR I-13769, para 28 and the case law cited therein; M Helios, 'Taxation of Non-Profit Organizations and EC Law' (2007) 16 EC Tax Rev 65, 69; Stevens, 'Tax Aid and Non-profit Organizations' (n 119) 159.

124 *Höfner* (n 15) para 21.

125 See above, n 19.

126 See above, n 39–44. For instance, see *Decision 2013/284/EU* (n 44) paras 164–176.

127 On selectivity, see A Bartosch, 'Is There a Need for a Rule of Reason in European State Aid Law? Or How to Arrive at a Coherent Concept of Material Selectivity?' (2010) 47 CML Rev 729.

128 See Perri, 'European Competition Law and the Non-Profit Sector' (n 2) 219–220.

129 *Banking Foundations* (n 18) paras 135–136. See also Helios, 'Taxation of Non-Profit Organizations and EC Law' (n 123) 71.

130 Case C-143/99 *Adria-Wien Pipeline GmbH and Wietersdorfer & Peggauer Zementwerke GmbH v Finanzlandesdirektion für Kärnten* [2001] ECR I-08365, para 42.

accepts that 'it may (...) be justified by the nature of the tax system that non-profit-making undertakings (...) are specifically exempt from the taxes on profits if they cannot actually earn any profits'.[131] Yet, where tax benefits are extended to taxes which do not require any income or to corporate taxation of specific profit-making activities of CSOs which are unrelated to their main activity, this justification does not hold any more,[132] for Member States cannot rely on objectives external to the tax system.[133]

Finally, for grants and preferential taxation to constitute state aid incompatible with the internal market, *trade between Member States* must be affected and *competition* must be distorted. The two criteria are inextricably linked and the thresholds to be met are particularly low.[134] The effect on trade is not affected by the local or regional character of the service supplied, or by the scale of the activity concerned so that 'the relatively small amount of aid or the relatively small size of the undertaking which receives it does not as such exclude the possibility that trade between Member States might be affected'.[135] Relief may still be found in the *de minimis* Regulation[136] which provides that aid not exceeding a ceiling of EUR 200 000 over any period of three years does not affect trade between Member States and/or does not distort or threaten to distort competition.[137] Yet, this exception only offers a solution for relatively small CSOs.[138]

To sum up, financial subsidies to CSOs, in principle, amount to state aid which is prohibited by Article 107(1) TFEU unless they have been notified to and been approved by the Commission in accordance with Article 107(2) or (3) TFEU. Article 107(2) a) TFEU, which finds aid having a social character granted to individual consumers to be compatible with the internal market, may be relevant for CSOs which are supported by vouchers or other demand-side subsidies.[139] Considering the central role assigned to CSOs in the construction

131 Commission, 'Notice on the Application of the State Aid Rules to Measures relating to Direct Business Taxation' [1998] OJ C384/3, para 25.

132 Helios, 'Taxation of Non-Profit Organizations and EC Law' (n 123) 71.

133 Commission, 'Notice on the Application of the State Aid Rules to Measures relating to Direct Business Taxation' (n 131) para 26. See also *Banking Foundations* (n 18) para 137; *Decision 2013/284/EU* (n 44) para 126. This is contested in Bartosch, 'Is There a Need for a Rule of Reason in European State Aid Law' (n 127) 745–746.

134 P Nicolaides, M Kekelekis and M Kleis, *State Aid Policy in the European Community* (2nd edn, Kluwer 2008) 36–41.

135 Case C-280/00 *Altmark Trans GmbH and Regierungspräsidium Magdeburg v Nahverkehrs-gesellschaft Altmark GmbH, and Oberbundesanwalt beim* Bundesverwaltungsgericht (Altmark) [2003] ECR I-07747, paras 81–82.

136 Commission Regulation (EU) 1407/2013 of 18 December 2013 on the application of Articles 107 and 108 of the Treaty on the Functioning of the European Union to de minimis aid [2013] OJ L352/1.

137 Ibid Article 3 (2).

138 Stevens, 'Tax Aid and Non-profit Organizations' (n 119) 163.

139 See J Baquero Cruz, 'Social Services of General Interest and the State Aid Rules' in U Neergaard, E Szyszczak, JW van de Gronden and M Krajewski (eds), *Social Services of General Interest in the EU* (TMC Asser Press 2013) 296–299.

of social Europe, one could also argue that funding civil society promotes the execution of an important project of common European interest which may be compatible with the internal market according to Article 107(3) b) TFEU.[140] Finally, aid which facilitates the development of certain economic activities may be saved by virtue of Article 107(3) c) TFEU. On this basis, the Commission has already taken a favourable view towards aid schemes which promote the not-for-profit sector.[141] CSOs have also benefited from the preferential regime instituted by the General Block Exemption Regulation for certain categories of aid to small and medium-sized enterprises (SMEs).[142] Possibilities for saving CSOs' financial subsidies from the prohibition of state aid therefore exist.[143] A task for the future would be for the Commission to formulate its policy towards CSOs into a proper regulation or set of guidelines which would shed light upon the specific circumstances allowing financial support.[144]

However, it is still important to note that financial subsidies to CSOs will not classify as state aid if they compensate for services CSOs provide in the general economic interest.[145] In its famous *Altmark* ruling, the ECJ has enumerated a number of conditions for public service compensations (PSCs) to escape classification as state aid:

> First, the recipient undertaking must actually have public service obligations to discharge, and the obligations must be clearly defined (...) Second, the parameters on the basis of which the compensation is calculated must be established in advance in an objective and transparent manner (...) Third, the compensation cannot exceed what is necessary to cover all or part of the costs incurred in the discharge of public service obligations, taking into account the relevant receipts and a reasonable profit

---

140 Helios, 'Taxation of Non-Profit Organizations and EC Law' (n 123) 72. *Contra*, see Perri, 'European Competition Law and the Non-Profit Sector' (n 2) 221; Stevens, 'Tax Aid and Non-profit Organizations' (n 119) 163.

141 See Coursin, 'La Politique Européenne de Concurrence et les Entreprises de l'Économie Sociale' (n 5) 34; Quigley, *European State Aid Law and Policy* (n 122) 137. Both cite Commission, *Twenty-First Report on Competition Policy* (Publications Office 1991) point 272.

142 Commission Regulation (EU) 651/2014 of 17 June 2014 declaring certain categories of aid compatible with the internal market in application of Articles 107 and 108 of the Treaty (General Block Exemption Regulation) [2014] OJ L187/1. On the preferential regime of SMEs, see Quingley, *European State Aid Law and Policy* (n 122) 216–237. Under previous versions of that Regulation, Spain has, for instance, communicated to the Commission an aid scheme for the stimulation of the cooperative, mutual and non-profit sector ([2002] OJ C275/3), while Austria has communicated support for non-profit associations which build housing units and care facilities for elderly people ([2007] OJ C222/8; [2004] OJ C72/10).

143 For a more pessimistic view, see Perri, 'European Competition Law and the Non-Profit Sector' (n 2) 221.

144 In this sense, see Coursin, 'La Politique Européenne de Concurrence et les Entreprises de l'Économie Sociale' (n 5) 35. For the more radical view that Article 107 TFEU needs to be amended, see Perri, 'European Competition Law and the Non-Profit Sector' (n 2) 221.

145 See Stevens, 'Tax Aid and Non-profit Organizations' (n 119) 164–169. For a definition of SGEI, see Commission, 'A Quality Framework for Services of General Interest in Europe' (Communication) COM (2011) 900 final, 3.

> for discharging those obligations (...) Fourth, where the undertaking which is to discharge public service obligations, in a specific case, is not chosen pursuant to a public procurement procedure which would allow for the selection of the tenderer capable of providing those services at the least cost to the community, the level of compensation needed must be determined on the basis of an analysis of the costs which a typical undertaking, well run and adequately provided with means (...) so as to be able to meet the necessary public service requirements, would have incurred in discharging those obligations, taking into account the relevant receipts and a reasonable profit for discharging the obligations.[146]

The practice of the Commission shows that very few PSCs meet those high standards.[147] This is particularly true for grants and preferential taxation directed to CSOs,[148] so that authorities willing to finance civil society's delivery of public services through such channels will often have no other choice but to rely on Article 106(2) TFEU and show that disrespecting state aid rules is necessary for CSOs entrusted with the operation of a Service of General Economic Interest (SGEI) to perform the particular tasks assigned to them under economically acceptable conditions.[149]

On this basis, the Commission adopted a new SGEI package on 20 December 2011 to replace the 2005 'Post-Altmark' package.[150] In many respects, this package shields CSOs which deliver SGEI from the full rigour of state aid rules. First, the SGEI Regulation provides that aid granted to undertakings for the provision of a SGEI shall be deemed not to meet all the criteria of Article 107(1) TFEU and shall therefore be exempted from the notification requirement of

146 *Altmark* (n 135) paras 88–94. On *Altmark*, see F Louis and A Vallery, '*Ferring* Revisited: The *Altmark* Case and State Financing of Public Service Obligations' (2004) 27 World Competition 53.

147 J De Beys, 'Aide d'État et Financement des Services Publics: Un Bilan après l'Adoption du Paquet Post-*Altmark*' [2006] JDE 1, 2. Yet, since *BUPA* (Case T-289/03 *British United Provident Association Ltd (BUPA), BUPA Insurance Ltd and BUPA Ireland Ltd v Commission* [2008] ECR II-81), the GC has taken a more relaxed approach towards the *Altmark* conditions (SA de Vries, '*BUPA*: A Healthy Case, in the light of a Changing Constitutional Setting in Europe?' in JW van de Gronden, E Szyszczak, U Neergaard and M Krajewski (eds), *Health Care and EU Law* (TMC Asser Press 2011) 316).

148 Stevens, 'Tax Aid and Non-profit Organizations' (n 119) 167–168.

149 On Article 106 (2) TFEU, see Sauter and Schepel, *State and Market in European Union Law* (n 27) 164–192.

150 Commission Decision 2012/21/EU of 20 December 2011 on the application of Article 106(2) of the Treaty on the Functioning of the European Union to State aid in the form of public service compensation granted to certain undertakings entrusted with the operation of services of general economic interest [2012] OJ L7/3 (SGEI Decision); Commission Regulation (EU) 360/2012 of 25 April 2012 on the application of Articles 107 and 108 of the Treaty on the Functioning of the European Union to de minimis aid granted to undertakings providing services of general economic interest [2012] OJ L114/8 (SGEI Regulation); Commission, 'The Application of the European Union State Aid Rules to Compensation Granted for the Provision of Services of General Economic Interest' (n 44); Commission, 'European Union Framework for State Aid in the Form of Public Service Compensation' (Communication) [2012] OJ C8/15.

Article 108(3) TFEU if it does not exceed EUR 500 000 over any period of three fiscal years.[151] Second, there is a 'social exception'[152] contained in the SGEI Decision which deems compatible with the internal market and exempts from notification compensations for the provision of a wide array of social SGEI.[153] The same Decision contains a *de minimis* threshold of maximum EUR 15 million on a yearly basis which will render compatible with the internal market and exempt from notification most social services which would not enter the scope of the social exception.[154] Compensations that are covered by the SGEI Decision have to abide by criteria which clarify the first three *Altmark* conditions, while compensations falling outside its scope are subject to notification and may be permitted in accordance with similar, yet stricter, criteria.[155] The exclusion of the fourth *Altmark* criterion from the SGEI Decision can only bring relief to CSOs. For, neither choosing by tender the undertaking able to provide the SGEI at the least cost to the community, nor the alternative of comparing the SGEI provider with a typical, well-run undertaking looking for reasonable profit, seems adapted to the non-commercial nature of CSOs.[156]

5.5. CONCLUSIONS

Is the likely impact of European competition law on CSOs better characterised as integrationist or assimilationist? An investigation limited to the jurisdictional scope of competition law would suggest that CSOs have good reasons to fear assimilation to for-profit companies. The social aims of CSOs reflected in their not-for-profit status do not exempt them from compliance with competition rules; the ECJ assigns to the notion of 'undertaking' a functional meaning so that all social services CSOs provide are in principle considered economic. At

151 SGEI Regulation, Articles 2 (1) and (2).

152 W Sauter, 'The Altmark Package Mark II: New Rules for State Aid and the Compensation of Services of General Economic Interest' (2012) 33 ECLR 307, 310.

153 SGEI Decision, Articles 2 (1) c) and d). Commission Decision 2005/842/EC of 28 November 2005 on the application of Article 86(2) of the EC Treaty to State aid in the form of public service compensation granted to certain undertakings entrusted with the operation of services of general economic interest [2005] OJ L312/67 (ex-Decision 2012/21) only exempted from notification PSCs granted to *hospitals* and *social housing* undertakings (Article 2 (1) b)). For its application to public hospitals, see *CBI* (n 43). For the application of the same Decision to Dutch social housing, see Commission Decision on State Aid E 2/2005 and N 642/2009 – The Netherlands: Existing and special project aid to housing corporations C (2009) 9963 final, 15 December 2009.

154 SGEI Decision, Article 2 (1) a).

155 See Commission, 'European Union Framework for State Aid in the Form of Public Service Compensation' (n 150).

156 See *Germany v Commission* (n 19) paras 74–89; E Van den Abeele, 'Les Services d'Intérêt Général. État du Débat Européen' (2005) 1901–1902 Courrier Hebdomadaire du CRISP 21; M Dony, *Contrôle des Aides d'État* (Ed. de l'Université de Bruxelles 2007) 161.

the moment, only social solidarity engineered or endorsed by the state may bring CSOs outside the remit of competition law (*5.2*).

Thorough examination of the substance of competition law makes room for a less pessimistic view. *Wouters* indicates that the ECJ is willing to balance, under Article 101(1) TFEU, competition against the social goals pursued by CSOs' anti-competitive agreements, while the Commission allows social considerations to be taken into account for granting exemption under Article 101(3) TFEU to the extent that they translate into economic benefits. This economic approach to competition law does not necessarily mean assimilation, for there is a good case to be made that CSOs deserve to be treated differently on economic grounds. This would imply abandoning the object test and making a flexible use of the market power screen when considering the anti-competitive effect of an agreement, while condoning an inventive use of qualitative efficiencies as allowed in the Commission Guidelines (*5.3*).

Competition law also rejects an assimilationist approach if we take the perspective of the ban on state aid contained in Article 107(1) TFEU. Subsidies for CSOs, whether provided directly through grants or indirectly through preferential taxation, will in most cases fall foul of the prohibition of state aid found in Article 107(1) TFEU. As a result, they must be notified to the Commission. Yet, the Commission may declare them compatible with the internal market by reference to the justifications contained in Article 107(2) and (3) TFEU. Or, subsidies might not constitute state aid at all if they compensate for the delivery of a SGEI in accordance with the *Altmark* criteria. If, as is often the case, all the criteria are not fulfilled, state aid will be present. But, it will most probably evade notification as a result of the social and *de minimis* exceptions contained in the SGEI package (*5.4*).

This chapter illustrates the point that European economic law has developed into a reflexive legal system able to integrate social concerns. More particularly, European competition law reflects the social values pursued by CSOs with the help of the same two mechanisms described for internal market law. On the one hand, the ECJ shows it may be willing to limit the wide jurisdiction of competition rules over CSOs by resorting to a 'social solidarity' shield. On the other hand, substantive competition rules strike a balance between economic and social goals. As a consequence, CSOs may conclude anti-competitive agreements that are necessary for the pursuit of social objectives, while Member States may subsidise CSOs where it is needed for reaching objectives compatible with the internal market or necessary for the delivery of SGEI.

***

The latter two chapters have approached European economic law from a civil perspective which had so far been overlooked. Developing this approach to its full extent would require further avenues for research to be explored. This will be the task of the last, conclusive, chapter of this book (*Chapter 8*). In the meantime, one can provisionally conclude that European economic law does not – necessarily – threaten civil society as a third sector between state and market. As shown by *Chapter 4*, internal market law does not prevent Member States from erecting their welfare systems along civil lines if they so wish. As illustrated by *Chapter 5*, European competition law does not oblige Member States to withdraw financial support for CSOs; nor does it preclude CSOs from concluding anti-competitive agreements when their social objectives so require. These are important findings from the perspective of this book which investigates whether participatory democracy can succeed in multilevel social Europe. For, it could hardly be the case if organised civil society, on which social Europe relies for its democratisation, was colonised by the market imperative of European economic law.

The latter two chapters also confirm previous findings as to the reflexive, that is to say, the self-limiting capacity of European economic law with regard to social policy more narrowly defined as citizens' equal entitlement to social services provided by the state. As explained in *section 3.2*, reflexivity entails the setting-up of procedural rules that make the economic subsystem sensitive to side-effects and externalities. European economic law is a reflexive legal system in the sense that it limits the impact of the economic subsystem on the social realm within which civil society can flourish by resorting to a social solidarity shield which as much valid for social services provided by the state as it is for social services provided by CSOs. For those social services which nevertheless enter the scope of European economic law, proportionality is the procedural device through which social and economic concerns are balanced to such an extent that economic restrictions will be accepted so long as they are necessary for the pursuit of social goals.

These positive conclusions as to the capacity of European economic law to integrate social concerns are to be taken with cautious optimism in view of the new European economic governance framework set up in the context of the current euro crisis. The latter draws criticism for increasing trends towards welfare retrenchment in many Member States. This complex institutional framework will be summarily described in *chapter 8*. So will its (potentially) negative impact on national social policies. For many, the only way out would be for social Europe to provide an effective counterweight to the ever stronger market imperative of European economic integration. The extent to which social Europe has so far managed to do so will be discussed in *Chapter 8*.

In the meantime, there is another challenge to be tackled if social Europe wants to realise its participatory turn. European governance needs to close the gap with European citizens. It will be the task of the next two chapters to verify whether participatory-democratic tools such as the Commission consultation regime or the social OMC open the governance of social Europe to civil society's influence without subjecting it to its bureaucratising tendencies.

CHAPTER 6

THE CIVIL DIALOGUE

A Magic Cure for the Democratic Ailments of the Community Method?

6.1. INTRODUCTION

Among the many channels of influence arising from the fragmented nature of EU law-making, the Commission is often chosen as the foremost venue for interest representation.[1] This preference mainly stems from the lead the Commission takes in agenda-setting through the use of its exclusive power to initiate legislation. Interest groups knock on an open door,[2] for the Commission has a long tradition of consulting interest representatives.[3] DG Employment, in particular, has developed early on a dense relationship with social CSOs which it sees as agents contributing with support, expertise and knowledge, to the development of its policies.[4]

Nevertheless, since the first European social policy forum held in 1996, DG Employment and supportive networks of social CSOs have hedged their bets and undertaken to establish 'a strong civil dialogue at European level to take its place alongside the policy dialogue with the national authorities and the social dialogue with the social partners'.[5] This political commitment went mainstream with the 2001 White Paper on European Governance (White Paper), leading the Commission to portray civil society's participation in European

---

1 K Karr, *Democracy and Lobbying in the European Union* (Campus Verlag 2007) 155; J Greenwood, *Interest Representation in the European Union* (3rd edn, Palgrave Macmillan 2011) 24.

2 S Mazey and J Richardson, 'Pluralisme Ouvert ou Restreint? Les Groupes d'Intérêt dans l'Union Européenne' in R Balme, D Chabanet and V Wright (eds), *L'Action Collective en Europe-Collective Action in Europe* (Presses de Sciences Po 2002) 137.

3 Commission, 'An Open and Structured Dialogue between the Commission and Special Interest Groups' (Communication) [1993] OJ C63/2, 2.

4 L Cram, 'Civil Society, Participatory Democracy and the Governance of the Union: The Institutionalisation of a Fiction' (2006) paper delivered at the 2–4 November 2006 Osnabrück conference on governance and policy-making in the EU, 6 <http://web.uvic.ca/jmtrg/Papers_files/cram_paper_1.pdf> accessed 1st September 2015.

5 Commission, 'Promoting the Role of Voluntary Organisations and Foundations in Europe' (Communication) COM (97) 241 final, 7.

governance as a chance to get citizens more actively involved in achieving the Union's objectives, thereby contributing to participatory democracy in the EU.[6] The normative appeal of this discourse became such that, eventually, the Lisbon Treaty has elevated participatory democracy to the rank of a legal principle which European institutions are now bound to implement.[7]

The White Paper conveys the belief that wide participation is indubitably good, for it enhances democratic governance and, at the same time, improves the effectiveness of EU law-making.[8] Yet, it might be misleading to present participation as the new magic cure for the democratic ailments of the old CM. There is, as Dahl noted long ago, a democratic dilemma between citizen participation and system effectiveness:

> [i]n very small political systems a citizen may be able to participate extensively in decisions that do not matter much but cannot participate much in decisions that really matter a great deal; whereas very large systems may be able to cope with problems that matter more to a citizen, the opportunities for the citizen to participate in and greatly influence decisions are vastly reduced.[9]

Top-down law-making through the CM has confronted this dilemma by expanding Member States' ability to address problems with which they could not deal on their own to the detriment of European citizens' capacity for self-rule.[10] This has, in its turn, created a democratic deficit which has been addressed over time by increasing the legislative powers of the European Parliament. Article 11 TEU now directs European institutions to complement these efforts at building a proper representative democracy at EU level by engaging directly with organised civil society.[11]

What the White Paper does is simply mask the aforementioned dilemma. The Lisbon Treaty leaves European institutions, and the Commission in

---

6 Commission, 'European Governance: a White Paper' COM (2001) 428 final, 15. See also Commission, 'The Commission and Non-Governmental Organisations: Building a Stronger Partnership' (Discussion Paper) COM (2000) 11 final, 4; Commission, 'Towards a Reinforced Culture of Consultation and Dialogue – General Principles and Minimum Standards for Consultation of Interested Parties by the Commission' (Communication) COM (2002) 704 final, 5.

7 See Article 11 TEU, which lies under title II entitled 'Provisions on Democratic Principles'. On participatory democracy as a *legal* principle, see J Mendes, 'Participation and the Role of Law after Lisbon: A Legal View on Article 11 TEU' (2011) 48 CML Rev 1849.

8 Commission, 'White Paper' (n 6) 10; Commission, 'General Principles and Minimum Standards' (n 6) 5.

9 RA Dahl, 'A Democratic Dilemma: System Effectiveness versus Citizen Participation' (1994) 109 Political Science Quarterly 23, 28.

10 R Dahl, *On Democracy* (Yale University Press 1998) 115.

11 See R Bieber and F Maiani, 'Bringing the Union Closer to its Citizens? "Participatory Democracy" and the Potential Contribution of the Lisbon Treaty' (2009) Annuaire Suisse de Droit Européen 229, 232–235.

particular, with no choice but to address it. Either the Commission allows wide *democratic* participation in the elaboration of European laws, knowing that this will, at some point, interfere with its bureaucratic capacity to deal with problems efficiently;[12] or it consults so long as needed for bringing expertise, knowledge and information to the table of decision-making.[13] The latter *functional* use of participation would leave civil society, seen as an autonomous sphere of society between state and market, with no other choice but to trade civic participation for *elite* representation in the process of influencing EU law-making effectively.[14] Therefore, the question raised by the turn to participatory democracy is not *if*, but *how* and *where* the Commission strikes the balance between the conflicting demands for wide participation and effective administration.

With a view to answer this question, the consultations which the Commission holds prior to proposing any major instrument of social law will be analysed as a structure of opportunities which influences, through the funding opportunities provided and the instruments of consultation used, social CSOs seen as the subject of those consultations.[15] A rather elitist picture of European civil society will emerge from this examination, to some extent mitigated by the flourishing of new public consultation instruments (*6.2*). Nonetheless, elitism, which seems quite symptomatic of the democratic deficiencies of the Commission's consultation regime more generally, is increasingly tamed by procedural rules aiming at, on the one hand, opening consultations to a wider audience (*6.3*) and, on the other, democratising European civil society (*6.4*). However, in both cases, a legally-binding approach is resisted by the Commission, which leaves us wondering about the reasons preventing further

---

12 On the trade-off between democracy, efficiency and effectiveness, see K Heard-Lauréote, *European Union Governance: Effectiveness and Legitimacy in European Commission Committees* (Routledge 2010) 21–24.

13 See Commission, 'White Paper' (n 6) 15, which alludes to the latter use of consultations.

14 For more detail on the notion of civil society to which this book subscribes, see Sec 3.2. The process by which civil society adapts to the functional requirements of European administration may be explained by the iron law of oligarchy. For more detail, see R Michels, *Political Parties: A Sociological Study of the Oligarchical Tendencies of Modern Democracy* (Free Press 1949). On functional participation in the White Paper, see P Magnette, 'European Governance and Civic Participation: Can the European Union be Politicised?' in C Joerges, Y Mény and JHH Weiler (eds), *Mountain or Molehill? A Critical Appraisal of the Commission White Paper on Governance* (2001) Jean Monnet Working Paper no. 6/01, paras 1–5 <http://centers.law.nyu.edu/jeanmonnet/archive/papers/01/010901.html> accessed 1st September 2015; MT Greven, 'Some Considerations on Participation in Participatory Governance' in B Kohler-Koch and B Rittberger (eds), *Debating the Democratic Legitimacy of the European Union* (Rowman & Littlefield 2007) 236.

15 For a similar approach, see Mazey and Richardson, 'Pluralisme Ouvert ou Restreint?' (n 2); S Mazey and J Richardson, 'Interest Groups and EU Policy-Making: Organisational Logic and Venue Shopping' in J Richardson (ed), *European Union: Power and Policy-Making* (3rd edn, Routledge 2006).

legalisation of the civil dialogue and whether that self-restraint is compatible with Article 11 TEU (*6.5*).

6.2. EUROPEAN CIVIL SOCIETY: AN ELITE GAME

According to Greenwood, citizens' interests represent 'the second largest category of EU interest groups, possibly now accounting for one third of the total, and have been the largest growth sector of all EU level groups in recent years'.[16] Many of these organisations are active in the social field, with the Social Platform as a leader for the sector.[17] Social CSOs have not acquired a European dimension spontaneously.[18] Europeanization has rather taken place as a consequence of the opportunities provided by the EU political system.[19]

Although it is usually political opportunities that attract interest groups to Brussels, most European networks of social CSOs are proliferating in a field where the EU only holds residual power. Why moving to Brussels if it is to shoot where the ducks are not?[20] European social CSOs have emerged not despite but *because* of the EU's lack of legislative power in social affairs,[21] with the Commission, and DG Employment more particularly, providing institutional and funding opportunities so as to create a constituency able to support its quest for expanding the frontiers of European integration, both in terms of developing the catalogue of EU social competences and of bridging the gap with grass-roots citizens.[22]

The origins of the Social Platform can, for instance, be traced back to the publication of the Green Paper on European social policy in 1993, following which a group of CSOs decided to create a permanent framework for co-operation, with the aim to establish a broader and on-going dialogue with the European institutions on questions of social policy.[23] DG Employment reacted positively to this initiative and supplied funding for the establishment of the

---

16 Greenwood, *Interest Representation* (n 1) 129–130.

17 A headcount of the NGOs registered in the transparency register (http://ec.europa.eu/transparencyregister/info/homePage.do) reveals that more than one third of the NGOs registered have declared an interest in employment and social affairs (743 out of 2120).

18 R Sánchez Salgado, 'Giving a European Dimension to Civil Society Organizations' (2007) 3 Journal of Civil Society 253, 253. See also L Cram, *Policy-Making in the European Union: Conceptual Lenses and the Integration Process* (Routledge 1997) 126.

19 Sánchez Salgado, 'Giving a European Dimension' (n 18) 255.

20 Cram, 'Civil Society, Participatory Democracy and the Governance of the Union' (n 4) 5.

21 L Cram, 'In the Shadow of Hierarchy: Governance as a Tool of Government' in R Dehousse, *The "Community Method": Obstinate or Obsolete?* (Palgrave Macmillan 2011) 156.

22 J Greenwood, 'Organized Civil Society and Democratic Legitimacy in the European Union' (2007) 37 British Journal of Political Science 333, 344. See also Cram, *Policy-Making in the European Union* (n 18) 128–129.

23 See B Kohler-Koch, 'Post-Maastricht Civil Society and Participatory Democracy' (2012) 34 Journal of European Integration 809, 811.

Social Platform in 1995.[24] The latter is now funded by a multiannual grant from the Commission to support its running costs, which covers 90% of its budget for the years 2014–2017.[25] The Social Platform brings together around forty European CSOs, federations and networks involved in social policy issues. While some of its members were established independently, most of them emerged directly from Commission programs and initiatives.[26] This cosy relationship with the Commission is confirmed by the fact that many members of the Social Platform are heavily financed through the EU budget.[27]

This institutional strategy marks an attempt to organise the civil dialogue with confederated structures of CSOs.[28] The Commission's preference for Euro-groups has to do with the wish to fight input overload and to simplify consultative life in the confidence that less consultation will lead to better policy outcomes.[29] Institutionalising European civil society for such output-enhancing purposes, may, however, run contrary to the aim discursively endorsed by the Commission to build Europe bottom-up, in partnership with a civil society of active citizens. How can a European civil society whose creation and survival depend on the Commission possess the participatory-democratic virtues for which civil society as an independent sphere of society is so often praised?[30] European CSOs are well aware of that contradiction, often complaining about the cheerleading function imposed by current EU funding arrangements.[31]

---

24 P Cullen, 'Pan-European NGOs and Social Rights: Participatory Democracy and Civil Dialogue' in J Joachim and B Locher (eds), *Transnational Activism in the UN and EU: a Comparative Study* (Routledge 2008) 142.

25 See <https://eacea.ec.europa.eu/sites/eacea-site/files/efc-results-og-2014_en.pdf> accessed 1st September 2015.

26 Cullen, 'Pan-European NGOs and Social Rights' (n 24) 144.

27 R Geyer, 'Can European Union (EU) Social NGOs Co-Operate to Promote EU Social Policy?' (2001) 30 Jnl Soc Pol 477, 479. This is confirmed by R Sánchez Salgado and K Parthenay, 'Fostering Regional Democracy Through Civic Organisations: Comparing EU Mechanisms in Europe and Central America' (2013) 35 Journal of European Integration 151, table 4.

28 J Greenwood, 'The Search for Input Legitimacy through Organised Civil Society in the EU' (2004) 2 Transnational Associations 145, 149.

29 J Greenwood, 'Advocacy, Influence and Persuasion: Has it all been Overdone?' in A Warleigh and J Fairbrass (eds), *Influence and Interests in the European Union: the New Politics of Persuasion and Advocacy* (Europa Publications 2002) 28–29. See also B Harvey, 'Lobbying in Europe: The Experience of Voluntary Organizations' in S Mazey and J Richardson (eds), *Lobbying in the European Community* (OUP 1993) 191. Other reasons for supporting federations of CSOs such as reinforcing accountability or creating a constituency of support are often invoked. For further detail, see Greenwood, *Interest Representation in the European Union* (n 1).

30 This paradox has been highlighted by: K Armstrong, 'Rediscovering Civil Society: The European Union and the White Paper on Governance' (2002) 8 ELJ 102, 127; D Obradovic, 'Civil Society and the Social Dialogue in European Governance' (2005) 24 YEL 261, 296; M Piewitt, M Rodekamp and J Steffek, 'Civil Society in World Politics: How Accountable are Transnational CSOs?' (2010) 6 Journal of Civil Society 237, 241.

31 Cullen, 'Pan-European NGOs and Social Rights' (n 24) 149–150; Cram, 'In the Shadow of Hierarchy' (n 21) 160. This cheerleading function is illustrated by the Progress axis of the new EaSI programme which subordinates funding to European social CSOs' capacity 'to develop,

That CSOs resemble more the European governance structure in which they are institutionally and financially embedded than the civic sphere to which they claim to belong is exactly the criticism which has been raised against this so-called European civil society. Warleigh, for instance, found that, 'although NGOs can score highly on their ability to influence EU policy and are developing higher profiles as political campaigners, their internal governance is far too elitist to allow supporters a role in shaping policies, campaigns and strategies, even at one remove'.[32] Similarly, Saurugger claims that 'these groups are not the bottom-up, citizen-initiated phenomenon as often portrayed'.[33] The European Commission does not seem content with this situation where Brussels is definitely talking to Brussels,[34] and we will see below that new consultation instruments aiming precisely at expanding participation beyond the Brussels bubble are progressively being used.

The Commission consults with non-state actors using a wide range of instruments.[35] Consultation practices vary from one DG to another. More particularly, the instruments used by DG Employment may be categorised into three groups according to the addressees of consultation: *expert* consultation, consultation with *civil society*, and *public* consultation.[36] These instruments are generally combined and used successively during the preparation of a proposal, depicting some kind of 'chameleon pluralism' where level of access diminishes over time, from an early public consultation stage through to a late expert-focused discussion time.[37]

DG Employment retrieves the expertise it needs for elaborating its policies through the organisation of expert seminars. Experts are further consulted

---

promote and support the implementation of Union instruments and policies [...] and relevant Union law.' ([2013] OJ L347/238, Article 15).

32 A Warleigh, '"Europeanizing" Civil Society: NGOs as Agents of Political Socialization' (2001) 39 JCMS 619, 635.

33 S Saurugger, 'Interest Groups and Democracy in the European Union' in J Beyers, R Eising and W Maloney (eds), *Interest Group Politics in Europe: Lessons from EU Studies and Comparative Politics* (Routledge 2010) 177. For a similar view, see I Sudbery, 'Bridging the Legitimacy Gap in the EU: Can Civil Society Help to Bring the Union Closer to its Citizens?' (2003) 26 Collegium 75; Kohler-Koch, 'Post-Maastricht Civil Society and Participatory Democracy' (n 23).

34 See Commission, 'General Principles and Minimum Standards' (n 6) 12.

35 See Commission, 'Review of the Commission Consultation Policy Accompanying the Communication on EU Regulatory Fitness' (Staff Working Document) SWD (2012) 422 final, 5–7.

36 See C Quittkat and B Finke, 'The EU Commission Consultation Regime' in B Kohler-Koch, D De Bièvre and W Maloney (eds), *Opening EU-Governance to Civil Society – Gains and Challenges* (2008) CONNEX Report Series no.5, 195 <www.mzes.uni-mannheim.de/projekte/typo3/site/index.php?id=596> accessed 1st September 2015; C Quittkat, 'Consultation in Daily Practice' in B Kohler-Koch and C Quittkat with V Buth and C Altides, *De-Mystification of Participatory Democracy: EU Governance and Civil Society* (OUP 2013) 63.

37 Greenwood, *Interest Representation in the European Union* (n 1) 215. See also C Quittkat and P Kotzian, 'Lobbying via Consultation – Territorial and Functional Interests in the Commission's Consultation Regime' (2011) 33 Journal of European Integration 401, 405.

through the creation of expert groups.[38] DG Employment adopts a narrow view as to the notion of expert. From all the expert groups and similar entities under the lead of DG Employment, only the group of EU Stakeholders for the Platform against Poverty and the High Level Group on Disability have CSOs as members.[39] CSOs are however present in expert groups and similar entities of direct relevance for social policy, which are under the lead of other DGs, such as the EU Health Forum,[40] and the Regional Policy Structured Dialogue with Civil Society Organisations.[41] Expert groups mainly comprise European-level CSOs.

Besides consulting experts, the Commission, DG Employment and DG Justice in particular, cooperates with social CSOs through the European civil dialogue. The civil dialogue started off as a result of two consultative conferences, the social policy forums held in 1996 and in 1998, after which DG Employment agreed to hold bi-annual meetings with the members of the Social Platform so as to discuss matters of common interest. One of the strengths of these meetings has been the Employment Directorate's ability to involve key officials from other services to attend.[42] These bi-annual meetings are complemented by ad-hoc meetings with the Commission's services as required.[43] One may question the extent to which this dialogue is any more civil than the dialogues occurring within expert groups such as the EU Health Policy Forum or the Regional Policy Structured Dialogue with Civil Society Organisations. The same pattern seems indeed to prevail where the Commission consults with a narrow constituency of European-level CSOs considered as experts who will improve the epistemic quality of its decisions.[44]

Bridging the gap between European citizens and their Europe therefore requires that more inclusive tools of consultation be elaborated so that participation is extended beyond the Brussels' beltway. In this respect, *online consultations* and *citizen initiatives* may be setting the example of

---

38 Quittkat and Finke, 'The EU Commission Consultation Regime' (n 36) 195. See also Commission, 'Framework for Commission Expert Groups: Horizontal Rules and Public Register' (Communication) C (2010) 7649 final.

39 See <http://ec.europa.eu/transparency/regexpert/index.cfm?do=groupDetail.groupDetail&groupID=2247> accessed 1st September 2015; <http://ec.europa.eu/transparency/regexpert/index.cfm?do=groupDetail.groupDetail&groupID=1259> accessed 1st September 2015.

40 See <http://ec.europa.eu/transparency/regexpert/index.cfm?do=groupDetail.groupDetail&groupID=878> accessed 1st September 2015.

41 See <http://ec.europa.eu/transparency/regexpert/index.cfm?do=groupDetail.groupDetail&groupID=2677> accessed 1st September 2015.

42 G Alhadeff and S Wilson, 'European Civil Society Coming of Age' (2002) <www.globalpolicy.org/component/content/article/177/31558.html> accessed 1st September 2015.

43 See <www.socialplatform.org/what-we-do/civil-dialogue/eu-institutions/> accessed 1st September 2015.

44 For the minutes of the bi-annual meetings of the Social Platform with DG Employment, see <http://ec.europa.eu/social/keyDocuments.jsp?policyArea=85&subCategory=330&type=0&country=0&year=0&advSearchKey=&mode=advancedSubmit&langId=en> accessed 1st September 2015.

a new generation of instruments which aims at opening participation to a wider public.[45] Online consultations are accessible through 'Your Voice in Europe', the European Commission's single access point to a wide variety of consultations, discussions and other tools which enable citizens to play an active role in European policy-making.[46] Online consultations are now frequently used by the Commission services, although with important variations from one DG to the other.[47] Formally, online consultations are truly public in the sense that they provide all actors with equal chances to participate. More than any other instrument, they therefore contribute to lowering the thresholds for participation, thereby drawing a wide spectrum of actors into the decision-making process.[48] Yet, they have so far failed to overcome the well-known participatory imbalances which afflict the EU consultation regime, characterised by the dominance of business over diffuse interests,[49] the over-representation of old Member States, and a north-south divide in terms of associational involvement.[50] On the bright side, an imbalance which does seem to have receded is the one separating European federations of social CSOs from local, grassroots associations which have finally found 'their way to Europe' through this instrument.[51]

The European citizens' initiative (ECI), introduced during the last days of the Convention on the Future of Europe, is another interesting innovation. According to Article 11 TEU,

---

45 B Kohler-Koch and B Finke, 'The Institutional Shaping of EU-Society Relations: A Contribution to Democracy Via Participation?' (2007) 3 Journal of Civil Society 205, 211–212; Quittkat and Finke, 'The EU Commission Consultation Regime' (n 36) 189–190. For another example of public instrument, see L Boussaguet and R Dehousse, 'L'Europe des Profanes: L'Expérience des Conférences Citoyennes' in O Costa and P Magnette (eds), *Une Europe des Élites? Réflexions sur la Fracture Démocratique de l'Union Européenne* (Editions de l'Université de Bruxelles 2007).

46 < http://ec.europa.eu/yourvoice/index_en.htm> accessed 1st September 2015.

47 C Quittkat, 'The European Commission's Online Consultations: A Success Story?' (2011) 49 JCMS 653, 658–659.

48 Ibid 670. See also E Bozzini, 'The Role of Civil Society Organisations in Written Consultation Processes: From the European Monitoring Centre to the European Fundamental Rights Agency' in V Della Sala and C Ruzza (eds), *Governance and Civil Society in the European Union: Exploring Policy Issues* (vol 2, Manchester University Press 2007) 99–100; T Persson, 'Civil Society Participation and Accountability' in S Gustavsson, C Karlsson and T Persson (eds), *The Illusion of Accountability in the European Union* (Routledge 2009) 150.

49 T Persson, 'Democratizing European Chemicals Policy: Do Consultations Favour Civil Society Participation?' (2007) 3 Journal of Civil Society 223, 236.

50 Quittkat, 'The European Commission's Online Consultations' (n 47) 671; C Quittkat, 'New Instruments Serving Democracy – Do Online Consultations Benefit Civil Society?' in B Kohler-Koch and C Quittkat with V Buth and C Altides, *De-Mystification of Participatory Democracy: EU Governance and Civil Society* (OUP 2013) 109–110.

51 Quittkat and Finke, 'The EU Commission Consultation Regime' (n 36) 212. See also Quittkat and Kotzian, 'Lobbying via Consultation' (n 37) 410.

> [n]ot less than one million citizens who are nationals of a significant number of Member States may take the initiative of inviting the European Commission, within the framework of its powers, to submit any appropriate proposal on matters where citizens consider that a legal act of the Union is required for the purpose of implementing the Treaties.

The Regulation which specifies the procedures and conditions required for filing an ECI entered into force on 1st April 2012.[52] This new instrument might be of enormous significance for democracy in the EU.[53] It is the first time in history that citizens are given the right to collectively shape the political agenda beyond national borders.[54] The ECI departs from the consultation instruments analysed so far in two ways. First, instead of reacting to Commission's consultations, the citizenry is here asked to take a proactive stance, by participating in a truly bottom-up process through which it can shape the legislative agenda of the EU.[55] Another welcome improvement upon the existing consultation regime is that the ECI is guaranteed as of right.[56] This right in no way hinders the Commission's monopoly of initiative, for citizens may only invite the Commission to act. It, however, obliges the Commission to comply with good administration requirements, in particular regarding the transparency of the whole process and the duty to give reasons for refusal to register the initiative or to act upon it.[57] The effectiveness of this tool is, unfortunately, constrained in many ways.[58] In particular, the fact that the Regulation does not provide for any kind of assistance, financial or other, to citizen's committees is open to criticism, since one can fear that only large and well-established, mostly EU-funded, organisations will be able to gather the resources needed to run transnational campaigns on the scale imposed by the Regulation.[59] With no steps taken to level resources, it will be difficult to bring the initiative of the initiative outside

52 Regulation (EU) 211/2011 of the European Parliament and of the Council of 16 February 2011 on the citizens' initiative [2011] OJ L65/1 (ECI Regulation).

53 A Warleigh, 'On the Path to Legitimacy? A Critical Deliberativist Perspective on the Right to the Citizens' Initiative' in C Ruzza and V Della Sala (eds), *Governance and Civil Society in the European Union: Normative Perspectives* (vol 1, Manchester University Press 2007) 64.

54 B Kaufmann, 'Citizen Power Beyond the Nation-State' in C Berg, P Carline, B Kaufmann, J Leinen and D Wallis (eds), *Initiative for Europe Handbook 2008 – The Guide to Transnational Democracy in Europe* (Initiative & Referendum Institute Europe 2007) 10 <www.iri-europe.org/publications/handbooks/european-citizens-initiative-handbook/> accessed 1st September 2015.

55 Warleigh, 'On the Path to Legitimacy' (n 53) 66. See also EESC, 'The Implementation of the Lisbon Treaty: Participatory Democracy and the Citizens' Initiative (Article 11)' (Opinion) [2010] OJ C354/59, point 4.3.1.

56 For a legal analysis of the ECI, see M Dougan, 'What are We to Make of the Citizens' Initiative?' (2011) 48 CML Rev 1807.

57 ECI Regulation, Articles 4(3) and 10.

58 For an overview, see Warleigh, 'On the Path to Legitimacy' (n 53).

59 C Berg, 'The European Citizen's Initiative Process' in Berg et al, *Initiative for Europe Handbook 2008* (n 54) 57.

Brussels. Yet, a democratic hope remains, namely that the ECI will at last provide EU insiders with an incentive to better communicate with grassroots activists and, more widely, with lay citizens for fear of being marginalised by the emergence of new organisations competing for citizens' signatures.[60]

6.3. PROCEDURAL RULES I: OPENING CONSULTATIONS

Since Declaration no. 17 on the right of access to information was annexed to the Maastricht Treaty,[61] the Union has been treading the path of transparency in the hope that it will strengthen 'the democratic nature of the institutions (...)',[62] and, more to the point, support the right for citizens to participate in the political life of the Union.[63] Making no exception to that rule, the Commission has early on embraced transparency as a means to secure wider participation in its consultation processes. In a 1992 Communication aiming at 'Increased Transparency',[64] the Commission proposed to give advanced information about its initiatives through the publication of its annual work and legislative programmes in the Official Journal of the EU. At the same time, it committed itself to more public participation in its work. Broad consultation on certain key proposals at an early stage through wider use of Green Papers and recourse to a notification procedure was therefore proposed.[65] Consulting widely before proposing legislation as well as publishing consultation documents became a duty imposed on the Commission by Protocol no. 30 on the application of the principles of subsidiarity and proportionality annexed to the Amsterdam Treaty.[66] The need to increase the transparency of consultations was reiterated

60 J Greenwood, 'The European Citizens' Initiative and EU Civil Society Organisations' (2012) 13 Perspectives on European Politics and Society 325, 333.

61 [1992] OJ C191/101.

62 Ibid.

63 The link between democratic participation and openness is squarely made in Article 10(3) TEU and Article 15 (1) TFEU. See also D Curtin, 'Citizens' Fundamental Right of Access to EU Information: An Evolving Digital Passepartout?' (2000) 37 CML Rev 7, 41. On the evolution of transparency and openness in the EU, see D Curtin and AJ Meijer, 'Does Transparency Strengthen Legitimacy? A Critical Analysis of European Union Policy Documents' (2006) 11 Information Polity 109; ME De Leeuw, 'Openness in the Legislative Process in the European Union' (2007) 32 EL Rev 295.

64 Commission, 'Increased Transparency in the Work of the Commission' (Communication) [1993] OJ C63/8. On the implementation of the commitments made therein, see Commission, 'Openness in the Community' (Communication) [1993] OJ C166/4.

65 For a follow-up on these measures, see Commission, 'Report on the Operation of the Treaty on European Union' SEC (95) 731 final, 32. Most of them have been followed through except the notification procedure which has had limited use so far.

66 [1997] OJ C340/105.

by the Commission in its White Paper,[67] following which a Communication setting out 'general principles and minimum standards for consultation of interested parties by the Commission'[68] was adopted as a part of the better law-making agenda.[69]

This Communication subjects the Commission's consultations to the five principles of good governance put forward in the White Paper: participation, openness, accountability, effectiveness and coherence. In addition, it requires the Commission to comply with some minimum standards:

- The content of the consultation process should be clear;
- When defining the target group(s) in a consultation process, the Commission should ensure that relevant parties have an opportunity to express their opinions;
- The Commission should also ensure adequate awareness-raising publicity and adapt its communication channels to meet the needs of all target audiences. Open public consultations should at least be announced via the 'Your Voice in Europe' web portal (the single access point for consultations);
- The Commission should strive to allow at least 8 weeks for reception of responses to written public consultations and 20 working days' notice for meetings;
- Receipt of contributions should be acknowledged and adequate feedback provided.

By making clear what issues are being developed, what mechanisms are being used to consult, who is being consulted, why, and, finally, what has influenced decisions, the standards and principles were indubitably meant to further wide and equitable access to consultations.[70] Yet, procedural impact was constrained by their restricted scope.[71] The principles and standards only applied to consultations taking place in the policy-shaping phase *prior* to a decision by the Commission. Consequently, they did not cover consultation frameworks provided for in the Treaties,[72] in secondary legislation, or in international

67 Commission, 'White Paper' (n 6) 15–17. See also Commission, 'Promoting the Role of Voluntary Organisations' (n 5); Commission, 'The Commission and Non-Governmental Organisations' (n 6).

68 See above, n 6.

69 See Interinstitutionnal agreement between the European Parliament, the Council and the Commission of 16 December 2003 on better law-making [2003] OJ C321/1.

70 See Commission, 'General Principles and Minimum Standards' (n 6) 17.

71 Ibid 15–16. See Obradovic, 'Civil Society and the Social Dialogue' (n 30) 301; I Tanasescu, *The European Commission and Interest Groups: Towards a Deliberative Interpretation of Stakeholder Involvement in EU Policy-Making* (VUB Press 2009) 74.

72 See, eg, social dialogue (Articles 153–155 TFEU); EESC (Article 304 TFUE) and CoR (Article 307 TFUE) in their advisory function; subsidiarity monitoring by national parliaments (Article 5(3) TEU and Protocol no. 2 on the application of the principles of subsidiarity and proportionality [2012] OJ C326/206).

agreements,[73] nor did they cover comitology procedure.[74] Moreover, they only concerned Green Papers and those major policy initiatives which were subject to impact assessment (IA),[75] a process by which the Commission collects evidence on the advantages and disadvantages of possible policy options by assessing their potential impacts.[76] Consulting interested parties was a compulsory part of every IA prepared by the Commission. Participation therein was facilitated by the prior publication of a roadmap outlining a consultation plan.[77] For any other consultation exercises they intended to launch, the services of the Commission were merely encouraged to apply the principles and standards where possible.

This was the state of affairs until the adoption of the 'guidelines on stakeholder consultation' as part of the Commission's 2015 'better regulation' package.[78] The guidelines complement and further define the aforementioned general principles and minimum standards, while extending their scope of application beyond major initiatives subject to impact assessment. In a nutshell, the Commission commits to holding a 12-week internet-based public consultation as part of its consultation strategy for initiatives subject to impact assessment, evaluation and fitness check as well as for green papers, while a simple consultation strategy must in any case be set up for each initiative, fitness check or evaluation. The latter is set out in a roadmap which plans consultation work ahead, after approval by the Inter Service Group (ISG) set up to follow the initiative or, if no ISG has been established, by the Secretariat General. The guidelines further provide that any of the above consultation activity must fulfil the Commission's minimum standards for consultation, while a report outlining overall results of the consultation work and providing feedback must be published on the consultation website and, where applicable, added as an annex to the impact assessment/evaluation report. Finally, beside consultation proper, the guidelines now allow for feedback to be provided for each roadmap on legislative and policy proposals as well as for draft delegated and implementing acts, which is a major improvement in terms of openness of the policy-making process in its implementation phase.

---

73 See, eg, Regulation (EC) 1367/2006 of the European Parliament and of the Council of 6 September 2006 on the application of the provisions of the Aarhus convention on access to information, public participation in decision-making and access to justice in environmental matters to community institutions and bodies [2006] OJ L264/13.

74 See Article 291(3) TFEU; Regulation (EU) 182/2011 of the European Parliament and of the Council of 16 February 2011 laying down the rules and general principles concerning mechanisms for control by member states of the Commission's exercise of implementing powers [2011] OJ L55/13.

75 For the initiatives which are subject to IA, see Commission, 'Impact Assessment Guidelines' SEC (2009) 92, 6.

76 Ibid 4.

77 Ibid 7–8, 19–20.

78 Commission, 'Better Regulation Guidelines' SWD (2015) 111 final, 63. See also Commission, 'Better Regulation for Better Results – an EU Agenda' (Communication) SWD (2015) 110 final.

Yet, relying on *soft* rules (communications, guidelines, etc....) remains a defining feature of the Commission's consultation regime. The Commission justifies this stance on efficiency grounds:

> A situation must be avoided in which a Commission proposal could be challenged in the Court on the grounds of alleged lack of consultation of interested parties. Such an over-legalistic approach would be incompatible with the need for timely delivery of policy, and with the expectations of the citizens that the European Institutions should deliver on substance rather than concentrating on procedures.[79]

The Commission claims that soft law is anyway harder than what its contenders think,[80] for, when the Commission enacts rules, even non-binding, its services do have to act accordingly.[81] Compliance with consultation rules is monitored by the ISG set up to follow each initiative and through the annual report on 'better law-making'[82] and, for those major initiatives which are subject to IA, a complex and many-layered quality control system has been organised within the Commission.[83] Moreover, consultation rules are open to outside scrutiny by the European Ombudsman who considers their violation as an instance of maladministration regarding which complaint may be lodged before him.[84]

Nonetheless, a consequence of proceeding by way of bureaucratic accommodation, as the Commission has done so far, is that citizens have no participation rights as such.[85] With no legal means to compel the Commission to act according to the rules it sets for itself, participation ultimately depends on the grace and favour of EU officials.[86] This plays to the advantage of insiders, while the voices traditionally excluded from consultations are left with no

79 Commission, 'General Principles and Minimum Standards' (n 6) 10.

80 This expression is borrowed from DM Trubek and LG Trubek, 'The Open Method of Co-Ordination and the Debate Over "Hard" and "Soft" Law' in J Zeitlin, P Pochet and L Magnusson (eds), *The Open Method of Co-Ordination in Action: the European Employment and Social Inclusion Strategies* (PIE-Peter Lang 2005) 83.

81 Commission, 'General Principles and Minimum Standards' (n 6) 10; Commission, 'Better Regulation Guidelines' (n 78) 4.

82 Commission, 'Better Regulation Guidelines' (n 78) 69; Commission, 'General Principles and Minimum Standards' (n 6) 14. The 'better law-making' reports are available at <http://ec.europa.eu/smart-regulation/better_regulation/reports_en.htm> accessed 1st September 2015.

83 Commission, 'Better Regulation Guidelines' (n 78) 17–18. See also A Alemanno, 'The Better Regulation Initiative at the Judicial Gate: A Trojan Horse within the Commission's Walls or the Way Forward?' (2009) 15 ELJ 382, 388–391.

84 Decision 948/2004/OV of 4 May 2005, para 3.8. Recently, see also Decision 2097/2011/RA of 25 January 2013; Decision 1151/2008/(DK)ANA of 9 July 2013; Decision 1682/2010/(ANA) BEH of 19 December 2013; Decision 240/2014/FOR of 28 April 2015.

85 P Craig, 'Democracy and Rule-Making within the EC: An Empirical and Normative Assessment' (1997) 3 ELJ 105, 124.

86 D Friedrich, *Democratic Participation and Civil Society in the European Union* (Manchester University Press 2011) 113.

right to force their way in. Only the enactment of a demanding procedural law guaranteeing participation rights and subjecting them to judicial review would confer as open and as inclusive a section of the public as possible a voice in policy-making.[87] In that regard, it is sometimes suggested that the Commission be bound by a notice and comment provision akin to that which operates in the US Administrative Procedure Act (APA)[88] or in the United Nations Aarhus Convention[89].[90] The notification procedure contemplated in the 'increased transparency' Communication[91] was a first step in that direction, but it has received limited use so far.[92]

Judicial activism has been an essential ingredient in making the APA the powerful democratic device it is today. On the bare bones of a provision which stipulated that, when making rules, an agency must give notice of the proposed rule, afford an opportunity for outsiders to comment, and finally publish the rule accompanied by a concise and general statement of its basis and purpose,[93] the federal courts have superimposed judicial demands for total transparency, complete participation and, ultimately, perfect rationality of the rule-making process.[94] Despite the Commission's uneasiness with legal activism in this matter, the possibility of procedural rights being imposed on the Commission by judicial means should therefore not be discarded, especially considering that the societal demands for transparency and participation which have driven judges to question the legitimacy of technocratic government in the US are now firmly embedded in the Treaties which the EU Courts must uphold.[95]

---

87 D Curtin, 'Private Interest Representation or Civil Society Deliberation? A Contemporary Dilemma for European Union Governance' (2003) 12 Social & Legal Studies 55, 69.

88 5 USC §553.

89 Convention on Access to Information, Public Participation in Decision-Making and Access to Justice in Environmental Matters, signed in Aarhus, Denmark, 25 June 1998, United Nations, Treaty Series, vol 2161, 447.

90 This proposal finds support in G Majone, 'Regulatory Legitimacy' in G Majone and P Baake (eds), *Regulating Europe* (Routledge 1996) 291–294; Craig, 'Democracy and Rule-Making' (n 85) 120–124; F Bignami, 'The Democratic Deficit in European Community Rulemaking: A Call for Notice and Comment in Comitology' (1999) 40 Harvard International Law Review 451; C Joerges, '"Good Governance" through Comitology?' in C Joerges and E Vos (eds), *EU Committees: Social Regulation, Law and Politics* (Hart 1999) 337; R Dehousse, 'European Governance in Search of Legitimacy: The Need for a Process-Based Approach' in O De Schutter, N Lebessis and J Paterson (eds), *Governance in the European Union* (Office for Official Publications of the European Communities 2001); Curtin, 'Private Interest Representation' (n 87) 69. *Contra*, see C Harlow, 'Codification of EC Administrative Procedures? Fitting the Foot to the Shoe or the Shoe to the Foot' (1996) 2 ELJ 3, 11; F Bignami, 'Three Generations of Participation Rights before the European Commission' (2004) 68 Law and Contemporary Problems 61, 82–83.

91 See above, n 64.

92 See Commission, 'Openness in the Community' (n 64) 7.

93 5 USC §553.

94 M Shapiro, 'Codification of Administrative Law: The US and the Union' (1996) 2 ELJ 26, 38.

95 Articles 10–11 TEU; Article 15 TFEU. See also Shapiro, 'Codification of Administrative Law' (n 94) 42–43.

Yet, an examination of the case law pertaining to the grounds for annulment of EU legal acts provided for in Article 263 TFEU reveals that, while the EU Courts are keen on bringing transparency within the remit of their control of legality, upholding participation or participation through dialogue is much less of a priority. The EU Courts do not hesitate to uphold consultation rights *qua* essential procedural requirements wherever these are expressly provided for in the Treaties or secondary legislation;[96] but they have systematically opposed the recognition of a general right to participate or be consulted in the making of EU legislation.[97] Mounting a legal challenge against a legislative act for which no or inadequate consultations have been organised by the Commission appears therefore extremely difficult, so long as consultation rules remain soft, non-legally binding rules, as such outside the scope of the control of legality exercised by the EU Courts.[98] Likewise, the duty to give reasons enshrined in Article 296 TFEU is an essential procedural requirement which gives plaintiffs ground to challenge the absence or the inadequacy of the reasons stated in a legal act.[99] This duty finds its roots into the desire for transparency of government affairs.[100] It also guarantees that the EU Courts hold sufficient information so as to exercise their powers of substantive judicial review.[101] However, it does not require European institutions to abide by a dialogue requirement which would oblige them to respond to all the arguments raised by interested parties during the preparation of the act.[102]

---

96 See, eg, Case 138/79 *SA Roquette Frères* v *Council* [1980] ECR 3333.

97 P Craig and G De Búrca, *EU Law: Text, Cases, and Materials* (5th edn, OUP 2011) 521. See Case T-521/93 *Atlanta AG and others v Council and Commission* [1996] ECR II-1707, para 71; Case C-104/97 P *Atlanta AG and Others* v *Commission and Council* [1999] ECR I-6983, para 38; Case C-258/02 P *Bactria Industriehygiene-Service Verwaltungs GmbH v Commission* [2003] ECR I-15105, para 43; T-526/10 *Inuit Tapiriit Kanatami and Others v Commission* (GC, 25 April 2013) para 113. For a critical appraisal of that position, see J Mendes, *Participation in EU Rule-Making: a Rights-Based Approach* (OUP 2011) chap 5.

98 *Nevertheless*, according to Alemanno, 'The Better Regulation Initiative at the Judicial Gate' (n 83) 392–394, the consultation standards and principles may produce legal effects arising from the duty for the Commission to abide by the rules it has set for itself, disregard of which could amount to breach of an essential procedural requirement likely to entail annulment of the act finally adopted in cases where no consultation or no IA has been conducted. For a similar position, see W Voermans and Y Schuurmans, 'Better Regulation by Appeal' (2011) 17 EPL 507.

99 Case C-367/95 P *Commission* v *Chambre syndicale nationale des entreprises de transport de fonds et valeurs (Sytraval) and Brink's France SARL* (Sytralaval) [1998] ECR I-01719, para 67. See also Craig and De Búrca, *EU Law* (n 97) 522–524.

100 M Shapiro, 'The Giving Reasons Requirement' [1992] U Chic Legal Forum 179, 200.

101 Case C-17/99 *France v Commission* [2001] ECR I-2481, para 35.

102 Joined Cases 240, 241, 242, 261, 262, 268 and 269/82 *Stichting Sigarettenindustrie and others v Commission* [1985] ECR 3831, para 88: '[the Commission] is not required to discuss all the issues of fact and law raised by every party during the administrative proceedings'. In *Sytralaval* (n 99) para 58, the Court reiterated that the Commission is under no obligation to conduct an exchange of views with the complainant. For more detail, see Craig and De Búrca, *EU Law* (n 97) 523–524.

Will the consecration by the TEU of an unspecified, but express, right for every citizen to *participate* in the democratic life of the Union, combined with the correlative obligation for European institutions to maintain an open, transparent and regular *dialogue* with organised civil society, bring the EU Courts to reconsider their restrictive stance toward participation or participation through dialogue in the post-Lisbon era?[103] We might argue that the EU Courts already recognise the democratic principle as a legal principle which they must uphold.[104] However, they have so far done so in a representative mode. More particularly in the *UEAPME* case, the GC has ruled that a legislative act implementing an agreement concluded by the social partners at EU level may be challenged in court by a representative of management or labour that has been excluded from the negotiating process where it appears that his participation was necessary with a view to raise the collective representativity of the signatories to the required level. According to the GC, the principle of democracy requires that, in the absence of the participation of the European Parliament in the legislative implementation of collective agreements, the participation of the people be otherwise assured, in this case through the social partners claiming sufficient representativity.[105]

The fact that the European Parliament is fully involved in the ordinary legislative procedure might prevent the EU courts from developing a similar kind of reasoning for the civil dialogue. So does the programmatic nature of new 11 TEU.[106] The same can be said for Article 2 of Protocol no. 2 attached to the Lisbon Treaty,[107] to the extent that it provides that the Commission shall consult widely, the width of consultations leaving the Commission with much leeway in that respect. At the same time, it is undeniable that the same Protocol compels the Commission to organise consultations and, in case no consultations have been organised before proposing legislation, imposes that consultations be not conducted only in cases of exceptional urgency and that reasons be provided in

---

103 See Articles 10(3) and 11 (2) TEU. Voermans and Schuurmans, 'Better Regulation by Appeal' (n 98) suggests that it might. So does Meuwese ('Embedding Consultation Procedures: Law or Institutionalization?' (2011) 17 EPL 527, 532–533) and Mendes ('Participation and the Role of Law after Lisbon' (n 7) 1873–1875).

104 JP Jacqué, *Droit Institutionnel de l'Union Européenne* (6th edn, Dalloz 2010) 87.

105 Case T-135/96 *Union Européenne de l'artisanat et des petites et moyennes entreprises (UEAPME) v Council* [1998] ECR II-2335, paras 88–90. See also Case 138/79 *SA Roquette Frères v Council* [1980] ECR 3333, para 33; Case 139/79 *Maizena GmbH v Council* [1980] ECR 3393, para 34; Case C-409/13 *Council v Commission* (ECJ, 14 April 2015) para 96.

106 C Kaddous, 'L'Initiative Citoyenne: Un Instrument de Démocratie Directe à l'Échelle de l'Union Européenne' in C Kaddous and A Auer (eds), *Les Principes Fondamentaux de la Constitution Européenne* (Bruylant 2006) 318; R Bieber and F Maiani, 'Bringing the Union Closer to its Citizens? "Participatory Democracy" and the Potential Contribution of the Lisbon Treaty' [2009] Annuaire Suisse de Droit Européen 229, 233–234; Alemanno, 'The Better Regulation Initiative at the Judicial Gate' (n 83) 394–395.

107 Protocol no. 2 (ex-Protocol no. 7 annexed to the Amsterdam Treaty [1997] OJ C340/105) on the application of the principles of subsidiarity and proportionality [2012] OJ C326/206.

the proposal for such a decision.[108] Whether the EU Courts will deem a breach of this new procedural requirement to be essential enough to justify annulment of the legislative act finally adopted remains to be seen.[109]

Meanwhile, recent rulings already hold the promise to uphold participation indirectly by using impact assessments as an aid to the parties and to the judge for reviewing compliance with the principles of conferral, subsidiarity and proportionality.[110] In particular, the established practice of carrying out impact assessments for all major commission initiatives has led the EU Courts to refer back to the analysis contained in the IA report so as to evaluate compliance of legislative acts with the principle of proportionality.[111] Inversely, the EU Courts have questioned the proportionality of EU legislative actions based on shaky factual foundations when no such assessment has been conducted.[112] In areas where the EU has wide legislative powers, review by the European judicature is traditionally limited to verifying whether the exercise of such powers has been vitiated by a manifest error of assessment.[113] This new strand of case law, however, suggests that this discretion is now constrained by the need for the European legislature to base its choice on objective criteria,[114] 'which presupposes the taking into consideration of all the relevant factors and circumstances of the situation the act was intended to regulate'.[115] Absent the recognition by the EU Courts of a general right of participation as a correlate to the principle of transparency, the judicial embrace of evidence-based decision-making may offer a realistic opening towards indirect judicial review of consultation rules. By scrutinising the rationality of EU legislation, the EU Courts incidentally require procedures allowing for organised civil society's views to be put forward so that

108 Ibid Article 2. Cp Protocol no. 7 annexed to the Amsterdam Treaty, Article 9.

109 G Garzón Clariana, 'Les Droits Politiques des Citoyens de l'Europe: les Vingt Premières Années' (2013) 13 ERA Forum 545, 562.

110 A Alemanno, 'A Meeting of Minds on Impact Assessment' (2011) 17 EPL 485. See also J Scott and S Sturm, 'Courts as Catalysts: Re-Thinking the Judicial Role in New Governance' (2006–2007) 13 CJEL 565, 582–587.

111 Case C-58/08 *The Queen, on the application of Vodafone Ltd and Others v Secretary of State for Business, Enterprise and Regulatory Reform* (Vodafone) [2010] ECR I-04999, para 55; Case C-176/09 *Luxemburg v Parliament and Council* (ECJ, 12 May 2011), para 65; Case T-368/11 *Polyelectrolyte Producers Group and others v Commission* (GC, 1 February 2013) paras 83–95.

112 Case C-310/04 *Spain v Council* [2006] ECR I-07285, para 103.

113 *Vodafone* (n 111) para 52.

114 *Vodafone* (n 111) para 53; *Luxemburg v Parliament and Council* (n 111) para 63; *Inuit* (n 97) para 89; Case C-101/12 *Herbert Schaible v Land Baden-Württemberg* (ECJ, 17 October 2013) para 49; Case C-356/12 *Wolfgang Glatzel v Freistaat Bayern* (ECJ, 22 May 2014) para 53. See also Case C-269/90 *Technische Universität München v Hauptzollamt München-Mitte* [1991] ECR I-05469, para 14; Case T-13/99 *Pfizer Animal Health SA v Council* [2002] ECR II-03305, paras 171–172.

115 Case C-343/09 *Afton Chemical Limited v Secretary of State for Transport* [2010] ECR I-07027, para 34; *Spain v Council* (n 112) para 122; *Polyelectrolyte Producers Group and others v Commission* (n 111) para 31. See also Case C-450/98 P *International Express Carriers Conference (IECC) v Commission* [2001] ECR I-03947, para 57; Case C-12/03 P *Commission v Tetra Laval BV* [2005] ECR I-987, para 39.

all relevant factors and circumstances are taken into account. Protocol no. 2 confirms that the duty for the Commission to consult widely guarantees that the principles of proportionality and subsidiarity are respected.

Further embedding participation into the EU judicial arena would however require that the EU Courts be accessible to their most likely advocates, that is, private litigants keen to challenge violations of consultation rules. The current *locus standi* rules are so restrictive that the chance for that to happen is almost close to zero. Natural and legal persons are only allowed to institute proceedings against decisions as acts of individual application and against acts of general application which are of direct and individual concern to them.[116] The latter, 'individual', requirement has made it almost impossible for private applicants to challenge acts of general application which directly affect them and has often resulted in the denial of standing for associations which represent collective or general interests.[117] Although the 'individual' concern is moderated by a *participation* exception–participation in a procedure leading to the adoption of a legal act confers standing to challenge it–, this is cold comfort for applicants up against legislative acts, for the EU Courts adopt a rights-based approach when construing this exception.[118]

Likewise, it is unlikely that the EU Courts would, as they did in the *UEAPME* case for the social partners, deem to be 'individually' concerned a CSO that has been excluded from the consultation process on the grounds that its consultation was necessary with a view to raise the collective representativity of the consultation to the required level.[119] As explained before, this ruling was based on the principle of democracy which requires that the participation of the people be otherwise assured in a procedure where the European Parliament was excluded, mainly the legislative implementation of collective agreements. No similar reasoning can be held for the civil dialogue which does not replace but rather complements the ordinary legislative procedure wherein the European Parliament is fully involved.

Following calls for more effective judicial protection,[120] the TFEU has dropped the 'individual' requirement for actions directed by private litigants

---

116 See Case T-18/10 *Inuit Tapiriit Kanatami and Others v Parliament and Council* (Inuit) (GC, 6 September 2011), para 41, citing Case 25/62 *Plaumann v Commission* [1963] ECR 95, para 107, and Case C-50/00 P *Unión de Pequeños Agricultores v Council* [2002] ECR I-6677, para 36. See also Article 230 (4) TEC (now Article 263 (4) TFEU).

117 See, eg, Joined Cases 16/62 and 17/62 *Confédération nationale des producteurs de fruits et légumes and others v Council* [1962] ECR 471; Case T-585/93 *Stichting Greenpeace Council (Greenpeace International) and others v Commission* [1995] ECR II-02205, para 59. For exceptions to the exclusion of associational standing, see O De Schutter, 'Public Interest Litigation before the European Court of Justice' (2006) 13 MJ 9, 18–26.

118 Scott and Sturm, 'Courts as Catalysts' (n 110) 579. See, eg, Case C-10/95 P *Asociación Española de Empresas de la Carne (Asocarne) v Council* [1995] ECR I-04149, para 40.

119 *UEAPME* (n 105) paras 88–90.

120 See C Koch, 'Locus Standi of Private Applicants under the EU Constitution: Preserving Gaps in the Protection of Individuals' Right to an Effective Remedy' (2005) 30 EL Rev 511.

against 'regulatory acts which are of direct concern to them and do not entail implementing measures'.[121] According to a recent order of the GC upheld by the ECJ on appeal, the notion of regulatory act 'must be understood as covering all acts of general application apart from legislative acts'.[122] *A contrario*, this means that private parties up against EU legislation which directly affects them are still left with the unsavoury alternative of bringing their case before a national judge and convince him to make a reference to the ECJ for a preliminary ruling on validity.

Deferring judicial protection of participation to its prior legalisation was a reasonable choice before Lisbon. Although Article 11 TEU explicitly requires all institutions, the EU Courts included, to implement participatory democracy, there are still good reasons for the EU judges to proceed with caution on this path. We are first dealing with politico-legal institutions very much different from those found on the other side of the Atlantic.[123] The notice and comment provision was adopted with a view to harness the discretion of US agencies when adopting delegated or supplementary legislation. Its beneficial effects were supposed to be two-fold: reinforcing bureaucrats' accountability to a divided law-maker, and ensuring the fairness of administrative processes.[124] These considerations remain persuasive for cases where the Commission executes European law,[125] but much less so concerning the Commission *qua* initiator of the law-making process. In that case, the division of law-making powers between Commission, Parliament and Council already provides strong checks and balances, while participation of the people is channelled through the European and national parliaments. Experience of the APA, moreover, supports the Commission's view that were consultation rights to be upheld, an unnecessary dose of proceduralism might be purchased at the price of inefficiency and immobilism.[126] More importantly, the principle of representative democracy on which the EU is founded would be threatened if a legislative act reflecting the will of the citizens of Europe was annulled because of the legal activism of a few functional interests claiming that their consultation rights have not been respected.[127] These are well-grounded concerns. They remind the EU Courts that the participatory principle will have to be implemented with an

121 Article 263 (4) TFEU.

122 *Inuit* (n 116) para 56; Case C-583/11 P *Inuit Tapiriit Kanatami and Others v Parliament and Council* (ECJ, 3 October 2013).

123 See Shapiro, 'Codification of Administrative Law' (n 94) 26–31.

124 Bignami, 'The Democratic Deficit in European Community Rulemaking' (n 90) 451.

125 Articles 290–291 TFEU.

126 A Meuwese, Y Schuurmans and W Voermans, 'Towards a European Administrative Procedure Act' (2009) 2 Review of European Administrative Law 3, 26, speaks of the ossification of the decision-making process which arises from the APA. Bignami, 'The Democratic Deficit in European Community Rulemaking' (n 90) 503, similarly, presents the slowness of US rule-making has one of its main drawbacks.

127 See Article 10 (1) TEU.

eye to conflicting demands for representative democracy and administrative effectiveness.

6.4. PROCEDURAL RULES II: DEMOCRATISING EUROPEAN CIVIL SOCIETY

In 1992, the Commission decided, for the first time, to formalise its open dialogue with special interest groups.[128] A concern for the transparency of interest representation was leading the way. To this effect, the Commission undertook to set up a single directory of non-profit making organisations, while encouraging the profit making sector to draw up its own directory. Closer cooperation with the European Parliament would lead in the longer term to the establishment of a common database. Special interest groups (both profit and non-profit making) were also encouraged to draw up voluntarily codes of conduct including some specific minimum requirements. The latter measure came in reaction to a few cases of unethical lobbying behaviour of which the Commission was the victim. Probity was not meant as a one-way street though, since the Commission also contemplated possible improvements to staff regulations.[129]

Since the White Paper has announced that 'with better involvement comes greater responsibility',[130] organised civil society is expected to follow the principles of good governance imposed on European administration.[131] Organised civil society ought to abide by norms of *transparency* and *accountability*; but those requirements are ill-defined. Transparency, or more widely openness, implies that interested parties must improve their visibility to the outside world, so that the public is aware of the parties involved in the consultation processes and how they conduct themselves.[132] Accountability, which is inherently linked to transparency, enjoins CSOs to explain and take responsibility for what they do in Europe.[133] These injunctions translate the Commission's irritation over the charge often being made against European civil society that it is elitist, lacks supporters' input and is not internally democratic.[134] Reforming the internal structures of organised civil society has

128 Commission, 'An Open and Structured Dialogue between the Commission and Special Interest Groups' (n 3). See also AM McLaughlin and J Greenwood, 'The Management of Interest Representation in the European Union' (1995) 33 JCMS 143.
129 As to the implementation of the measures contemplated, see Commission, 'Openness in the Community' (n 64).
130 Commission, 'White Paper' (n 6) 15.
131 Commission, 'General Principles and Minimum Standards' (n 6) 15.
132 Ibid 17.
133 Ibid 17.
134 A Vizcaino, M Jose and D Obradovic, 'Good Governance Requirements Concerning the Participation of Interest Groups in EU Consultations' (2006) 43 CML Rev 1049, 1075–1076. See also above, n 32–33.

become a priority for the Commission looking for a friend, rather than a foe, in its quest for legitimising its institutional position.[135]

The concept of *representativeness* also made its first apparition in the White Paper.[136] The Commission does not elaborate on this concept and does not make clear how it relates to representativeness as defined within other institutional frameworks such as the social dialogue.[137] It seems that the Commission equates representativeness with a preference for EU-level organisations having members in a sufficient number of EU countries.[138] Geographical representativeness, as it were, draws from the eligibility requirements devised by the EESC for the civil dialogue.[139] Representativeness is difficult to disentangle from transparency and accountability, but should not be confused with them. The latter two principles clearly share the same democratic pedigree. Transparency guarantees full participation in decision-making, while accountability entails mechanisms guaranteeing that the ruler's actions are scrutinised by the ruled.[140] Representation, on the other hand, is a diminished form of participation which arose as a concession by democrats to the functional need to govern effectively large-size societies.[141] It serves the same purpose in the Commission's consultations. The representativeness criterion has been advanced by the Commission with a view to legitimise its long-held preference for EU-level organisations as a way to manage input overload. It detracts from the pursuit of democratic legitimacy, rather than further it, since it excludes on efficiency grounds local and national organisations not adequately represented at European level as well as groups which advocate for a cause rather than for their members.[142]

If correcting the democratic failures of (representative) European civil society through transparency and accountability may be seen as a laudable end in itself, caution is in order regarding the means through which such democratisation is pursued, for, the imposition, through public regulation, of excessive bureaucratic burdens on organised civil society could have the unintended effect of further threatening the independent structures and pluralist values for which the

---

135 J Greenwood, 'The Future of Consultation with, and Participation by, Interests Groups in the European Union' (2005) 4 Transnational Associations 219, 219.

136 Commission, 'White Paper' (n 6) 17.

137 Obradovic, 'Civil Society and the Social Dialogue' (n 30) 292. See also Commission, 'Adapting and Promoting the Social Dialogue at Community Level' (Communication) COM (1998) 322 final, 6.

138 Greenwood, *Interest Representation in the European Union* (n 1) 218–223.

139 Commission, 'General Principles and Minimum Standards' (n 6) 11. See also EESC, 'The Representativeness of European Civil Society Organisations in Civil Dialogue' (Opinion) [2006] OJ C88/41.

140 See M Bovens, 'Two Concepts of Accountability: Accountability as a Virtue and as a Mechanism' (2010) 33 West European Politics 946, 951.

141 RA Dahl, *On Democracy* (Yale University Press 1998) 103–104.

142 J Greenwood, *Interest Representation in the European Union* (2nd edn, Palgrave Macmillan 2007) 195. See also Obradovic, 'Civil Society and the Social Dialogue' (n 30) 292–295.

Commission turned to civil society as a civic space in the first place.[143] The question therefore is: do the regulatory means put in place by the Commission conform to this need for self-restraint?

Interested parties that wish to submit comments on a policy proposal by the Commission must be ready to make apparent to the Commission and the public at large which interests they represent and how inclusive that representation is.[144] This information used to be provided through the CONECCS database, an online voluntary directory for non-profit-making CSOs active at European level. After the launch of the European Transparency Initiative,[145] CONECCS was replaced in spring 2008 by the Register of Interest Representatives, a web-based Commission-managed voluntary registration system open to all entities carrying out activities with the objective of influencing EU policy-making.[146]

The Register improved upon CONECCS in two ways. Firstly, the incentives to join the Register were strengthened.[147] In exchange for providing information on who they represent, what their mission is and how and by whom they are funded, interest groups were automatically alerted to consultations taking place in their areas of interest.[148] The Register was also increasingly used as a reference by Commission services which invited organisations to join the Register before attending meetings otherwise risking being overlooked in case of non-registration.[149] This added to the incentive existing under CONECCS that consultation responses of non-participants were considered as individual, rather than representative, contributions.[150] Secondly, the Register was assigned, in addition to its informative function, a regulatory function, for registration was made conditional upon adherence to a code of conduct established by the Commission or to a professional code that had comparable rules.[151] The former prescribed integrity rules largely inspired by the minimum requirements of 1992. Breach of the rules, including false or misleading information entered into the Register, would eventually lead to suspension or exclusion from the Register.[152] This tightening aimed at overcoming the limits of the self-regulatory

143 See above, n 30.

144 Commission, 'General Principles and Minimum Standards' (n 6) 17.

145 Commission, 'Proposing the Launch of a European Transparency Initiative' (Communication) SEC (2005) 1300/5.

146 Commission, 'European Transparency Initiative: A Framework for Relations with Interest Representatives (Register and Code of Conduct)' (Communication) COM (2008) 323 final.

147 D Obradovic, 'Regulating Lobbying in the European Union' in D Coen and J Richardson (eds), *Lobbying the European Union: Institutions, Actors, and Issues* (OUP 2009) 309–313.

148 Commission, 'European Transparency Initiative' (Green Paper) COM (2006) 194 final, 8.

149 Greenwood, *Interest Representation in the European Union* (n 1) 58.

150 Commission, 'Follow-up to the Green Paper "European Transparency Initiative"' (Communication) COM (2007) 127 final, 4.

151 Commission, 'European Transparency Initiative' (n 146) annex.

152 Ibid 4–5.

approach which had so far developed codes which applied unevenly and with limited checks on compliance.[153]

With a view to implement Article 11 TEU, the Parliament and the Commission have agreed to establish and operate a common Transparency Register which replaces the Commission's Register of Interest Representatives.[154] Its scope is somewhat wider and better-defined than its predecessor;[155] while the content, that is the information to be provided by registrants, has been enhanced.[156] A Joint Transparency Register Secretariat has been created so as to ease implementation.[157] More importantly for our purpose, observance of the Commission's code of conduct has become compulsory for those that wish to register, although registrants can still provide the text of a professional code by which they are bound.[158] The compliance mechanism has also been strengthened. And albeit the registration scheme is still voluntary, a further incentive now comes from the fact that the Parliament's 1-year entry pass can be made available only for those that have registered.[159]

A new version of the Transparency Register was launched in January 2015.[160] The revised Transparency Register includes a number of improvements and clarifications, among which an overhauling of the alerts and complaints procedure, a strengthening of the code of conduct and the setting up of new incentives to encourage registration. For instance, the Commission will advise all departments to encourage their stakeholders and expert group members to register. Also, Commissioners will no longer accept to be patrons of events where the event organisers should be registered but are not.[161] Interest representatives must finally be registered in order to hold meetings with Commissioners, Cabinet members and Directors-General. Since 1st December 2014, these officials are moreover bound to publish basic information about these meetings so that the wider public can know about the date of the meeting,

---

153 Commission, 'European Transparency Initiative' (n 148) 9–10. See also Obradovic, 'Regulating Lobbying' (n 147) 301.

154 Agreement between the European Parliament and the European Commission of 23 June 2011 on the establishment of a transparency register for organisations and self-employed individuals engaged in EU policy- making and policy implementation [2011] OJ L191/29 (Agreement).

155 Ibid 30.

156 Ibid annex II.

157 Ibid 31.

158 Ibid 31. See FAQs available at <http://ec.europa.eu/transparencyregister/info/your-organisation/faq.do?locale=en#en> accessed 1st September 2015.

159 Ibid 31.

160 See Agreement between the European Parliament and the European Commission of 16 April 2014 on the Transparency Register for Organisations and Self-Employed Individuals Engaged in EU Policy-Making and Policy Implementation [2014] OJ L277/11.

161 Commission, 'The revised Transparency Register: more information, more incentives, tougher on those who break the rules' (MEMO/14/302) 15 April 2014.

the location, the name of the people or organisations attending and the subject of the meeting.[162]

The above developments illustrate the normative tensions with which the Commission is struggling the moment it tries to regulate European civil society: as a matter of principle, the Commission wants its dialogue with organised civil society to be as open and as inclusive as possible, which leads to a refusal of any system of accreditation or registration. Yet, for the sake of enhancing its own democratic legitimacy, the Commission needs organised civil society to be more transparent and accountable. With a view to prevent exclusionary effects and so as to avoid the bureaucratic interference which would arise from imposing the latter regulatory commitments on organised civil society, the Commission adopts a minimal, low-key approach which prefers resorting to self-regulation and other soft law mechanisms rather than inflicting high administrative, *a fortiori* legal, burdens on organised civil society.

A consequence of this soft approach is that some will see the pluralist glass half-full and rejoice that respecting the independence of civil society and ensuring wide participation has been a recurring theme in the regulatory interventions of the Commission. This would explain the Commission's initial preference for self-regulation and minimal rules as regards the enactment of a code of conduct,[163] and its reluctance towards the setting-up of a mandatory register. After all, asking CSOs to provide, on a voluntary basis, and to update every year, basic information on their mission, membership and finances can hardly be said to impose excessive bureaucratic hurdles on organised civil society, while it may play, in return, a catalytic role for its democratisation. The optimists would therefore find in the recent emergence of a third generation of public consultation instruments, as well as in the constant reaffirmation of openness as a guiding principle for European administration, sufficient proof that the Register is not meant to restrict access to consultations.[164]

A contrario, others will express the fear that, despite having resisted, on pluralist grounds, the putting into place of an accreditation system akin to the ones in place at the Council of Europe[165] or the UN Economic and

---

162 Commission Decision 2014/838/EU of 25 November 2014 on the Publication of Information on Meetings Held Between Directors-General of the Commission and Organisations or Self-employed Individuals [2014] OJ L343/19; Commission Decision 2014/839/EU of 25 November 2014 on the Publication of Information on Meetings Held Between Members of the Commission and Organisations or Self-employed Individuals [2014] OJ L343/22.

163 The remains of which can still be found in the Agreement which encourages European federations of interest representatives, as part of their self-regulatory efforts, to draw up guidelines aimed at identifying activities falling within the scope of the Register.

164 See Articles 1 and 10(3) TEU; Article 15 (1) TFEU.

165 See Committee of Ministers of the Council of Europe, 'Resolution (2003) 8 of 19 November 2003 on the Participatory Status for International Non-Governmental Organisations with the Council of Europe'.

Social Council,[166] the Commission is *de facto* running a mechanism of the sort.[167] Voluntary directories have been replaced by the Transparency Register, registration in which is almost mandatory considering the incentives attached to registration. Besides, minimum rules of conduct enforced through self-regulation have given way to a Commission-devised code of conduct, compliance with which is compulsory to enter and stay on the Register. The purely informative purpose of the early days has been overtaken by the Commission's wider concerns related to restoring legitimacy in times of trouble. The Commission may use registration as a catalyst to improve CSO's governance in terms of increased transparency and accountability, which may seem laudable, but it may also use it as a device for providing the information necessary to select organisations that are representative at European level, thereby reinforcing the impression that 'Brussels is talking to Brussels'[168] rather than fighting it.[169]

In that respect, the White Paper had suggested that more 'extensive partnership arrangements' be set up in exchange for civil society organisations promising to 'tighten up their internal structures, furnish guarantees of openness and representativity, and prove their capacity to relay information or lead debates in the Member States'.[170] The European Parliament, rightly, opposed this proposal on the grounds that such *quid pro quo* would jeopardise the independence of civil society which is so essential to a vibrant democracy.[171] As seen in *Section 6.2*, the problem is that the practices that those arrangements were meant to solemnise live on and already suffer from the weaknesses the European Parliament foresaw.[172] Privileged partners such as the social Platform are keen proponents of their formalisation into a proper accreditation process based on geographical representativeness. The Register might just bring us a little closer to it.[173]

---

166 See Economic and Social Council, 'Resolution 31 of 25 July 1996 on the Consultative Relationship between the United Nations and Non-Governmental Organizations' UN Doc E/1996/96.

167 J Greenwood and D Halpin, 'The European Commission and the Public Governance of Interest Groups in the European Union: Seeking a Niche between Accreditation and Laissez-Faire' (2007) 8 Perspectives on European Politics and Society 189, 197. See also Commission, 'An Open and Structured Dialogue between the Commission and Special Interest Groups' (n 3) 2–3.

168 Commission, 'General Principles and Minimum Standards' (n 6) 12.

169 J Greenwood, 'The Lobby Regulation Element of the European Transparency Initiative: Between Liberal and Deliberative Models of Democracy' (2011) 9 Comparative European Politics 317, 327.

170 Commission, 'White Paper' (n 6) 17.

171 European Parliament, 'Resolution of 29 November 2001 on the Commission White Paper on European Governance' [2002] OJ C153E/314, paras 11–12.

172 Greenwood, *Interest Representation in the European Union* (n 1) 218–223.

173 See S Smismans, 'Interest Representation in the EU-Is There Any?' in S Kröger and D Friedrich (eds), *The Challenge of Democratic Representation in the European Union* (Palgrave Macmillan 2012) 224.

6.5. CONCLUSIONS

How and where does the Commission strike the balance between the conflicting demands for wide participation and effective administration? A quick analysis of the funding opportunities offered to social CSOs and the instruments of consultation which the Commission uses prior to proposing any major instrument of social legislation conjures up the picture of a consultation regime which, on efficiency grounds, confines participation to a European elite of civil society representatives whose democratic credentials are highly contested, albeit a new generation of public consultation instruments, such as the ECI and online consultations, seems to be finally, but hardly, reaching beyond the Brussels' beltway (*6.2*).

So as to get citizens on board, the Commission has enacted procedural rules with a view to open consultations to new entrants. But the Commission refuses conferring them a legally-binding nature, a stand deemed incompatible with the need for effective administration. This soft stand is opposed by those who would like to see consultations evolving towards a right-based participatory regime supervised by the EU Courts. The EU Courts have so far been unwilling to uphold, at least directly, civil society's participation in EU law-making. Yet, increased judicial scrutiny of EU law as to its rationality as well as the recent constitutional embrace of participatory democracy may be signs that the tide is turning (*6.3*).

Beside opening consultations through new instruments and soft procedures, the Commission has invited (representative) European civil society to democratise its internal structures. Regulatory demands for more openness and accountability are being made in the hope that European civil society will, at last, bridge the gap with EU citizens. However, for fear that any kind of *de jure* accreditation would threaten further the independence and pluralist values for which civil society's contribution to democracy is celebrated, the Commission enforces those demands through self-regulation and other soft law mechanisms (*6.4*).

This chapter attests to the growing role played by soft law in the Commission's consultation regime, which seems to increasingly act as a convenient meeting ground for democracy and effectiveness. Whether the Commission regulates consultations with a view to further wide access (*6.3*) or regulates organised civil society so as to democratise its structures (*6.4*), soft rules are preferred to hard solutions. However, the reasons for doing so differ: soft law in rescue of administrative effectiveness in the first case and soft law in support of participatory democracy in the second case. While true rights-based participation is resisted for efficiency reasons, soft procedures are enacted by the Commission as a less disruptive option which furthers the wider involvement of civil society in governance. While imposing any kind of legal-administrative obligations on civil society would unduly interfere with the pluralist values and structural independence on which its democratic contribution rests, soft law and self-regulation are chosen as less intrusive ways to incite much needed reforms.

This soft consultation regime is reflexive in the sense that it makes the EU bureaucratic system sensitive to the concerns of CSOs through procedural rules which give them a voice in lawmaking without at the same threatening their autonomy to a great extent. These procedural rules are broadly in line with the participatory ideal, for they strive for more open, transparent and wide participation. Yet, are *soft* rules adequate for embedding participatory democracy in EU law-making? Ideally, truly bottom-up participation would require that civil society be granted proper participatory rights with no corresponding obligations, but further legalisation of the civil dialogue on this model might be incompatible with the CM whose effectiveness is premised upon top-down law-making.[174] The CM was born and remains, by design, hierarchical; as such, it is hardly amenable to wide participation. Empowering the European Parliament was a first step towards correcting that birth defect. Yet, already, a compromise had to be reached. Representative democracy was above all chosen because it was a well-tested means to govern effectively large-size societies. The participatory turn now requires European institutions to bring civil society directly in. Because civic participation inevitably takes place in the shadow of the CM's hierarchy,[175] a balance has once again to be struck between the conflicting demands for democracy and effectiveness.

The Commission's soft consultation regime reflects a quite successful attempt at striking that balance: organised civil society benefit from (non-enforceable) consultation rules without assuming any (proper) legal obligation. It is also compatible with new Article 11 TEU which does not seem to require further legalisation in terms of increasing rights or responsibilities. Paragraph 1 of the article admits that there are several means to implement participatory democracy, not necessarily legal but also political;[176] while, only paragraph 4, on the ECI, contains a proper legal basis for implementing the principle of participatory democracy. Besides, paragraph 3 provides that the Commission shall consult broadly with parties concerned with a view to ensure that the EU's actions are coherent. This entails a functional use of participation which would hardly be compatible with granting proper participatory rights. Meanwhile, paragraph 2 obliges the Commission to maintain an open dialogue with organised civil society. The setting-up of a *de jure* accreditation process would certainly run contrary to that aim. Last but not least, Article 11 TEU should be read in combination with Article 10 TEU which recalls that 'the functioning of the Union shall be founded on representative democracy'. As seen

174 See Craig and De Búrca, *EU Law* (n 97) 160.

175 This expression is borrowed from A Héritier and M Rhodes (eds), *New Modes of Governance in Europe: Governing in the Shadow of Hierarchy* (Palgrave Macmillan 2011).

176 See P Craig, *The Lisbon Treaty: Law, Politics, and Treaty Reform* (OUP 2010) 70.

in *Section 6.3*, further legalisation of consultation rules might undermine that founding principle of the EU legal order rather than support it.

In the next chapter, civil society's participation in the social OMC will be examined. This will offer an interesting point of comparison with the current chapter, for the OMC is portrayed by its proponents as a decentralised governance tool which combines radical democratic aspirations with problem-solving capacities unavailable under the CM. Whether it is really the case will now be assessed critically.

CHAPTER 7
THE OPEN METHOD OF COORDINATION
Radicalising Participatory Democracy in the EU?

7.1. INTRODUCTION

At the Lisbon European summit in 2000,[1] the Union set itself an ambitious goal for the next decade: 'to become the most competitive and dynamic knowledge-based economy in the world capable of sustainable economic growth with more and better jobs and greater social cohesion'.[2] With a view to realise this socio-economic agenda, 'a [new] open method of coordination' (OMC) was introduced 'as the means of spreading best practice and achieving greater convergence towards the main EU goals'.[3] The Lisbon strategy built upon previous coordination processes in the economic (Broad Economic Policy Guidelines, 1992) and employment (European Employment Strategy, 1997) fields so that the OMC was new only to the extent that it provided a new legitimising discourse around which past and novel practices could crystallise.[4]

Since then, the OMC has become 'the central tool of EU social policy-making in the new millennium',[5] for, the *social inclusion process*, established in 2000 with a view 'to make a decisive impact on the eradication of poverty',[6] would later be complemented by a *pensions process* (2001) and a *health care*

1 European Council, 23–24 March 2000, Lisbon, presidency conclusions.

2 Ibid para 5 (italics omitted).

3 Ibid para 37.

4 CM Radaelli, 'The Open Method of Coordination: A New Governance Architecture for the European Union?' (2003) Sieps Report no. 1, 17 <http://eucenter.wisc.edu/OMC/Papers/radaelli.pdf> accessed 1st September 2015.

5 J Zeitlin, 'The Open Method of Co-Ordination in Question' in J Zeitlin, P Pochet and L Magnusson (eds), *The Open Method of Co-Ordination in Action: the European Employment and Social Inclusion Strategies* (PIE-Peter Lang 2005) 19.

6 Lisbon European Council (n 1) para 32. See also European Council, 7–9 December 2000, Nice, presidency conclusions, para 20.

and long-term care process (2004).[7] As from 2006, the three processes were streamlined into a single social OMC with the following elements:[8]

- *Common objectives* were endorsed by the European Council in March 2006, with both overarching and specific objectives for each strand of the social OMC;
- *Common indicators* were also agreed by the Social Protection Committee (SPC) with a view to measure Member States' progress towards the common objectives;
- Every three years, Member States would translate common objectives into *National Strategies for Social Protection and Social Inclusion*, with a common section presenting their overall strategic approach and three thematic plans covering, respectively, social inclusion, pensions, and healthcare and long-term care;
- The strategies would then be sent to the Commission with a view to monitor progress in a *Joint Social Protection and Social Inclusion Report* to be drafted every year for Council/Commission adoption prior to each Spring European Council;
- The different elements of the social OMC were supported by *Progress*,[9] a programme which financed the implementation of the objectives of the European Union in the fields of employment and social affairs for the period 2007–2013.

The social OMC was not Member States' first attempt to cooperate on social policy issues.[10] Already in 1992, the Council adopted two Recommendations which instated what would later be seen as some kind of 'unfinished OMC' in the social field.[11] In 1999, social cooperation was given new impetus when the Council endorsed the Commission's concerted strategy for modernising social

---

7 For more detail, see E Marlier, T Atkinson, B Cantillon and B Nolan, *The EU and Social Inclusion: Facing the Challenges* (Policy Press 2007) 22–26.

8 See Commission, 'Strengthening the Social Dimension of the Lisbon Strategy: Streamlining Open Coordination in the Field of Social Protection' (Communication) COM (2003) 261 final; Commission, 'Working Together, Working Better: A New Framework for the Open Coordination of Social Protection and Inclusion Policies in the European Union' (Communication) COM (2005) 706 final.

9 Decision 1672/2006/EC of the European Parliament and of the Council of 24 October 2006 establishing a Community Programme for Employment and Social Solidarity – Progress [2006] OJ L315/1 (Progress Decision).

10 See Marlier et al, *The EU and Social Inclusion* (n 7) 17–21.

11 Council Recommendation 92/441/EEC of 24 June 1992 establishing common criteria concerning sufficient resources and social assistance in social protection systems [1992] OJ L245/46; Council Recommendation 92/442/EEC of 27 July 1992 on the convergence of social protection objectives and policies [1992] OJ L245/49. See also P Pochet, 'The Open Method of Co-Ordination and the Construction of Social Europe. A Historical Perspective' in J Zeitlin, P Pochet and L Magnusson (eds), *The Open Method of Co-Ordination in Action: The European Employment and Social Inclusion Strategies* (PIE-Peter Lang 2005) 64.

protection in the EU.[12] With Lisbon, the social OMC became the political tool chosen by Member States to modernise the European social model with proper regard for the diversity of national welfare systems. The Lisbon strategy came to an end in 2010 and was replaced by the Europe 2020 strategy for smart, sustainable and inclusive growth.[13] As the social OMC underwent reforms within the context of this new strategy, time is ripe for asking whether this tool has delivered on its promises and, if not, whether current reforms are likely to fill that delivery gap.

From a theoretical perspective, the social OMC is often depicted as a form of Directly-Deliberative Polyarchy (DDP) in action. As a consequence, many embrace it as a tool for making social Europe both more democratic and more effective than under the CM: more democratic because its bottom-up philosophy would give a chance to radicalise participatory democracy in the EU, more effective because the social OMC would be an opportunity for social Europe to address common challenges while respecting the diversity of national welfare traditions (*7.2*).[14] Yet, empirical evidence pertaining to the social OMC tells a story of practical disappointments in the face of high theoretical expectations. Despite its strong democratic credentials, the social OMC is not directly-deliberative, nor is it polyarchic for that matter. Its effectiveness is also at stake, for it has so far failed to solve the problems of social Europe (*7.3*). To close the delivery gap, experts have called for a reflexive reform strategy. This strategy found echo in the 2011 Opinion of the SPC on the future of the social OMC within the framework of the Europe 2020 strategy.[15] Nevertheless, it is argued that the reflexive reforms envisaged so far will hardly make the social OMC more democratic and effective because they merely try to approximate the institutional ideal proposed by DDP, whereas DDP itself overlooks the bureaucratic and economic threats to the realisation of its own socio-democratic aspirations. Rather, a critical assessment of DDP is needed in the first place, which would shed light on the legal, political and constitutional requirements underpinning any genuine democratic reform of the social OMC (*7.4*). Provided such reforms are implemented, radical participatory democracy might become a reality in social Europe. This offers an interesting point of contrast with the

12 Commission, 'A Concerted Strategy for Modernising Social Protection' (Communication) COM (99) 347 final; Council, 'Conclusions of 17 December 1999 on the Strengthening of Cooperation for Modernising and Improving Social Protection' [2000] OJ C08/7.

13 See Commission, 'Europe 2020: A Strategy for Smart, Sustainable and Inclusive Growth' (Communication) COM (2010) 2020 final.

14 See C de la Porte and P Pochet (eds), *Building Social Europe through the Open Method Co-Ordination* (PIE-Peter Lang 2002); O De Schutter and S Deakin (eds), *Social Rights and Market Forces: Is the Open Coordination of Employment and Social Policies the Future of Social Europe?* (Bruylant 2005); Zeitlin et al, *The Open Method of Co-Ordination in Action* (n 5).

15 SPC, 'Reinvigorating the Social OMC in the Context of the Europe 2020 Strategy' (Opinion) (2011) Doc 10405/11.

previous chapter. For, we have seen that the civil dialogue cannot be the magic cure for the democratic ailments of the CM because of its inherently top-down features (7.5).

7.2. THEORETICAL PROMISES

The OMC, as a means to coordinate national policies according to a fully decentralised approach,[16] has been pinpointed as an example of DDP in action.[17] This theoretical model accounts for democratic experiments in which:

> (...) collective decisions are made through public deliberation in arenas open to citizens who use public services, or who are otherwise regulated by public decisions. But in deciding, those citizens must examine their own choices in the light of the relevant deliberations and experiences of others facing similar problems in comparable jurisdictions or subdivisions of government. Ideally, then, directly-deliberative polyarchy combines the advantages of local learning and self-government with the advantages (and discipline) of wider social learning and heightened political accountability that result when the outcomes of many concurrent experiments are pooled to permit public scrutiny of the effectiveness of strategies and leaders.[18]

DDP 'is directly deliberative because local agents (...) can participate directly in problem-solving, representing as it were themselves (...) It is polyarchic because, even as they gain freedom of initiative, locales (...) remain accountable to a public informed by the doing of their peers'.[19]

Directly-deliberative polyarchy, contrary to anarchy, relies on a centre which provides the relevant infrastructure for learning among directly-deliberative units to occur.[20] DDP therefore entails a transformation of hierarchically-ordered government whose principal role becomes 'to encourage and coordinate (...) decentralized decisionmaking'.[21] Within such an experimentalist framework, 'the task of the legislature is to authorize these deliberations and

---

16 Lisbon European council (n 1) para 38.

17 O Gerstenberg and CF Sabel, 'Directly-Deliberative Polyarchy: An Institutional Ideal for Europe?' in C Joerges and R Dehousse (eds), *Good Governance in Europe's Integrated Market* (OUP 2002) 333–334; J Cohen and CF Sabel, 'Sovereignty and Solidarity: EU and US' in J Zeitlin and DM Trubek (eds), *Governing Work and Welfare in a New Economy: European and American Experiments* (OUP 2003) 364–366; CF Sabel and J Zeitlin, 'Learning from Difference: The New Architecture of Experimentalist Governance in the EU' (2008) 14 ELJ 271, 289–292.

18 J Cohen and C Sabel, 'Directly-Deliberative Polyarchy' (1997) 3 ELJ 313, 313–314.

19 Gerstenberg and Sabel, 'Directly-Deliberative Polyarchy: An Institutional Ideal for Europe?' (n 17) 340–341. For an alternative formulation, see MC Dorf and CF Sabel, 'A Constitution of Democratic Experimentalism' (1998) 98 CLR 267, 320.

20 Cohen and Sabel, 'Sovereignty and Solidarity' (n 17) 366.

21 Dorf and Sabel, 'A Constitution of Democratic Experimentalism' (n 19) 340.

finance the ensuing experiments', while 'the task of the administrative agencies is to provide the infrastructure of coordination'.[22] Finally, 'the courts (...) are charged with the familiar tasks of policing government and safeguarding rights', but 'these judicial activities are now more conspicuously than ever in the service of the common end of increasing citizen participation in political decisions'.[23]

DDP describes itself as 'an attractive kind of radical, participatory democracy with problem-solving capacities useful under current conditions and unavailable to representative systems'.[24] Considering that EU leaders initially agreed on top-down law-making through the CM and taking for granted that democratising the CM through further parliamentary involvement and Commission's enhanced dialogue with civil society has so far failed to overcome those elitist origins,[25] the rise of the OMC as DDP could be seen as a move in the direction of a more democratic Europe. For, the OMC offers the promise to decentralise EU decision-making by bringing powers back to Member States working in partnership with civil society.[26] The OMC as DDP could also become key to the integration of social Europe, by allowing Member States to address collectively, while respecting diversity, problems arising in a sensitive policy field where the CM is often unavailable due to lack of legal competence or political will and would, in any case, be ineffective in view of the complexity and uncertainty of the issues to be addressed.[27] To what extent do those theoretical hopes find confirmation in practice?

7.3. PRACTICAL DISAPPOINTMENTS

The social OMC possesses strong democratic credentials. Suffice it to remind the reader that one of the objectives of the social inclusion process has from the beginning been to 'involve all relevant bodies'.[28] The third social inclusion objective of the streamlined social OMC reformulates that objective by insisting that 'social inclusion policies are well-coordinated and involve all levels of government and relevant actors, including people experiencing poverty'.[29]

22 Ibid 340.

23 Ibid 340.

24 Cohen and Sabel, 'Directly-Deliberative Polyarchy' (n 18) 313.

25 On the elitist origins of the CM, see G Majone, 'Is the Community Method still Viable?' in R Dehousse (ed), *The "Community Method": Obstinate or Obsolete?* (Palgrave Macmillan 2011) 23–26.

26 See Cohen and Sabel, 'Sovereignty and Solidarity' (n 17) 362–373; J Zeitlin, 'Social Europe and Experimentalist Governance: Towards a New Constitutional Compromise?' in G De Búrca (ed), *EU Law and the Welfare State: in Search of Solidarity* (OUP 2005) 223–227.

27 See the references cited above, n 14.

28 See Council, 'Fight against Poverty and Social Exclusion' (2000) Doc 14110/00.

29 See SPC and EPC, 'Joint Opinion on the Communication "Working Together, Working Better"' (2006) Doc 6801/06, annex I.

Of particular importance is also the uploading of the participatory objective of the social inclusion process as an overarching concern over 'good governance, transparency and the involvement of stakeholders in the design, implementation and monitoring of policy', and its percolation within the specific objectives of the health and pensions strands of the social OMC.[30] Besides, the joint reports have reviewed national strategies' compliance with the aforementioned participatory objectives, while comparing performance and highlighting best practices in that respect.[31] At the same time, *Progress* has supported the participatory architecture of the social OMC by funding transnational networks of CSOs involved in social affairs as well as awareness-raising campaigns pertaining thereto.[32]

Empirical evidence currently available as to the impact of the social OMC on Member States also confirms that it has broadened stakeholders' involvement in social policy-making by creating or reinforcing vertical and horizontal links within government, while at the same time extending participation opportunities beyond government.[33] Regarding the latter, Zeitlin observes that:

> (...) in many countries (...) the social OMCs have led to the creation or reinforcement of consultative and participatory structures for the involvement of social partners and civil society organizations in policy formation, implementation, monitoring, and evaluation at national and (in some cases) subnational levels.[34]

This is especially true for the social inclusion strand of the social OMC which, he says, 'has the best record of stakeholder involvement'.[35]

Demands for involving stakeholders as well as people experiencing poverty in the social inclusion strand of the social OMC have also been taken seriously by European authorities. Since 2002, European Round Tables on Poverty and Social Exclusion have been organised annually by the country holding the Presidency

---

30 Ibid annex I.

31 See, eg, Commission and Council, 'Joint Report on Social Protection and Social Inclusion' (2009) Doc 7503/09.

32 See Progress Decision, Article 5.

33 J Zeitlin, 'The Open Method of Co-Ordination in Action: Theoretical Promise, Empirical Realities, Reform Strategy' in J Zeitlin, P Pochet and L Magnusson (eds), *The Open Method of Co-Ordination in Action: The European Employment and Social Inclusion Strategies* (PIE-Peter Lang 2005) 457–476; J Zeitlin, 'The Open Method of Coordination and Reform of National Social and Employment Policies: Influences, Mechanisms, Effects' in M Heidenreich and J Zeitlin (eds), *Changing European Employment and Welfare Regimes: The Influence of the Open Method of Coordination on National Reforms* (Routledge 2009) 221–226; B Vanhercke, 'Delivering the Goods for Europe 2020? The Social OMC's Adequacy and Impact Re-Assessed' in E Marlier and D Natali (eds), *Europe 2020: Towards a More Social EU?* (PIE-Peter Lang 2010) 129–131.

34 Zeitlin, 'The Open Method of Coordination and Reform of National Social and Employment Policies' (n 33) 223.

35 J Zeitlin, 'Towards a Stronger OMC in a More Social Europe 2020: A New Governance Architecture for EU Policy Coordination' in E Marlier and D Natali (eds), *Europe 2020: Towards a More Social EU?* (PIE- Peter Lang 2010) 268.

of the EU with the support of the Commission.[36] They bring together European and national policy-makers, NGOs and other stakeholders to discuss the problem of poverty in Europe. The Round Table was transformed into a wider Annual Convention of the European Platform against Poverty and Social Exclusion held with a view to taking stock of progress made towards meeting the Europe 2020 headline target for lifting at least 20 million people out of poverty and social exclusion by 2020, and discussing how to take this forward.[37]

In addition, the Belgian Presidency of the EU initiated in 2001 a process of yearly European Meetings of People Experiencing Poverty.[38] These meetings aim at giving a voice to the poor and socially excluded people and are a first step towards their involvement in the social inclusion process. The meetings are supported by the Commission and build on the expertise of the European Anti-Poverty Network (EAPN) in empowering people experiencing poverty.[39]

Beside these quasi 'institutionalised' EU events, European networks of social CSOs involved in the fight against poverty such as EAPN and the European Federation of National Organisations working with the Homeless (FEANTSA), are regularly consulted on the development of the social OMC to which they contribute through independent reports and position papers based on detailed information supplied by national affiliates. All of these networks are heavily funded by the Commission and regularly organise EU-wide conferences and round tables in collaboration with the Commission.[40] One can finally mention the supportive role played by the CoR and the EESC. Both advocate, through their advisory opinions, wide ownership of the social OMC, while monitoring progress through networks established with, respectively, the functional and regional/local interests they represent.[41]

Are the above participatory features enough for the social OMC to qualify as Directly-Deliberative? A qualified 'no' seems appropriate. While it is undeniable that stakeholders' involvement in the social OMC has improved, there are still wide variations between Member States and important change over time,[42]

---

36 Marlier et al, *The EU and Social Inclusion* (n 7) 230.

37 The latest Convention was held from 20 to 21 November 2014. For more detail, see <http://ec.europa.eu/social/main.jsp?langId=en&catId=88&eventsId=1008&furtherEvents=yes> accessed 1st September 2015.

38 Marlier et al, *The EU and Social Inclusion* (n 7) 230–231.

39 Ibid 231.

40 Zeitlin, 'The Open Method of Coordination and Reform of National Social and Employment Policies' (n 33) 225.

41 See CoR, 'The European Platform against Poverty and Social Exclusion' (Opinion) [2011] OJ C166/18; EESC, 'The Open Method of Coordination and the Social Clause in the Context of Europe 2020' (Opinion) [2011] OJ C44/23.

42 Vanhercke, 'Delivering the Goods for Europe 2020?' (n 33) 130. For a comparative outlook, see C de la Porte and P Pochet, 'Participation in the Open Method of Co-Ordination. The Cases of Employment and Social Inclusion' in J Zeitlin, P Pochet and L Magnusson (eds), *The Open Method of Co-Ordination in Action: the European Employment and Social Inclusion Strategies* (PIE-Peter Lang 2005).

with some Member States even going backwards.[43] In many Member States, governance arrangements for mobilising all relevant actors are still too weak.[44] Arguably, broader stakeholders' involvement has not benefited all types of actors equally.[45] Many complain that the preparation of national strategies is essentially a bureaucratic process,[46] piloted by the national administrations to the detriment of local and regional authorities,[47] with the executive intervening late in the decision-making stage.[48]

CSOs representing people experiencing poverty are now widely involved but their involvement encounters serious limits. While involvement is achieved at the implementation stage, it remains less entrenched during the drafting and design phase of national strategies.[49] The depth of their involvement is also subject to important changes, ranging from mere information in some Member States to full partnership in others.[50] CSOs are often disillusioned by a process which, they consider, works under too tight time constraints and fails to produce impact on national social policy processes and outcomes.[51] The poor themselves are involved in only half of the Member States,[52] while the CSO representatives that do get involved in the process find it difficult to mobilise their constituencies.[53]

---

43 EAPN, 'Building Security, Giving Hope: EAPN Assessment of the National Strategic Reports on Social Protection and Social Inclusion (2008–10)' (2008) 12–13.

44 H Frazer and E Marlier, 'Strengthening Social Inclusion in the Europe 2020 Strategy by Learning from the Past' in E Marlier and D Natali (eds), *Europe 2020: Towards a More Social EU?* (PIE- Peter Lang 2010) 234; H Frazer, E Marlier and I Nicaise, *A Social Inclusion Roadmap for Europe 2020* (Garant 2010) 22.

45 See INBAS GmbH and ENGENDER asbl, 'Study on Stakeholders' Involvement in the Implementation of the Open Method of Coordination (OMC) in Social Protection and Social Inclusion – Final Report' (2010) 9, 26–27 <www.stakeholders-socialinclusion.eu/site/en/outputs/finrep> accessed 1st September 2015.

46 S Kröger, 'The End of Democracy as we Know it? The Legitimacy Deficits of Bureaucratic Social Policy Governance' (2007) 29 Journal of European Integration 565, 578–579; S Kröger, *Soft Governance in Hard Politics* (VS Verlag 2008) 212–213. See also J Berghman and KGH Okma, 'The Method of Open Co-Ordination: Open Procedures or Closed Circuit? Social Policy Making between Science and Politics' (2002) 4 European Journal of Social Security 331; M Büchs and D Friedrich, 'Surface Integration: The National Action Plans for Employment and Social Inclusion in Germany' in J Zeitlin, P Pochet and L Magnusson (eds), *The Open Method of Co-Ordination in Action: the European Employment and Social Inclusion Strategies* (PIE-Peter Lang 2005).

47 A Michalski, 'Social Welfare and Levels of Democratic Government in the EU' (2012) 34 Journal of European Integration 397, 416; Public Policy and Management Institute, 'Evaluation of the Effectiveness and Impact of the Social OMC since 2006 – Suggestions for Improvement and Strengthening of the Effectiveness and Impact of the Social OMC'(2011) 132.

48 INBAS and ENGENDER, 'Study on Stakeholders' Involvement' (n 45) 26–27.

49 Ibid 27.

50 Ibid 35–36.

51 D Friedrich, 'Policy Process, Governance and Democracy in the EU: The Case of the Open Method of Co-Ordination on Social Inclusion in Germany' (2006) 34 Policy & Politics 367, 375.

52 INBAS and ENGENDER, 'Study on Stakeholders' Involvement' (n 45) 9.

53 See S Kröger, 'The OMC Inclusion and National Social NGOs: From Enthusiasm to Reality' (2006) Fourth ESPAnet annual conference, 21–23 September 2006, Bremen.

Wider public involvement is also severely constrained by the low participation of national parliaments and lack of media attention to social OMC issues which, in the few cases where they are reported, are depicted as national issues.[54] Ultimately, this lack of public interest for the social OMC is related to the crucial fact that national strategies are in most Member States considered as 'backward-looking activity reports to the EU and government documents "owned" by the relevant ministries rather than as forward-looking action plans or strategic programming instruments subject to normal public scrutiny and debate'.[55] In sum, the social OMC is certainly not directly-deliberative; rather the opposite, it is a bureaucratic process driven by a small circle of civil servants supported by a narrow group of CSO experts who fail to mobilise those they represent and the wider public more generally.[56]

Exactly for the same reasons, the social OMC cannot be said to be polyarchic. The Parliament, which is the central assembly, does not play even the residual function assigned thereto by DDP. It is duly informed about the process' main developments[57] and makes its views known through resolutions, despite repeated calls for its 'unrestricted and equal participation'.[58] Weak parliamentary supervision is not compensated by a democratisation of the administrative centrepiece of the process. Indeed, the SPC, which plays a pivotal role for monitoring progress towards the common objectives, is often accused of working behind a veil of secrecy.[59] To be fair, the SPC's transparency has greatly improved over time. Its membership, work agenda and formal opinions are now available online[60] and the SPC is, since 2004, bound to establish appropriate contacts with social NGOs.[61] Yet, only EAPN and FEANTSA have so far been regularly consulted, mostly on an informal basis.[62] This narrow participation of civil society is problematic considering that the two networks are not

54 M Büchs, 'How Legitimate is the Open Method of Coordination?' (2008) 46 JCMS 765, 775–780; R de Ruiter, 'Full Disclosure? The Open Method of Coordination, Parliamentary Debates and Media Coverage' (2013) 14 European Union Politics 95, 112; Public Policy and Management Institute, 'Evaluation of the Effectiveness and Impact of the Social OMC since 2006' (n 47) 121.

55 Zeitlin, 'The Open Method of Co-Ordination in Action' (n 33) 461.

56 See S Kröger, 'When Learning Hits Politics or: Social Policy Coordination Left to the Administrations and the NGOs?' (2006) 10 EIoP 10 <http://eiop.or.at/eiop/texte/2006-003a.htm> accessed 1st September 2015.

57 See Article 156 TFEU; Council Decision (EU) 2015/773 of 11 May 2015 establishing the Social Protection Committee and repealing Decision 2004/689/EC [2015] OJ L121/16, Article 2 (4).

58 European Parliament, 'Resolution of 15 March 2006 on Social Protection and Social Inclusion' [2006] OJ C291E/304, para 61.

59 Kröger, 'The End of Democracy as we Know it?' (n 46) 576; Büchs, 'How Legitimate is the Open Method of Coordination?' (n 54) 775–778.

60 See <http://ec.europa.eu/social/main.jsp?langId=en&catId=758> accessed 1st September 2015.

61 Council Decision (EU) 2015/773 of 11 May 2015 establishing the Social Protection Committee and repealing Decision 2004/689/EC [2015] OJ L121/16, Article 2 (4). As opposed to the social partners, the obligation to consult social NGOs is not mentioned in Article 160 TFEU.

62 Kröger, 'The End of Democracy as we Know it?' (n 46) 573.

representative of the wide range of actors likely to be affected by the social OMC.[63] They, moreover, both rely on EU funding for their survival which raises questions as to their independence and ability to communicate with grassroots, while more critical voices might be side-lined.[64] Limited openness is all the more worrying that the national civil servants members of the SPC can hardly be held accountable through normal parliamentary channels. The meetings of the SPC are not held in public, its minutes are not made available and the Council to which goes the final decision is under no obligation to deliberate in public on non-legislative matters,[65] so that respective national positions on the social OMC cannot be easily identified by national parliaments which, as a result, cannot scrutinise their executive agents effectively.

The democratic shortcomings of the social OMC may also be related to the widespread perception that it is an ineffective tool. Is that perception mistaken? There is no consensus as to the kind of results the social OMC is expected to deliver and disagreement exists as to whether the said results have been achieved or not.[66] Empirical research demonstrates that, aside from triggering procedural shifts in national policy-making, the social OMC has also been a source of substantive change in terms of national policy thinking, discourse and agendas.[67] Yet, once the more ambitious target of making a decisive impact on the eradication of poverty is taken as a benchmark, the social OMC appears as a failure.[68] According to Eurostat, in 2013, 122.9 million people, or 24.5% of the population in the EU-28 were at risk of poverty or social exclusion, compared with 24.7% in 2012 and 24.3% in 2011.[69]

The social OMC may also disappoint those that would see therein a third way for European social policy between legislative harmonisation and regulatory competition.[70] A major cause for concern is that the social OMC is subordinated to the wider growth agenda pursued by the Lisbon, now Europe 2020, strategy. The originality of the Lisbon strategy was to create an integrated

63 See de la Porte and Pochet, 'Participation in the Open Method of Co-ordination' (n 42) 375–376.

64 Kröger, 'The End of Democracy as we Know it?' (n 46) 579.

65 See Article 15 (2) TFEU.

66 Büchs, 'How Legitimate is the Open Method of Coordination?' (n 54) 769.

67 J Zeitlin, 'Is the Open Method of Coordination an Alternative to the Community Method?' in R Dehousse (ed), *The "Community Method": Obstinate or Obsolete?* (Palgrave Macmillan 2011) 142–143; Public Policy and Management Institute, 'Evaluation of the Effectiveness and Impact of the Social OMC since 2006' (n 47) 121.

68 K Armstrong, *Governing Social Inclusion: Europeanization through Policy Coordination* (OUP 2010) 263.

69 For more details, see <http://appsso.eurostat.ec.europa.eu/nui/submitViewTableAction.do> accessed 1st September 2015.

70 See de la Porte and Pochet, *Building Social Europe through the Open Method Co-ordination* (n 14); De Schutter and Deakin, *Social Rights and Market Forces: Is the Open Coordination of Employment and Social Policies the Future of Social Europe?* (n 14); Zeitlin et al, *The Open Method of Co-ordination in Action* (n 5).

policy framework with separate but mutually reinforcing growth, employment and social cohesion pillars.[71] The social inclusion process, and later the health and long-term care processes, were set up to implement the social strand of the strategy, while the economic and employment strands of the strategy were subject to separate coordination mechanisms. With a view to improve delivery, the governance of Lisbon was revised in 2005 with the adoption of a set of 'integrated guidelines' bringing the economic and employment processes under a common reporting mechanism.[72] In the meantime, the Commission had proposed to refocus Lisbon's priorities on growth and employment.[73] After fears were expressed that social policy would be kept on the sidelines of the Lisbon strategy, the European Council pledged that social cohesion would remain an integral part of the renewed Lisbon strategy for growth and jobs,[74] with the streamlined social OMC feeding in to economic and employment objectives while Lisbon would feed out to advance social cohesion goals.[75] But, in practice, feeding in and out ended up as a one-way street where the Lisbon strategy systematically pursued growth to the detriment of social cohesion.[76]

The Lisbon strategy came to an end in 2010 and was replaced by Europe 2020. A substantive rebalancing has occurred, for Europe 2020 is a strategy for smart, sustainable and inclusive growth which purports to lift at least 20 million people out of poverty and social exclusion by 2020.[77] The Commission has also established a European Platform against Poverty (EPP) as one of the seven flagship initiatives launched to tackle the Europe 2020 goals.[78] The governance of Europe 2020 is organised around the European semester, a yearly cycle of economic policy coordination where National Reform Programmes (NRPs)

---

71 M Dawson, 'Transforming into What? New Governance in the EU and the "Managerial Sensibility" in Modern Law' [2010] Wisconsin Law Review 389, 402.

72 See European Council, 22–23 March 2005, Brussels, presidency conclusions.

73 Commission, 'Working Together for Growth and Jobs: A New Start for the Lisbon Strategy' (Communication) COM (2005) 24 final.

74 European Council, 13–14 March 2008, Brussels, presidency conclusions, para 5. See also J Zeitlin, 'The Open Method of Co-Ordination and the Governance of the Lisbon Strategy' (2008) 46 JCMS 436, 437–438.

75 Commission, 'Working Together for Growth and Jobs' (n 73) 4.

76 M Dawson, 'The Ambiguity of Social Europe in the Open Method of Coordination' (2009) 34 EL Rev 55, 73, and the evidence cited therein.

77 European Council, 25–26 March 2010, presidency conclusions; European Council, 17 June 2010, presidency conclusions. See also Commission, 'Europe 2020: A Strategy for Smart, Sustainable and Inclusive Growth' (n 13) 3. For an overview, see H Frazer and E Marlier, with D Natali, R Van Dam and B Vanhercke, 'Europe 2020: Towards a More Social EU?' in E Marlier and D Natali (eds), *Europe 2020: Towards a More Social EU?* (PIE- Peter Lang 2010).

78 Commission, 'The European Platform against Poverty and Social Exclusion: A European Framework for Social and Territorial Cohesion' (Communication) COM (2010) 758 final. EPP builds upon the momentum created by the 2010 European year for combatting poverty and social exclusion (see Decision 1098/2008/EC of the European Parliament and of the Council of 22 October 2008 on the European year for combating poverty and social exclusion [2008] OJ L298/20).

based on the 'Europe 2020 integrated guidelines' are assessed by the Commission and Council which may issue policy recommendations to Member States where appropriate.[79] Whether this governance architecture adequately reflects the new socio-economic compromise struck by Europe 2020 will be critically assessed in the next chapter with a particular emphasis on its progressive overhaul within the context of the current eurocrisis. In the meantime, one may wonder what the future of the social OMC ought to be in the context of that new strategy. The Communication setting out Europe 2020 suggested that the social OMC would be transformed into a platform for cooperation, peer-review and exchange of good practice.[80] The EPP later identified the need to merely adapt the working methods of the social OMC to the new governance of Europe 2020 while leaving the details of that reform to further elaboration.[81]

7.4. REFORMING THE SOCIAL OMC

There has been a long-standing debate as to the reforms that would be most appropriate for strengthening the OMC. Although experts agree that the iterative nature of OMC processes makes them particularly prone to learn from experience, they still disagree as to *what* has to be learnt from past. For Zeitlin, the experience of the social OMC, more precisely of its social inclusion strand, offers a model for improving OMC processes through a reflexive strategy where the method would be applied to its own procedures through benchmarking, peer review, monitoring, and iterative redesign.[82] This strategy would address OMCs' procedural shortcomings by increasing transparency, enhancing stakeholder participation, mainstreaming OMC processes into domestic policy-making and reinforcing mutual learning.[83]

The Commission takes the opposite view, arguing that the social OMC could be strengthened by learning from the successful methods applied under the Treaty-based economic and employment coordination processes.[84] It proposes four priority areas for action: increasing political commitment and visibility, strengthening the positive interaction with other EU policies, reinforcing the analytical tools, and enhancing ownership through peer reviews, mutual

79 On the European semester, see <http://ec.europa.eu/europe2020/making-it-happen/index_en.htm> accessed 1st September 2015.

80 Commission, 'Europe 2020: A Strategy for Smart, Sustainable and Inclusive Growth' (n 13) 19.

81 Commission, 'The European Platform against Poverty and Social Exclusion' (n 78) 18.

82 Zeitlin, 'The Open Method of Co-Ordination in Action' (n 33) 447–448. For a recent reformulation, see Public Policy and Management Institute, 'Evaluation of the Effectiveness and Impact of the Social OMC since 2006' (n 47) 137–140.

83 Ibid 483–493. See also Armstrong, *Governing Social Inclusion* (n 68) 292–298.

84 Commission, 'A Renewed Commitment to Social Europe: Reinforcing the Open Method of Coordination for Social Protection and Social Inclusion' (Communication) COM (2008) 418 final, 4–5.

learning and involvement of all relevant actors.[85] These objectives are broadly in line with those of the reflexive reform strategy. Where the difference lies is in the tools that are supposed to deliver reforms. While Zeitlin wants the social OMC to reflect upon its own experience, the Commission takes the setting of targets and the use of recommendations as successful examples of how the social OMC could be strengthened on the model of the Lisbon strategy.[86]

The SPC refuses to tread that harder path and invites the Commission 'to make extensive use of the experience accumulated by the SPC and by its Indicators Sub-Group with a view to (...) fully exploiting the potential of the Social OMC'.[87] In an Opinion endorsed by the EPSCO Council of June 2011,[88] the SPC sets out the future of the social OMC in the context of Europe 2020. Therein, Europe 2020 as well as the new provisions of the Lisbon Treaty are depicted as a window of opportunity to reinvigorate the social OMC as a visible expression of 'Social Europe'. As to concrete reforms, the SPC opts for incremental change. The common social objectives are reaffirmed,[89] while regular strategic reporting on progress towards these covering the three strands of the OMC with a multiannual perspective is retained. Reporting takes place every year through National Social Reports (NSRs) submitted at the same time as NRPs.[90] So as to avoid overlap with the Commission's assessment of the Europe 2020 integrated guidelines, regular joint reports are dropped in favour of annual reports of the SPC on progress towards the common social objectives and the implementation of the social dimension of Europe 2020 submitted to the EPSCO Council in time to feed into the Spring European Council. Yet, thematic work in the SPC, to be reflected in national reporting and other aspects of the OMC, may still lead to specific Commission-Council joint reports. Finally, stakeholders' involvement will be enhanced and synergies be developed with EPP. Although the SPC does not specify how stakeholders' involvement will be enhanced, one may think that the EPP's commitment to create voluntary guidelines on stakeholders' involvement in social policy-making would be central to this endeavour.[91]

---

85 Ibid 4–8.

86 Ibid 5–6. See also H Frazer and E Marlier, 'Building a Stronger EU Social Inclusion Process: Analysis and Recommendations of the EU Network of Independent National Experts on Social Inclusion' (2008) <http://ec.europa.eu/social/main.jsp?catId=1025&langId=en&newsId=1410&furtherNews=yes> accessed 1st September 2015.

87 SPC, 'A Renewed Commitment to Social Europe: Reinforcing the Open Method of Coordination for Social Protection and Social Inclusion' (Opinion) (2008) Doc 15308/08, 3.

88 SPC, 'Reinvigorating the Social OMC in the Context of the Europe 2020 Strategy' (Opinion) (2011) Doc 10405/11. See also ad-hoc group on reinvigorating the social OMC in the context of the Europe 2020 strategy, 'Draft Background Paper' (SPC /2011.09/1).

89 For a technical update, see SPC, 'Reinvigorating the Social OMC' (n 88) annex.

90 See SPC, 'Preparation of the 2012 National Social Reports (NSR)' (Guidance Note) (2012) SPC/2012.2/4.

91 Commission, 'The European Platform against Poverty and Social Exclusion' (n 78) 17.

The SPC did not associate itself with any specific reform proposal. Yet, its incremental approach seems to be largely inspired by Zeitlin's reflexive reform strategy. The latter takes DDP as the institutional ideal against which OMC processes ought to be benchmarked.[92] However, it is argued that any reform proposal willing to bring the social OMC into line with the socio-democratic aspirations of DDP ought first to account for the bureaucratic and economic barriers which stand in the way of their practical realisation. The theoretical limits of DDP have already been explored and used to explain the failings of the OMC in practice.[93] What has been missing so far is a counter model which could give theoretical grounding to that claim and help put institutional flesh on alternative reform proposals.

The tripartite framework developed by Cohen and Arato seems quite apposite to that task.[94] Civil society is depicted therein as an autonomous sphere of democratic participation to be differentiated from the state and market subsystems. The challenge of modernity, say Cohen and Arato, is for civil society to assert influence over the state and market subsystems, while, at the same time, erecting barriers against their colonising tendencies. The two steps presuppose one another since 'only an adequately defended, differentiated, and organized civil society can monitor and influence the outcomes of steering processes, but only a civil society capable of influencing the state and economy can help to restrain or redirect the expansive tendencies of the media'.[95]

By contrast, DDP collapses the systemic boundaries which characterise modern societies into undifferentiated problem-solving by actors gathered in directly-deliberative settings.[96] By so doing, it loses sight of the fact that actor-centred problem-solving takes place within societies which are still dominated by power and money. There are *bureaucratic* and *economic* threats against the participatory-democratic ideal of DDP. Yet, DDP cannot see them because it discards the dangers that materialise whenever the administrative and economic subsystems act beyond their boundaries, colonising, as it were, civil society.[97] Mimicking DDP might therefore be dangerous, for that ideal does not provide civil society with any safeguard against the colonising forces of power and money. The social OMC already provides a practical instance of DDP facing those theoretical limits. The previous section has indeed shown how civil

---

92 Sabel and Zeitlin, 'Learning from Difference' (n 17) 289–292.

93 See Büchs, 'How Legitimate is the Open Method of Coordination?' (n 54) 775–780; M Dawson, *New Governance and the Transformation of European Law: Coordinating EU Social Law and Policy* (CUP 2011) chaps 3–4.

94 See JL Cohen and A Arato, *Civil Society and Political Theory* (MIT Press 1992) chap 9.

95 Ibid 471–472.

96 See Cohen and Sabel, 'Directly-Deliberative Polyarchy' (n 18) 314–315. See also K Armstrong, 'Inclusive Governance? Civil Society and the Open Method of Co-Ordination' in S Smismans (ed), *Civil Society and Legitimate European Governance* (Edward Elgar 2006) 63.

97 On the colonisation thesis, see J Habermas, *The Theory of Communicative Action /Vol.2, Lifeworld and System: A Critique of Functionalist Reason* (Polity Press 1987) 332–373.

society finds itself squeezed by a process which is deeply bureaucratic while, at the same time, unable to protect it against the market imperative. With a view to overcome the bureaucratic threat, the social OMC needs to undergo a wide range of legal, political and constitutional reforms. The economic threat will be addressed further below as well as in the next chapter.

7.4.1. LEGAL REFORMS

Insufficient attention is paid by DDP enthusiasts to the power struggles that take place at the local level. While increasing participation, that is, reducing exclusion, is precisely one of their central concerns, they fail to see that direct deliberation could, on the contrary, have exclusionary effects if steps are not taken to correct power asymmetries.[98] There is, according to Magnette, an inequality bias attached to direct deliberation.[99] Most citizens do not have the time, the will or the knowledge to participate in directly-deliberative experiments. They prefer to leave the business of participating to functional representatives.[100] As for bureaucrats, limited time and staff allocated to direct-deliberation often means that consultations are directed to insiders, leaving less powerful and more critical groups voiceless.[101] These theoretical concerns are well grounded and they fit with the practical disappointments of stakeholders' involvement in the social OMC.

Equalising stakeholders' resources and strengthening national administrations' capacity to deal with their involvement would be a first step towards correcting the power asymmetries which plague the social OMC at Member States' level. In that respect, it is important that the *Progress* axis of the new EU Programme for Employment and Social Innovation (EaSI) supports awareness-raising projects devised by domestic CSOs while developing the capacity of key European networks of social CSOs to mobilise national affiliates.[102] However, funding the capacity of civil society to engage with the social OMC would be worthless without a *legal* strategy aiming at opening national administrations to its influence. Cohen and Arato indeed

98 Büchs, 'How Legitimate is the Open Method of Coordination?' (n 54) 779.

99 P Magnette, 'Democracy in the European Union: Why and How to Combine Representation and Participation?' in S Smismans (ed), *Civil Society and Legitimate European Governance* (Edward Elgar 2006) 32–36.

100 S Smismans, 'Civil Society and European Governance: The Interdisciplinary Challenge of Reflexive Deliberative Polyarchy' in S Smismans (ed), *Civil Society and Legitimate European Governance* (Edward Elgar 2006) 306.

101 Kröger, 'The End of Democracy as we Know it?' (n 46) 579.

102 See Regulation (EU) 1296/2013 of the European Parliament and of the Council of 11 December 2013 on a European Union Programme for Employment and Social Innovation ("EaSI") and amending Decision 283/2010/EU establishing a European Progress Microfinance Facility for employment and social inclusion [2013] OJ L347/238, Article 16.

claim that the bureaucratic rationality of the administrative subsystem needs to be tamed by some kind of reflexive law. They call for a strategy which would democratise administration through procedures upholding the right of citizens to participate in decision-making. This would make administrative governance sensitive to the concerns of civil society by securing its involvement therein as a matter of right rather than power.[103] Earlier versions of DDP were the first to account for bureaucratic power when they proposed right-based safeguards as a guarantee against it and asked courts, taking on a procedural role, to uphold the participatory rights of citizens.[104] The challenge is now for the social OMC to retrieve that legal-critical edge.

Proponents of the social OMC were initially reluctant to frame reform proposals in legal terms. They felt that legally guaranteeing direct-deliberation might be counterproductive because new governance tools such as the social OMC stand in opposition to European law's values and premises; soft instruments of that kind were precisely meant to depart from the values traditionally related to legality.[105] This corresponds to what Dawson calls the first wave of new governance literature where governance could only be understood as external to law.[106] The reflexive reform strategy which inspires the SPC is characteristic of a second wave where law finds itself absorbed by new governance in the process of taking-up its experimentalist features, with the result that strengthening the social OMC means building on past experience rather than looking up to traditional rule of law virtues for reform.[107]

The time has come for the establishment of a third, complementary, relationship between law and new governance, where legal rules would provide the institutional infrastructure through which the social OMC can at last realise its experimentalist promises.[108] Prior reforms of the social OMC already point

103 On the use of reflexive law with a view to secure the influence of civil society over the administrative system, see Cohen and Arato, *Civil Society and Political Theory* (n 94) 480–487.

104 Dorf and Sabel, 'A Constitution of Democratic Experimentalism' (n 19) 340, 388–404.

105 J Scott and DM Trubek, 'Mind the Gap: Law and New Approaches to Governance in the European Union' (2002) 8 ELJ 1, 8–9; G De Búrca and J Scott, 'Introduction: New Governance, Law and Constitutionalism' in G De Búrca and J Scott (eds), *Law and New Governance in the EU and the US* (Hart 2006) 4–6. See also DM Trubek and LG Trubek, 'The Open Method of Co-Ordination and the Debate Over "Hard" and "Soft" Law' in J Zeitlin, P Pochet and L Magnusson (eds), *The Open Method of Co-Ordination in Action: the European Employment and Social Inclusion Strategies* (PIE-Peter Lang 2005).

106 M Dawson, 'Three Waves of New Governance in the European Union' (2010) 36 EL Rev 208, 211–213.

107 Ibid 213–216. On the absorption thesis, see N Walker and G De Búrca, 'Reconceiving Law and New Governance' (2006–2007) 13 CJEL 519, 522.

108 Ibid 217. See also G De Búrca and J Scott, 'Introduction: New Governance, Law and Constitutionalism' in G De Búrca and J Scott (eds), *Law and New Governance in the EU and the US* (Hart 2006) 6–9.

in that direction.[109] The path of *uniformity* has been trodden, with the setting up of common objectives and indicators with due respect for the diversity of local circumstances. The transition towards uniformity is particularly clear regarding the participatory objective of the social inclusion process which has been streamlined into a common social objective. As part of the commitments made in the EPP, the Commission now elaborates common European guidelines on stakeholders' involvement with a view to monitor and report on Member States' performance in that regard.[110] Ensuring the *stability* of the rules of the game has also justified the move from yearly to three-yearly national strategies, while the successive reforms through which the process has gone nevertheless attest to its adaptability over time. A concern for *clarifying* the process and its interaction with the economic and employment coordination processes has finally pushed for streamlining and rationalisation, while maintaining the autonomy of the social inclusion process within the social OMC has remained a core objective.

Strikingly, this shows how the values of uniformity, stability and clarity, usually associated with legal rules, have been rediscovered in the process of reforming the social OMC. Strengthening the social OMC entails a difficult balancing exercise, but what is still missing is a proper legal dimension that would make flexible governance strong enough to resist bureaucratic threats to its democratic aspirations. What shape could *legalisation* of the social OMC take? The Commission and some experts have suggested that greater use be made of recommendations and framework directives so as to formalise convergence of views whenever it arises from the social OMC.[111] It was further proposed that the Commission be able to make individual recommendations to Member States that deviate from the social OMC discipline.[112] Albeit this remains legalisation with a soft touch – recommendations produce legal effects but do not bind, while directives leave Member states free to choose the means by which to attain EU objectives–[113], the SPC did not consider this a serious option in its last opinion.

---

109 See Commission, 'Strengthening the Social Dimension of the Lisbon Strategy' (n 8); Commission, 'Working Together, Working Better' (n 8).

110 Commission, 'The European Platform against Poverty and Social Exclusion' (n 78) 17.

111 Commission, 'A Renewed Commitment to Social Europe' (n 84) 5–6; H Frazer and E Marlier, 'Strengthening Social Inclusion in the Europe 2020 Strategy by Learning from the Past' in E Marlier and D Natali (eds), *Europe 2020: Towards a More Social EU?* (PIE-Peter Lang 2010) 247; H Frazer, E Marlier and I Nicaise, *A Social Inclusion Roadmap for Europe 2020* (Garant 2010) 34–35. A precedent for this exists with Commission Recommendation of 3 October 2008 on the active inclusion of people excluded from the labour market [2008] OJ L307/11.

112 Frazer and Marlier, 'Building a Stronger EU Social Inclusion Process' (n 86) 6; Frazer and Marlier, 'Strengthening Social Inclusion in the Europe 2020 Strategy' (n 111) 239; Frazer et al, *A Social Inclusion Roadmap for Europe 2020* (n 111) 33.

113 See Article 288 TFEU.

That is a mistake because EU law of that kind could be used to tame the social OMC's bureaucratic tendencies at Member States' level. The Commission could, for instance, address individual recommendations to Member States that neglect the social OMC's participatory objectives, while the voluntary guidelines on stakeholders' involvement that it elaborates might become a general recommendation on key governance issues. A more radical step would be to legalise the voluntary guidelines into a directive akin to those implementing the Aarhus convention on access to information, public participation in decision-making and access to justice in environmental matters.[114] This would be consistent with the need to maintain flexibility as directives, especially framework directives, leave a wide margin of appreciation to Member States. By analogy with the Aarhus convention,[115] the public would be given a right of access to social information together with the right to participate in the elaboration and implementation of NSRs under the control of a court of law to which access would be granted for the purpose of securing those rights. Public participation in the social OMC would be scrutinised as to its legality by national judges with the possibility of asking the ECJ for a preliminary ruling on the interpretation of the directive, while the Commission could start infringement proceedings against recalcitrant Member States.

Even if legal reforms of that kind would have the advantage of bringing the social OMC under the rule of law, one may doubt their feasibility. For, Article 153 TFEU explicitly prohibits any kind of harmonisation, procedural or other, in the field of social inclusion and social protection. It is, moreover, certain that most Member States would find this move politically unacceptable. Experience of the social OMC finally shows that involving stakeholders is a messy and time consuming affair,[116] and, as such, represents a huge human investment for an administration which is often tight with resources.[117] OMC processes have been simplified over time with a view to ease the administrative burden imposed on national authorities. Still, legal proceduralism might have the undesired effect of paralysing the administrations in charge of running the social OMC.

---

114 Directive 2003/4/EC of the European Parliament and of the Council of 28 January 2003 on public access to environmental information and repealing Council Directive 90/313/EEC [2003] OJ L41/26; Directive 2003/35/EC of the European Parliament and of the Council of 26 May 2003 providing for public participation in respect of the drawing up of certain plans and programmes relating to the environment and amending with regard to public participation and access to justice Council Directives 85/337/EEC and 96/61/EC [2003] OJ L156/17.

115 Convention on Access to Information, Public Participation in Decision-Making and Access to Justice in Environmental Matters, signed in Aarhus, Denmark, 25 June 1998, United Nations, Treaty Series, vol 2161, 447.

116 See W Scheuerman, 'Democratic Experimentalism or Capitalist Synchronization? Critical Reflections on Directly Deliberative Polyarchy' (2004) 17 Can J L & Jurisprudence 101, 118.

117 Frazer et al, *A Social Inclusion Roadmap for Europe 2020* (n 111) 203.

The previous considerations impede, but they do not definitely preclude, legal reforms of the kind advocated above. What is legally feasible may be subject to Treaty changes. Besides, convergent application of common participatory guidelines might, in the long run, soften up Member States' political disagreement so that a recommendation or even a directive on governance issues would become acceptable. Finally, where to strike the balance between the efficient use of administrative resources and the slowness that comes with democratic processes remains a political issue better settled by the people's representatives than by the bureaucrats themselves. If the EU legislature does not manage to strike that balance in a directive, national parliaments should step in.

7.4.2. POLITICAL REFORMS

The critics of DDP accuse it of dismantling some of the most notable features of modern representative democracy.[118] While parliamentary oversight is the best means we have found so far to keep bureaucratic power in check, DDP replaces it with a new model of horizontal accountability through peer review which is ill-suited to perform that function.[119] On the contrary, Cohen and Arato consider that the political society of parliaments and parties are the primary means for civil society to control the administration.[120] For, without a strong parliament acting as a receptacle for the deliberations of citizens in civil society, politics hardly leaves the remit of a narrow circle of stakeholders with the time, money and energy to find interest in such matters.

The above criticism is valid if we take DDP to be accountability without a sovereign.[121] Yet, it might come as too radical a statement once we accept that DDP was not initially meant to replace the institutions of modern representative government but only to transform them.[122] In the American context, Dorf and Sabel have explained that the National Congress should authorise and finance experiments in whatever field it finds appropriate, whereas its loss of supervisory powers ought to be compensated by democratising central executive agencies through a procedure akin the APA notice and comment procedure.[123] They have also claimed that DDP should reinvigorate, rather than replace, local politics by making public officials accountable to a public which is informed, through

118 Scheuerman, 'Democratic Experimentalism or Capitalist Synchronization?' (n 116) 116.

119 Büchs, 'How Legitimate is the Open Method of Coordination?' (n 54) 779.

120 See JL Cohen, 'Civic Innovation in America: Towards a Reflexive Politics' (2003) 12 The Good Society 56, 60–61.

121 See CF Sabel and WH Simon, 'Epilogue: Accountability without Sovereignty' in G De Búrca and J Scott (eds), *Law and New Governance in the EU and the US* (Hart 2006).

122 Dorf and Sabel, 'A Constitution of Democratic Experimentalism' (n 19) 340.

123 Ibid 442–444.

benchmarking, by the doing of their peers.[124] This critical edge somehow got lost as democratic experimentalism crossed the Atlantic, for parliaments, both national and European, have taken a backseat in the development of the OMC and current reform proposals reassert their importance only reluctantly.[125]

The time has come for a political reform of the social OMC, where the Parliament, as it requests,[126] would be fully involved on equal terms with the Council and the Commission. 'Co-decision' of the objectives pursued by the social OMC together with parliamentary scrutiny of the SPC's activities would be enshrined in an interinstitutional agreement. At the same time, the SPC would democratise its relationship with organised civil society through a procedure akin the APA's notice and comment procedure. A softer alternative could be for the Commission to apply its 'general principles and minimum standards' when consulting civil society prior to taking part in the SPC activities or for the SPC itself to adopt such standards.[127] Meanwhile, national parliaments would be well advised to seize the information generated by the social OMC as an opportunity to increase scrutiny of their executive, by benchmarking its failures and successes against those of other Member States.[128] This is a move that the EU could encourage by providing parliamentary committees with financial incentives to engage with the social OMC and by setting the example with the European Parliament taking a greater role in OMC processes.[129]

7.4.3. CONSTITUTIONAL REFORMS

Would the legal-political reform strategy articulated above gain any added value by being enshrined in the Treaties which make the constitutional charter of the EU? This possibility surfaced during the debates of the Convention tasked with drafting the Constitutional Treaty. A relatively broad agreement emerged among the working groups as to the necessity to include the OMC within the

124 Gerstenberg and Sabel, 'Directly-Deliberative Polyarchy: An Institutional Ideal for Europe?' (n 17) 341.

125 See, however, M Tsakatika, 'A Parliamentary Dimension for EU Soft Governance' (2007) 29 Journal of European Integration 549; Dawson, 'Transforming into What?' (n 71) 420–430.

126 European Parliament, 'Resolution of 15 March 2006 on Social Protection and Social Inclusion' (n 58) para 61.

127 See Commission, 'Towards a Reinforced Culture of Consultation and Dialogue – General Principles and Minimum Standards for Consultation of Interested Parties by the Commission' (Communication) COM (2002) 704 final.

128 A Cygan, 'The Parliamentarisation of EU Decision-Making? The Impact of the Treaty of Lisbon on National Parliaments' (2011) 36 EL Rev 478, 496. See also F Duina and T Raunio, 'The Open Method of Coordination and National Parliaments: Further Marginalization or New Opportunities?' (2007) 14 JEPP 489.

129 Dawson, 'Transforming into What?' (n 71) 429.

Constitutional Treaty.[130] A solution of the kind would have endowed the method with legitimacy and clarity[131] and would have been an opportunity to address some persisting weaknesses of this new governance tool, particularly regarding transparency and wide participation.[132]

The initial consensus quickly ran against two kinds of arguments.[133] The first was that the OMC would displace the use of hard legislation in fields where the EU is already competent. The second was that that embedding the OMC into the Treaties would rigidify the instrument in a way that would undermine its flexibility. Nevertheless, both concerns could have been met through a generic provision defining only the fundamental characteristics of the method and specifying that it would not undermine or weaken the existing EU *acquis*, nor become a permanent substitute for Union legislative action permissible under the Constitutional Treaty.[134] This generic provision could have conferred a clear consultative role to the European Parliament and included explicit requirements for transparency and participation in all OMC processes. It was also proposed to include a specific article on the social OMC so as to preserve the soft *acquis* in the fields of social inclusion and social protection.[135]

In the end, the above concerns prevailed during the final negotiations so that no generic OMC provision can be found in the revised Treaties. Only in Article 5 TFEU, remains a vague reference to coordination in the field of economic, employment and social policies. Regarding the latter, the Union *may* take measures to ensure coordination, whereas it *shall* do so in the two other cases. The relationship between that provision and the more detailed Treaty articles on social policy is not entirely clear.[136] The most natural linkage might be with Article 156 TFEU which has been revised with a view to empower the Commission to take further initiatives to develop some key features of the social OMC (guidelines, indicators, exchange of best practice, periodic monitoring and evaluation), albeit without referring thereto by name.[137] At the same time, a significant democratic improvement is that the practice of informing the European Parliament as to social OMC's developments is now legally guaranteed by Article 156 TFEU.

130 G De Búrca and J Zeitlin, 'Constitutionalizing the Open Method of Coordination: What Should the Convention Propose?' (2003) CEPS Policy Brief no. 31, 1.

131 M Tsakatika, 'The Open Method of Co-Ordination in the European Convention: An Opportunity Lost?' in L Dobson and A Follesdal (eds), *Political Theory and the European Constitution* (Routledge 2004) 94.

132 G De Búrca, 'The Constitutional Challenge of New Governance in the European Union' (2003) 28 EL Rev 814, 830–839.

133 De Búrca and Zeitlin, 'Constitutionalizing the Open Method of Coordination' (n 130) 2.

134 Ibid 2–3.

135 Ibid 3–4.

136 P Craig and G De Búrca, *EU Law: Text, Cases, and Materials* (5th edn, OUP 2011) 88.

137 Zeitlin, 'Social Europe and Experimentalist Governance' (n 26) 240.

This remains a very light constitutional foundation for the wider legal-political strategy advocated by this book. As to *legal* reforms, stakeholders' involvement and transparency are not among the constitutive features of the process mentioned in Article 156 TFEU. There is, moreover, no specific Treaty basis for the Council or the Commission to make recommendations to Member States within the framework of the social OMC; nor is the flexibility clause, which had been used for adopting the 1992 Council Recommendations on social protection,[138] available since the Union is now competent in the social field.[139] When adopting its 2008 Recommendation on the active inclusion of people excluded from the labour market,[140] the Commission had overcome these legal constraints by relying on Article 211 TEC which provided that the Commission could formulate recommendations on matters dealt with in the Treaty if deemed necessary.[141] This provision has been replaced by Article 292 TFEU which stipulates that the Commission may adopt recommendations *in the specific cases provided for in the Treaties*. If read literally, this article precludes the Commission from making further recommendations based on the social OMC. However, this has not prevented the Commission from recently adopting a Recommendation on child poverty which takes the exact same article as its legal basis,[142] which raises question as to its legality. Anyway, 153 TFEU explicitly prohibits legislative harmonisation, procedural or other, regarding social exclusion and the modernisation of social protection systems, so that a recommendation arising from the social OMC could never be transformed into a directive.

As to *political* reforms, the Parliament is informed, whereas it was asking for full involvement on equal terms with the Council and Commission. National parliaments are not mentioned in Article 156 TFEU, nor are social OMC documents among the 'draft legislative acts' which are forwarded to them as part of the subsidiarity monitoring exercise.[143] Article 160 TFEU compels the SPC to establish appropriate contacts with the social partners, but new Article 11 TEU does not oblige it to enter into a dialogue with civil society. The SPC is now bound to respect the right of access to documents. Yet, publicity is still confined to the Council when acting in a legislative capacity.[144] All the above suffices to highlight how inimical the current Treaty framework is to new governance processes such as the social OMC.

---

138 [1992] OJ L245/46; [1992] OJ L245/49.

139 See Article 352 TFEU which requires that the flexibility clause be used only when the Treaties have not provided the necessary powers.

140 [2008] OJ L307/11.

141 On the difficult choice of legal basis for this Recommendation, see Armstrong, *Governing Social Inclusion* (n 68) 279–284.

142 Commission Recommendation 2013/112/EU of 20 February 2013 Investing in children: breaking the cycle of disadvantage [2013] OJ L59/5.

143 See Protocol no. 2 on the application of the principles of subsidiarity and proportionality, annexed to the Lisbon treaty [2012] OJ C326/206.

144 See new Article 15 TFEU.

7.5. CONCLUSIONS

This chapter has illustrated the practical limits of the social OMC as a tool for radicalising participatory democracy in the EU. Contrary to theoretical expectations (*7.2*), the social OMC is not directly-deliberative, nor is it polyarchic (*7.3*). The reflexive reform strategy embraced by the SPC in its latest opinion will not succeed in bridging this expectation gap because it merely tries to approximate DDP without questioning DDP itself as an ideal. A critical appraisal of DDP informed by the tripartite framework of Cohen and Arato, on the contrary, reveals that there are bureaucratic and economic barriers which prevent DDP from realising its own socio-democratic promises. The social OMC very much provides a practical instance of DDP facing those theoretical limits, for it remains a bureaucratic process which fails to protect civil society from the market imperative. With a view to counter the bureaucratic threat, a legal/political/constitutional reform strategy has been articulated so that civil society could regain control over the social OMC. As regards legal reform in particular, it is a kind of reflexivity different from the one embraced by the SPC which is advocated. Rather than learning from its own experience, the social OMC would enact stronger procedural rules aiming at securing civil society's influence therein as a matter of right rather than favour (*7.4*).

Provided the above-mentioned reforms are implemented, it is claimed that radical participatory democracy might become a reality in social Europe. This offers an interesting point of contrast with the CM. As the previous chapter illustrates, the civil dialogue cannot be the magic cure for the democratic ailments of the CM. The CM is by design hierarchical and as such hardly amenable to wide participation so that any attempt at embedding participatory democracy therein will necessarily entail that a compromise be struck. A successful instance of such a compromise is provided by the commission's consultation regime which manages to tread a soft path between democracy and effectiveness. On the contrary, the social OMC as DDP requires no such compromise for it combines a new kind of radical democracy with effective problem-solving capacities unavailable under the CM. The social OMC in action has yet to fully exploit that potential. The reforms which have been proposed would surely make the social OMC stronger and better equipped to realise its democratic promises but they offer no guarantee that the social OMC would become truly effective in the sense advocated by Cohen and Arato. In line with their tripartite framework, effectiveness depends on the social OMC's capacity to defend civil society against the market imperative. Whether it can do so considering the constraints set by Europe 2020 within the context of the strengthened European economic governance will be critically assessed in the next, conclusive, chapter.

CHAPTER 8
LOOKING BACK – MOVING FORWARD

8.1. INTRODUCTION

Relying on the tripartite framework of Cohen and Arato,[1] this book takes the view that civil society should be seen as a pluralist sphere of participation between state and market wherein deliberative democracy realises its full potential. Democratisation proceeds whenever civil society manages to assert influence over state and market without falling prey to their colonising tendencies. This emancipatory process has so far taken place within the context of national welfare states. The fundamental question raised by the turn to civil society is whether multilevel social Europe will continue this emancipatory process or, on the contrary, bring about its collapse under the colonising forces of power and money. This raises two sets of questions which have been explored in detail through the case studies contained in *Chapters 4 to 7*, the first pertaining to the reflexive tendencies of European economic law and the second to the participatory-democratic credentials of social Europe.

Whether multilevel social Europe protects civil society from state and market forces is an issue that cannot be fully addressed without answering a last question relating to the *effectiveness* of EU social law and policy making. In line with our tripartite framework, assessing the effectiveness of social Europe comes down to asking whether it is strong enough to protect civil society from the colonising tendencies of European economic integration. This issue necessarily comes at the end of our inquiry and finds itself deeply intertwined with the two previous questions. What social Europe *must* achieve in order to provide effective protection against markets very much depends on the constraints negative integration imposes on civil society in the first place. What social Europe *can* legitimately hope to achieve very much hinges upon its ability to draw democratic support from its dialogue with civil society. This final chapter is therefore an opportunity to bring the threads of this book together.

Looking back, this book' findings as to the reflexive capacity of European economic law (*8.2*) and democratic support available for social Europe (*8.3*) will be summarised. The limits of those findings will be exposed as well as

---

1 JL Cohen and A Arato, *Civil Society and Political Theory* (MIT Press 1992) chap 9.

their relevance for the issue of effective social Europe. Moving forward, the *effectiveness* of multilevel social Europe will be appraised through a preliminary assessment of the achievements of the *hard* CM and the *soft* OMC. Our main conclusion will be that, taken together, EU social law and policy making are currently unable to protect civil society from the market imperative of European economic integration which is growing all the more stronger in the context of the current euro crisis (*8.4*).

8.2. EUROPEAN ECONOMIC LAW: COLONISING?

The case for a European economic constitution that systematically threatens national social policy has been exaggerated.[2] On the contrary, European economic law contains reflexive elements that make it receptive to the social values embedded in national welfare states. This reflexivity has been demonstrated from a *civil* perspective which emphasises the importance of active citizens coming together with a view to provide welfare outside state and market structures. The impact of European economic law on this dimension of welfare delivery had so far been overlooked, although there is a growing body of case-law that directly addresses the issue.[3]

As illustrated in *Chapter 4*, internal market law does not prevent Member States from erecting their social welfare systems along civil lines if they so whish. The reflexive capacity of internal market law manifests itself through two mechanisms: on the one hand, the ECJ carefully draws the state/market boundary according a 'social solidarity' benchmark which, in some cases, suffices to shield the delivery of social services by CSOs from internal market rules, while, on the other, it condones an inventive use of the proportionality test so as to balance civil with economic concerns.

As shown in *Chapter 5*, European competition law does not oblige Member States to withdraw financial subsidies granted to CSOs; nor does it preclude CSOs from concluding anti-competitive agreements when their social objectives so require. European competition law reflects the social values promoted by CSOs with the help of the same two mechanisms found in internal market law. On the one hand, the ECJ limits the wide jurisdiction of competition rules over CSOs as undertakings by resorting to a 'social solidarity' shield. On the other hand, substantive competition rules strike a balance between economic and

2 K Armstrong, *Governing Social Inclusion: Europeanization through Policy Coordination* (OUP 2010) 226.

3 See C-70/95 *Sodemare SA, Anni Azzurri Holding SpA and Anni Azzurri Rezzato Srl v Regione Lombardia* [1997] ECR I-3395; Case C-475/99 *Firma Ambulanz Glöckner v Landkreis Südwestpfalz* [2001] ECR I-8089; C-113/13 *Azienda sanitaria locale n. 5 "Spezzino" and Others v San Lorenzo Soc. coop. sociale and Croce Verde Cogema cooperativa sociale Onlus* (ECJ, 11 December 2014).

social goals: CSOs may conclude anti-competitive agreements that are necessary for the pursuit of social objectives, while Member States may subsidise civil society where it is needed for reaching objectives compatible with the internal market or necessary for the delivery of SGEI.

These are important findings from the perspective of this book which investigates whether participatory democracy can succeed in multilevel social Europe. For, it could hardly be the case if organised civil society, on which social Europe relies for its democratisation, was colonised by the market imperative of European economic law. Developing a civil approach on European economic law to its full extent would, however, require that the limits of our findings be discussed and further avenues for research be explored.

For practical reasons, our analysis has omitted several parts of European economic law that might be relevant for organised civil society. Free movement of goods, workers and capital has been left aside. So has Article 102 TFEU on abuse of dominant position.[4] Our aim has not been to provide a comprehensive assessment of the impact of European economic law on CSOs but only to highlight, through relevant case studies, key issues that could frame future debates.

Some may also question whether focusing on European economic law makes sense at all considering that, as is the case with educational services,[5] the Treaty provisions on Union citizenship are often used to subvert the ring-fencing of non-economic activities in the ECJ's case law.[6] The remark is valid but one should bear in mind that European economic law remains the only source of rights and obligations for legal, as opposed to natural, persons. European companies are not EU citizens but they are treated the same as EU citizens for the purpose of applying internal market law,[7] while European competition law only applies to undertakings.[8] Focusing on European economic law therefore seemed like the most logical approach for a book which is about *organised* civil society rather than EU citizenship.

Why then assess European economic law as a threat against civil society, while at the same time overlooking the opportunity it offers for CSOs to operate in a bigger and more exciting market?[9] European economic law might enable

4 For the application of the latter article to CSOs, see Case C-475/99 *Firma Ambulanz Glöckner v Landkreis Südwestpfalz* [2001] ECR I-08089.

5 See, eg, Case C-76/05 *Herbert Schwarz and Marga Gootjes-Schwarz v Finanzamt Bergisch Gladbach* [2007] ECR I-6849; Case C-318/05 *Commission v Germany* [2007] ECR I-6957.

6 S O'Leary, 'Free Movement of Persons and Services' in P Craig and G De Búrca (eds), *The Evolution of EU Law* (2nd edn, OUP 2011) 532.

7 Article 54 TFEU.

8 See Articles 101, 102, 106, 107 TFEU.

9 6 Perri, 'European Competition Law and the Non-Profit Sector' (1992) 3 Voluntas 215, 243. See also I Wendt and A Gideon, 'Services of General Interest Provision through the Third Sector under EU Competition Law Constraints: The Example of Organising Healthcare in England, Wales and the Netherlands' in D Schiek, U Liebert and H Schneider (eds), *European Economic and Social Constitutionalism after the Treaty of Lisbon* (CUP 2011).

civil society to act across national borders but the Treaties still provide an inauspicious place for the creation of such a legally enabling environment.[10] Article 49 TFEU states that:

> [f]reedom of establishment shall include the right to take up and pursue activities as self employed persons and to set up and manage undertakings, in particular companies or firms within the meaning of the second paragraph of Article 54, under the conditions laid down for its own nationals by the law of the country where such establishment is effected (...).

Article 54 TFEU specifies that '"[c]ompanies or firms" means companies or firms constituted under civil or commercial law, including cooperative societies, and other legal persons governed by public or private law, save for those which are non-profit-making'. The same limitation applies for the right to provide services by virtue of Article 62 TFEU.

The scope to be given to the latter provision remains a bone of contention. Should it be understood widely as refusing all non-profit-making organisations the freedom of establishment and the right to provide services in other Member States, or more narrowly as disregarding their non-economic activities only?[11] The ECJ has condoned a narrow interpretation of the exclusion in *Commission v Belgium*,[12] ruling that a law requiring the presence of a Belgian member in the administration of an association or a minimum, and majority, presence of members of Belgian nationality in order for the legal personality of an association to be recognised, was contrary to the freedom of establishment.[13] Besides, the ECJ has ruled in *Stauffer*[14] and subsequent cases[15] that CSOs may rely on the free movement of capital in order to challenge discriminatory access to other Member States' preferential tax schemes. In line with this case law, the Commission has proposed that a Statute for a European Foundation be created so as to remove the obstacles that foundations face when operating across

---

10 OB Breen, 'EU Regulation of Charitable Organizations: The Politics of Legally Enabling Civil Society' (2008) 10 IJNFPL 50, 61.

11 For a narrow, functional, interpretation of Article 54 TFEU, see Perri, 'European Competition Law and the Non-Profit Sector' (n 9) 230; P Craig and G De Búrca, *EU Law: Text, Cases, and Materials* (5th edn, OUP 2011) 780; S Lombardo, 'Some Reflections on Freedom of Establishment of Non-Profit Entities in the European Union' (2013) 14 EBOR 225. For a wide, organic, interpretation of the same terms contained in Article 13 of the Sixth VAT Directive ([1977] OJ L145/1), see Case C-174/00 *Kennemer Golf & Country Club v Staatssecretaris van Financiën* [2002] ECR I-03293, paras 16–23.

12 Case C-172/98 *Commission v Belgium* [1999] ECR I-03999. See, however, *Sodemare* (n 3) para 25.

13 Ibid para 14.

14 Case C-386/04 *Centro di Musicologia Walter Stauffer v Finanzamt München für Körperschaften* [2006] ECR I-08203.

15 Case C-318/07 *Hein Persche v Finanzamt Lüdenscheid* [2009] ECR I-00359; Case C-10/10 *Commission v Austria* [2011] ECR I-05389; Case C-25/10 *Missionswerk Werner Heukelbach eV v Belgian State* [2011] ECR I-00497.

borders within the Union, but this proposal has recently been withdrawn after failure to reach unanimity within the Council.[16] A similar statute was proposed for European associations but was also withdrawn by the Commission in 2006 due to a lack of progress in the legislative process.[17]

It might finally appear reductionist to present state-based social solidarity as a shield protecting organised civil society from European economic law whereas the welfare state will often colonise organised civil society in the name of its own protection.[18] The extent to which the bureaucratic welfare state interferes with the autonomy of CSOs is an empirical question which falls outside the ambit of this book. The answer will necessarily depend on the modalities of the relationship that a state chooses to establish with organised civil society. What is important for our purpose is that European economic law adopts a neutral stance on the issue and leaves Member States free to define this relationship on their own terms. Once they decide to restrict the provision of social services to CSOs as opposed to market operators in accordance with the *Sodemare* case,[19] Member States may implement that preference through any administrative means they deem appropriate such as public contracts, service concessions or licensing regimes provided that they respect internal market law.[20] They enjoy the same freedom when funding civil society. Member States may use subsidies, preferential taxation or public contracts so long as they respect state aid law.[21]

With the aforementioned caveats in mind, it can be concluded that European economic law does not colonise organised civil society as the proponents of negative integration would expect us to believe.[22] European economic law rather exercises self-restraint through careful policing of the state/market boundary according to a 'social solidarity' benchmark and cautious use of the proportionality test at the justificatory stage. This is in line with the conclusions of recent studies regarding the impact of European economic law on more traditional aspects of welfare policy.[23] These studies

---

16 Commission, 'Proposal for a Council Regulation on the Statute for a European Foundation (FE)' COM (2012) 35 final.

17 Commission, 'Proposal for a Council Regulation (EEC) on the Statute for a European Association' COM (91) 273 final.

18 See J Habermas, *The Theory of Communicative Action /Vol.2, Lifeworld and System: A Critique of Functionalist Reason* (Polity Press 1987) 361; Cohen and Arato, *Civil Society and Political Theory* (n 1) 470.

19 *Sodemare* (n 3).

20 Commission, 'Guide to the Application of the European Union Rules on State Aid, Public Procurement and the Internal Market to Services of General Economic Interest, and in particular to Social Services of General Interest' (Staff Working Document) SWD (2013) 53 final/2, 88–89, 95, 100, 105.

21 Ibid 39.

22 For the opposite view, see FW Scharpf, *Governing Europe: Effective and Democratic?* (OUP 1999) 50–71.

23 K Armstrong, *Governing Social Inclusion: Europeanization through Policy Coordination* (OUP 2010) 226–228; L Nistor, *Public Services and the European Union: Healthcare, Health Insurance and Education Services* (TMC Asser Press 2011) 399–412.

agree that European economic law is endowed with a reflexive, that is to say, self-limiting capacity which enables it to strike a balance between social and economic concerns. European economic law is a reflexive legal system in the sense that it limits the impact of the economic imperative on the social realm within which civil society can flourish, by resorting to a social solidarity shield which as much valid for social services provided by the state as it is for social services provided by CSOs. For those social services which nevertheless enter the scope of European economic law, proportionality is the procedural device through which social and economic concerns are balanced, to such an extent that economic restrictions will be accepted so long as they are necessary for the pursuit of social goals. This is an important finding from the perspective of this chapter, for the reflexive capacity of European economic law will lower the expectations we place upon effective social Europe as a counterweight to negative integration.

The new social provisions of the Lisbon Treaty might even further tip the balance in favour of national social policies. According to new Article 3 TFEU, the Union shall have as an objective the establishment of 'a highly competitive social market economy, aiming at full employment and social progress (...)'.[24] This ambitious objective does not translate into an extension of the EU's law-making powers in the social field.[25] This rhetorical flourish does not remain toothless though, for Article 9 TFEU contains a new social mainstreaming clause obliging the Union to take into consideration social concerns when defining and implementing its policies and actions. This social clause tallies with the duty for the Union to respect the social rights contained in the now legally binding Charter of Fundamental Rights.[26] Another legal change comes from Protocol no. 26 which introduces for the first time into EU primary law the notion of 'non-economic services of general interest', only to reassert that the EU cannot in any way affect Member States' competence in that field.[27] Taken together, these provisions might prompt the ECJ to give more consideration to social concerns when applying and interpreting European economic law in the future.[28]

Our optimistic conclusions about the reflexive capacity of European economic law call for a final note of caution. For, there are also indirect *de*

24 See also Article 2 TFEU for a new reference to solidarity as a value of the Union.

25 M Dawson and B De Witte, 'The EU Legal Framework of Social Inclusion and Social Protection: Between the Lisbon Strategy and the Lisbon Treaty' in B Cantillon, H Verschueren and P Ploscar (eds), *Social Inclusion and Social Protection in the EU: Interactions between Law and Policy* (Intersentia 2012) 54.

26 Charter of Fundamental Rights of the European Union [2012] OJ C326/393, esp Articles 14, 34–36.

27 Protocol no. 26 on services of general interest [2012] OJ C326/308.

28 Dawson and De Witte, 'The EU Legal Framework of Social Inclusion and Social Protection' (n 25) 55; E Szyszczak, U Neergaard and JW van de Gronden, 'Conclusions' in U Neergaard, E Szyszczak, JW van de Gronden and M Krajewski (eds), *Social Services of General Interest in the EU* (TMC Asser Press 2013) 604–608.

facto pressures that the European process of economic integration imposes on national social policy.[29] It is often claimed that Member States are engaging into 'a race to the bottom' as a consequence of deepening the single market, although evidence of social dumping actually occurring between Member States remains scarce.[30] In our view, a more pressing issue might relate to the Europe-wide turn to budgetary rigour in the context of the current euro crisis. It is not the purpose of this book to undertake a systematic analysis of the measures that have been taken with a view to save the euro but only to highlight potential sources of conflict with national social policy.[31]

In the wake of the financial crisis of 2008 and of the economic and social crises which followed from 2009, Member States of the EU – and in particular those of the euro area – have injected large sums of money into their financial and economic sectors, with the inevitable consequence that budget deficits – and so public debt – have started to rise to unprecedented high levels.[32] Ironically enough, the financial sector that triggered this chain of events eventually started to lose confidence in the Euro area so that collective measures had to be taken with a view to bail out Member States that were unable to finance themselves on the credit market (previously through the European Financial Stabilisation Mechanism and the European Financial Stability Facility and currently through the European Stability Mechanism (ESM)).[33] Most importantly for our purpose, a new set of regulations, procedures and institutions known as 'new European economic governance' was set up to overcome the sovereign debt crisis.[34] As highlighted by Majone, the aim of this new regime 'is to ensure that members of the euro zone fulfil three main duties: to achieve a balanced budget; to avoid an excessive government deficit; and to prevent or correct macroeconomic imbalances'.[35]

As to *balanced budget*, it was already an obligation before the euro crisis that Member States sharing the euro currency submit every year a 'Stability Programme', while Member States that have not adopted the euro submit a 'Convergence Programme'. These documents are used by the Commission and by the Council to assess whether Member States are on track towards reaching

---

29 See S Leibfried, 'Social Policy: Left to the Judges and the Markets?' in H Wallace, M Pollack and A Young (eds), *Policy-Making in the European Union* (6th edn, OUP 2010) 274–277.

30 See, eg, G Majone, *Europe as the Would-Be World Power: the EU at Fifty* (CUP 2009) 134–138; C Hay and D Wincott, *The Political Economy of European Welfare Capitalism* (Palgrave Macmillan 2012) 66–96.

31 For a historical overview, see C Degryse, 'The New European Economic Governance' (2012) ETUI Working Paper no. 2012/14.

32 Ibid 5.

33 Ibid 5.

34 Ibid 6.

35 G Majone, *Rethinking the Union of Europe Post-Crisis: Has Integration Gone Too Far?* (CUP 2014, ebook) loc 4237.

their Medium-Term Budgetary Objectives (MTBOs).[36] Before the euro crisis, the Council would address recommendations to Member States that would significantly deviate from their adjustment path and no consequence would arise in case of non-compliance.[37] For Member States of the euro area, an interest-bearing deposit will now be imposed by the Council unless it decides by a qualified majority not do so.[38] The Stability Treaty has moreover placed parameters on the content of the MTBO, by stating that the budget of all States must be 'balanced or in surplus' with an automatic correction mechanism to be activated in case of significant deviations therefrom.[39] This 'golden rule' has to bet set in a national provision of binding force and permanent character, preferably of a constitutional nature.[40] In case of non-compliance therewith, any state party may bring the matter before the ECJ.[41]

The second duty of Member States is to avoid *excessive deficits* which occur when there is a planned or actual government budget deficit of more than 3% of GDP or total government debt of more than 60% of GDP.[42] Before the euro crisis, the Council would address recommendations to the Member State concerned by an excessive deficit with no proper sanctioning power.[43] For Member States of the euro area, the Council is now bound to impose a non-interest bearing deposit then a fine except if it decides not to do so by a qualified majority.[44] If the recommendations are still not followed, the Council may adopt additional measures such as inviting the European Investment Bank to reconsider its lending policy towards the Member State concerned.[45] Under the Stability Treaty, the finding of an excessive deficit entails the additional obligation for Member States to set up a budgetary and economic partnership programme to be approved by the Commission and the Council, including a detailed description of the structural reforms that the Member State undertakes to implement with a

---

36 Council Regulation (EC) 1466/97 of 7 July 1997 on the strengthening of the surveillance of budgetary positions and the surveillance and coordination of economic policies [1997] OJ L209/1, as amended by Regulation (EU) 1175/2011 of the European Parliament and of the Council of 16 November 2011 [2011] OJ L306/12, Article 2.a.

37 Ibid Articles 6 and 10.

38 Regulation (EU) 1173/2011 of the European Parliament and of the Council of 16 November 2011 on the effective enforcement of budgetary surveillance in the euro area [2011] OJ L306/1, Article 4.

39 Treaty on Stability, Coordination and Governance (TSCG) (including Fiscal Compact) (March 2012) Article 3 (1).

40 Ibid Article 3 (2).

41 Ibid Article 8.

42 Protocol no.12 on the excessive deficit procedure [2008] OJ C 115/279; Article 126 TFEU.

43 Article 126 (7) and (8).

44 Regulation (EU) 1173/2011 of the European Parliament and of the Council of 16 November 2011 on the effective enforcement of budgetary surveillance in the euro area [2011] OJ L306/1, Articles 5–6.

45 Article 126 (9) TFEU.

view to correct the excessive deficit.[46] Since the entry into force of the two pack legislation, the Commission may decide to subject to enhanced surveillance a Member State of the euro area experiencing or threatened with serious difficulties with respect to its financial stability. If these difficulties become so serious that the Member State in question has to request financial assistance from the EU, the IMF or any third country, a macroeconomic adjustment programme will have to be drafted subject to approval by the Commission and the Council. In the most likely case of ESM support, the structural reforms it contains will become conditions for financial assistance according to a memorandum of understanding negotiated by the Commission in liaison with the ECB and the IMF.[47]

The third – and last – duty of Member States is to prevent or correct *macroeconomic imbalances*.[48] This new procedure supplements the multilateral surveillance of economic policies with specific rules for the detection of macroeconomic imbalances, as well as the prevention and correction of excessive macroeconomic imbalances within the EU. It establishes an alert mechanism for the early detection of emerging macroeconomic imbalances based on a 'scoreboard' of indicators with indicative thresholds.[49] On this basis, the Commission may detect the Member States for which an 'in-depth review' is necessary.[50] If macroeconomic imbalances are identified during the 'in-depth review', the Council may address recommendations to the Member State concerned to provide guidance on appropriate policy responses, while in case of 'excessive' macroeconomic imbalances, the Council may recommend that the Member State concerned take corrective action to be detailed in a corrective action plan subject to Commission and Council approval.[51] Non-compliance with the recommendations issued under the excessive imbalance procedure does not call for any kind of sanction, except for Member States of the euro area for which an interest-bearing deposit or a fine will be imposed by the Council unless a qualified majority votes against it.[52]

---

46 Treaty on Stability, Coordination and Governance (TSCG) (including Fiscal Compact) (March 2012) Article 5. See also Regulation (EU) 473/2013 of the European Parliament and of the Council of 21 May 2013 on common provisions for monitoring and assessing draft budgetary plans and ensuring the correction of excessive deficit of the Member States in the euro area [2013] OJ L140/11, Article 9.

47 Regulation (EU) 472/2013 of the European Parliament and of the Council of 21 May 2013 on the strengthening of economic and budgetary surveillance of Member States in the euro area experiencing or threatened with serious difficulties with respect to their financial stability [2013] OJ L 140/1, Article 7.

48 See Regulation (EU) 1176/2011 of the European Parliament and of the Council of 16 November 2011 on the prevention and correction of macroeconomic imbalances [2011] OJ L306/25.

49 Ibid Articles 3 and 4.

50 Ibid Article 5.

51 Ibid Articles 6–12.

52 Regulation (EU) 1174/2011 of the European Parliament and of the Council of 16 November 2011 on enforcement measures to correct excessive macroeconomic imbalances in the euro area [2011] OJ L306/8.

From a governance perspective, the three aforementioned strands are integrated into a yearly cycle of economic and budgetary policy coordination called the *European Semester*. Its functioning may be summarized as follows:

> The European Semester starts every year with the publication by the Commission of the Annual Growth Survey. It outlines general economic priorities for the EU. It is debated by the other institutions and feeds the discussion leading to the spring European Council. Member States present national programmes in the spring of each year. The Commission then proposes country-specific policy recommendations to each Member State, based on its assessment of national economic situations and programmes. All relevant policy areas are covered: fiscal, macro-economic and structural reforms. The recommendations are discussed in the Council and endorsed by the June European Council, before being finally adopted by the Council. Member States are expected to reflect the recommendations in their budgetary and policy plans for the subsequent year and to implement them in the coming 12 months.[53]

The impact of new – strengthened – European economic governance on national social policy should not be underestimated. Chalmers insightfully remarks that 'sound public finances require borrowing to be limited and the problem of accumulated debt to be remedied, thereby putting upward pressure on levels of taxation and downward pressure on levels of welfare provision'.[54] If the EMU was not historically associated with welfare retrenchment, it was mainly for lack of compliance with the 'sound public finances' paradigm upon which it rested.[55] Things might change now that the 'golden rule' is enshrined in national law with an automatic correction mechanism to guarantee compliance therewith. Besides, the structural reforms conveyed by the recommendations of the Council – many of which depict social policy as the main adjustment variable through which Member States may regain competitivess in the EMU[56] – cannot be discarded as cheap talk anymore. For, the sanctioning power of the Council has been significantly reinforced – especially for euro area Member States –, while the automaticity of the sanctions it adopts has been increased through the introduction of the 'reversed' qualified majority principle. Moreover, the structural reforms proposed by the Commission are *de facto* compulsory for Member States of the euro area that request financial assistance considering the strict conditionality attached to ESM support.

Multilevel social Europe is developing as a response to these increasing pressures for national welfare retrenchment, but will it be strong enough to reclaim social ground lost to European economic integration? This will depend

53 Commission, 'Annual Growth Survey 2015' (Communication) COM (2014) 902 final, 18.

54 D Chalmers, 'The European Redistributive State and a European Law of Struggle' (2012) 18 ELJ 667, 669.

55 See Article 119(3) TFEU.

56 C Degryse, M Jepsen and P Pochet, 'The Euro Crisis and its Impact on National and European Social Policies' (2013) ETUI Working Paper no. 2013/05, 38.

on social Europe's capacity to protect civil society from the colonising forces of markets, a question to which we will come back later on in this chapter. The strength of social Europe's achievements will also depend on the democratic support on which it can count. This is the issue to which we now turn.

8.3. SOCIAL EUROPE: DEMOCRATIC?

This book has assessed the participatory-democratic credentials of European governance by analysing the involvement of civil society in the two main methods through which multilevel social Europe is built, the CM and the OMC respectively. Has the participatory turn been successful? Success depends on the extent to which civil society was given the opportunity to participate in the governance of social Europe without succumbing to its bureaucratising tendencies. In other words, is the governance of social Europe merely driven by bureaucratic power, or has it institutionalised reflexive structures which open European governance to the democratic influence of civil society?

8.3.1 THE COMMUNITY METHOD

Top-down law-making through the CM has enhanced Member States' ability to solve problems to the detriment of European citizens' capacity for self-rule.[57] This democratic gap has been filled over time by empowering the European Parliament. The participatory turn now requires European institutions to complement those efforts at building a proper representative democracy at EU level by engaging directly with organised civil society. A central argument of this book has been that the civil dialogue cannot be the magic cure for the democratic ailments of the CM, for the CM was born and remains by design hierarchical. As such, it is hardly amenable to wide participation so that any attempt at embedding participatory democracy therein necessarily entails that a compromise be struck with effective problem-solving. The question raised by the turn to participatory democracy, therefore, is not if, but how and where European institutions strike that balance.

With a view to answer this question, *Chapter 6* has analysed the consultations which the Commission holds prior to proposing any major instrument of social law as a structure of opportunities which exerts influence on social CSOs. A rather elitist picture of European civil society has emerged therefrom. Nonetheless, this elitism is increasingly tamed by procedural rules aiming at, on the one hand, opening consultations to a wider audience and, on the other, democratising European civil society. In both cases, a legally-binding approach

---

57 R Dahl, *On Democracy* (Yale University Press 1998) 115.

is resisted by the Commission. This soft consultation regime has been described as a quite successful attempt at striking a balance between the conflicting demands for democracy and effectiveness and one that has the advantage of being compatible with representative democracy as a founding principle of the EU legal order. It is also reflexive in the sense that it makes the EU bureaucratic system sensitive to the concerns of CSOs through procedural rules which give them a voice in lawmaking without at the same threatening their autonomy to a great extent.

The participatory turn might have run its course with regard to the Commission's consultation regime because the latter has reached a satisfactory compromise which any further step towards legalisation might threaten. This does not mean that the balance has been drawn satisfactorily by different or the same institutions at other stages of the law-making process. Further research is required in that regard. It could, for instance, convincingly be argued that moving towards a notice and comment procedure akin to that found in the US APA might remain compatible with effective problem-solving where the Commission executes European law through delegated or implementing acts.[58] In that case, participatory rights could perform the same democratic function as in the APA in terms of reinforcing bureaucrats' accountability to a divided law-maker and ensuring the fairness of administrative processes.[59]

As *Chapter 6* illustrates, the participatory turn provides the most active segments of the citizenry, organised civil society as it were, with new opportunities to influence EU law-making and for that reason it may be seen as a success. At the same time, one should realise that the participatory turn does not guarantee a progress of 'enlightened understanding' in the EU citizenry at large.[60] For ordinary citizens who do not have the time, the will or the resources to participate in the Commission's consultations, representative democracy will often remain the only way to get involved in EU law-making.[61] This brings us back to square one for, as we have already seen, EU representative democracy as it was embedded in the CM is reaching limits that are difficult to overcome.

To repeat the point made in *Chapter 1*, the dilemma is such that either we accept that the CM is sufficiently democratic, or we admit that the CM is far from democratic yet cannot/should not be democratised as this requires a constitutional revolution that national governments and the people they

58 Articles 290–291 TFEU.

59 F Bignami, 'The Democratic Deficit in European Community Rulemaking: A Call for Notice and Comment in Comitology' (1999) 40 Harvard International Law Review 451. For a right-based approach with regard to participation more generally, see J Mendes, *Participation in EU Rule-Making: a Rights-Based Approach* (OUP 2011).

60 See P Magnette, 'Democracy in the European Union: Why and How to Combine Representation and Participation?' in S Smismans (ed), *Civil Society and Legitimate European Governance* (Edward Elgar 2006) 33.

61 Ibid 33.

represent do not support.[62] The Parliament and the Commission are trying to find a way out of that dilemma. With a view to the 2014 parliamentary elections, they have urged European political parties to nominate candidates for the Presidency of the Commission and expected that these candidates would defend their political programme in all Member States of the Union prior to the elections.[63] Politicising European elections through their linkage with the designation of the President of the Commission is a novelty that might enhance the democratic legitimacy of the EU, although the jury is still out as to its actual impact on voting behaviour.[64] At the same time, it threatens one of the founding principles of the CM which lies in the neutrality of the Commission acting as a guardian of the general interest of the Union.[65] The Parliament and the Commission seem ready to give up on this basic tenet of the CM if it means alleviating the democratic deficit of EU law-making. The extent to which they can lawfully do so within the boundaries of the current Treaty framework remains, however, to be seen.

8.3.2. THE OPEN METHOD OF COORDINATION

The democratic shortcomings of EU law-making have triggered the search for new modes of governance which depart from the top-down logic of the old CM.[66] Emblematic of that search is the OMC which was depicted in the Lisbon conclusions as a fully decentralised approach in which civil society would be actively involved.[67] The proponents of the OMC pretend that it does not require the kind of compromises that characterise the CM, since it combines radical participatory democracy with effective problem-solving. Instead of a counterweight to hierarchy, participatory democracy would become the constitutive feature of a new form of Directly-Deliberative Polyarchy (DDP).[68]

Chapter 7 has shown the practical limits of the OMC as a tool for radicalising participatory democracy in the EU. Contrary to theoretical expectations, the

---

62 G Majone, *Europe as the Would-Be World Power* (n 30) 154.

63 European Parliament, 'Resolution of 22 November 2012 on the Elections to the European Parliament in 2014' (P7_TA-PROV(2012)0462), point 1; Commission Recommendation 2013/142/EU of 12 March 2013 on enhancing the democratic and efficient conduct of the elections to the European Parliament [2013] OJ L79/29, point 3.

64 See A Follesdal and S Hix, 'Why There is a Democratic Deficit in the EU: A Response to Majone and Moravcsik' (2006) 44 JCMS 533, 557; R Corbett, "European Elections are Second-Order Elections': Is Received Wisdom Changing?' (2014) 52 JCMS 1194, 1198.

65 Article 17 TEU. See also Magnette, 'Democracy in the European Union' (n 35) 35; Majone, *Europe as the Would-Be World Power* (n 30) 154.

66 See J Scott and DM Trubek, 'Mind the Gap: Law and New Approaches to Governance in the European Union' (2002) 8 ELJ 1.

67 European Council, 23–24 March 2000, Lisbon, presidency conclusions, point 38.

68 See J Cohen and C Sabel, 'Directly-Deliberative Polyarchy' (1997) 3 ELJ 313, 313.

social OMC does not translate the ideal of DDP into action. The SPC has recently articulated a reflexive reform strategy which will not succeed in bridging this expectation gap,[69] because it attempts to mimic DDP without questioning DDP itself as a normative ideal. There are bureaucratic and economic barriers which prevent DDP from realising its own socio-democratic promises. The social OMC already provides a practical instance of DDP stumbling over these barriers, for it remains a bureaucratic process which fails to protect civil society from the market imperative.

However, provided that proper legal, political and constitutional reforms are implemented, radical participatory democracy might become a realistic prospect for the social OMC and one that would have the advantage of being compatible with effective problem-solving. As regards legal reform in particular, it is a kind of reflexivity different from the one embraced by the SPC which is advocated. Rather than learning from its own experience, the social OMC would enact stronger procedural rules aiming at securing civil society's influence therein as a matter of right rather than favour.

8.3.3. COMPARATIVE ASSESSMENT

Social Europe has made great efforts to put institutional flesh on the bare bones of its new participatory rhetoric. Institutional structures have been set up with a view to open European governance to the democratic influence of civil society, with more or less success depending on the method under scrutiny.

If we take the participatory turn in its moderate version, the Commission may be credited with various initiatives taken in favour of more open, inclusive and transparent consultations which have surely shaken the hierarchical bases of the CM. The Commission's soft consultation regime is not without democratic flaws, but those flaws are inevitable so long as the CM's effectiveness will be premised upon top-down law-making by the Commission, the Council and the Parliament.

If we take the participatory turn in its more radical version, greater disappointment arises because the social OMC fails to exploit its democratic potential. At the same time, there is cause for more optimism; the democratic potential of the OMC is there, waiting to be unleashed through appropriate reforms, and there are no legitimate reasons for procrastination since such reforms will improve, rather than impede, effective problem-solving.

69 SPC, 'Reinvigorating the Social OMC in the Context of the Europe 2020 Strategy' (Opinion) (2011) Doc 10405/11.

8.4. SOCIAL EUROPE: EFFECTIVE?

Effectiveness is commonly defined as 'the degree to which something is successful in producing a desired result'.[70] Since there is no consensus as to the result that social Europe is expected to deliver, disagreement persists as to whether social Europe has been effective or not.[71] In line with Cohen and Arato's tripartite framework,[72] this book takes effectiveness to mean social Europe's capacity to protect civil society from the colonising tendencies of European economic integration. Effectiveness will be appraised through the achievements of, respectively, the *hard* CM and the *soft* OMC. These are the two main tools through which the EU builds its social dimension. Our assessment does not pretend to be exhaustive. It simply aims to provide a brief overview on the question of effective social Europe and show how this links up with previous findings as to the reflexive capacity of European economic law and democratic support available for social Europe.

The examination of two highly debated pieces of legislation which harmonise or coordinate rules pertaining to social services will reveal that the social dimension which emerges from EU law-making is definitely one that is subordinated to the market imperative. In those circumstances, social Europe cannot adequately protect civil society from the colonising tendencies of European economic integration. Because the EU will not be able to adopt proper social legislation any time soon, the social OMC has been proposed as a way forward. The problem is that the social OMC also fails to deliver on the promise of building a European social dimension and might even lead to a colonisation of national social policies by the market imperative of European economic integration if appropriate reforms are not taken with a view to reinforce its influence over the EU 2020 strategy within the wider context of strengthened European economic governance.

8.4.1. THE COMMUNITY METHOD

The CM may be used to *harmonise* national legislations with the twofold purpose of filling the regulatory gaps induced by the process of negative integration as well as preventing a race to the bottom between different regulatory regimes competing for mobile factors of production.[73] Legislative harmonisation is

[70] A Stevenson, *Oxford Dictionary of English* (3rd edn, OUP 2010).

[71] M Büchs, 'How Legitimate is the Open Method of Coordination?' (2008) 46 JCMS 765, 769.

[72] Cohen and Arato, *Civil Society and Political Theory* (n 1) chap 9.

[73] See T Hervey, *European Social Law and Policy* (Longman 1998) 34–37; O De Schutter, 'The Democratic Experimentalist Approach to Governance: Protecting Social Rights in the European Union' in O De Schutter and J Lenoble (eds), *Reflexive Governance: Redefining the Public Interest in a Pluralistic World* (Hart 2010) 116.

in principle not directly relevant for social services since the TFEU explicitly prohibits any harmonisation of the laws and regulations pertaining thereto.[74] Nevertheless, the boundaries which separate the internal market for which the EU is competent from the social sphere for which Member States remain sovereign are not so neatly drawn. As *Chapters 4 and 5* have amply demonstrated, the ECJ's expansive interpretation of the notion of economic activity often means that European economic law will reach into sensitive welfare domains such as health, education or social security. When this is the case, social services may become subject to legislative harmonisation as economic services able to circulate freely within the internal market.

The most illustrious example of social harmonisation occurring as a spill-over from the ECJ's internal market case law is the 2011 Directive on the application of patients' rights in cross-border healthcare.[75] The Directive was adopted on the basis of Article 114 TFEU because the majority of its provisions aim to improve the functioning of the internal market. The main objective of the Directive is to provide rules for facilitating the access to safe and high quality cross-border healthcare in the Union. The Directive perfectly fits the mould of the standard interaction between positive and negative integration: first the ECJ upholds the right of EU citizens to be reimbursed for health services received abroad with a destabilising effect for the welfare states from which payment is sought and then the European legislature comes in to fill the regulatory gap created by the Court's intervention by striking a more liberal balance between the freedom to receive economic services and Member States' responsibility for organising their healthcare systems.[76] The Directive clarifies the Court's case law on patient mobility that is summarised in *Chapter 4*. It also creates new rights to accountability and transparency for mobile patients, while taking into account broader principles of universality, access to good quality care, equity and solidarity. Legally, harmonisation is limited to cross-border healthcare but, politically, it might become unsustainable for Member States to confer new rights to mobile patients without doing likewise for static patients.[77]

The CM may also be used to *coordinate* national social legislations. It is much more acceptable to Member States because, instead of replacing national rules by European ones, as harmonisation would do, social coordination enacts legal rules which ensure the peaceful coexistence of divergent welfare regimes.[78] Legal coordination of national social policy initially occurred

---

74 Articles 153 (2), 165 (4), 166 (4) and 168 (5) TFEU.

75 Directive 2011/24/EU of the European Parliament and of the Council of 9 March 2011 on the application of patients' rights in cross-border healthcare [2011] OJ L88/45 ('health' Directive).

76 W Sauter, 'Harmonization in Health Care: The EU Patients' Rights Directive' in B Cantillon, H Verschueren and P Ploscar (eds), *Social Inclusion and Social Protection in the EU: Interactions between Law and Policy* (Intersentia 2012) 126.

77 Ibid 124.

78 Hervey, *European Social Law* (n 73) 37–38.

through Regulation 1612/68[79] and Regulation 1408/71.[80] Their aim was to facilitate free movement of workers by requiring that national and non-national EU workers be treated alike with respect to social security, social and tax advantages.[81] The benefits of social coordination have progressively been extended to other categories of EU citizens, both economically and non-economically active. This process has culminated with the adoption of Directive 2004/38 on the right of citizens of the Union and their family members to move and reside freely within the territory of the Member States,[82] together with Regulation 883/2004 on the coordination of social security systems.[83] Social coordination redefines the boundaries of national welfare states in the sense that they cannot unjustifiably discriminate between EU citizens and their nationals with regard to access to social benefits. However, in the main, Member States are left free to organise their welfare systems as they wish.[84]

Legal coordination reaches deeper into welfare sovereignty when social services benefit as economic services from EU legislation allowing free circulation in the internal market. In that respect, the 'services' Directive[85] deserves particular attention. For, it is the first horizontal piece of legislation which coordinates, at EU level, the modernisation of national systems for regulating service activities.[86] In its initial proposal, the Commission provided for the application of the country of origin principle according to which a service provider would be subject only to the law of the country in which he is established.[87] The latter principle became the focus of social CSOs' criticism as it would have forced the most benevolent Member States to allow delivery of cheaper, and potentially

79 Council Regulation (EEC) 1612/68 of 15 October 1968 on freedom of movement for workers within the Community [1968] OJ L257/2. The latter Regulation was replaced Regulation (EU) 492/2011 of the European Parliament and of the Council of 5 April 2011 on freedom of movement for workers within the Union [2011] OJ L141/1.

80 Council Regulation (EEC) 1408/71 of 14 June 1971 on the application of social security schemes to employed persons and their families moving within the Community [1971] OJ L149/2.

81 D Damjanovic and B De Witte, 'Welfare Integration through EU Law: The overall Picture in the Light of the Lisbon Treaty' in U Neergaard, R Nielsen and L Roseberry (eds), *Integrating Welfare Functions into EU Law: from Rome to Lisbon* (DJOF Publishing 2009) 61.

82 Directive 2004/38/EC of the European Parliament and of the Council of 29 April 2004 on the right of citizens of the Union and their family members to move and reside freely within the territory of the Member States amending Regulation (EEC) 1612/68 and repealing Directives 64/221/EEC, 68/360/EEC, 72/194/EEC, 73/148/EEC, 75/34/EEC, 75/35/EEC, 90/364/EEC, 90/365/EEC and 93/96/EEC [2004] OJ L158/77.

83 Regulation (EC) 883/2004 of the European Parliament and of the Council of 29 April 2004 on the coordination of social security systems [2004] OJ L166/1.

84 P Watson, *EU Social and Employment Law: Policy and Practice in an Enlarged Europe* (OUP 2009) 95.

85 Directive 2006/123/EC of the European Parliament and of the Council of 12 December 2006 on services in the internal market [2006] OJ L376/36.

86 Commission, 'Proposal for a Directive of the European Parliament and of the Council on Services in the Internal Market' COM (2004) 2 final, 9.

87 Ibid Article 16.

lower quality, social services from other Member States. Social CSOs made their case before the European Parliament which eventually secured the withdrawal of the country of origin principle from the Directive and obtained that health services, as well as many other social services, be exempted from its scope.[88] For the few social services that remain in, restrictions to the freedom of establishment that are not justified by an overriding reason relating to the public interest shall be lifted.[89] This merely codifies the ECJ's case law on the matter. The Directive's liberalising tendencies are more visible as regards free movement of services.[90] The usual list of overriding reasons relating to the public interest found in the ECJ's case law have been narrowed down to reasons of public policy, public security, public health and the protection of the environment,[91] even though a derogation has been introduced for the temporary provision of SGEI.[92]

This preliminary examination of the aforementioned legislative instruments illustrates that the hard CM suffers from an economic bias. When social services are harmonised or coordinated through EU legislation, it is as a precondition for the proper functioning of the internal market or as part of the internal market project itself. But we should not be too quick to judge: our brief assessment also shows that legal safeguards have been put in place in order to protect national social policy from undue market interference. The 'services' Directive has abandoned the country of origin principle. It also integrates the notion of social solidarity acting as a shield against internal market law for non-economic services which are delivered by the state or on behalf of the state.[93] Meanwhile, for those few social services which are economic yet cannot benefit from the social exemption,[94] the 'services' Directive balances the social objectives pursued by authorisation schemes as overriding reasons of public interest against the freedom of establishment under a proportionality test,[95] while it excludes social SGEI from the provisions on temporary services.[96] Likewise, the 'health' Directive allows Member States to balance the economic benefits of cross-border healthcare with the necessity to ensure the proper functioning of their healthcare systems through prior authorisation schemes while upholding respect for broader principles of universality, access to good quality care, equity and solidarity.[97]

---

88 IJ Butler, 'Non-Governmental Organisation Participation in the EU Law-Making Process: The Example of Social Non-Governmental Organisations at the Commission, Parliament and Council' (2008) 14 ELJ 558, 568–569. See 'services' Directive, Article 2 (2) f) and j).

89 'Services' Directive, Articles 9, 10 and 15.

90 C Barnard, 'Unravelling the Services Directive' (2008) 45 CML Rev 323, 366–368.

91 'Services' Directive, Article 16.

92 Ibid Article 17.

93 Ibid recital 34.

94 Ibid Article 2 (2) j).

95 Ibid Articles 9, 10 and 15.

96 Ibid Article 17.

97 'Health' Directive, Articles 4 (1) and (3), 8 and 9.

Drawing a parallel with judicially-enforced European economic law, we may say that internal market legislation shows respect for the social sovereignty of Member States through careful policing of the state/market boundary and generous use of proportionate derogations and justifications. Nevertheless, the fact remains that internal market legislation, as the ECJ's case law, promotes a thin social agenda that treats national social policy as derogation to free movement rules.[98] Legislative self-restraint is useful as far as it goes, but it does not enhance national welfare states' capacity to protect social policy from the indirect constraints imposed by European economic integration.[99] Social policy must europeanise if it wants to catch up with market forces and, ideally, Europeanization should have the character of European law in order to establish constitutional parity with the rules of European economic integration.[100] And so we fall into Europe's well-known 'social dilemma', for the European legal dimension that social Europe desperately needs is precisely what it cannot achieve within the boundaries of the current Treaty framework.[101]

The new social provisions of the Lisbon Treaty fail to offer a way out of this stalemate. The ambitious objective of establishing 'a highly competitive social market economy'[102] is introduced in the TEU but it does not translate into an extension of the EU's law-making powers in the social field.[103] The European legislature is only compelled to mainstream, as it already does, social rights into internal market legislation.[104] A narrow window of opportunity opens with the new legislative competence of the EU in respect of SGEI. Article 14 TFEU provides for the adoption of a regulation stating principles and conditions which would enable SGEI to fulfil their missions. This article has triggered demands for a European legislation on social SGEI.[105] Harmonisation would be limited since non-economic services of general interest would be excluded from the regulation in accordance with Protocol no. 26[106] as well as social services which are not provided in the general interest, but it would be a chance for the EU to take a first step towards the creation of a European social model which truly balances

98 FW Scharpf, 'The Asymmetry of European Integration, or Why the EU Cannot Be a "Social Market Economy"' (2010) 8 Socio-Economic Review 211, 219.

99 See Leibfried, 'Social Policy: Left to the Judges and the Markets?' (n 29) 274–277.

100 FW Scharpf, 'The European Social Model: Coping with the Challenges of Diversity' (2002) 40 JCMS 645, 666.

101 See M Dawson, 'The Ambiguity of Social Europe in the Open Method of Coordination' (2009) 34 EL Rev 55, 57.

102 Article 3 (3) TEU.

103 Dawson and De Witte, 'The EU Legal Framework of Social Inclusion and Social Protection' (n 25) 54.

104 See Article 9 TFEU; Charter of Fundamental Rights, Articles 14, 34–36.

105 See COLLECTIF SSIG (ed), *Social Services of General Interest in the Internal Market of the 21st Century – The Reform Treaty: The New State of Affairs* (2008) <http://cor.europa.eu/en/documentation/brochures/Documents/7bc13269-7368-4afe-b12f-825be1a9e33c.pdf> accessed 1st September 2015.

106 Protocol no. 26 on services of general interest [2012] OJ C326/308, Article 2.

economic with social progress.[107] Unfortunately, the initiative has so far failed to gather support from the European legislature which remains strongly divided over the necessity to legislate on such a sensitive issue.[108]

8.4.2. THE OPEN METHOD OF COORDINATION

If the EU fails to legislate beyond market-making, it is as a consequence of the current division of powers where it is explicitly denied the right to harmonise national welfare policies. It is also because the diversity of European welfare states has increased to such an extent that it becomes politically unfeasible for them to agree on common legislative solutions in what it is deemed to be a very sensitive policy field.[109] These constraints have triggered the search for a new way to develop a European social dimension. Social Europe has always been characterised by its heavy reliance on soft law. Non-binding measures as varied as opinions, recommendations, resolutions and action-programmes were adopted by the EU with a view to encourage Member States' cooperation in social affairs long before the Treaties came to acknowledge the EU's competence in that respect. Against this background, the Lisbon European Council has innovated by proposing the soft OMC as a fully-fledged alternative to the hard CM.[110]

From thereon, the OMC rapidly became the governance instrument of choice for EU social policy-making.[111] Separate coordination processes in the social inclusion, health and pension fields were streamlined into a single social OMC, while another OMC was instituted for education policy. This enthusiastic embrace of the OMC attests a progressive move away in national and EU debates from harmonisation in favour of coordination as the preferred tool for advancing the agenda of social Europe.[112] Instead of striving for uniformity, the social OMC takes the diversity of Europe as an opportunity to start a deliberative process by which Member States can discover and experiment with new solutions to the intractable problems their welfare systems are collectively facing.[113] For

---

107 Damjanovic and De Witte, 'Welfare Integration through EU Law' (n 81) 87. See also M Ross, 'Article 16 E.C. and Services of General Interest: from Derogation to Obligation?' (2000) 25 EL Rev 22.

108 S Rodrigues,'Towards a General EC Framework Instrument related to SGEI? Political Considerations and Legal Constraints' in M Krajewski, U Neergaard and JW van de Gronden (eds), *The Changing Legal Framework for Services of General Interest in Europe: Between Competition and Solidarity* (TMC Asser Press 2009) 257–259.

109 Scharpf, 'The European Social Model' (n 100) 650–652.

110 Scott and Trubek, 'Mind the Gap' (n 66) 4.

111 J Zeitlin, 'Social Europe and Experimentalist Governance: Towards a New Constitutional Compromise?' in G De Búrca (ed), *EU Law and the Welfare State: In Search of Solidarity* (OUP 2005) 215–216.

112 Ibid 214–215.

113 DM Trubek and LG Trubek, 'The Open Method of Co-Ordination and the Debate Over "Hard" and "Soft" Law' in J Zeitlin, P Pochet and L Magnusson (eds), *The Open Method of*

that reason, the social OMC has been emulated as a third way for European social policy between legislative harmonisation and regulatory competition, by which Member States would address common concerns in a way that respects their diversity.[114] These were, at least, the theoretical promises that laid behind the social OMC when it was proclaimed in Lisbon, but has it delivered in practice?

Empirical research confirms that the social OMC has triggered procedural shifts in national policy-making, 'including reinforced horizontal coordination and cross-sectoral integration between interdependent policy fields (...) improvements in national steering and statistical capacities (...) enhanced vertical coordination between levels of governance (...) increased involvement of non-state actors in policy-making processes (...) and development of horizontal and diagonal networks for the involvement of non-state and subnational actors in European policy-making processes'.[115] The social OMC has also been a source of substantive policy change causing ideational, agenda-setting, and programmatic shifts in national policy-making.[116]

Nevertheless, these influences greatly differ between Member States and across the three strands of the social OMC.[117] We may also doubt their ability to contribute to the ultimate objective of poverty alleviation embraced by the EU 2020 strategy. It seems important to repeat that, in 2013, 122.9 million people, or 24.5% of the population in the EU-28 were at risk of poverty or social exclusion, compared with 24.7% in 2012 and 24.3% in 2011.[118] This is far from the decisive impact on the eradication of poverty that was promised by the Lisbon European Council in 2000.[119] Since the launch of the EU 2020 strategy, the EU has drifted further away from its target of lifting at least 20 million people out of the risk of poverty and social exclusion and the Commission itself admits that there is no sign of rapid progress to remedy this situation.[120]

Co-Ordination in Action: The European Employment and Social Inclusion Strategies (PIE-Peter Lang 2005) 87.

114 J Zeitlin, 'The Open Method of Co-Ordination in Question' in J Zeitlin, P Pochet and L Magnusson (eds), *The Open Method of Co-Ordination in Action: The European Employment and Social Inclusion Strategies* (PIE-Peter Lang 2005) 22.

115 J Timo Weishaupt, 'The Social OMCs at Work: Identifying and Explaining Variations in National Use and Influence' in E Barcevicius, J Timo Weishaupt, and J Zeitlin, *Assessing the Open Method of Coordination: Institutional Design and National Influence of EU Social Policy Coordination* (Palgrave Macmillan 2014) 204. See also J Zeitlin, 'Is the Open Method of Coordination an Alternative to the Community Method?' in R Dehousse (ed), *The "Community Method": Obstinate or Obsolete?* (Palgrave Macmillan 2011) 142–143.

116 Ibid 204.

117 Ibid 227.

118 For more details, see <http://appsso.eurostat.ec.europa.eu/nui/submitViewTableAction.do> accessed 1st September 2015.

119 Büchs, 'How Legitimate is the Open Method of Coordination?' (n 71) 769–770. See European Council, 23-24 March 2000, Lisbon, presidency conclusions, para 32.

120 Commission, 'Taking stock of the Europe 2020 strategy for smart, sustainable and inclusive growth' (Communication) COM (2014) 130 final/2, 14.

The social OMC might also come as a disappointment for those that were hoping to build a third way between harmonisation and deregulation once they realise that this soft tool does not alter the constitutional asymmetry which characterises European integration. As Scharpf explains, 'when responding to OMC guidelines (...) Member States continue to operate under exactly the same legal and economic constraints of economic integration which limit their policy choices when they are acting individually'.[121] In other words, the social OMC leaves Member States with no other choice but to optimise the downward adjustment of their welfare systems to market forces because they continue to act in the shadow of a European economic constitution promoting liberalism over any other values.[122]

It could be retorted that European economic law preserves national policy choices to a greater extent that the term 'negative integration' so dear to Scharpf would lead us to believe. Our case studies have sufficiently shown that European economic law is endowed with a reflexive capacity which enables it to strike a balance between social and economic concerns. Nonetheless, the argument that the European economic constitution encourages national welfare retrenchment without legally requiring it is becoming more compelling than ever.[123] The noise made around the 'country of origin' principle originally inserted in the proposal for the 'services' Directive has amplified worries that the single market might trigger a race to the bottom between national welfare states competing for mobile factors of production. A growing number of Member States are also waking up to the fact that EMU's membership may require structural reforms of their welfare system with a view to consolidate state finances. In other words, it becomes increasingly difficult to deny that the single market and EMU constrain the range of national policy choices available under the social OMC.

Aside from its subordinate position with regard to the European economic constitution, the social OMC also fails to deliver effective protection against markets because it is integrated into a wider political framework which systematically favours economic over social concerns. The social OMC was created in the wake of the Lisbon strategy hailed as (possibly) Europe's Maastricht for welfare. For the first time, the EU tried to bring the economic and social dimension of European integration into a coherent policy framework.[124] As said in the previous chapter, those hopes were short-lived. For, the Lisbon strategy took a neo-liberal turn in 2005 when the European Council decided to refocus its priorities on growth and jobs.[125]

---

121 Scharpf, 'The European Social Model' (n 100) 655.

122 Ibid 658. See also C Offe, 'The European Model of "Social" Capitalism: Can it Survive European Integration?' (2003) 11 The Journal of Political Philosophy 437, 462–463.

123 Leibfried, 'Social Policy: Left to the Judges and the Markets?' (n 29) 274–277.

124 D Wincott, 'Beyond Social Regulation? New Instruments and/or a New Agenda for Social Policy at Lisbon?' (2003) 81 Public Administration 533, 533.

125 Hay and Wincott, *The Political Economy of European Welfare Capitalism* (n 29) 152.

The new Europe 2020 strategy addresses the social imbalances of its predecessor. It re-establishes a three-pillar structure based on smart, sustainable and inclusive growth.[126] At the same time, the strategy purports to lift at least 20 million people out of poverty and social exclusion by 2020. To support this aim, the Commission has initiated a 'European platform against poverty' (EPP) as one of the seven flagship initiatives launched to tackle the Europe 2020 goals.[127] Besides, better integration of social OMC outcomes into Europe 2020 is ensured through a revision of the Lisbon integrated guidelines. The 'Europe 2020 integrated guidelines'[128] on which NRPs are now based contain new employment guideline no. 10 which is entirely dedicated to 'promoting social inclusion and combating poverty'. Meanwhile, one of the social OMC's overarching objectives remains to interact effectively with Europe 2020 as was previously the case with Lisbon.[129]

For all those efforts at rebalancing, the mood remains pessimistic. EAPN comments that '[t]here is a growing disillusionment with both the content and process of Europe 2020, which is failing to reduce poverty, and is seen as responsible for generating more poverty and inequality through its austerity approach'.[130] This viewpoint is confirmed by Degryse, Jepsen and Pochet who conclude their analysis of the country-specific recommendations issued under the Europe 2020 strategy as follows:

> Because of a failure to commit to a real economic union, that is to say, to a voluntary process of convergence of the economic performance and social cohesion of the eurozone member states [...] social policies – in the broad sense – have today been designated as the main adjustment variables of monetary union. What the dominant discourse states is that forms of internal devaluation – affecting wages, labour law and social protection – must from now on replace the practice of currency devaluation as it was practised in the past.[131]

---

126 See Commission, 'Europe 2020: A Strategy for Smart, Sustainable and Inclusive Growth' (Communication) COM (2010) 2020 final.

127 Commission, 'The European Platform against Poverty and Social Exclusion: A European Framework for Social and Territorial Cohesion' (Communication) COM (2010) 758 final.

128 Council Recommendation of 13 July 2010 on broad guidelines for the economic policies of the Member States and of the Union [2010] OJ L191/28; Council Decision 2010/707/EU of 21 October 2010 on guidelines for the employment policies of the Member States [2010] OJ L308/46.

129 SPC, 'Reinvigorating the Social OMC in the Context of the Europe 2020 Strategy' (Opinion) (2011) Doc 10405/11, annex.

130 EAPN, 'An EU Worth Defending – Beyond Austerity to Social Investment and Inclusive Growth: EAPN Analysis of the 2012 National Reform Programmes (NRPs) and National Social Reports (NSRs)' (Report) (2012) 6. See also EAPN, 'Widening the Gap: EAPN Assessment of the National Reform Programmes 2013' (Report) (2013).

131 Degryse, Jepsen and Pochet, 'The Euro Crisis and its Impact on National and European Social Policies' (n 56) 38.

In our view, there are three major weaknesses which prevent Europe 2020 from achieving parity between economic and social goals. Firstly, the social discourse promoted by the social OMC fails to find its way into Europe 2020 because of a lack of political will to depart from the hegemonic economic proposition that inevitably there is a 'trade-off' between social equity and economic efficiency. The launch of the Commission's social investment package as well as the ongoing debate on the social dimension of EMU may however be signs that common wisdom is at last being challenged from within the Commission itself.[132]

A second major weakness is that proper mechanisms which would institutionalize social influence within Europe 2020 are currently lacking. It is striking that guideline no. 10 is the only one dedicated to the fight against poverty and social exclusion whereas it should have been made an overarching objective to be mainstreamed in all Europe 2020 guidelines in accordance with new Article 9 TFEU.[133] In this respect, we may find reassuring that the new Europe 2020 guidelines recently proposed by the Commission provide much more space to social values than it is the case with the current guidelines. From now on, structural reforms will have to pursue growth and employment while *at the same time* 'ensuring access for all to high quality, affordable and sustainable social services and benefits'.[134]

The third, and main, weakness of Europe 2020 is that it is a mere political strategy which continues to work in the shadow of the constitutional hierarchy we have denounced earlier on. With sound public finances becoming the overriding priority in the context of the current euro crisis, legal incentives to comply with the country-specific recommendations issued under the economic and budgetary strands of the strategy have been strengthened through various means,[135] while the employment strand of Europe 2020 remains as soft as before. This reinforces the domination of the already stronger economic and budgetary disciplines over their weaker employment counterpart.[136]

---

132 A Hemerijck, 'The Euro-Crisis – Welfare State Conundrum' in MJ Rodrigues and E Xiarchogiannopoulou (eds), *The Eurozone Crisis and the Transformation of EU Governance: Internal and External Implications* (Ashgate 2014, ebook) loc 3324. See also Commission, 'Towards Social Investment for Growth and Cohesion – including implementing the European Social Fund 2014–2020' (Communication) COM (2013) 83 final; J-C Juncker with D Tusk, J Dijsselbloem, M Draghi and M Schulz, 'Completing Europe's Economic and Monetary Union' (Report) (2015) 8–9.

133 See H Frazer and E Marlier, 'Strengthening Social Inclusion in the Europe 2020 Strategy by Learning from the Past' in E Marlier and D Natali (eds), *Europe 2020: Towards a More Social EU*? (PIE- Peter Lang 2010) 240–241.

134 Commission, 'Annex to the Recommendation for a Council Recommendation on broad guidelines for the economic policies of the Member States and of the Union' COM(2015) 99 final, guideline 2. See also Commission, 'Annex to the Proposal for a Council Decision on guidelines for the employment policies of the Member States' COM (2015) 98 final.

135 See *section 8.2.*

136 K Armstrong, 'EU Social Policy and the Governance Architecture of Europe 2020' (2012) 18 Transfer 285, 290.

The legal imbalance of Europe 2020 could be curtailed by increasing the potential for sanction in case of deviations from country-specific employment recommendations, including those based on the poverty guideline.[137] But, social policy would not effectively influence Europe 2020 without a correlative strengthening of the social OMC itself. Proposals for reinforcing the democratic credentials of the social OMC have already been made in the previous chapter. Ways to improve its effectiveness are now considered. According to the Commission, this could be done by formalising convergence of views whenever they arise from the OMC into proper legal instruments.[138] The social OMC has already paved the ground for the adoption of two policy Recommendations, one on child poverty[139] and the other on active inclusion.[140] Further steps towards correcting the EU's constitutional asymmetry would require that binding European legislation be adopted on the basis of the social OMC. It goes without saying that such legislation would also need to be sufficiently differentiated so as to accommodate the growing diversity of national welfare regimes.[141]

The most likely candidate for a first legislative initiative in the field of social inclusion might be the introduction of a pan-European adequate minimum income scheme.[142] In a Resolution of 20 October 2010, the Parliament instructs the Commission to investigate the impact such an initiative would have on Member States.[143] The social OMC has created the conditions for the debate on the necessity of a pan-European minimum income scheme to occur and that illustrates its main merit: to pave the way for European social legislation as the principal means to reinstate constitutional parity between economic and social Europe.[144] At the same time, this example reminds us of the great distance that separates dream from reality.[145] For, the two Recommendations on child poverty and active inclusion were adopted on shaky legal foundations and there are good reasons to believe that the proposal for a pan-European minimum

137 EAPN, 'An EU Worth Defending' (n 130) 11.

138 Commission, 'A Renewed Commitment to Social Europe: Reinforcing the Open Method of Coordination for Social Protection and Social Inclusion' COM (2008) 418 final, 5.

139 Commission Recommendation 2013/112/EU of 20 February 2013 on investing in children: breaking the cycle of disadvantage [2013] OJ L59/5.

140 Commission Recommendation of 3 October 2008 on the active inclusion of people excluded from the labour market [2008] OJ L307/11.

141 Scharpf, 'The European Social Model' (n 100) 666.

142 B Cantillon and N Van Mechelen, 'Between Dream and Reality... On Anti-Poverty, Minimum Income Protection and the European Social Model' in B Cantillon, H Verschueren and P Ploscar (eds), *Social Inclusion and Social Protection in the EU: Interactions between Law and Policy* (Intersentia 2012) 201.

143 European Parliament, 'Resolution of 20 October 2010 on the Role of Minimum Income in Combating Poverty and Promoting an Inclusive Society in Europe' [2012] OJ C70E/8.

144 T Idema and RD Kelemen, 'New Modes of Governance, the Open Method of Co-Ordination and Other Fashionable Red Herring' (2006) 7 Perspectives on European Politics and Society 108, 118.

145 Cantillon and Van Mechelen, 'Between Dream and Reality' (n 142).

income scheme would even have a harder time finding a proper legal basis in the Treaties.[146]

8.4.3. COMPARATIVE ASSESSMENT

We can conclude from the above that multilevel social Europe fails to protect civil society from the market imperative of European economic integration. When social services are harmonised or coordinated through EU legislation, it is as a precondition for the proper functioning of the internal market or as part of the internal market project itself. Legal safeguards were put in place to protect national social policy from internal market legislation but they do not enhance national welfare states' capacity to protect civil society from the indirect constraints of European economic integration. Because the CM fails to legislate beyond market-making, the social OMC has been proposed as a way forward. Yet, the social OMC does not deliver on the promise of building a European social dimension and might even lead to a colonisation of national social policies by the market imperative of European economic integration if appropriate reforms are not taken with a view to reinforce its influence over the economic and budgetary pillars of Europe 2020.

These findings allow us to come back on previous findings as to the democratic credentials of social Europe, for we have said that the achievements of social Europe will need to rest on a sound legitimacy basis. In that respect, Majone convincingly argues that the EU does not need democratic legitimacy so long as it focuses on market regulation which he describes as antithetical to social redistribution pursued at the national level. For Majone a clear separation should be kept between economics and politics.[147] Markets are more effectively regulated by non-democratic EU while redistributive policies should remain the domain of democratic welfare states.[148]

Multilevel social Europe has already gone beyond that clear division of tasks on which Majone's vision of a non-democratic EU rests.[149] We have seen that EU decision-making blurs the boundaries between market regulation and social redistribution. The CM brings social services within the purview of internal market legislation, while the OMC is unable to protect national social policy from the destabilising pressures of European economic integration. If we follow

---

146 H Verschueren, 'Union Law and the Fight against Poverty: Which Legal Instruments?' in B Cantillon, H Verschueren and P Ploscar (eds), *Social Inclusion and Social Protection in the EU: Interactions between Law and Policy* (Intersentia 2012) 213.

147 G Majone, 'Europe's "Democratic Deficit": The Question of Standards' (1998) 4 ELJ 5, 7.

148 G Majone, 'Regulatory Legitimacy' in G Majone and P Baake (eds), *Regulating Europe* (Routledge 1996) 285–287.

149 For a similar argument, see Wincott, 'Beyond Social Regulation?' (n 124) 542–544; Follesdal and Hix, 'Why There is a Democratic Deficit in the EU' (n 64) 542–544.

Majone's reasoning to its logical conclusion, the supposedly clear separation between market regulation and social policy has become an argument for democracy at EU level rather than an obstacle to it. At the same time, this book demonstrates that we cannot realistically expect the democratisation of social Europe to proceed at the same pace for the CM and the OMC.

Because representative democracy through the CM may be reaching its limits, the EU has turned to a moderate version of participatory democracy which the aim to revitalise the CM through enhanced dialogue with organised civil society. The civil dialogue has been useful as far as it goes but it cannot provide a magic cure for the democratic ailments of the CM which is bound to strike a balance between the conflicting demands for democracy and effectiveness. Whether the current democratic deadlock is acceptable from the perspective of European legislation interfering with democratically-legitimated national social policy, is debatable. 'No' might be the answer if we take the principled standpoint that regulatory politics requires majoritarian democracy the moment it impacts redistributive policies. A more balanced view might be that EU law-making does not demand full-blown democratisation so long as its market-making incursions into national welfare policy are subject to legal safeguards set under the control of the ECJ. The stand taken depends on the judgement we make about the ECJ's willingness to guard the border between social and market forces. Our views on that subject are quite positive and we would therefore feel comfortable with the likely persistence of the status quo.

On the other hand, we find unacceptable that the OMC be authorised to coordinate Member States' social protection and social inclusion policies without proper democratic support. We are dealing with a political tool that impacts national redistributive policies. For that reason, it requires democratic legitimation, all the more so because it deals with redistributive issues in a way that subordinate them to the market imperative of European economic integration without the legal safeguards applicable for the CM.[150] The social OMC has so far failed to radicalise participatory democracy in the EU but it should not give up on this promise. Provided that a proper reform strategy is implemented through legal, political and constitutional means, radical participatory democracy might become a reality for the social OMC. There are no valid reasons to resist such reforms, for the OMC does not face the kind of compromise that characterises the CM: radical democracy will enhance, not impede, effective problem-solving.

---

150 Büchs, 'How Legitimate is the Open Method of Coordination?' (n 71) 766–767.

TABLE OF LEGISLATION

EUROPEAN UNION

TREATIES

Charter of Fundamental Rights of the European Union [2012] OJ C326/393

Consolidated versions of the Treaty on European Union and the Treaty on the Functioning of the European Union [2012] OJ C326/01

Declaration no. 17 on the right of access to information, annexed to the Maastricht Treaty [1992] OJ C191/101

Declaration no. 23 on cooperation with charitable associations, annexed to the Maastricht Treaty [1992] OJ C191/103

Declaration no. 38 on voluntary service activities, annexed to the Amsterdam Treaty [1997] OJ C340/01

Declaration no. 23 on the future of the Union, annexed to the Nice Treaty [2001] C80/01

Protocol no. 30 on the application of the principles of subsidiarity and proportionality, annexed to the Amsterdam Treaty [1997] OJ C340/105

Protocol no. 12 on the excessive deficit procedure [2008] OJ C115/279

Protocol no. 1 on the role of national parliaments in the European Union, annexed to the Lisbon Treaty [2012] OJ C326/203

Protocol no. 2 on the application of the principles of subsidiarity and proportionality, annexed to the Lisbon Treaty [2012] OJ C326/206

Protocol no. 26 on services of general interest, annexed to the Lisbon Treaty [2012] OJ C326/308

Protocol no. 27 on the internal market and competition, annexed to the Lisbon Treaty [2012] OJ C326/309

Treaty establishing the European Economic Community, signed in Rome, 25 March 1957

Treaty establishing the European Community (consolidated version 1992) [1992] OJ C224/01

Treaty establishing the European Community (consolidated version 1997) [1997] OJ C340/03

Treaty establishing the European Community (consolidated version 2002) [2002] OJ C325/01

Treaty establishing a Constitution for Europe [2004] OJ C310/01

Treaty of Lisbon amending the Treaty on European Union and the Treaty establishing the European Community, signed at Lisbon, 13 December 2007 [2007] OJ C306/01

Treaty on Stability, Coordination and Governance (TSCG) (including Fiscal Compact) (March 2012)

REGULATIONS

Commission Regulation (EC) 1998/2006 of 15 December 2006 on the application of Articles 87 and 88 of the Treaty to de minimis aid [2006] OJ L379/5

Commission Regulation (EC) 800/2008 of 6 August 2008 declaring certain categories of aid compatible with the common market in application of Articles 87 and 88 of the Treaty (General Block Exemption Regulation) [2008] OJ L214/3

Commission Regulation (EU) 360/2012 of 25 April 2012 on the application of Articles 107 and 108 of the Treaty on the Functioning of the European Union to de minimis aid granted to undertakings providing services of general economic interest [2012] OJ L114/8

Commission Regulation (EU) 1407/2013 of 18 December 2013 on the application of Articles 107 and 108 of the Treaty on the Functioning of the European Union to de minimis aid [2013] OJ L352/1

Commission Regulation (EU) 651/2014 of 17 June 2014 declaring certain categories of aid compatible with the internal market in application of Articles 107 and 108 of the Treaty (General Block Exemption Regulation) [2014] OJ L187/1

Council Regulation (EEC) 1612/68 of 15 October 1968 on freedom of movement for workers within the Community [1968] OJ L257/2

Council Regulation (EEC) 1408/71 of 14 June 1971 on the application of social security schemes to employed persons and their families moving within the Community [1971] OJ L149/2

Council Regulation (EC) 1466/97 of 7 July 1997 on the strengthening of the surveillance of budgetary positions and the surveillance and coordination of economic policies [1997] OJ L209/1, as amended by Regulation (EU) 1175/2011 of the European Parliament and of the Council of 16 November 2011 [2011] OJ L306/12

Council Regulation (EC) 1/2003 of 16 December 2002 on the implementation of the rules on competition laid down in Articles 81 and 82 of the Treaty [2003] OJ L1/1

Council Regulation (EU) 1177/2011 of 8 November 2011 amending Regulation (EC) 1467/97 on speeding up and clarifying the implementation of the excessive deficit procedure [2011] OJ L306/33

Council Regulation (EU) 390/2014 of 14 April 2014 Establishing the 'Europe for Citizens' Programme for the Period 2014–2020 [2014] OJ L115/3

Regulation (EC) 1049/2001 of the European Parliament and of the Council of 30 May 2001 regarding public access to European Parliament, Council and Commission documents [2001] OJ L145/43

Regulation (EC) 883/2004 of the European Parliament and of the Council of 29 April 2004 on the coordination of social security systems [2004] OJ L166/1

Regulation (EC) 1367/2006 of the European Parliament and of the Council of 6 September 2006 on the application of the provisions of the Aarhus convention on access to information, public participation in decision-making and access to justice in environmental matters to Community institutions and bodies [2006] OJ L264/13

Regulation (EU) 182/2011 of the European Parliament and of the Council of 16 February 2011 laying down the rules and general principles concerning mechanisms for control by member states of the Commission's exercise of implementing powers [2011] OJ L55/13

Regulation (EU) 211/2011 of the European Parliament and of the Council of 16 February 2011 on the citizens' initiative [2011] OJ L65/1

Regulation (EU) 492/2011 of the European Parliament and of the Council of 5 April 2011 on freedom of movement for workers within the Union [2011] OJ L141/1

Regulation (EU) 1173/2011 of the European Parliament and of the Council of 16 November 2011 on the effective enforcement of budgetary surveillance in the euro area [2011] OJ L306/1

Regulation (EU) 1174/2011 of the European Parliament and of the Council of 16 November 2011 on enforcement measures to correct excessive macroeconomic imbalances in the euro area [2011] OJ L306/8

Regulation (EU) 1176/2011 of the European Parliament and of the Council of 16 November 2011 on the prevention and correction of macroeconomic imbalances [2011] OJ L306/25

Regulation (EU) 472/2013 of the European Parliament and of the Council of 21 May 2013 on the strengthening of economic and budgetary surveillance of Member States in the euro area experiencing or threatened with serious difficulties with respect to their financial stability [2013] OJ L140/1

Regulation (EU) 473/2013 of the European Parliament and of the Council of 21 May 2013 on common provisions for monitoring and assessing draft budgetary plans and ensuring the correction of excessive deficit of the Member States in the euro area [2013] OJ L140/11

Regulation (EU) 1296/2013 of the European Parliament and of the Council of 11 December 2013 on a European Union Programme for Employment and Social Innovation ("EaSI") and amending Decision 283/2010/EU establishing a European Progress Microfinance Facility for employment and social inclusion [2013] OJ L347/238

DIRECTIVES

Directive 2003/4/EC of the European Parliament and of the Council of 28 January 2003 on public access to environmental information and repealing Council Directive 90/313/EEC [2003] OJ L41/26

Directive 2003/35/EC of the European Parliament and of the Council of 26 May 2003 providing for public participation in respect of the drawing up of certain plans and programmes relating to the environment and amending with regard to public participation and access to justice Council Directives 85/337/EEC and 96/61/EC [2003] OJ L156/17

Directive 2004/18/EC of the European Parliament and of the Council of 31 March 2004 on the coordination of procedures for the award of public works contracts, public supply contracts and public service contracts [2004] OJ L134/114

Directive 2004/38/EC of the European Parliament and of the Council of 29 April 2004 on the right of citizens of the Union and their family members to move and reside freely within the territory of the Member States amending Regulation (EEC) 1612/68 and repealing Directives 64/221/EEC, 68/360/EEC, 72/194/EEC, 73/148/EEC, 75/34/EEC, 75/35/EEC, 90/364/EEC, 90/365/EEC and 93/96/EEC [2004] OJ L158/77

Directive 2006/123/EC of the European Parliament and of the Council of 12 December 2006 on services in the internal market [2006] OJ L376/36

Directive 2011/24/EU of the European Parliament and of the Council of 9 March 2011 on the application of patients' rights in cross-border healthcare [2011] OJ L88/45

Directive 2014/24/EU of the European Parliament and of the Council of 26 February 2014 on public procurement and repealing Directive 2004/18/EC [2014] OJ L94/65

Sixth Council Directive 77/388/EEC of 17 May 1977 on the harmonization of the laws of the Member States relating to turnover taxes – Common system of value added tax: uniform basis of assessment [1977] OJ L145/1

DECISIONS

NAVEWA-ANSEAU (Case IV / 29.995) Decision 82/371/EEC [1982] OJ L167/39

BPCL / ICI (Case IV / 30.863) Commission Decision 84/387/EEC [1984] OJ L212/1

ENI / Montedison (Case IV / 31.055) Commission Decision 87/3/EC [1987] OJ L5/13

Ford Volkswagen (Case IV / 33.814) Commission Decision 93/49/EEC [1993] OJ L20/14

Grundig's EC Distribution System (Case IV / 29.420) Commission Decision 94/29/EC [1994] OJ L20/15

Stichting Baksteen (Case IV / 34.456) Commission Decision 94/296/EC [1994] OJ L131/15

CECED (Case IV.F.1/36.718) Commission Decision 2000/475/EC [2000] OJ L187/47

Joint Selling of the Commercial Rights of the UEFA Champions League (Case COMP / C.2–37.398) Commission Decision 2003/778/EC [2003] OJ L291/25

Commission Decision 2005/842/EC of 28 November 2005 on the application of Article 86(2) of the EC Treaty to State aid in the form of public service compensation granted to certain undertakings entrusted with the operation of services of general economic interest [2005] OJ L312/67

Commission Decision 2006/225/EC of 2 March 2005 on the aid scheme implemented by Italy for the reform of the training institutions [2006] OJ L81/25

Commission Decision on State Aid NN 54/2006 – Czech Republic: Přerov logistics College C (2006) 5228, 8 November 2006

Commission Decision on State Aid NN 54/2009 (ex- CP 244/2005) – Belgique: Financement des hôpitaux publics du réseau IRIS de la Région Bruxelles-Capitale C (2009) 8120 final, 28 October 2009

Commission Decision on State Aid E 2/2005 and N 642/2009 – The Netherlands: Existing and special project aid to housing corporations C (2009) 9963 final, 15 December 2009

Commission Decision 2012/21/EU of 20 December 2011 on the application of Article 106(2) of the Treaty on the Functioning of the European Union to State aid in the form of public service compensation granted to certain undertakings entrusted with the operation of services of general economic interest [2012] OJ L7/3

Commission Decision 2013/284/EU of 19 December 2012 on State Aid SA.20829 (C 26/2010, ex NN 43/2010 (ex CP 71/2006)) Scheme concerning the municipal real estate tax exemption granted to real estate used by non-commercial entities for specific purposes implemented by Italy [2013] OJ L166/24

Commission Decision 2013/767/EU of 16 December 2013 Setting Up a Framework for Civil Dialogue in Matters Covered by the Common Agricultural Policy and Repealing Decision 2004/391/EC [2013] OJ L338/115

Commission Decision 2014/838/EU of 25 November 2014 on the Publication of Information on Meetings Held Between Directors-General of the Commission and Organisations or Self-employed Individuals [2014] OJ L343/19

Commission Decision 2014/839/EU of 25 November 2014 on the Publication of Information on Meetings Held Between Members of the Commission and Organisations or Self-employed Individuals [2014] OJ L343/22

Council Decision 75/458/EEC of 22 July 1975 concerning a programme of pilot schemes and studies to combat poverty [1975] OJ L199/34

Council Decision 85/8/EEC of 19 December 1984 on specific Community action to combat poverty [1985] OJ L2/24

Council Decision 89/457/EEC of 18 July 1989 establishing a medium-term Community action programme concerning the economic and social integration of the economically and socially less privileged groups in society [1989] OJ L224/10

Council Decision 2000/436/EC of 29 June 2000 setting up a Social Protection Committee [2000] OJ L172/26

Council Decision 2004/100/EC of 26 January 2004 establishing a Community action programme to promote active European citizenship (civic participation) [2004] OJ L30/6

Council Decision 2004/689/EC of 4 October 2004 establishing a Social Protection Committee and repealing Decision 2000/436/EC [2004] OJ L314/8

Council Decision 2010/707/EU of 21 October 2010 on guidelines for the employment policies of the Member States [2010] OJ L308/46

Decision 1686/98/EC of the European Parliament and the Council of 20 July 1998 establishing the Community action programme 'European Voluntary Service for Young People' [1998] OJ L214/1

Decision 50/2002/EC of the European Parliament and of the Council of 7 December 2001 establishing a programme of Community action to encourage cooperation between Member States to combat social exclusion [2002] OJ L10/1

Decision 1672/2006/EC of the European Parliament and of the Council of 24 October 2006 establishing a Community Programme for Employment and Social Solidarity – Progress [2006] OJ L315/1

Decision 1904/2006/EC of the European Parliament and of the Council of 12 December 2006 establishing for the period 2007 to 2013 the programme Europe for Citizens to promote active European citizenship [2006] OJ L378/32

Decision 1098/2008/EC of the European Parliament and of the Council of 22 October 2008 on the European year for combating poverty and social exclusion [2008] OJ L298/20

Decision 1093/2012/EU of the European Parliament and of the Council of 21 November 2012 on the European Year of Citizens (2013) [2012] OJ L325/1

RECOMMENDATIONS

Commission Recommendation of 3 October 2008 on the active inclusion of people excluded from the labour market [2008] OJ L307/11

Commission Recommendation 2013/112/EU of 20 February 2013 on investing in children: breaking the cycle of disadvantage [2013] OJ L59/5

Commission Recommendation 2013/142/EU of 12 March 2013 on enhancing the democratic and efficient conduct of the elections to the European Parliament [2013] OJ L79/29

Council Recommendation 92/441/EEC of 24 June 1992 establishing common criteria concerning sufficient resources and social assistance in social protection systems [1992] OJ L245/46

Council Recommendation 92/442/EEC of 27 July 1992 on the convergence of social protection objectives and policies [1992] OJ L245/49

Council Recommendation of 13 July 2010 on broad guidelines for the economic policies of the Member States and of the Union [2010] OJ L191/28

INTERINSTITUTIONAL AGREEMENTS

Agreement between the European Parliament and the European Commission of 23 June 2011 on the Establishment of a Transparency Register for organisations and self-employed individuals engaged in EU policy- making and policy implementation [2011] OJ L191/29

Agreement between the European Parliament and the European Commission of 16 April 2014 on the Transparency Register for Organisations and Self-Employed Individuals Engaged in EU Policy-Making and Policy Implementation [2014] OJ L277/11

Interinstitutionnal agreement between the European Parliament, the Council and the Commission of 16 December 2003 on better law-making [2003] OJ C321/1

UNITED STATES

5 USC §553

INTERNATIONAL

Convention on Access to Information, Public Participation in Decision-Making and Access to Justice in Environmental Matters, signed in Aarhus, Denmark, 25 June 1998, United Nations, Treaty Series, vol 2161, 447

TABLE OF CASES

EUROPEAN UNION

EUROPEAN COURT OF JUSTICE

16/62 and 17/62 *Confédération nationale des producteurs de fruits et légumes and others v Council* [1962] ECR 471

25/62 *Plaumann v Commission* [1963] ECR 95

56 and 58/64 *Établissements Consten S.à.R.L. and Grundig-Verkaufs-GmbH v Commission* (Consten and Grundig) [1966] ECR 0299

32/65 *Italy v Council and Commission* [1966] ECR 389

56/65 *Société Technique Minière (L.T.M.) v Maschinenbau Ulm GmbH (M.B.U.)* [1966] ECR 235

23/67 *Brasserie De Haecht v Wilkin* [1967] ECR 407

14/68 *Walt Wilhelm and others v Bundeskartellamt* [1969] ECR 1

6/72 *Europemballage Corporation and Continental Can Company Inc. v Commission* [1973] ECR 215

173/73 *Italy v Commission* [1974] ECR 0709

36/74 *B.N.O. Walrave and L.J.N. Koch v Association Union cycliste internationale, Koninklijke Nederlandsche Wielren Unie et Federación Española Ciclismo* [1974] ECR 1405

43/75 *Gabrielle Defrenne v Société anonyme belge de navigation aérienne Sabena* [1976] ECR 0455

26/76 *Metro SB-Großmärkte GmbH & Co. KG v Commission* (Metro) [1977] ECR 1875

78/76 *Steinike & Weinlig v Germany* [1977] ECR 0595

209 to 215 and 218/78 *Heintz van Landewyck SARL and others v Commission* (FEDETAB) [1980] ECR 3125

258/78 *L.C. Nungesser KG and Kurt Eisele v Commission* [1982] ECR 2015

138/79 *SA Roquette Frères v Council* [1980] ECR 3333

139/79 *Maizena GmbH v Council* [1980] ECR 3393

60/81 *International Business Machines Corporation v Commission* [1981] ECR 2639

238/82 *Duphar BV and others v The Netherlands* [1984] ECR 523

240, 241, 242, 261, 262, 268 and 269/82 *Stichting Sigarettenindustrie and others v Commission* [1985] ECR 3831

286/82 and 26/83 *Graziana Luisi and Giuseppe Carbone v Ministero del Tesoro* [1984] ECR 377

270/83 *Commission v France* [1986] ECR 273

293/83 *Françoise Gravier v City of Liège* [1985] ECR 593

42/84 *Remia BV and others v Commission* [1985] ECR 2545

161/84 *Pronuptia de Paris GmbH v Pronuptia de Paris Irmgard Schillgallis* [1986] ECR 0353
118/85 *Commission v Italy* [1987] ECR 2599
352/85 *Bond van Adverteerders and others v The Netherlands State* (Bond) [1988] ECR 2085
263/86 *Belgian State v René Humbel and Marie-Thérèse Edel* (Humbel) [1988] ECR 5365
46/87 and 227/88 *Hoechst AG v Commission* [1989] ECR 2859
85/87 *Dow Benelux NV v Commission* [1989] ECR 3137
97/87, 98/87 and 99/87 *Dow Chemical Ibérica, SA, and others v Commission* [1989] ECR 3165
374/87 *Orkem v Commission* [1989] ECR 3283
C-3/88 *Commission v Italy* [1989] ECR 4035
C-221/89 *The Queen v Secretary of State for Transport, ex parte Factortame Ltd and others* [1991] ECR I-3905
C-234/89 *Stergios Delimitis v Henninger Bräu AG* [1991] ECR I-00935
C-288/89 *Stichting Collectieve Antennevoorziening Gouda and others v Commissariaat voor de Media* [1991] ECR I-4007
C-353/89 *Commission v The Netherlands* [1991] ECR I-4069
C-41/90 *Klaus Höfner and Fritz Elser v Macrotron GmbH* (Höfner) [1991] ECR I-1979
C-269/90 *Technische Universität München v Hauptzollamt München-Mitte* [1991] ECR I-05469
C-159/91 and C-160/91 *Christian Poucet v Assurances Générales de France (AGF) and Caisse Mutuelle Régionale du Languedoc-Roussillon (Camulrac) and Daniel Pistre v Caisse Autonome Nationale de Compensation de l'Assurance Vieillesse des Artisans (Cancava)* (Poucet and Pistre) [1993] ECR I-637
C-272/91 *Commission v Italy* [1994] ECR I-1409
C-109/92 *Stephan Max Wirth v Landeshauptstadt Hannover* (Wirth) [1993] ECR I-6447
C-364/92 *SAT Fluggesellschaft mbH v Eurocontrol* (Eurocontrol) [1994] ECR I-00043
C-415/93 *Union royale belge des sociétés de football association ASBL v Jean-Marc Bosman, Royal club liégeois SA v Jean-Marc Bosman and others and Union des associations européennes de football (UEFA) v Jean-Marc Bosman* (Bosman) [1995] ECR I-4921
C-39/94 *Syndicat français de l'Express international (SFEI) and others v La Poste and others* [1996] ECR I-3547
C-55/94 *Reinhard Gebhard v Consiglio dell'Ordine degli Avvocati e Procuratori di Milano* (Gebhard) [1995] ECR I-4165
C-101/94 *Commission v Italy* [1996] ECR I-2691
C-244/94 *Fédération Française des Sociétés d'Assurance, Société Paternelle-Vie, Union des Assurances de Paris-Vie and Caisse d'Assurance et de Prévoyance Mutuelle des Agriculteurs v Ministère de l'Agriculture et de la Pêche* (FFSA) [1995] ECR I-4013
C-10/95 P *Asociación Española de Empresas de la Carne (Asocarne) v Council* [1995] ECR I-04149
C-70/95 *Sodemare SA, Anni Azzurri Holding SpA and Anni Azzurri Rezzato Srl v Regione Lombardia* (Sodemare) [1997] ECR I-3395
C-120/95 *Nicolas Decker v Caisse de maladie des employés privés* [1998] ECR I-1831
C-343/95 *Diego Calì & Figli Srl v Servizi ecologici porto di Genova SpA (SEPG)* (Diego Calì) [1997] ECR I-1547
C-367/95 P *Commission v Chambre syndicale nationale des entreprises de transport de fonds et valeurs (Sytraval) and Brink's France SARL* (Sytralaval) [1998] ECR I-01719

C-51/96 and C-191/97 *Christelle Deliège v Ligue francophone de judo et disciplines associées ASBL, Ligue belge de judo ASBL, Union européenne de judo (C-51/96) and François Pacquée (C-191/97)* [2000] ECR I-2549
C-67/96 *Albany International BV v Stichting Bedrijfspensioenfonds Textielindustrie* (Albany) [1999] ECR I-5751
C- 106/96 *United Kingdom v Commission* [1998] ECR I-2729
C-158/96 *Raymond Kohll v Union des caisses de maladie* [1998] I-01931
C-75/97 *Belgium v Commission* [1999] ECR I-03671
C-104/97 P *Atlanta AG and others v Commission and Council* [1999] ECR I-6983
C-115/97 to C-117/97 *Brentjens' Handelsonderneming BV v Stichting Bedrijfspensioenfonds voor de Handel in Bouwmaterialen* [1999] ECR I-6025
C-219/97 *Maatschappij Drijvende Bokken BV v Stichting Pensioenfonds voor de Vervoer* [1999] ECR I-6121
C-172/98 *Commission v Belgium* [1999] ECR I-03999
C-180/98 to C-184/98 *Pavel Pavlov and Others v Stichting Pensioenfonds Medische Specialisten* (Pavlov) [2000] ECR I-6451
C-222/98 *Hendrik van der Woude v Stichting Beatrixoord* [2000] ECR I-7111
C-281/98 *Roman Angonese v Cassa di Risparmio di Bolzano SpA* [2000] ECR I-04139
C-368/98 *Abdon Vanbraekel and Others v Alliance nationale des mutualités chrétiennes (ANMC)* [2001] ECR I-5363
C-450/98 P *International Express Carriers Conference (IECC) v Commission* [2001] ECR I-03947
C-17/99 *France v Commission* [2001] ECR I-2481
C-143/99 *Adria-Wien Pipeline GmbH and Wietersdorfer & Peggauer Zementwerke GmbH v Finanzlandesdirektion für Kärnten* [2001] ECR I-08365
C-157/99 *B.S.M. Geraets-Smits v Stichting Ziekenfonds VGZ and H.T.M. Peerbooms v Stichting CZ Groep Zorgverzekeringen* (Smits and Peerbooms) [2001] I-05473
C-309/99 *J.C.J. Wouters, J.W. Savelbergh and Price Waterhouse Belastingadviseurs BV v Algemene Raad van de Nederlandse Orde van Advocaten* (Wouters) [2002] ECR I-1577
C-385/99 *V.G. Müller-Fauré v Onderlinge Waarborgmaatschappij OZ Zorgverzekeringen UA and E.E.M. van Riet v Onderlinge Waarborgmaatschappij ZAO Zorgverzekeringen* (Müller-Fauré) [2003] ECR I-4509
C-439/99 *Commission v Italy* [2002] ECR I-305
C-475/99 *Firma Ambulanz Glöckner v Landkreis Südwestpfalz* (Ambulanz Glöckner) [2001] ECR I-8089
C-50/00 P *Unión de Pequeños Agricultores v Council* [2002] ECR I-6677
C-174/00 *Kennemer Golf & Country Club v Staatssecretaris van Financiën* [2002] ECR I-03293
C-218/00 *Cisal di Battistello Venanzio & C. Sas v Istituto nazionale per l'assicurazione contro gli infortuni sul lavoro (INAIL)* (Cisal) [2002] ECR I-691
C-280/00 *Altmark Trans GmbH and Regierungspräsidium Magdeburg v Nahverkehrsgesellschaft Altmark GmbH, and Oberbundesanwalt beim* Bundesverwaltungsgericht (Altmark) [2003] ECR I-07747
C-355/00 *Freskot AE v Elliniko Dimosio* (Freskot) [2003] ECR I-05263
C-126/01 *Ministère de l'Économie, des Finances et de l'Industrie v GEMO SA* [2003] ECR I-13769

C-243/01 *Criminal proceedings against Piergiorgio Gambelli and Others* [2003] ECR I-13031
C-264/01, C-306/01, C-354/01 and C-355/01 *AOK Bundesverband and others* (AOK) [2004] ECR I-2493
C-422/01 *Försäkringsaktiebolaget Skandia (publ) and Ola Ramstedt v Riksskatteverket* [2003] ECR I-6817
C-153/02 *Valentina Neri v European School of Economics (ESE Insight World Education System Ltd)* [2003] ECR I-13555
C-258/02 P *Bactria Industriehygiene-Service Verwaltungs GmbH v Commission* [2003] ECR I-15105
C-12/03 P *Commission v Tetra Laval BV* [2005] I-987
C-147/03 *Commission v Austria* [2005] ECR I-5969
C-172/03 *Wolfgang Heiser v Finanzamt Innsbruck* [2005] ECR I-0162
C-205/03 P *Federación Española de Empresas de Tecnología Sanitaria (FENIN) v Commission* [2006] ECR I-6295
C-532/03 *Commission v Ireland* [2007] ECR I-11353
C-310/04 *Spain v Council* [2006] ECR I-07285
C-222/04 *Ministero dell'Economia e delle Finanze v Cassa di Risparmio di Firenze SpA, Fondazione Cassa di Risparmio di San Miniato and Cassa di Risparmio di San Miniato SpA* (Banking Foundations) [2006] ECR I-289
C-237/04 *Enirisorse SpA v Sotacarbo SpA* [2006] ECR I-2843
C-338/04, C-359/04 and C-360/04 *Criminal proceedings against Massimiliano Placanica (C-338/04), Christian Palazzese (C-359/04) and Angelo Sorricchio (C-360/04)* [2007] ECR I-1891
C-372/04 *The Queen, on the application of Yvonne Watts v Bedford Primary Care Trust and Secretary of State for Health* (Watts) [2006] ECR I-4325
C-386/04 *Centro di Musicologia Walter Stauffer v Finanzamt München für Körperschaften* (Stauffer) [2006] ECR I-08203
C-519/04 P *David Meca-Medina and Igor Majcen v Commission of the European Communities* (Meca-Medina) [2006] ECR I-6991
C-76/05 *Herbert Schwarz and Marga Gootjes-Schwarz v Finanzamt Bergisch Gladbach* (Schwarz) [2007] ECR I-6849
C-318/05 *Commission v Germany* [2007] ECR I-6957
C-341/05 *Laval un Partneri Ltd v Svenska Byggnadsarbetareförbundet, Svenska Byggnadsarbetareförbundets avdelning 1, Byggettan and Svenska Elektrikerförbundet* [2007] ECR I-11767
C-438/05 *International Transport Workers' Federation and Finnish Seamen's Union v Viking Line ABP and OÜ Viking Line Eesti* [2007] ECR I-10779
C-444/05 *Aikaterini Stamatelaki v NPDD Organismos Asfaliseos Eleftheron Epangelmation (OAEE)* (Stamatelaki) [2007] ECR I-3185
C-281/06 *Hans-Dieter Jundt and Hedwig Jundt v Finanzamt Offenburg* (Jundt) [2007] ECR I-12231
C-487/06 P *British Aggregates Association v Commission* [2008] ECR I-10515
C-501/06 P, C-513/06 P, C-515/06 P and C-519/06 P, *GlaxoSmithKline and others v Commission* [2009] I-09291
C-531/06 *Commission v Italy* [2009] ECR I-4103

C-49/07 *Motosykletistiki Omospondia Ellados NPID (MOTOE) v Elliniko Dimosio* (MOTOE) [2008] ECR I-4863
C-94/07 *Andrea Raccanelli v Max-Planck-Gesellschaft zur Förderung der Wissenschaften eV* [2008] ECR I-5939
C-169/07 *Hartlauer Handelsgesellschaft mbH v Wiener Landesregierung and Oberösterreichische Landesregierung* [2009] ECR I-1721
C-171/07 and C-172/07 *Apothekerkammer des Saarlandes and Others (C-171/07) and Helga Neumann-Seiwert (C-172/07) v Saarland and Ministerium für Justiz, Gesundheit und Soziales* (DocMorris) [2009] ECR I-4171
C-208/07 *Petra von Chamier-Glisczinski v Deutsche Angestellten-Krankenkasse* [2009] ECR I-6095
C-209/07 *Competition Authority v Beef Industry Development Society Ltd and Barry Brothers (Carrigmore) Meats Ltd* [2008] ECR I-08637
C-318/07 *Hein Persche v Finanzamt Lüdenscheid* [2009] ECR I-00359
C-350/07 *Kattner Stahlbau GmbH v Maschinenbau- und Metall- Berufsgenossenschaft* (Kattner) [2009] ECR I-01513
C-58/08 *The Queen, on the application of Vodafone Ltd and Others v Secretary of State for Business, Enterprise and Regulatory Reform* (Vodafone) [2010] ECR I-04999
C-211/08 *Commission v Spain* [2010] ECR I-05267
C-280/08 P *Deutsche Telekom AG v Commission* [2010] ECR I-09555
C-512/08 *Commission v France* [2010] ECR I-08833
C-52/09 *Konkurrensverket v TeliaSonera Sverige AB* (Konkurrensverket) [2011] ECR I-00527
C-56/09 *Emiliano Zanotti v Agenzia delle Entrate – Ufficio Roma 2* (Zanotti) [2010] ECR I-04517
C-89/09 *Commission v France* [2010] ECR I-12941
C-173/09 *Georgi Ivanov Elchinov v Natsionalna zdravnoosiguritelna kasa* [2010] ECR I-08889
C-176/09 *Luxemburg* v *Parliament and Council* (ECJ, 12 May 2011)
C-221/09 *AJD Tuna Ltd* v *Direttur tal-Agrikoltura u s-Sajd and Avukat Generali* [2011] ECR I-01655
C-255/09 *Commission v Portugal* (ECJ, 27 October 2011)
C-343/09 *Afton Chemical Limited v Secretary of State for Transport* [2010] ECR I-07027
C-437/09 *AG2R Prévoyance v Beaudout Père et Fils SARL* (AG2R) [2011] ECR I-00973
C-490/09 *Commission v Luxemburg* [2011] ECR I-00247
C-10/10 *Commission v Austria* [2011] ECR I-05389
C-25/10 *Missionswerk Werner Heukelbach eV v Belgian State* [2011] ECR I-00497
C-124/10 P *Commission v Électricité de France* (EDF) (ECJ, 5 June 2012)
C-562/10 *Commission v Germany* (ECJ, 12 July 2012)
C-84/11 *Marja-Liisa Susisalo, Olli Tuomaala and Merja Ritala* (ECJ, 21 June 2012)
C-138/11 *Compass-Datenbank GmbH v Republik Österreich* (ECJ, 12 July 2012)
C-583/11 P *Inuit Tapiriit Kanatami and Others v Parliament and Council* (ECJ, 3 October 2013)
C-1/12 *Ordem dos Técnicos Oficiais de Contas v Autoridade da Concorrência* (Chartered accountants) (ECJ, 28 February 2013)
C-101/12 *Herbert Schaible v Land Baden-Württemberg* (ECJ, 17 October 2013)

C-136/12 *Consiglio nazionale dei geologi v Autorità garante della concorrenza e del mercato and Autorità garante della concorrenza e del mercato v Consiglio nazionale dei geologiparas* (ECJ, 18 July 2013)

C-356/12 *Wolfgang Glatzel v Freistaat Bayern* (ECJ, 22 May 2014)

C-113/13 *Azienda sanitaria locale n. 5 "Spezzino" and Others v San Lorenzo Soc. coop. sociale and Croce Verde Cogema cooperativa sociale Onlus* (ECJ, 11 December 2014)

C-184/13 to C-187/13, C-194/13, C-195/13 and C-208/13 *API – Anonima Petroli Italiana SpA v Ministero delle Infrastrutture e dei Trasporti and Ministero dello Sviluppo economico and others* (ECJ, 4 September 2014)

C-409/13 *Council v Commission* (ECJ, 14 April 2015)

C-413/13 *FNV Kunsten Informatie en Media v Staat der Nederlanden* (ECJ, 4 December 2014)

GENERAL COURT

T-30/89 *Hilti AG v Commission* [1991] ECR II-1439

T-83/91 *Tetra Pak International SA v Commission* [1994] ECR II-755

T-17/93 *Matra Hachette SA v Commission* [1994] ECR II-00595

T-521/93 *Atlanta AG and others v Council and Commission* [1996] ECR II-1707

T-528/93, T-542/93, T-543/93 and T-546/93 *Metropole télévision SA and Reti Televisive Italiane SpA and Gestevisión Telecinco SA and Antena 3 de Televisión v Commission of the European Communities* (Metropole) [1996] ECR II-649

T-585/93 *Stichting Greenpeace Council (Greenpeace International) and others v Commission* [1995] ECR II-02205

T-86/95 *Compagnie générale maritime and Others v Commission* [2002] ECR II-1011

T-135/96 *Union Européenne de l'artisanat et des petites et moyennes entreprises (UEAPME) v Council* [1998] ECR II-2335

T-13/99 *Pfizer Animal Health SA v Council* [2002] ECR II-03305

T-319/99 *Federación Nacional de Empresas de Instrumentación Científica, Médica, Técnica y Dental (FENIN) v Commission* (FENIN) [2003] ECR II-357

T-185/00, T-216/00, T-299/00 and T-300/00 *Métropole Télévision SA (M6) (T-185/00), Antena 3 de Televisión, SA (T-216/00), Gestevisión Telecinco, SA (T-299/00) and SIC – Sociedade Independente de Comunicação, SA (T-300/00) v Commission* [2002] ECR II-3805

T-213/00 *CMA CGM and Others v Commission* [2003] ECR II-00913

T-168/01 *GlaxoSmithKline Services Unlimited v Commission* (Glaxo) [2006] ECR II-02969

T-193/02 *Laurent Piau v Commission* (Piau) [2005] ECR II-00209

T-289/03 *British United Provident Association Ltd (BUPA), BUPA Insurance Ltd and BUPA Ireland Ltd v Commission* [2008] ECR II-81

T- 99/04 *AC-Treuhand AG v Commission* [2008] ECR II-01501

T-155/04 *SELEX Sistemi Integrati SpA v Commission* [2006] ECR II-04797

T-347/09 *Germany v Commission* (GC, 12 September 2013)

T-18/10 *Inuit Tapiriit Kanatami and Others v Parliament and Council* (Inuit) (GC, 6 September 2011)

T-137/10 *Coordination bruxelloise d'institutions sociales et de santé (CBI) v Commission* (GC, 7 November 2012)
T-526/10 *Inuit Tapiriit Kanatami and Others v Commission* (GC, 25 April 2013)
T-90/11 *Ordre national des pharmaciens (ONP) and Others v Commission* (GC, 10 December 2014)
T-368/11 *Polyelectrolyte Producers Group and others v Commission* (GC, 1 February 2013)

EFTA

E-5/07 *Private Barnehagers Landsforbund v EFTA surveillance authority* [2008] EFTA CR 62

UNITED STATES

US v Brown University 805 F Supp 288 (ED Pa 1992)
US v Brown University 5 F 3d 658 (3rd Cir 1993)

BIBLIOGRAPHY

—. 'Direct Democracy and the European Union... Is that a Threat or a Promise?' (2008) 45 CML Rev 929

—. 'Europe 2020 - A Promising Strategy?' (2010) 45 Intereconomics 136

—. 'Strenghtening Economic Governance in the EU – Report of the Task Force to the European Council' (2010)

—. 'Symposium on Democracy and New Modes of Governance' (2011) 46 Government and Opposition 56

Abromeit H, 'How to Democratise a Multi-Level, Multi-Dimensional Polity' in Weale A and Nentwich M (eds), *Political Theory and the European Union* (Routledge 1998)

Ad-hoc group on reinvigorating the social OMC in the context of the Europe 2020 strategy, 'Draft Background Paper' (SPC /2011.09/1)

Alemanno A, 'The Better Regulation Initiative at the Judicial Gate: A Trojan Horse within the Commission's Walls or the Way Forward?' (2009) 15 ELJ 382

—. 'A Meeting of Minds on Impact Assessment' (2011) 17 EPL 485

—. 'Le Principe d'Ouverture en Droit Européen: d'un Instrument de Lutte contre l'Opacité Institutionnelle à un Outil de Démocratie Participative' [2012] RDUE 627

Alhadeff G and Wilson S, 'European Civil Society Coming of Age' (2002) <www.globalpolicy.org/component/content/article/177/31558.html> accessed 1 September 2015

Allen F, Carletti E and Gray J, *Political, Fiscal and Banking Union in the Eurozone* (FIC Press 2013)

—. Carletti E and Simonelli S, *Governance for the Eurozone: Integration or Disintegration* (FIC Press 2012)

Andenas M and Roth W (eds), *Services and Free Movement in EU law* (OUP 2002)

Andersen SS and Burns TR, 'The European Union and the Erosion of Parliamentary Democracy: A Study of Post-Parliamentary Governance' in Andersen SS and Eliassen KA (eds), *The European Union: How Democratic is it?* (SAGE Publications 1996)

Andersen SS and Eliassen KA (eds), *The European Union: How Democratic is it?* (SAGE Publications 1996)

Andreev SA, 'The EU "Crisis of Legitimacy" Revisited: Concepts, Causes, and Possible Consequences for the European Politics and Citizens' (2007) 2 Political Perspectives EPRU 1 <www.politicalperspectives.org.uk/wp-content/uploads/2010/08/EPRU-2007-S1-07.pdf> accessed 29 August 2013

Anheier HK, *Nonprofit Organizations: Theory, Management, Policy* (Routledge 2004)

—. 'Third Sector-Third Way: Comparative Perspectives and Policy Reflections' in Lewis J and Surender R (eds), *Welfare State Change: Towards a Third Way?* (OUP 2004)

Areeda P, *The "Rule of Reason" in Antitrust Analysis: General Issues* (Federal Judicial Center 1981)

Armstrong K, 'Legal Integration: Theorizing the Legal Dimension of European Integration' (1998) 36 JCMS 155

—. 'Rediscovering Civil Society: The European Union and the White Paper on Governance' (2002) 8 ELJ 102

—. 'Tackling Social Exclusion through OMC: Reshaping the Boundaries of European Governance' in Börzel TA and Cichowski RA (eds), *State of the Union: Law, Politics and Society* (vol 6, OUP 2003)

—. 'Inclusive Governance? Civil Society and the Open Method of Co-Ordination' in Smismans S (ed), *Civil Society and Legitimate European Governance* (Edward Elgar 2006)

—. 'The "Europeanisation" of Social Exclusion: British Adaptation to EU Co-Ordination' (2006) 8 British Journal of Politics and International Relations 79

—. 'Governance and Constitutionalism after Lisbon' (2008) 46 JCMS 415

—. *Governing Social Inclusion: Europeanization through Policy Coordination* (OUP 2010)

—. 'EU Social Policy and the Governance Architecture of Europe 2020' (2012) 18 Transfer 285

—. 'The Lisbon Strategy and Europe 2020: from the Governance of Co-Ordination to the Co-Ordination of Governance' in Copeland P and Papadimitriou D (eds), *The EU's Lisbon Strategy: Evaluating Success, Understanding Failure* (Palgrave Macmillan 2012)

—. Begg I and Zeitlin J, 'JCMS Symposium: EU Governance after Lisbon' (2008) 46 JCMS 413

—. and Kilpatrick C, 'Law, Governance, or New Governance – the Changing Open Method of Coordination' (2006–2007) 13 CJEL 649

Atkinson T, 'Social Inclusion and the European Union' (2002) 40 JCMS 625

Auer A and Flauss JF (eds), *Le Référendum Européen* (Bruylant 1997)

Bachrach P, *The Theory of Democratic Elitism* (Little, Brown and Company 1967)

Balme R and Chabanet D, *European Governance and Democracy: Power and Protest in the EU* (Rowman and Littlefield 2008)

—. and Wright V (eds), *L'Action Collective en Europe-Collective Action in Europe* (Presses de Sciences Po 2002)

Baquero Cruz J, *Between Competition and Free Movement: The Economic Constitutional Law of the European Community* (Hart 2002)

—. 'Beyond Competition: Services of General Interest and European Community Law' in De Búrca G (ed), *EU Law and the Welfare State: In Search of Solidarity* (OUP 2005)

—. 'The Case Law of the European Court of Justice on the Mobility of Patients: an Assessment' in van de Gronden JW, Szyszczak E, Neergaard U and Krajewski M (eds), *Health Care and EU Law* (TMC Asser Press 2011)

—. 'Social Services of General Interest and the State Aid Rules' in Neergaard U, Szyszczak E, van de Gronden JW, and Krajewski M (eds), *Social Services of General Interest in the EU* (TMC Asser Press 2013)

Barber B, *Strong Democracy: Participatory Politics for a New Age* (University of California Press 1984)

—. 'Three Challenges to Reinventing Democracy' in Hirst PQ and Khilnani S (eds), *Reinventing Democracy* (Blackwell 1996)

—. 'How to Make Society Civil and Democracy Strong' in Giddens A (ed), *The Global Third Way Debate* (Polity Press 2001)
Barnard C, 'EC "Social" Policy' in Craig P and De Búrca G (eds), *The Evolution of EU Law* (1st edn, OUP 1999)
—. 'EU Citizenship and the Principle of Solidarity' in Spaventa E and Dougan M (eds), *Social Welfare and EU Law* (Hart 2005)
—. 'Solidarity and New Governance in Social Policy' in De Búrca G and Scott J (eds), *Law and New Governance in the EU and the US* (Hart 2006)
—. *The Substantive Law of the EU: The Four Freedoms* (2nd edn, OUP 2007)
—. 'Unravelling the Services Directive' (2008) 45 CML Rev 323
—. *The Substantive Law of the EU: The Four Freedoms* (3rd edn, OUP 2010)
—. 'The Shaky Legal Foundations for Institutional Action under the Employment, Lisbon and EU2020 Strategies' (2010) 12 CYELS 1
—. *EU Employment Law* (4th edn, OUP 2012)
—. and Odudu O (eds), *The Outer Limits of European Law* (Hart 2009)
—. and Scott J (eds), *The Law of the Single European Market: Unpacking the Premises* (Hart 2002)
Bartholomew A, 'Democratic Citizenship, Social Rights and the "Reflexive Continuation" of the Welfare State' (1993) 42 Studies in Political Economy 141
Bartosch A, 'Social Housing and European State Aid Control' (2007) 28 ECLR 563
—. 'Is There a Need for a Rule of Reason in European State Aid Law? Or How to Arrive at a Coherent Concept of Material Selectivity?' (2010) 47 CML Rev 729
Bauer MW, 'Limitations to Agency Control in European Union Policy-Making: The Commission and the Poverty Programmes' (2002) 40 JCMS 381
Baynes K, 'A Critical Theory Perspective on Civil Society and the State' in Rosenblum NL and Post RC (eds), *Civil Society and Government* (Princeton University Press 2002)
Bee C and Bozzini E (eds), *Mapping the European Public Sphere: Institutions, Media and Civil Society* (Ashgate, 2010)
Beetham D, 'Market Economy and Democratic Polity' in Fine R and Rai S (eds), *Civil Society: Democratic Perspectives*, (Frank Cass 1997)
—. and Lord C, *Legitimacy and the EU* (Longman 1998)
Begg I, 'Is There a Convincing Rationale for the Lisbon Strategy?' (2008) 46 JCMS 427
Behning U, 'Implementing the "New Open Method of Coordination" in the Field of Social Inclusion' (2003) 9 Transfer 737
Bekker S and Klosse S, 'EU Governance of Economic and Social Policies: Chances and Challenges for Social Europe' [2013] EJSL 103
Bellamy R and Castiglione D, 'Legitimizing the Euro-"Polity" and its "Regime": The Normative Turn in EU Studies' (2003) 2 European Journal of Political Theory 7
—. Follesdal A and Weale A, 'Evaluating Trustworthiness, Representation and Political Accountability in New Modes of Governance' in Héritier A and Rhodes M (eds), *New Modes of Governance in Europe: Governing in the Shadow of Hierarchy* (Palgrave Macmillan 2011)
—. and Shaw J, 'Introduction: From National to Transnational Citizenship' in Bellamy R, Castiglione D and Shaw J (eds), *Making European Citizens: Civic Inclusion in a Transnational Context* (Palgrave Macmillan 2006)

—. and Shaw J (eds), *Making European Citizens: Civic Inclusion in a Transnational Context* (Palgrave Macmillan 2006)
Bellamy R and Warleigh A, 'From an Ethics of Integration to an Ethics of Participation: Citizenship and the Future of the European Union' (1998) 27 Millenium 447
—. (eds), *Citizenship and Governance in the European Union* (Continuum 2001)
Belot C and Cautrès B (eds), *La Vie Démocratique de l'Union Européenne* (Documentation française 2006)
Benz A and Papadopoulos Y (eds), *Governance and Democracy: Comparing National, European and International Experiences* (Routledge 2006)
Bercusson B, 'The Lisbon Treaty and Social Europe' (2009) 10 ERA Forum 87
Berg C, 'The European Citizen's Initiative Process' in Berg C, Carline P, Kaufmann B, Leinen J and Wallis D (eds), *Initiative for Europe Handbook 2008 – The Guide to Transnational Democracy in Europe* (Initiative & Referendum Institute Europe 2007) <www.iri-europe.org/publications/handbooks/european-citizens-initiative-handbook/> accessed 29 August 2013
—. Carline P, Kaufmann B, Leinen J and Wallis D (eds), *Initiative for Europe Handbook 2008 – the Guide to Transnational Democracy in Europe* (Initiative & Referendum Institute Europe 2007) <www.iri-europe.org/publications/handbooks/european-citizens-initiative-handbook/> accessed 29 August 2013
Berger N, 'Participatory Democracy: Organised Civil Society and the "New" Dialogue' (2004) Online Paper 09/04, the Federal Trust
Berghman J and Okma KGH, 'The Method of Open Co-Ordination: Open Procedures or Closed Circuit? Social Policy Making between Science and Politics' (2002) 4 European Journal of Social Security 331
Bernard E, 'La Démocratie Participative sous l'Angle du Dialogue Civil et du Dialogue Social' in Constantinesco V, Gautier Y and Michel V (eds), *Le Traité établissant une Constitution pour l'Europe: Analyses & Commentaires* (Presses universitaires de Strasbourg 2005)
Beyers J, Eising R and Maloney W (eds), *Interest Group Politics in Europe: Lessons from EU Studies and Comparative Politics* (Routledge 2010)
Bieber R and Maiani F, 'Bringing the Union Closer to its Citizens? "Participatory Democracy" and the Potential Contribution of the Lisbon Treaty' [2009] Annuaire Suisse de Droit Européen 229
Bignami F, 'The Democratic Deficit in European Community Rulemaking: A Call for Notice and Comment in Comitology' (1999) 40 Harvard International Law Review 451
—. 'Three Generations of Participation Rights in European Administrative Proceedings' (2003) Jean Monnet Working Paper no. 11/03
—. 'Three Generations of Participation Rights before the European Commission' (2004) 68 Law and Contemporary Problems 61
Binon JM, 'Solidarité et Assurance: Mariage de Coeur ou de Raison? Réflexion sur la Ligne de Partage entre l'Assurance Publique et l'Assurance Privée à la Lumière des Arrêts Poucet/Pistre, Coreva et Garcia de la Cour de Justice des Communautés Européennes' [1997] RMUE 87
Biondi A and Rubini L, 'Aims, Effects and Justifications: EC State Aid Law and its Impact on National Social Policies' in Spaventa E and Dougan M (eds), *Social Welfare and EU Law* (Hart 2005)

Blackstone EA and Fuhr Jr JP, 'An Antitrust Analysis of Non-Profit Hospital Mergers' (1992) 8 Review of Industrial Organization 473

Blankart CB and Mueller DC (eds), *A Constitution for the European Union* (MIT Press 2004)

Blauberger M, Puntscher Riekmann S and Wydra D, *Conventional Wisdoms under Challenge: Reviewing the EU's Democratic Deficit in Times of Crisis* (Symposium) (2014) 52 JCMS 1171

Boeger N, '"New" Social Democracy before the Court of Justice' (2006) 8 CYELS 95

—. 'Solidarity and EC Competition Law' (2007) 32 EL Rev 319

Bork RH, *The Antitrust Paradox: A Policy at War with Itself* (Free Press 1993)

Borrás S and Conzelmann T, 'Democracy, Legitimacy and Soft Modes of Governance in the EU: The Empirical Turn' (2007) 29 Journal of European Integration 531

Borrás S and Jacobsson K, 'The Open Method of Co-Ordination and New Governance Patterns in the EU' (2004) 11 JEPP 185

Borrás S and Radaelli CM, 'Recalibrating the Open Method of Coordination: Towards Diverse and More Effective Usages' (2010) SIEPS Report No 72

Boual JC (ed), *Vers une Société Civile Européenne?* (Éd de l'Aube 1999)

Boussaguet L, 'À l'Écoute des Citoyens: Bilan des Premières Expériences Participatives à l'Échelle Communautaire' (2011) Notre Europe Policy Paper no. 44 <www.notre-europe.eu/media/policy44-crdemocratie_01.pdf?pdf=ok> accessed 31 August 2013

—. and Dehousse R, 'L'Europe des Profanes: L'Expérience des Conférences Citoyennes' in Costa O and Magnette P (eds), *Une Europe des Élites? Réflexions sur la Fracture Démocratique de l'Union Européenne* (Editions de l'Université de Bruxelles 2007)

Bouza García L, 'How Could the New Article 11 TEU Contribute to Reduce the EU's Democratic Malaise?' in Dougan M, Shuibhne NN and Spaventa E (eds), *Empowerment and Disempowerment of the European Citizen* (Hart 2012)

—. and Greenwood J (eds), *The European Citizens' Initiative: a First for Participatory Democracy?* (2012) 13 Perspectives on European Politics and Society (special issue) 251

Bovens M, 'Two Concepts of Accountability: Accountability as a Virtue and as a Mechanism' (2010) 33 West European Politics 946

Bowman J, 'The European Union Democratic Deficit: Federalists, Skeptics, and Revisionists' (2006) 5 European Journal of Political Theory 191

Bozzini E, 'The Role of Civil Society Organisations in Written Consultation Processes: From the European Monitoring Centre to the European Fundamental Rights Agency' in Della Sala V and Ruzza C (eds), *Governance and Civil Society in the European Union: Exploring Policy Issues* (vol 2, Manchester University Press 2007)

Brandsen T, Pavolini E, Ranci C, Sittermann B and Zimmer A, 'The National Action Plan on Social Inclusion: an Opportunity for the Third Sector?' (2005) Third Sector European Policy Working Paper no. 14 <http://eprints.lse.ac.uk/29023/1/14TSEP.pdf> accessed 1st September 2015

Breen OB, 'EU Regulation of Charitable Organizations: The Politics of Legally Enabling Civil Society' (2008) 10 IJNFPL 50

Brisimi V, 'Abuse of a Dominant Position and Public Policy Justifications: A Question of Attribution' (2013) 24 EBLR 261

Bruun N, Lörcher K and Schömann I (eds), *The Lisbon Treaty and Social Europe* (Hart 2012)

Büchs M, 'How Legitimate is the Open Method of Coordination?' (2008) 46 JCMS 765

—. and Friedrich D, 'Surface Integration: The National Action Plans for Employment and Social Inclusion in Germany' in Zeitlin J, Pochet P and Magnusson L (eds), *The Open Method of Co-Ordination in Action: The European Employment and Social Inclusion Strategies* (PIE-Peter Lang 2005)

Buendia Sierra JL, *Exclusive Rights and State Monopolies under EC Law: Article 86 (Formerly Article 90) of the EC Treaty* (OUP 1999)

Busschaert G, 'Revisiting the Fundamentals of Internal Market Law: Civil Society as a Third Sector between the State and the Market' (2011) 22 EBLR 725

Butler IJ, 'Non-Governmental Organisation Participation in the EU Law-Making Process: The Example of Social Non-Governmental Organisations at the Commission, Parliament and Council' (2008) 14 ELJ 558

Cahill D, 'The Ebb and Flow, the Doldrums and the Raging Tide: Single Market Law's Ebb and Flow over Services of General Economic Interest, the Legal Doldrums over Services of General Interest, and the Raging Tide of Article 106(2) (ex Art 86(2)) over State Aid and Public Procurement' (2010) 21 EBLR 629

Cantillon B and Van Mechelen N, 'Between Dream and Reality… On Anti-Poverty, Minimum Income Protection and the European Social Model' in Cantillon B, Verschueren H and Ploscar P (eds), *Social Inclusion and Social Protection in the EU: Interactions between Law and Policy* (Intersentia 2012)

Cantillon B, Verschueren H and Ploscar P (eds), *Social Inclusion and Social Protection in the EU: Interactions between Law and Policy* (Intersentia 2012)

Carlton DW, Bamberger GE and Epstein RJ, 'Antitrust and Higher Education' (1994) Working Paper no. 107, Center for the Study of the Economy and the State, University of Chicago <http://research.chicagobooth.edu/economy/research/articles/107.pdf> accessed 1st September 2015

Carmel E, 'What is European and Social about European Social Policy? Some Remarks on the Open Methods of Coordination' (2003) Paper presented at the first ESPAnet annual conference, Copenhagen, 14–17 November 2003

Carter A, *The Political Theory of Global Citizenship* (Routledge 2001)

—. and Stokes G (eds), *Democratic Theory Today: Challenges for the 21st Century* (Polity 2002)

Chalmers D, 'The European Redistributive State and a European Law of Struggle' (2012) 18 ELJ 667

—. and Lodge M, 'The Open Method of Co-Ordination and the European Welfare State' (2003) ESRC Centre for Analysis of Risk and Regulation Discussion Paper no. 11 <www2.lse.ac.uk/researchAndExpertise/units/CARR/pdf/DPs/Disspaper11.pdf> accessed 1 September 2015

Chambers S, 'A Critical Theory of Civil Society' in Chambers S and Kymlicka W (eds), *Alternative Conceptions of Civil Society* (Princeton University Press 2001)

—. and Kymlicka W (eds), *Alternative Conceptions of Civil Society* (Princeton University Press 2001)

Chari R, Murphy G and Hogan J, 'Regulating Lobbyists: A Comparative Analysis of the United States, Canada, Germany and the European Union' (2007) 78 The Political Quarterly 422

Cheema GS and Popovski V (eds), *Engaging Civil Society: Emerging Trends in Democratic Governance* (United Nations University Press 2010)
Cheneviere C and Duchenne G (eds), *Les Modes d'Expression de la Citoyenneté Européenne: Actes de la Journée d'Étude Organisée à Louvain-la-Neuve le 19 Mars 2010* (Presses Universitaires de Louvain UCL 2011)
Cicoria C, 'European Competition Law and Nonprofit Organizations: A Law and Economics Analysis' (2006) 6 Global Jurist Topics <www.degruyter.com/view/j/gj.2006.6.1/issue-files/gj.2006.6.issue-1.xml> accessed 1 September 2015
—. *Nonprofit Organizations Facing Competition: The Application of United States, European and German Competition Law to Not-for-Profit Entities* (Peter Lang 2006)
Clauwaert S, 'The Country-Specific Recommendations (CSRs) in the Social Field: An Overview and Initial Comparison' (2013) ETUI Background Analysis 2013.02
Cohen J and Sabel CF, 'Directly-Deliberative Polyarchy' (1997) 3 ELJ 313
—. 'Sovereignty and Solidarity: EU and US' in Zeitlin J and Trubek DM (eds), *Governing Work and Welfare in a New Economy: European and American Experiments* (OUP 2003)
Cohen JL, 'Civic Innovation in America: Towards a Reflexive Politics' (2003) 12 The Good Society 56
—. and Arato A, *Civil Society and Political Theory* (MIT Press 1992)
Cole GDH, *Social Theory* (Methuen & Co 1920)
COLLECTIF SSIG (ed), *Social Services of General Interest in the Internal Market of the 21st Century - The Reform Treaty: The New State of Affairs* (2008) <http://cor.europa.eu/en/documentation/brochures/Documents/7bc13269-7368-4afe-b12f-825be1a9e33c.pdf> accessed 1 September 2015
Commission, *Twenty-First Report on Competition Policy* (Publications Office 1991)
—. 'Proposal for a Council Regulation (EEC) on the Statute for a European Association' COM (91) 273 final
—. 'An Open and Structured Dialogue between the Commission and Special Interest Groups' (Communication) [1993] OJ C63/2
—. 'Increased Transparency in the Work of the Commission' (Communication) [1993] OJ C63/8
—. 'Openness in the Community' (Communication) [1993] OJ C166/4
—. 'European Social Policy: Options for the Union' (Green Paper) COM (93) 551
—. 'European Social Policy: a Way Forward for the Union' (White Paper) COM (94) 333 final
—. 'The Future of Social Protection: a Framework for a European Debate' (Communication) COM (95) 466 final
—. 'Report on the Operation of the Treaty on European Union' SEC (95) 731 final
—. 'Modernising and Improving Social Protection in the European Union' (Communication) COM (97) 102 final
—. 'Promoting the Role of Voluntary Organisations and Foundations in Europe' (Communication) COM (97) 241 final
—. 'Adapting and Promoting the Social Dialogue at Community Level' (Communication) COM (98) 322 final
—. 'Notice on the Application of the State Aid Rules to Measures relating to Direct Business Taxation' [1998] OJ C384/3

—. 'A Concerted Strategy for Modernising Social Protection' (Communication) COM (99) 347 final
—. 'White Paper on Modernisation of the Rules Implementing Articles 85 and 86 of the EC Treaty' [1999] OJ C132/1
—. 'The Commission and Non-Governmental Organisations: Building a Stronger Partnership' (Discussion Paper) COM (2000) 11 final
—. 'Building an Inclusive Europe' COM (2000) 79 final
—. 'Services of General Interest in Europe' (Communication) COM (2000) 580 final
—. 'Guidelines on the Applicability of Article 81 of the EC Treaty to Horizontal Cooperation Agreements' [2001] OJ C3/2
—. 'European Governance: a White Paper' COM (2001) 428 final
—. 'The Lisbon Strategy: Making Change Happen' (Communication) COM (2002) 14 final
—. 'Consultation Document: Towards a Reinforced Culture of Consultation and Dialogue – Proposal for General Principles and Minimum Standards for Consultation of Interested Parties by the Commission' (Communication) COM (2002) 277 final
—. 'Streamlining the Annual Economic and Employment Policy Co-ordination Cycles' (Communication) COM (2002) 487 final
—. 'Towards a Reinforced Culture of Consultation and Dialogue – General Principles and Minimum Standards for Consultation of Interested Parties by the Commission' (Communication) COM (2002) 704 final
—. 'Strengthening the Social Dimension of the Lisbon Strategy: Streamlining Open Coordination in the Field of Social Protection' (Communication) COM (2003) 261 final
—. 'Green Paper on Services of General Interest' COM (2003) 270 final
—. 'Guidelines on the Application of Article 81(3) of the Treaty' [2004] OJ C101/97
—. 'Proposal for a Directive of the European Parliament and of the Council on Services in the Internal Market' COM (2004) 2 final
—. 'White Paper on Services of General Interest' COM (2004) 374 final
—. 'Working Together for Growth and Jobs: A New Start for the Lisbon Strategy' (Communication) COM (2005) 24 final
—. 'Working Together, Working Better: A New Framework for the Open Coordination of Social Protection and Inclusion Policies in the European Union' (Communication) COM (2005) 706 final
—. 'Lisbon Action Plan Incorporating EU Lisbon Programme and Recommendations for Actions to Member States for Inclusion in their National Lisbon Programmes' (Companion document) SEC (2005) 192
—. 'Delivering on Growth and Jobs: A New and Integrated Economic and Employment Co-Ordination Cycle in the EU' (Companion document) SEC (2005) 193
—. 'Proposing the Launch of a European Transparency Initiative' (Communication) SEC (2005) 1300/5
—. 'White Paper on a European Communication Policy' COM (2006) 35 final
—. 'Implementing the Community Lisbon Programme: Social Services of General Interest in the European Union' (Communication) COM (2006) 177 final
—. 'European Transparency Initiative' (Green Paper) COM (2006) 194 final

—. 'Follow-up to the Green Paper "European Transparency Initiative"' (Communication) COM (2007) 127 final
—. 'Services of General Interest, Including Social Services of General Interest: a New European Commitment' (Communication) COM (2007) 725 final
—. 'European Transparency Initiative: A Framework for Relations with Interest Representatives (Register and Code of Conduct)' (Communication) COM (2008) 323 final
—. 'Renewed Social Agenda: Opportunities, Access and Solidarity in 21st Century Europe' (Communication) COM (2008) 412 final
—. 'Proposal for a Directive of the European Parliament and of the Council on the Application of Patients' Rights in Cross-Border Healthcare' COM (2008) 414 final
—. 'Biennial Report on Social Services of General Interest' (Staff Working Document) COM (2008) 418 final
—. 'A Renewed Commitment to Social Europe: Reinforcing the Open Method of Coordination for Social Protection and Social Inclusion' (Communication) COM (2008) 418 final
—. 'A Renewed Commitment to Social Europe: Reinforcing the Open Method of Coordination for Social Protection and Social Inclusion-Impact Assessment' (Staff Working Document) SEC (2008) 2169
—. 'Impact Assessment Guidelines' SEC (2009) 92
—. 'Portfolio of Indicators for the Monitoring the European Strategy for Social Protection and Social Inclusion – September 2009 Update' (2009)
—. 'Smart Regulation in the European Union' (Communication) COM (2010) 543 final
—. 'The European Platform against Poverty and Social Exclusion: A European Framework for Social and Territorial Cohesion' (Communication) COM (2010) 758 final
—. 'Europe 2020: A Strategy for Smart, Sustainable and Inclusive Growth' (Communication) COM (2010) 2020 final
—. 'Lisbon Strategy Evaluation Document' SEC (2010) 114 final
—. 'Second Biennial Report on Social Services of General Interest' (Staff Working Document) SEC (2010) 1284 final
—. 'Guide to the Application of the European Union Rules on State Aid, Public Procurement and the Internal Market to Services of General Economic Interest, and in particular to Social Services of General Interest' (Staff Working Document) SEC (2010) 1545 final
—. 'Framework for Commission Expert Groups: Horizontal Rules and Public Register' (Communication) C (2010) 7649 final
—. 'Guidelines on the Applicability of Article 101 of the Treaty on the Functioning of the European Union to Horizontal Co-operation Agreements' [2011] OJ C11/1
—. 'Social Business Initiative: Creating a Favourable Climate for Social Enterprises, Key Stakeholders in the Social Economy and Innovation' (Communication) COM (2011) 682 final
—. 'Proposal for a Council Regulation Establishing for the Period 2014–2020 the Programme "Europe for Citizens"' COM (2011) 884 final
—. 'Proposal for a Directive of the European Parliament and of the Council on Public Procurement' COM (2011) 896 final

—. 'A Quality Framework for Services of General Interest in Europe' (Communication) COM (2011) 900 final
—. 'The Application of the European Union State Aid Rules to Compensation Granted for the Provision of Services of General Economic Interest' (Communication) [2012] OJ C8/4
—. 'European Union Framework for State Aid in the Form of Public Service Compensation' (Communication) [2012] OJ C8/15
—. 'Proposal for a Council Regulation on the Statute for a European Foundation (FE)' COM (2012) 35 final
—. 'EU Regulatory Fitness' (Communication) COM (2012) 746 final
—. 'Review of the Commission Consultation Policy Accompanying the Communication on EU Regulatory Fitness' (Staff Working Document) SWD (2012) 422 final
—. '3rd Biennial Report on Social Services of General Interest' (Staff Working Document) SWD (2013) 40 final
—. 'Guide to the Application of the European Union Rules on State Aid, Public Procurement and the Internal Market to Services of General Economic Interest, and in particular to Social Services of General Interest' (Staff Working Document) SWD (2013) 53 final/2
—. 'Social Europe: Current Challenges and the Way Forward – Annual Report of the Social Protection Committee (2012)' (Publications Office of the EU 2013)
—. 'Towards Social Investment for Growth and Cohesion – including implementing the European Social Fund 2014–2020' (Communication) COM (2013) 83 final
—. 'EU Citizenship Report 2013 – EU Citizens: Your Rights, Your Future' COM (2013) 269 final
—. 'Policy Roadmap for the 2013–2014 Implementation of the Social Investment Package' (2013)
—. 'Social Economy and Social Entrepreneurship' (Social Europe guide vol 4, Publication Office of the EU 2013)
—. 'The EU's Economic Governance Explained' (MEMO/13/318) 10 avril 2013
—. 'Taking stock of the Europe 2020 strategy for smart, sustainable and inclusive growth' (Communication) COM (2014) 130 final/2
—. 'Annual Growth Survey 2015' (Communication) COM (2014) 902 final
—. 'The revised Transparency Register: more information, more incentives, tougher on those who break the rules' (MEMO/14/302) 15 April 2014
—. 'The EU's Economic Governance Explained' (MEMO/13/979) 28 May 2014
—. 'Annex to the Proposal for a Council Decision on guidelines for the employment policies of the Member States' COM (2015) 98 final
—. 'Annex to the Recommendation for a Council Recommendation on broad guidelines for the economic policies of the Member States and of the Union' COM(2015) 99 final
—. 'Report on the Application of Regulation (EU) No 211/2011 on the Citizens' Initiative' COM (2015) 145 final
—. 'Better Regulation for Better Results – an EU Agenda' (Communication) SWD (2015) 110 final
—. 'Better Regulation Guidelines' SWD (2015) 111 final

Commission and Council, 'Joint Report on Social Protection and Social Inclusion' (2009) Doc 7503/09

Commission and EESC, 'Protocol on cooperation' [2012] OJ C102/1

Committee of Ministers of the Council of Europe, 'Resolution (2003) 8 of 19 November 2003 on the Participatory Status for International Non-Governmental Organisations with the Council of Europe'

Copeland P, 'Conclusion: The Lisbon Strategy - Evaluating Success and Understanding Failure' in Copeland P and Papadimitriou D (eds), *The EU's Lisbon Strategy: Evaluating Success, Understanding Failure* (Palgrave Macmillan 2012)

—. and Papadimitriou D (eds), *The EU's Lisbon Strategy: Evaluating Success, Understanding Failure* (Palgrave Macmillan 2012)

CoR, 'the Role of Voluntary Organizations - a Contribution to a European Society' (Opinion) [1998] C180/57

—. 'New Forms of Governance: Europe, a Framework for Citizens' Initiative' (Opinion) [2001] OJ C144/1

—. 'The White Paper on European Governance' (Opinion) [2002] OJ C192/24

—. 'Follow-up to the White Paper on European Governance' (Opinion) [2003] OJ C256/24

—. 'Proposing the Launch of a European Transparency Initiative' (Communication) SEC (2005) 1300/5

—. 'The Communication from the Commission - Implementing the Community Lisbon Programme - Social Services of General Interest in the European Union' (Opinion) [2007] OJ C57/34

—. 'The European Transparency Initiative' (Opinion) [2007] OJ C146/53

—. 'The "European Citizens' Initiative"' (Opinion) [2010] OJ C267/57

—. 'The European Platform against Poverty and Social Exclusion' (Opinion) [2011] OJ C166/18

—. 'White Paper on Multilevel Governance' [2011] OJ C211/1

—. 'The Role of Local and Regional Authorities in Achieving the Objectives of the Europe 2020 Strategy' [2012] OJ C9/53

—. 'Building a European Culture of Multilevel Governance: Follow-up to the Committee of the Regions' White Paper' (Opinion) [2012] OJ C113/62

—. 'European Platform against Poverty and Social Exclusion: Survey of the EU Local and Regional Authorities – Final Report' (2013)

Corbett R, "European Elections are Second-Order Elections': Is Received Wisdom Changing?' (2014) 52 JCMS 1194

Costa O and Magnette P (eds), *Une Europe des Élites? Réflexions sur la Fracture Démocratique de l'Union Européenne* (Editions de l'Université de Bruxelles 2007)

—. 'Introduction. L'Europe des Élites, Anatomie d'un Mythe' in Costa O and Magnette P (eds), *Une Europe des Élites? Réflexions sur la Fracture Démocratique de l'Union Européenne* (Editions de l'Université de Bruxelles 2007)

Council, 'Resolution of 21 January 1974 concerning a Social Action Programme' [1974] OJ C13/1

—. 'Conclusions of 17 December 1999 on the Strengthening of Cooperation for Modernising and Improving Social Protection' [2000] OJ C08/7

—. 'Fight against Poverty and Social Exclusion' (2000) Doc 14110/00

—. 'Implementation of the IIA of 23 June 2011 between the European Parliament and the European Commission on the Establishment of a Transparency Register–The Work and Functioning of the Joint Transparency Register Secretariat (JTRS)' (2012) Doc 13528/12

Coursin F, 'La Politique Européenne de Concurrence et les Entreprises de l'Économie Sociale' (1995) 1 Transnational Associations 26

Craig P, *Public Law and Democracy in the United Kingdom and the United States of America* (Clarendon Press 1990)

—. 'Democracy and Rule-Making within the EC: An Empirical and Normative Assessment' (1997) 3 ELJ 105

—. *EU Administrative Law* (OUP 2006)

—. *The Lisbon Treaty: Law, Politics, and Treaty Reform* (OUP 2010)

—. and De Búrca G, *EU Law: Text, Cases, and Materials* (4th edn, OUP 2008)

—. and De Búrca G, *EU Law: Text, Cases, and Materials* (5th edn, OUP 2011)

—. and De Búrca G, *The Evolution of EU Law* (2nd edn, OUP 2011)

Cram L, *Policy-Making in the European Union: Conceptual Lenses and the Integration Process* (Routledge 1997)

—. 'Civil Society, Participatory Democracy and the Governance of the Union: The Institutionalisation of a Fiction' (2006) paper delivered at the 2–4 November 2006 Osnabrück conference on governance and policy-making in the EU <http://web.uvic.ca/jmtrg/Papers_files/cram_paper_1.pdf> accessed 1 September 2015

—. 'In the Shadow of Hierarchy: Governance as a Tool of Government' in Dehousse R (ed), *The "Community Method": Obstinate or Obsolete?* (Palgrave Macmillan 2011)

Cuesta Lopez V, 'The Lisbon Treaty's Provisions on Democratic Principles: A Legal Framework for Participatory Democracy' (2010) 16 EPL 123

Cullen P, 'Pan-European NGOs and Social Rights: Participatory Democracy and Civil Dialogue' in Joachim J and Locher B (eds), *Transnational Activism in the UN and EU: A Comparative Study* (Routledge 2008)

—. 'The Platform of European Social NGOs: Ideology, Division and Coalition' (2010) 15 Journal of Political Ideologies 317

Curtin D, *'Civil Society' and the European Union: Opening Spaces for Deliberative Democracy?* (Collected courses of the Academy of European law 1996)

—. 'Citizens' Fundamental Right of Access to EU Information: An Evolving Digital Passepartout?' (2000) 37 CML Rev 7

—. 'Private Interest Representation or Civil Society Deliberation? A Contemporary Dilemma for European Union Governance' (2003) 12 Social & Legal Studies 55

—. 'Framing Public Deliberation and Democratic Legitimacy in the European Union' in Besson S and Martí JL (eds), *Deliberative Democracy and its Discontents* (Ashgate 2006)

—. Kellermann AE and Blockmans S (eds), *The EU Constitution: the Best Way Forward?* (TMC Asser Press 2005)

—. Mair P and Papadopoulos Y (eds), *Accountability and European Governance* (2010) 33 West European Politics 929

—. and Meijer AJ, 'Does Transparency Strengthen Legitimacy? A Critical Analysis of European Union Policy Documents' (2006) 11 Information Polity 109

—. and Wessel RA (eds), *Good Governance and the European Union: Reflections on Concepts, Institutions and Substance* (Intersentia 2005)
Cygan A, 'Public Healthcare in the European Union: Still a Service of General Interest?' (2008) 57 ICLQ 529
—. 'The Parliamentarisation of EU Decision-Making? The Impact of the Treaty of Lisbon on National Parliaments' (2011) 36 EL Rev 478
Dahl RA, 'A Democratic Dilemma: System Effectiveness versus Citizen Participation' (1994) 109 Political Science Quarterly 23
—. *On Democracy* (Yale University Press 1998)
Daly M, 'EU Social Policy after Lisbon' (2006) 44 JCMS 461
—. 'Whither EU Social Policy? An Account and Assessment of Developments in the Lisbon Social Inclusion Process' (2008) 37 Journal of Social Policy 1
—. 'Paradigms in EU Social Policy: a Critical Account of Europe 2020' (2012) 18 Transfer 273
Damjanovic D and De Witte B, 'Welfare Integration through EU Law: The overall Picture in the Light of the Lisbon Treaty' in Neergaard U, Nielsen R and Roseberry L (eds), *Integrating Welfare Functions into EU law: from Rome to Lisbon* (DJOF Publishing 2009)
Davies G, 'Welfare as a Service' (2002) 29 LIEI 27
—. 'Article 86 EC, the EC's Economic Approach to Competition Law, and the General Interest' (2009) 5 ECJ 549
Dawson M, 'EU Law "Transformed"? Evaluating Accountability and Subsidiarity in the "Streamlined" OMC for Social Inclusion and Social Protection' (2009) 13 EIoP <http://eiop.or.at/eiop/texte/2009-008a.htm> accessed 1 September 2015
—. 'The Ambiguity of Social Europe in the Open Method of Coordination' (2009) 34 EL Rev 55
—. 'Learning from Past Failures? New Governance in the European Union from Lisbon 2000 to Lisbon 2020' (2010) 17 MJ 2
—. 'Three Waves of New Governance in the European Union' (2010) 36 EL Rev 208
—. 'Transforming into What? New Governance in the EU and the "Managerial Sensibility" in Modern Law' [2010] Wisconsin Law Review 389
—. *New Governance and the Transformation of European Law: Coordinating EU Social Law and Policy* (CUP 2011)
—. and De Witte B, 'The EU Legal Framework of Social Inclusion and Social Protection: Between the Lisbon Strategy and the Lisbon Treaty' in Cantillon B, Verschueren H and Ploscar P (eds), *Social Inclusion and Social Protection in the EU: Interactions between Law and Policy* (Intersentia 2012)
De Beys J, 'Aide d'État et Financement des Services Publics: Un Bilan après l'Adoption du Paquet Post-Altmark' [2006] JDE 1
De Búrca G, 'The Constitutional Challenge of New Governance in the European Union' (2003) 28 EL Rev 814
—. (ed), *EU Law and the Welfare State: In Search of Solidarity* (OUP 2005)
—. 'New Modes of Governance and the Protection of Human Rights' in Alston P and De Schutter O (eds), *Monitoring Fundamental Rights in the EU: the Contribution of the Fundamental Rights Agency* (Hart 2005)

—. and Scott J, 'Introduction: New Governance, Law and Constitutionalism' in De Búrca G and Scott J (eds), *Law and New Governance in the EU and the US* (Hart 2006)

—. and Scott J (eds), *Law and New Governance in the EU and the US* (Hart 2006)

—. and Scott J, 'Narrowing the Gap: Law and New Approaches to Governance in the European Union' (2006–2007) 13 CJEL 513

—. and Zeitlin J, 'Constitutionalizing the Open Method of Coordination: What Should the Convention Propose?' (2003) CEPS Policy Brief no. 31

Decker F, 'Governance beyond the Nation-State. Reflections on the Democratic Deficit of the European Union' (2002) 9 JEPP 256

Deckmyn V (ed), *Increasing Transparency in the European Union* (European Institute of Public Administration 2002)

—. and Thomson I (eds), *Openness and Transparency in the European Union* (European Institute of Public Administration 1998)

De Grauwe P, 'The Governance of a Fragile Eurozone' (2011) CEPS Working Document no. 346

Degryse C, 'The New European Economic Governance' (2012) ETUI Working Paper no. 2012/14

—. Jepsen M and Pochet P, 'The Euro Crisis and its Impact on National and European Social Policies' (2013) ETUI Working Paper no. 2013/05

—. and Pochet P, 'Monetary Union, Economic Coordination and Democratic Legitimacy' (2011) ETUI Policy Brief, European Social Policy, issue 5/2011

Dehousse R, 'Constitutional Reform in the European Community: Are There Alternatives to the Majoritarian Avenue?' (1995) 18 West European Politics 118

—. 'European Governance in Search of Legitimacy: The Need for a Process-Based Approach' in De Schutter O, Lebessis N and Paterson J (eds), *Governance in the European Union* (Office for Official Publications of the European Communities 2001)

—. (ed), *L'Europe Sans Bruxelles? Une Analyse de la Méthode Ouverte de Coordination* (L'Harmattan 2004)

—. (ed), *The "Community Method": Obstinate or Obsolete?* (Palgrave Macmillan 2011)

de la Porte C, 'Is the Open Method of Coordination Appropriate for Organising Activities at European Level in Sensitive Policy Areas?' (2002) 8 ELJ 38

—. and Nanz P, 'The OMC – a Deliberative-Democratic Mode of Governance? The Cases of Employment and Pensions 1.' (2004) 11 JEPP 267

—. and Pochet P (eds), *Building Social Europe through the Open Method Co-Ordination* (PIE-Peter Lang 2002)

—. and Pochet P, 'The OMC Intertwined with the Debates on Governance, Democracy and Social Europe: Research on the Open Method of Co-Ordination and European Integration' (2003) Report prepared for Frank Vandenbroucke, Belgian Minister for Social Affairs and Pensions, Observatoire social européen, Brussels

—. and Pochet P, 'Participation in the Open Method of Co-Ordination. The Cases of Employment and Social Inclusion' in Zeitlin J, Pochet P and Magnusson L (eds), *The Open Method of Co-Ordination in Action: The European Employment and Social Inclusion Strategies* (PIE-Peter Lang 2005)

—. Pochet P and Room G, 'Social Benchmarking, Policy Making and New Governance in the EU' (2001) 11 JESP 291

De la Rosa S, 'The Directive on Cross-Border Healthcare or the Art of Codifying Complex Case Law' (2012) 49 CML Rev 15
De Leeuw ME, 'Openness in the Legislative Process in the European Union' (2007) 32 EL Rev 295
Della Porta D and Caiani M, *Social Movements & Europeanization* (OUP 2009)
Della Sala V and Ruzza C (eds), *Governance and Civil Society in the European Union: Exploring Policy Issues* (vol 2, Manchester University Press 2007)
Demoustier D, 'Économie Sociale et Construction Européenne: Rapports au Marché et à la Concurrence' [1997] Problèmes économiques 29
de Ruiter R, 'Full Disclosure? The Open Method of Coordination, Parliamentary Debates and Media Coverage' (2013) 14 European Union Politics 95
Deschouwer K and Jans T (eds), *Politics Beyond the State: Actors and Policies in Complex Institutional Settings* (VUB Press 2007)
De Schutter O, 'Europe in Search of its Civil Society' (2002) 8 ELJ 198
—. 'Public Interest Litigation before the European Court of Justice' (2006) 13 MJ 9
—. 'Fundamental Rights and the Transformation of Governance in the European Union' (2007) 9 CYELS 133
—. 'The Democratic Experimentalist Approach to Governance: Protecting Social Rights in the European Union' in De Schutter O and Lenoble J (eds), *Reflexive Governance: Redefining the Public Interest in a Pluralistic World* (Hart 2010)
—. and Deakin S (eds), *Social Rights and Market Forces: Is the Open Coordination of Employment and Social Policies the Future of Social Europe*? (Bruylant 2005)
—. Lebessis N and Paterson J (eds), *Governance in the European Union* (Office for Official Publications of the European Communities 2001)
—. and Lenoble J (eds), *Reflexive Governance: Redefining the Public Interest in a Pluralistic World* (Hart 2010)
de Tocqueville A, *Democracy in America* (first published 1899, Reeve H tr) Electronic Edition Deposited and Marked-Up by ASGRP, the American Studies Programs at the University of Virginia, June 1, 1997 <http://xroads.virginia.edu/~HYPER/DETOC/> accessed 1 September 2015
de Vries SA, '*BUPA*: A Healthy Case, in the light of a Changing Constitutional Setting in Europe?' in van de Gronden JW, Szyszczak E, Neergaard U and Krajewski M (eds), *Health Care and EU Law* (TMC Asser Press 2011)
De Witte B, 'A Competence to Protect: the Pursuit of Non-Market Aims through Internal Market Legislation' in Syrpis P (ed), *The Judiciary, the Legislature and the EU Internal Market* (CUP 2012)
Dobner P and Loughlin M (eds), *The Twilight of Constitutionalism?* (OUP 2010)
Dobson L and Follesdal A (eds), *Political Theory and the European Constitution* (Routledge 2004)
Domurath I, 'The Three Dimensions of Solidarity in the EU Legal Order: Limits of the Judicial and Legal Approach' (2013) 35 Journal of European Integration 459
Dony M, 'Services Sociaux d'Intérêt Général et Droit Communautaire' [2004] Transnational Associations 299
—. *Contrôle des Aides d'État* (Ed. de l'Université de Bruxelles 2007)
Dorf MC and Sabel CF, 'A Constitution of Democratic Experimentalism' (1998) 98 CLR 267

Dougan M, 'Fees, Grants, Loans and Dole Cheques: Who Covers the Costs of Migrant Education within the EU?' (2005) 42 CML Rev 943
—. 'Cross-Border Educational Mobility and the Exportation of Student Financial Assistance' (2008) 33 EL Rev 723
—. 'Expanding the Frontiers of Union Citizenship by Dismantling the Territorial Boundaries of the National Welfare States?' in Barnard C and Odudu O (eds), *The Outer Limits of European Law* (Hart 2009)
—. 'What Are We to Make of the Citizens' Initiative?' (2011) 48 CML Rev 1807
—. Shuibhne NN and Spaventa E (eds), *Empowerment and Disempowerment of the European Citizen* (Hart 2012)
Draetta U, 'The Democratic Principles of the European Union in the Treaty of Lisbon' (2008) 50 The Federalist: A Political Review 110
Driguez L and Rodrigues S, 'Services Sociaux d'Intérêt Général et Droit Communautaire: entre Spécificité et Banalisation' (2007) 64 AJDA Hebdo: L'Actualité Juridique. Droit Administratif 191
Dryzek JS, *Deliberative Democracy and Beyond* (OUP 2002)
Duez D, 'La Démocratie Participative Européenne: du Citoyen à la Société Civile Organisée' in Cheneviere C and Duchenne G (eds), *Les Modes d'Expression de la Citoyenneté Européenne: Actes de la Journée d'Étude Organisée à Louvain-la-Neuve le 19 Mars 2010* (Presses Universitaires de Louvain UCL 2011)
Duina F and Raunio T, 'The Open Method of Coordination and National Parliaments: Further Marginalization or New Opportunities?' (2007) 14 JEPP 489
Dunkerley D and Fudge S, 'The Role of Civil Society in European Integration: A Framework for Analysis' (2004) 6 European Societies 237
EAPN, 'National Action Plans on Inclusion 2003–2005: Where is the Political Energy? EAPN's Response to the Second Round of Plans' (2003)
—. 'Building Security, Giving Hope: EAPN Assessment of the National Strategic Reports on Social Protection and Social Inclusion (2008–10)' (2008)
—. 'EAPN Proposals on the "European Platform against Poverty"' (2010)
—. 'The Europe 2020 Strategy' (2010)
—. 'Deliver Inclusive Growth – Put the Heart Back in Europe! EAPN Analysis of the 2011 National Reform Programmes, Europe 2020' (2011)
—. 'Breaking Barriers–Driving Change: Case Studies of Building Participation of People Experiencing Poverty' (2012)
—. 'An EU Worth Defending – Beyond Austerity to Social Investment and Inclusive Growth: EAPN Analysis of the 2012 National Reform Programmes (NRPs) and National Social Reports (NSRs)' (Report) (2012)
—. 'EAPN Response to the Social Investment Package: Will it Reduce Poverty?' (Position Paper) (2013)
—. 'Widening the Gap: EAPN Assessment of the National Reform Programmes 2013' (Report) (2013)
Eberlein B and Kerwer D, 'Theorising the New Modes of European Union Governance' (2002) 6 EIoP <http://eiop.or.at/eiop/pdf/2002-005.pdf> accessed 1 September 2015

Economic and Social Council, 'Resolution 31 of 25 July 1996 on the Consultative Relationship between the United Nations and Non-Governmental Organizations' UN Doc E/1996/96

Eder K, 'The Construction of a Transnational Public: Prerequisites for Democratic Governance in a Transnationalising Society' in Della Sala V and Ruzza C (eds), *Governance and Civil Society in the European Union: Exploring Policy Issues* (vol 2, Manchester University Press 2007)

—. 'The Making of a European Civil Society: "Imagined", "Practised" and "Staged"' (2009) 28 Policy and Society 23

—. and Trenz HJ, 'Prerequisites of Transnational Democracy and Mechanisms for Sustaining it: The Case of the European Union' in Kohler-Koch B and Rittberger B (eds), *Debating the Democratic Legitimacy of the European Union* (Rowman & Littlefield 2007)

Edwards M, *Civil society* (2nd edn, Polity Press 2009)

EESC, 'Cooperation with Charitable Associations as Economic and Social Partners in the Field of Social Welfare' (Opinion) [1998] OJ C73/92

—. 'The Role and Contribution of Civil Society Organisations in the Building of Europe' (Opinion) [1999] OJ C329/10

—. 'The Commission Discussion Paper "The Commission and Non-Governmental Organisations: Building a Stronger Partnership"' (Opinion) [2000] OJ C268/67

—. 'Organised Civil Society and European Governance: the Committee's Contribution to the Drafting of the White Paper' (Opinion) [2001] OJ C193/117

—. 'Private Not-for-Profit Social Services in the Context of Services of General Interest in Europe' (Opinion) [2001] OJ C311/08

—. 'European Governance – a White Paper' (Opinion) [2002] OJ C125/61

—. 'The Representativeness of European Civil Society Organisations in Civil Dialogue' (Opinion) [2006] OJ C88/41

—. 'The Communication from the Commission Implementing the Community Lisbon Programme: Social Services of General Interest in the European Union COM (2006) 177 final' (Opinion) [2007] OJ C161/80

—. 'Civil Society Organisations and the EU Council Presidency' (Opinion) [2010] OJ C354/56

—. 'The Implementation of the Lisbon Treaty: Participatory Democracy and the Citizens' Initiative (Article 11)' (Opinion) [2010] OJ C354/59

—. 'The Open Method of Coordination and the Social Clause in the Context of Europe 2020' (Opinion) [2011] OJ C44/23

—. 'Communication from the Commission on the European Platform against Poverty and Social Exclusion – A European Framework for Social and Territorial Cohesion' (Opinion) [2011] OJ C248/130

—. 'Strengthening EU Cohesion and EU Social Policy Coordination through the New Horizontal Social Clause in Article 9 TFEU' (Opinion) [2012] OJ C24/29

—. 'Strengthening the Participatory Processes and the Involvement of Local Authorities, NGOs and the Social Partners in the Implementation of Europe 2020' (Opinion) [2012] JO C299/1

—. 'Principles, Procedures and Action for the Implementation of Article 11(1) and (2) of the Lisbon Treaty' (Opinion) [2013] OJ C11/8

Efler M and Berg C, 'Initiative for the European Citizens' Initiative: How the Convention got Convinced' (2003) <www.citizens-initiative.eu/?p=35> accessed 29 August 2013

Ehrenberg J, *Civil Society: The Critical History of an Idea* (New York University Press 1999)

Eicker K, 'Do the Basic Freedoms of the EC Treaty also Require an Amendment to the National Tax Laws on Charities and Non-Profit Organisations?' (2005) 14 EC Tax Rev 140

Eisenberg A, *Reconstructing Political Pluralism* (SUNY Press 1995)

Elster J (ed), *Deliberative Democracy* (CUP 1998)

—. 'Introduction' in Elster J (ed), *Deliberative Democracy* (CUP 1998)

Enchelmaier S, 'Always at Your Service (Within Limits): the ECJ's Case Law on Article 56 TFEU (2006–11)' (2011) 36 EL Rev 615

EPSC, 'The Social Dimension of Economic and Monetary Union: Towards Convergence and Resilience' (2015) EPSC Strategic Notes, issue no. 5/2015

Eriksen EO, 'Deliberative Supranationalism in the EU' in Eriksen EO and Fossum JE (eds), *Democracy in the European Union: Integration through Deliberation?* (Routledge 2000)

—. 'An Emerging European Public Sphere' (2005) 8 European Journal of Social Theory 341

—. 'A Comment on Schmalz-Bruns' in Kohler-Koch B and Rittberger B (eds), *Debating the Democratic Legitimacy of the European Union* (Rowman & Littlefield 2007)

—. and Fossum JE (eds), *Democracy in the European Union: Integration through Deliberation?* (Routledge 2000)

—. and Fossum JE, 'Post-National Integration' in Eriksen EO and Fossum JE (eds), *Democracy in the European Union: Integration through Deliberation?* (Routledge 2000)

—. and Fossum JE, 'Democracy through Strong Publics in the European Union?' (2002) 40 JCMS 401

—. and Fossum JE, 'A Done Deal? The EU's Legitimacy Conundrum Revisited' in Eriksen EO, Joerges C and Rodl F (eds), *Law, Democracy and Solidarity in a Post-National Union: the Unsettled Political Order of Europe* (Routledge 2008)

—. and Fossum JE (eds), *Rethinking Democracy and the European Union* (Routledge 2012)

—. Joerges C and Rodl F (eds), *Law, Democracy and Solidarity in a Post-National Union: the Unsettled Political Order of Europe* (Routledge 2008)

European Council, 3–4 June 1999, Cologne, presidency conclusions

—. 23–24 March 2000, Lisbon, presidency conclusions

—. 7–9 December 2000, Nice, presidency conclusions

—. 23–24 March 2001, Stockholm, presidency conclusions

—. 14–15 December 2001, Laeken, presidency conclusions

—. 15–16 March 2002, Barcelona, presidency conclusions

—. 22–23 March 2005, Brussels, presidency conclusions

—. 16–17 June 2005, Brussels, declaration on the ratification of the Treaty establishing a Constitution for Europe

—. 23–24 March 2006, Brussels, presidency conclusions

—. 13–14 March 2008, Brussels, presidency conclusions

—. 25–26 March 2010, presidency conclusions

—. 17 June 2010, presidency conclusions

European Ombudsman, Decision 948/2004/OV of 4 may 2005
—. Decision 3617/2006/JF of 3 July 2008
—. Decision 406/2008/(WP)VIK of 16 December 2009
—. Decision 640/2011/AN of 4 October 2012
—. Decision 2097/2011/RA of 25 January 2013
—. Decision 1151/2008/(DK)ANA of 9 July 2013
—. Decision 1682/2010/(ANA)BEH of 19 December 2013
—. Decision 240/2014/FOR of 28 April 2015
European Parliament, 'Resolution of 13 March 1987 on Non-Profit-Making Associations in the European Community' [1987] OJ C99/205
—. 'Resolution of 2 July 1998 on the Communication from the Commission on Promoting the Role of Voluntary Organizations and Foundations in Europe' [1998] OJ C226/66
—. 'Resolution of 29 November 2001 on the Commission White Paper on European Governance' [2002] OJ C153E/314
—. 'Resolution of 28 February 2002 on the Strategy for Full Employment and Social Inclusion in the Run-up to the Spring 2002 Summit in Barcelona: Lisbon Process and the Way to Follow' [2002] OJ C293E/75
—. 'Resolution of 11 June 2002 on the Communication from the Commission: Draft Joint Report on Social Inclusion' [2003] OJ C261E/136
—. 'Resolution of 5 June 2003 on the Application of the Open Method of Coordination' [2004] OJ C68E/604
—. 'Resolution of 5 June 2003 on Analysis of the Open Coordination Procedure in the Field of Employment and Social Affairs, and Future Prospects' [2004] OJ C68E/601
—. 'Resolution of 15 March 2006 on Social Protection and Social Inclusion' [2006] OJ C291E/304
—. 'Resolution of 14 March 2007 on Social Services of General Interest in the European Union' [2007] OJ C301E/140
—. 'Resolution of 8 May 2008 on the Development of the Framework for the Activities of Interest Representatives (Lobbyists) in the European Institutions' [2009] OJ C271E /48
—. 'Resolution of 9 October 2008 on Promoting Social Inclusion and Combating Poverty, Including Child Poverty, in the EU' [2010] OJ C9E/11
—. 'Resolution of 13 January 2009 on the Perspectives for Developing Civil Dialogue under the Treaty of Lisbon' [2010] OJ C46E/23
—. 'Resolution of 24 March 2009 on Active Dialogue with Citizens on Europe' [2010] OJ C117E/27
—. 'Resolution of 7 May 2009 on Parliament's New Role and Responsibilities in Implementing the Treaty of Lisbon' [2010] OJ C212E/37
—. 'Resolution of 20 October 2010 on the Role of Minimum Income in Combating Poverty and Promoting an Inclusive Society in Europe' [2012] OJ C70E/8
—. 'Resolution of 17 February 2011 on Europe 2020' [2012] OJ C188E/42
—. 'Resolution of 5 July 2011 on the Future of Social Services of General Interest' [2013] OJ C33E/65
—. 'Resolution of 15 November 2011 on the European Platform against Poverty and Social Exclusion' [2013] OJ C153E/57

—. 'Resolution of 22 November 2012 on the Elections to the European Parliament in 2014' (P7_TA-PROV(2012)0462)
—. 'Decision of 11 May 2011 on Conclusion of an Interinstitutional Agreement between the European Parliament and the Commission on a Common Transparency Register' [2012] OJ C377E/176
Evers A, 'Part of the Welfare Mix: The Third Sector as an Intermediate Area' (1995) 6 Voluntas 159
—. and Laville JL (eds), *The Third Sector in Europe* (Edward Elgar 2004)
—. and Zimmer A (eds), *Third Sector Organizations Facing Turbulent Environments: Sports, Culture and Social Services in Five European Countries* (Nomos 2010)
Fazi E and Smith J, 'Civil Dialogue: Making it Work Better' (2006) Study commissioned by the Civil Society Contact Group <http://act4europe.horus.be/module/FileLib/Civil%20dialogue,%20making%20it%20work%20better.pdf> accessed 1 September 2015
Feld LP and G Kirchgassner, 'The Role of Direct Democracy in the European Union' in Blankart CB and Mueller DC (eds), *A Constitution for the European Union* (MIT Press 2004)
Ferrera M, Matsaganis M and Sacchi S, 'Open Coordination against Poverty: The New EU "Social Inclusion Process"' (2002) 12 JESP 227
Fine R and Rai S (eds), *Civil Society: Democratic Perspectives* (Frank Cass 1997)
Finke B, 'Civil Society Participation in EU Governance' (2007) 2 Living Rev Euro Gov <www.livingreviews.org/lreg-2007–2> accessed 1 September 2015
Follesdal A, 'Legitimacy Theories of the European Union' (2004) ARENA Working Paper no. 15/2004
—. and Hix S, 'Why There is a Democratic Deficit in the EU: A Response to Majone and Moravcsik' (2006) 44 JCMS 533
—. and Koslowski P (eds), *Democracy and the European Union* (Springer 1998)
Frazer H and Marlier E, 'Building a Stronger EU Social Inclusion Process: Analysis and Recommendations of the EU Network of Independent National Experts on Social Inclusion' (2008) <http://ec.europa.eu/social/main.jsp?catId=1025&langId=en&newsId=1410&furtherNews=yes> accessed 1 September 2015
—. 'Strengthening Social Inclusion in the Europe 2020 Strategy by Learning from the Past' in Marlier E and Natali D (eds), *Europe 2020: Towards a More Social EU?* (PIE-Peter Lang 2010)
—. with Natali D, Van Dam R and Vanhercke B, 'Europe 2020: Towards a More Social EU?' in Marlier E and Natali D (eds), *Europe 2020: Towards a More Social EU?* (PIE- Peter Lang 2010)
—. and Nicaise I, *A Social Inclusion Roadmap for Europe 2020* (Garant 2010)
Freedland M, Craig P, Jacqueson C and Kountouris N, *Public Employment Services and European Law* (OUP 2007)
Freedland M and Sciarra S (eds), *Public Services and Citizenship in European Law: Public and Labour Law Perspectives* (Clarendon Press 1998)
Freise M (ed), *European Civil Society on the Road to Success?* (Nomos 2008)
—. Pyykkönen M and Vaidelyte E (eds), *A Panacea for All Seasons? Civil Society and Governance in Europe* (Nomos 2010)

Friedrich D, 'Participatory Democracy in the European Union? European Governance and the Inclusion of Civil Society Organisations in Migration and Environmental Policies' (2006) revised version of a paper presented at the fifteenth international conference of the Council for European Studies, March 29–April 2, 2006

—. 'Policy Process, Governance and Democracy in the EU: The Case of the Open Method of Co-Ordination on Social Inclusion in Germany' (2006) 34 Policy & Politics 367

—. 'Old Wine in New Bottles? The Actual and Potential Contribution of Civil Society Organisations to Democratic Governance in Europe' (2007) RECON Online Working Paper no. 2007/08 <www.proyectos.cchs.csic.es/euroconstitution/Treaties/Library%20(Since%20June%202007/Friedrich%202007.pdf> accessed 1 September 2015

—. 'Actual and Potential Contributions of Civil Society Organisations to Democratic EU Governance' in Freise M (ed), *European Civil Society on the Road to Success?* (Nomos 2008)

—. *Democratic Participation and Civil Society in the European Union* (Manchester University Press 2011)

Fung A, 'Associations and Democracy: Between Theories, Hopes, and Realities' (2003) 29 Annual Review of Sociology 515

—. and Wright EO (eds), *Deepening Democracy: Institutional Innovations in Empowered Participatory Governance* (Verso 2003)

Garzón Clariana G, 'Les Droits Politiques des Citoyens de l'Europe: les Vingt Premières Années' (2013) 13 ERA Forum 545

Georgakakis D and de Lassalle M (eds), *La 'Nouvelle Gouvernance Européenne': Genèses et Usages Politiques d'un Livre Blanc* (Presses universitaires de Strasbourg 2008)

Gerstenberg O and Sabel CF, 'Directly-Deliberative Polyarchy: An Institutional Ideal for Europe?' in Joerges C and Dehousse R (eds), *Good Governance in Europe's Integrated Market* (OUP 2002)

Geyer R, *Exploring European Social Policy* (Polity Press 2000)

—. 'Can European Union (EU) Social NGOs Co-Operate to Promote EU Social Policy?' (2001) 30 Jnl Soc Pol 477

Giddens A, *The Third Way: The Renewal of Social Democracy* (Polity Press 1998)

Goehring R, 'Interest Representation and Legitimacy in the European Union' in Warleigh A and Fairbrass J (eds), *Influence and Interests in the European Union: The New Politics of Persuasion and Advocacy* (Europa Publications 2002)

Goode L, *Jürgen Habermas: Democracy and the Public Sphere* (Pluto Press 2005)

Greaney TL, 'Quality of Care and Market Failure Defenses in Antitrust Health Care Litigation' (1989) 21 Connecticut Law Review 605

—. 'Antitrust and Hospital Mergers: Does the Nonprofit Form Affect Competitive Substance?' (2006) 31 JHPPL 511

Greenwood J, 'Advocacy, Influence and Persuasion: Has it all been Overdone?' in Warleigh A and Fairbrass J (eds), *Influence and Interests in the European Union: The New Politics of Persuasion and Advocacy* (Europa Publications 2002)

—. 'The Search for Input Legitimacy through Organised Civil Society in the EU' (2004) 2 Transnational Associations 145

—. 'The Future of Consultation with, and Participation by, Interests Groups in the European Union' (2005) 4 Transnational Associations 219

—. 'Organized Civil Society and Democratic Legitimacy in the European Union' (2007) 37 British Journal of Political Science 333
—. *Interest Representation in the European Union* (2nd edn, Palgrave Macmillan 2007)
—. *Interest Representation in the European Union* (3rd edn, Palgrave Macmillan 2011)
—. 'The Lobby Regulation Element of the European Transparency Initiative: Between Liberal and Deliberative Models of Democracy' (2011) 9 Comparative European Politics 317
—. 'The European Citizens' Initiative and EU Civil Society Organisations' (2012) 13 Perspectives on European Politics and Society 325
—. and Halpin D, 'The European Commission and the Public Governance of Interest Groups in the European Union: Seeking a Niche between Accreditation and Laissez-Faire' (2007) 8 Perspectives on European Politics and Society 189
Greven MT, 'Some Considerations on Participation in Participatory Governance' in Kohler-Koch B and Rittberger B (eds), *Debating the Democratic Legitimacy of the European Union* (Rowman & Littlefield 2007)
Grewal SS, 'Habermas, Law and European Social Policy: a Rejoinder to Murphy' (2010) 17 JEPP 282
Gustavsson S, Karlsson C and Persson T (eds), *The Illusion of Accountability in the European Union* (Routledge 2009)
Gyselen L, 'Anti-Competitive State Measures under the EC Treaty: Towards a Substantive Legality Standard' (1993) EL Rev Supp (competition law checklist) 55
—. 'Services of General Economic Interest and Competition under European Law-A Delicate Balance' (2010) 1 JECL&P 491
—. 'Public Service and EU Competition Law' (2011) 2 JECL&P 572
Habermas J, *The Theory of Communicative Action /Vol.2, Lifeworld and System: A Critique of Functionalist Reason* (Polity Press 1987)
—. *Between Facts and Norms: Contributions to a Discourse Theory of Law and Democracy* (Polity Press 1996)
—. *The Postnational Constellation: Political Essays* (MIT Press 2001)
—. 'Why Europe Needs a Constitution?' (2001) 11 New Left Review 5
—. *Une Époque de Transition: Écrits Politiques (1998–2003)* (Fayard 2005)
—. 'Bringing the Integration of Citizens into Line with the Integration of States' (2012) 18 ELJ 485
—. *The Crisis of the European Union: A Response* (Polity Press 2012)
—. 'The Crisis of the European Union in the Light of a Constitutionalization of International Law' (2012) 23 EJIL 335
Haltern UR, Mayer FC and Weiler JHH, 'European Democracy and its Critique' (1995) 18 West European Politics 4
Hancher L and Sauter W, 'One Foot in the Grave or One Step Beyond? From Sodemare to DocMorris: The EU's Freedom of Establishment Case Law concerning Healthcare' (2009) TILEC Discussion Paper no. 2009/28
—. 'One Step Beyond? From Sodemare to Docmorris: The EU's Freedom of Establishment Case Law concerning Healthcare' (2010) 47 CML Rev 117
Hansmann H, 'Economic Theories of Nonprofit Organization' in Powell WW (ed), *The Nonprofit Sector: A Research Handbook* (Yale University Press 1987)
Hantrais L, *Social Policy in the European Union* (3rd edn, Palgrave Macmillan 2007)

Harlow C, 'Codification of EC Administrative Procedures? Fitting the Foot to the Shoe or the Shoe to the Foot' (1996) 2 ELJ 3
—. 'Citizen Access to Political Power in the European Union' (1999) EUI Working Paper RSC no. 99/2
—. and Rawlings R, 'Promoting Accountability in Multilevel Governance: A Network Approach' (2007) 13 ELJ 542
Harvey B, 'Lobbying in Europe: The Experience of Voluntary Organizations' in Mazey S and Richardson J (eds), *Lobbying in the European Community* (OUP 1993)
Hatzopoulos V, 'Recent Developments of the Case Law of the ECJ in the Field of Services' (2000) 37 CML Rev 43
—. '*Killing* National Health and Insurance Systems but *Healing* Patients? The European Market for Health Care Services after the Judgments of the ECJ in *Vanbraekel* and *Peerbooms*' (2002) 39 CML Rev 683
—. 'Health Law and Policy: The Impact of the EU' in De Búrca G (ed), *EU Law and the Welfare State: In Search of Solidarity* (OUP 2005)
—. 'Why the Open Method of Coordination is Bad for You: A Letter to the EU' (2007) 13 ELJ 309
Hay C and Wincott D, *The Political Economy of European Welfare Capitalism* (Palgrave Macmillan 2012)
Hayward J (ed), *The Crisis of Representation in Europe* (Frank Cass & Co 1995)
Heard-Lauréote K, *European Union Governance: Effectiveness and Legitimacy in European Commission Committees* (Routledge 2010)
Heater D, *What is Citizenship?* (Polity Press1999)
Heidbreder EG, 'Civil Society Participation in EU Governance' (2012) 7 Living Rev Eur Gov <www.livingreviews.org/lreg-2012-2> accessed 31 August 2013
Heidenreich M and Bischoff G, 'The Open Method of Co-Ordination: A Way to the Europeanization of Social and Employment Policies?' (2008) 46 JCMS 497
Heinrich VF, 'Assessing and Strengthening Civil Society Worldwide: A Project Description of the CIVICUS Civil Society Index' (2003) CIVICUS Civil Society Index Paper Series vol 2, issue 1
Helios M, 'Taxation of Non-Profit Organizations and EC Law' (2007) 16 EC Tax Rev 65
Hemerijck A, 'The Euro-Crisis - Welfare State Conundrum' in Rodrigues MJ and Xiarchogiannopoulou E (eds), *The Eurozone Crisis and the Transformation of EU Governance: Internal and External Implications* (Ashgate 2014, ebook)
Hendriks CM, 'The Ambiguous Role of Civil Society in Deliberative Democracy' (2002) refereed paper presented to the jubilee conference of the Australasian Political Studies Association, Australian National University, Canberra, October 2002
—. 'Integrated Deliberation: Reconciling Civil Society's Dual Role in Deliberative Democracy' (2006) 54 Political Studies 486
Héritier A, 'Elements of Democratic Legitimation in Europe: An Alternative Perspective' (1999) 6 JEPP 269
—. and Rhodes M (eds), *New Modes of Governance in Europe: Governing in the Shadow of Hierarchy* (Palgrave Macmillan 2011)
Hervey T, *European Social Law and Policy* (Longman 1998)
—. '*Social Solidarity*: A Buttress against Internal Market Law?' in Shaw J (ed), *Social Law and Policy in an Evolving European Union* (Hart 2000)

—. 'The Current Legal Framework on the Right to Seek Health Care Abroad in the European Union' (2007) 9 CYELS 261
—. '"Adjudicating in the Shadow of the Informal Settlement?": The Court of Justice of the European Union, "New Governance" and Social Welfare' (2010) 63 Current Legal Problems 92
Hirst PQ, 'Can Associationalism Come Back?' in Hirst PQ and Bader V-M (eds), *Associative Democracy: The Real Third Way* (Frank Cass 2001)
—. 'Can Associationalism Come Back?' (2001) 4 Critical Review of International Social and Political Philosophy 15
—. and Bader V-M (eds), *Associative Democracy: The Real Third Way* (Frank Cass 2001)
Hix S, 'The Study of the European Union II: The "New Governance" Agenda and its Rival' (1998) 5 JEPP 38
—. *What's Wrong with the European Union and How to Fix it* (Polity Press 2008)
Hodson D and Maher I, 'The Open Method as a New Mode of Governance: The Case of Soft Economic Policy Co-Ordination' (2001) 39 JCMS 719
Hooghe L and Marks G, *Multi-Level Governance and European Integration* (Rowman & Littlefield 2001)
Horeth M, 'No Way Out for the Beast? The Unsolved Legitimacy Problem of European Governance' (1999) 6 JEPP 249
Hüller T, 'Conceptualising Democratic Associational Involvement in EU Decision Making -Contributions from Contemporary Political Theory' (2010) 45 Acta Politica 298
—. and Kohler-Koch B, 'Assessing the Democratic Value of Civil Society Engagement in the European Union' in Kohler-Koch B, De Bièvre D and Maloney W (eds), *Opening EU-Governance to Civil Society – Gains and Challenges* (2008) CONNEX Report Series no. 5 <www.mzes.uni-mannheim.de/projekte/typo3/site/index.php?id=596> accessed 1 September 2015
Hunold C, 'Green Political Theory and the European Union: The Case for a Non-Integrated Civil Society' (2005) 14 Environmental Politics 324
Idema T and Kelemen RD, 'New Modes of Governance, the Open Method of Co-Ordination and Other Fashionable Red Herring' (2006) 7 Perspectives on European Politics and Society 108
Imig D and Tarrow S (eds), *Contentious Europeans: Protest and Politics in an Emerging Polity* (Rowman & Littlefield 2001)
INBAS GmbH and ENGENDER asbl, 'Study on Stakeholders' Involvement in the Implementation of the Open Method of Coordination (OMC) in Social Protection and Social Inclusion – Final Report' (2010) <www.stakeholders-socialinclusion.eu/site/en/outputs/finrep> accessed 1 September 2015
Jachtenfuchs M, 'Democracy and Governance in the European Union' (1997) 1 EIoP <http://eiop.or.at/eiop/texte/1997-002a.htm> accessed 1 September 2015
Jacqué JP, *Droit Institutionnel de l'Union Européenne* (6th edn, Dalloz 2010)
Jensen MN, 'Concepts and Conceptions of Civil Society' (2006) 2 Journal of Civil Society 39
Jensen T, 'The Democratic Deficit of the European Union' (2009) 1 Living Rev Dem <www.livingreviews.org/lrd-2009-2> accessed 1 September 2015
Joachim J and Locher B (eds), *Transnational Activism in the UN and EU: A Comparative Study* (Routledge 2008)

Jobert B and Kohler-Koch B (eds), *Changing Images of Civil Society: From Protest to Governance* (Routledge 2008)

Joerges C, '"Good Governance" through Comitology?' in Joerges C and Vos E (eds), *EU Committees: Social Regulation, Law and Politics* (Hart 1999)

—. 'Reconceptualizing the Supremacy of European Law: A Plea for a Supranational Conflict of Laws' in Kohler-Koch B and Rittberger B (eds), *Debating the Democratic Legitimacy of the European Union* (Rowman & Littlefield 2007)

—. and Dehousse R (eds), *Good Governance in Europe's Integrated Market* (OUP 2002)

—. Mény Y and Weiler JHH (eds), *Mountain or Molehill? A Critical Appraisal of the Commission White Paper on Governance* (2001) Jean Monnet Working Paper no. 6/01 <www.eui.eu/DepartmentsAndCentres/RobertSchumanCentre/Research/ArchivesInstitutionsGovernanceDemocracy/MountainorMolehill.aspx> accessed 1st September 2015

—. and Neyer J, 'From Intergovernmental Bargaining to Deliberative Political Processes: The Constitutionalisation of Comitology' (1997) 3 ELJ 273

—. and Vos E (eds), *EU Committees: Social Regulation, Law and Politics* (Hart 1999)

Johansson H, 'Europeanization "from Below": The OMC Process on Social Inclusion in the Swedish Welfare State" in Hinden B and Johansson H (eds), *Citizenship in Nordic Welfare States: Dynamics of Choice and Participation* (Routledge 2007)

—. 'Whom Do They Represent? Mixed Modes of Representation in EU-Based CSOs' in Kröger S and Friedrich D (eds), *The Challenge of Democratic Representation in the European Union* (Palgrave Macmillan 2012)

Joint Transparency Register Secretariat, 'Annual Report on the Operations of the Transparency Register' (2012)

—. 'List of Measures and Elements to Take into Account in the Event of a Review of the Transparency Register and Result of Discussions of the WG' (2013)

Jordan G and Maloney W, *Democracy and Interest Groups: Enhancing Participation?* (Palgrave Macmillan 2007)

Jørgensen S, 'The Right to Cross-Border Education in the European Union' (2009) 46 CML Rev 1567

Judge D and Earnshaw D, 'The Future is Parliamentary? Parliamentarisation and Legitimation in the EU' (2003) paper prepared for the EUSA 8th international biennial conference, March 27–29, 2003, Nashville, Tennessee

Juncker J-C with Tusk D, Dijsselbloem J, Draghi M and Schulz M, 'Completing Europe's Economic and Monetary Union' (Report) (2015)

Kaddous C, 'L'Initiative Citoyenne: Un Instrument de Démocratie Directe à l'Échelle de l'Union Européenne' in Kaddous C and Auer A (eds), *Les Principes Fondamentaux de la Constitution Européenne* (Bruylant 2006)

Kamaris G, 'The Reform of EU State Aid Rules for Services of General Economic Interest in Times of Austerity' (2012) 33 ECLR 55

Karr K, *Democracy and Lobbying in the European Union* (Campus Verlag 2007)

Kauff-Gazin F, 'Education et Droit Communautaire: le Marché Prend-il le Pas sur l'Intérêt Général?' (2008) 184 Le Dalloz 666

Kaufmann B, 'Citizen Power Beyond the Nation-State' in Berg C, Carline P, Kaufmann B, Leinen J and Wallis D (eds), *Initiative for Europe Handbook 2008 – the Guide to Transnational Democracy in Europe* (Initiative & Referendum Institute Europe

2007) <www.iri-europe.org/publications/handbooks/european-citizens-initiative-handbook/> accessed 1 September 2015

Kendall J, *The Voluntary Sector: Comparative Perspectives in the UK* (Routledge 2003)

—. (ed), *Handbook on Third Sector Policy in Europe: Multi-Level Processes and Organized Civil Society* (Edward Elgar 2009)

—. and Anheier HK, 'The Third Sector and the European Union Policy Process: An Initial Evaluation' (1999) 6 JEPP 283

—. and Fraisse L, 'The European Statute of Association: Why Still an Obscure but Contested Symbol in a Sea of Indifference and Scepticism?' in Kendall J (ed), *Handbook on Third Sector Policy in Europe: Multi-Level Processes and Organized Civil Society* (Edward Elgar 2009)

—. Will C and Brandsen T, 'The Third Sector and the Brussels Dimension: Trans-EU Governance Work in Progress' in Kendall J (ed), *Handbook on Third Sector Policy in Europe: Multi-Level Processes and Organized Civil Society* (Edward Elgar 2009)

Kerschen N, 'The Social Partners in European Employment Strategy. Specific Guidelines and National Action Plans for Employment' in De Schutter O and Deakin S (eds), *Social Rights and Market Forces: Is the Open Coordination of Employment and Social Policies the Future of Social Europe?* (Bruylant 2005)

Klosse S, 'Balancing Europe's Economic and Social Goals: Fighting a Losing Battle?' [2012] EJSL 176

Koch C, 'Locus Standi of Private Applicants under the EU Constitution: Preserving Gaps in the Protection of Individuals' Right to an Effective Remedy' (2005) 30 EL Rev 511

Kohler-Koch B, 'The Evolution and Transformation of European Governance' in Kohler-Koch B and Eising R (eds), *The Transformation of Governance in the European Union* (Routledge 1999)

—. 'The Organization of Interests and Democracy in the European Union' in Kohler-Koch B and Rittberger B (eds), *Debating the Democratic Legitimacy of the European Union* (Rowman & Littlefield 2007)

—. 'Chapter 17: Does Participatory Governance Hold its Promises?' in Kohler-Koch B and Larat F (eds), *Efficient and Democratic Governance in the European Union* (2008) CONNEX Report Series no. 9 <www.mzes.uni-mannheim.de/projekte/typo3/site/index.php?id=596> accessed 1 September 2015

—. 'The Three Worlds of European Civil society – What Role for Civil Society for what Kind of Europe?' (2009) 28 Policy and Society 47

—. 'Civil Society and EU Democracy: "Astroturf" Representation?' (2010) 17 JEPP 100

—. 'How to Put Matters Right? Assessing the Role of Civil Society in EU Accountability' (2010) 33 West European Politics 1117

—. 'Post-Maastricht Civil Society and Participatory Democracy' (2012) 34 Journal of European Integration 809

—. and Buth V, 'Civil Society in European Governance – Lobby Groups Like any Others' (2009) TranState Working Paper no. 108 <www.sfb597.uni-bremen.de/pages/pubApBeschreibung.php?SPRACHE=en&ID=148> accessed 1 September 2015

—. De Bièvre D and Maloney W (eds), *Opening EU-Governance to Civil Society – Gains and Challenges* (2008) CONNEX Report Series no. 5 <www.mzes.uni-mannheim.de/projekte/typo3/site/index.php?id=596> accessed 1 September 2015

—. and Eising R (eds), *The Transformation of Governance in the European Union* (Routledge 1999)

—. and Finke B, 'The Institutional Shaping of EU-Society Relations: A Contribution to Democracy Via Participation?' (2007) 3 Journal of Civil Society 205

—. and Larat F (eds), *Efficient and Democratic Governance in the European Union* (2008) CONNEX Report Series no. 9 <www.mzes.uni-mannheim.de/projekte/typo3/site/index.php?id=596> accessed 1 September 2015

—. and Quittkat C, 'What is Civil Society and Who Represents Civil Society in the EU? – Results of an Online Survey among Civil Society Experts' (2009) 28 Policy and Society 11

—. and Quittkat C with Buth V and Altides C, *De-Mystification of Participatory Democracy: EU Governance and Civil Society* (OUP 2013)

—. and Rittberger B, 'Charting Crowded Territory: Debating the Democratic Legitimacy of the European Union' in Kohler-Koch B and Rittberger B (eds), *Debating the Democratic Legitimacy of the European Union* (Rowman & Littlefield 2007)

—. and Rittberger B (eds), *Debating the Democratic Legitimacy of the European Union* (Rowman & Littlefield 2007)

Kok W, 'Facing the Challenge: The Lisbon Strategy for Growth and Employment' (2004) <http://ec.europa.eu/research/evaluations/pdf/archive/fp6-evidence-base/evaluation_studies_and_reports/evaluation_studies_and_reports_2004/the_lisbon_strategy_for_growth_and_employment__report_from_the_high_level_group.pdf> accessed 1st September 2015

Komninos AP, 'Non-Competition Concerns: Resolution of Conflicts in the Integrated Article 81 EC' (2008) Working Paper (L) 08/05, Oxford Centre for Competition Law and Policy <www.eui.eu/RSCAS/Research/Competition/2004/200409-compet-Komninos.pdf> accessed 1st September 2015

Kopit WG and McCann RW, 'Toward a Definitive Antitrust Standard for Nonprofit Hospital Mergers' (1988) 13 JHPPL 635

Kotkas T, 'Who Needs Social Rights when We've got Solidarity: Juridification of Solidarity and the Depoliticisation of EU Social Policy' [2012] EJSL 84

Koukiadaki A, 'EU Governance and Social Services of General Interest: When even the UK is Concerned' in Barbier JC (ed), *EU Law, Governance and Social Policy* (2012) 16 EIoP <http://eiop.or.at/eiop/texte/2012–005a.htm> accessed 1st September 2015

Koutrakos P, 'Healthcare as an Economic Service' in Spaventa E and Dougan M (eds), *Social Welfare and EU Law* (Hart 2005)

Krajewski M and Farley M, 'Non-Economic Activities in Upstream and Downstream Markets and the Scope of Competition Law after FENIN' (2007) 32 EL Rev 111

Krajewski M, Neergaard U, and van de Gronden JW (eds), *The Changing Legal Framework for Services of General Interest in Europe: Between Competition and Solidarity* (TMC Asser Press 2009)

Kramer RM, *Voluntary Agencies in the Welfare State* (University of California Press 1981)

Kröger S, 'The OMC Inclusion and National Social NGOs: From Enthusiasm to Reality' (2006) Fourth ESPAnet annual conference, 21–23 September 2006, Bremen

—. 'When Learning Hits Politics or: Social Policy Coordination Left to the Administrations and the NGOs?' (2006) 10 EIoP <http://eiop.or.at/eiop/texte/2006–003a.htm> accessed 1st September 2015

—. 'The End of Democracy as we Know it? The Legitimacy Deficits of Bureaucratic Social Policy Governance' (2007) 29 Journal of European Integration 565
—. *Soft Governance in Hard Politics* (VS Verlag 2008)
—. 'The Effectiveness of Soft Governance in the Field of European Anti-poverty Policy: Operationalization and Empirical Evidence' (2009) 11 Journal of Comparative Policy Analysis: Research and Practice 197
—. 'Democracy Promoter or Interest Defender? How the European Commission Influences Non-Electoral Representation by Civil Society Organizations' in Kröger S and Friedrich D (eds), *The Challenge of Democratic Representation in the European Union* (Palgrave Macmillan 2012)
—. 'Creating a European Demos? The Representativeness of European Umbrella Organisations' (2013) 35 Journal of European Integration 583
—. and Friedrich D (eds), *The Challenge of Democratic Representation in the European Union* (Palgrave Macmillan 2012)
Kupler R, 'The Many Democratic Deficits of the European Union' in Weale A and Nentwich M (eds), *Political Theory and the European Union* (Routledge 1998)
Laffan B and Shaw C, 'Classifying and Mapping OMC in Different Policy Areas' (2009) NewGov Working Paper no. 02/D09
Laulom S, Mazuyer E, Teissier C, Triomphe CE and Vielle P, 'How Has the Crisis Affected Social Legislation in Europe?' (2012) ETUI Policy Brief no. 2/2012
Laurent S, 'Le Droit d'Initiative Citoyenne: En Attendant l'Entrée en Vigueur de la Constitution Européenne' (2006) 497 RMUE 221
Laxer G and Halperin S (eds), *Global Civil Society and its Limits* (Palgrave 2003)
Lee M and Abbot C, 'The Usual Suspects? Public Participation under the Aarhus Convention' (2003) 66 ML Rev 80
Legris G and Lehmann B, 'L'Initiative Européenne de Transparence et l'Encadrement des Activités de Lobbyisme par la Commission Européenne' [2008] RDUE 807
Legros M, 'La MOC Inclusion, Une Méthode Questionnée' (2005) Independent report for the European Commission, DG Employment, Social Affairs and Equal Opportunities
Leibfried S, 'Social Policy: Left to the Judges and the Markets?' in Wallace H, Wallace W and Pollack M (eds), *Policy-Making in the European Union* (5th edn, OUP 2005)
—. 'Social Policy: Left to the Judges and the Markets?' in Wallace H, Pollack M and Young A (eds), *Policy-Making in the European Union* (6th edn, OUP 2010)
—. and Pierson P (eds), *European Social Policy: Between Fragmentation and Integration* (The Brookings Institution 1995)
—. and Pierson P, 'Semisovereign Welfare States: Social Policy in a Multitiered Europe' in Leibfried S and Pierson P (eds), *European Social Policy: Between Fragmentation and Integration* (The Brookings Institution 1995)
Liebert U, 'Civil Society, Public Sphere and Democracy in the EU' in Eriksen EO and Fossum JE (eds), *Rethinking Democracy and the European Union* (Routledge 2012)
—. and Trenz HJ (eds), *The New Politics of European Civil Society* (Routledge 2011)
Lindgren KO and Persson T, *Participatory Governance in the EU: Enhancing or Endangering Democracy and Efficiency?* (Palgrave Macmillan 2011)
Lodge J, 'The European Parliament' in Andersen SS and Eliassen KA, *The European Union: How Democratic is it?* (SAGE 1996)

Lombardo S, 'Some Reflections on Freedom of Establishment of Non-Profit Entities in the European Union' (2013) 14 EBOR 225
Lonbay J, 'Education and Law: The Community Context' (1989) 14 EL Rev 363
Lord C, 'Does the EU Suffer from a Democratic Deficit?' (2008) 43 Intereconomics 316
—. 'Parliamentary Representation in a Decentered Polity' in Kohler-Koch B and Rittberger B (eds), *Debating the Democratic Legitimacy of the European Union* (Rowman & Littlefield 2007)
—. and Beetham D, 'Legitimizing the EU: Is There a "Post-Parliamentary Basis" for its Legitimation?' (2001) 39 JCMS 443
—. and Magnette P, 'E Pluribus Unum? Creative Disagreement about Legitimacy in the EU' (2004) 42 JCMS 183
Louis F and Vallery A, '*Ferring* Revisited: The *Altmark* Case and State Financing of Public Service Obligations' (2004) 27 World Competition 53
Louis JV and Rodrigues S (eds), *Les Services d'Intérêt Économique Général et l'Union Européenne* (Bruylant 2006)
Louri V, '"Undertaking" as a Jurisdictional Element for the Application of EC Competition Rules' (2002) 29 LIEI 143
Macpherson CB, *The Life and Times of Liberal Democracy* (OUP 1977)
Magnette P, 'European Governance and Civic Participation: Can the European Union be Politicised?' in Joerges C, Mény Y and Weiler JHH (eds), *Mountain or Molehill? A Critical Appraisal of the Commission White Paper on Governance* (2001) Jean Monnet Working Paper no. 6/01 <http://centers.law.nyu.edu/jeanmonnet/archive/papers/01/010901.html> accessed 1st September 2015
—. 'Democracy in the European Union: Why and How to Combine Representation and Participation?' in Smismans S (ed), *Civil Society and Legitimate European Governance* (Edward Elgar 2006)
—. 'European Democracy between Two Ages' in Barnard C (ed), *The Fundamentals of EU Law Revisited: Assessing the Impact of the Constitutional Debate* (OUP 2007)
Maher I, 'Economic Governance: Hybridity, Accountability and Control' (2006–2007) 13 CJEL 679
Mahoney C and Beckstrand MJ, 'Following the Money: European Union Funding of Civil Society Organizations' (2011) 49 JCMS 1339
Majone G, 'The European Community between Social Policy and Social Regulation' (1993) 31 JCMS 153
—. 'Regulatory Legitimacy' in Majone G and Baake P (eds), *Regulating Europe* (Routledge 1996)
—. 'Europe's "Democratic Deficit": The Question of Standards' (1998) 4 ELJ 5
—. 'The Common Sense of European Integration' (2006) 13 JEPP 607
—. *Europe as the Would-Be World Power: the EU at Fifty* (CUP 2009)
—. 'Transaction-Cost Efficiency and the Democratic Deficit' (2010) 17 JEPP 150
—. 'Is the Community Method still Viable?' in Dehousse R (ed), *The "Community Method": Obstinate or Obsolete?* (Palgrave Macmillan 2011)
—. *Rethinking the Union of Europe Post-Crisis: Has Integration Gone Too Far?* (CUP 2014, ebook)
—. and Baake P (eds), *Regulating Europe* (Routledge 1996)

Maloney W and van Deth JW, 'Is Local Civil Society Conducive to European Participatory Engineering?' in Kohler-Koch B, De Bièvre D and Maloney W (eds), *Opening EU-Governance to Civil Society – Gains and Challenges* (2008) CONNEX Report Series no. 5 <www.mzes.uni-mannheim.de/projekte/typo3/site/index.php?id=596> accessed 1st September 2015

—. (eds), *Civil Society and Governance in Europe: from National to International Linkages* (Edward Elgar 2008)

Marks G and Mc Adam D, 'Social Movements and the Changing Structure of Political Opportunity in the European Union' (1996) 19 West European Politics 249

Marlier E, Atkinson T, Cantillon B and Nolan B (eds), *The EU and Social Inclusion: Facing the Challenges* (Policy Press 2007)

Marlier E and Natali D (eds), *Europe 2020: Towards a More Social EU?* (PIE- Peter Lang 2010)

Marshall TH, 'Citizenship and Social Class' in Manza J and Sauder M (eds), *Inequality and Society* (W.W. Norton and Co. 2009)

Martin D, Morsa M and Gosseries P, *Droit du Travail Européen: Questions spéciales* (Larcier 2015)

Mazey S and Richardson J (eds), *Lobbying in the European Community* (OUP 1993)

—. 'Pluralisme Ouvert ou Restreint? Les Groupes d'Intérêt dans l'Union Européenne' in Balme R, Chabanet D and Wright V (eds), *L'Action Collective en Europe-Collective Action in Europe* (Presses de Sciences Po 2002)

—. 'Interest Groups and EU Policy-Making: Organisational Logic and Venue Shopping' in Richardson J (ed), *European Union: Power and Policy-Making* (3rd edn, Routledge 2006)

McKee M, Mossialos E and Baeten R (eds), *The Impact of EU Law on Health Care Systems* (PIE-Peter Lang 2002)

McLaughlin AM and Greenwood J, 'The Management of Interest Representation in the European Union' (1995) 33 JCMS 143

Mendes J, 'Participation and the Role of Law after Lisbon: A Legal View on Article 11 TEU' (2011) 48 CML Rev 1849

—. *Participation in EU Rule-Making: a Rights-Based Approach* (OUP 2011)

Mény Y, 'The People, the Elites and the Populist Challenge' (1998) Jean Monnet Chair Paper RSC no. 98/47 <www.eui.eu/RSCAS/WP-Texts/JM98_47.html> accessed 1st September 2015

—. 'De la Démocratie en Europe: Old Concepts and New Challenges' (2002) 41 JCMS 1

—. 'The "Democratic Principle" and the European Union: The Challenge of a Post-National Democracy' in Moury C and de Sousa L (eds), *Institutional Challenges in Post-Constitutional Europe: Governing Change* (Routledge 2009)

—. 'Can Europe be Democratic? Is it Feasible? Is it Necessary? Is the Present Situation Sustainable?' (2011) 34 Fordham Int'l LJ 1287

Meuwese A, 'Embedding Consultation Procedures: Law or Institutionalization?' (2011) 17 EPL 527

—. Schuurmans Y and Voermans W, 'Towards a European Administrative Procedure Act' (2009) 2 Review of European Administrative Law 3

Michalski A, 'Social Welfare and Levels of Democratic Government in the EU' (2012) 34 Journal of European Integration 397

Michels R, *Political Parties: A Sociological Study of the Oligarchical Tendencies of Modern Democracy* (Free Press 1949)
Mill JS, *Essays on Politics and Culture* (Anchor Books 1963)
Monaghan E, '"Communicating Europe": The Role of Organised Civil Society' (2008) 4 JCER 18
Monti G, 'Article 81 EC and Public Policy' (2002) 39 CML Rev 1057
—. *EC Competition Law* (CUP 2007)
Moravcsik A, 'In Defence of the "Democratic Deficit": Reassessing Legitimacy in the European Union' (2002) 40 JCMS 603
—. 'The Myth of Europe's "Democratic Deficit"' (2008) 43 Intereconomics 331
Moreau MA (ed), *Before and After the Economic Crisis: What Implications for the "European Social Model"?* (Edward Elgar 2011)
Moury C and de Sousa L (eds), *Institutional Challenges in Post-Constitutional Europe: Governing Change* (Routledge 2009)
Murphy M, 'Between Facts, Norms and a Post-National Constellation: Habermas, Law and European Social Policy' (2005) 12 JEPP 143
Nanz P, 'Les Voix Multiples de l'Europe. Une Idée Interdiscursive de la Sphère Publique' (2003) 2 Raisons Politiques 69
Nazzini R, 'Article 81 EC between Time Present and Time Past: A Normative Critique of Restriction of Competition in EU Law' (2006) 43 CML Rev 487
Neergaard U, Nielsen R and Roseberry L (eds), *Integrating Welfare Functions into EU Law: From Rome to Lisbon* (DJOF Publishing 2009)
—. (eds), *The Services Directive - Consequences for the Welfare State and the European Social Model* (DJOF Publishing 2008)
Neergaard U, Szyszczak E, van de Gronden JW and Krajewski M (eds), *Social Services of General Interest in the EU* (TMC Asser Press 2013)
Nentwich M, 'Opportunity Structures for Citizens' Participation: The Case of the European Union' in Weale A and Nentwich M (eds), *Political Theory and the European Union* (Routledge 1998)
Newdick C, 'Citizenship, Free Movement and Health Care: Cementing Individual Rights by Corroding Social Solidarity' (2006) 43 CML Rev 1645
Nickless J, 'The Internal Market and the Social Nature of Health Care' in McKee M, Mossialos E and Baeten R (eds), *The Impact of EU Law on Health Care Systems* (PIE-Peter Lang 2002)
Nicolaides P, Kekelekis M and Kleis M, *State Aid Policy in the European Community* (2nd edn, Kluwer 2008)
Nieuwenburg P, 'Democratic Life in Europolis' in Kinneging A (ed), *Rethinking Europe's Constitution* (Wolf Legal Publishers 2007)
Nistor L, *Public Services and the European Union Healthcare, Health Insurance and Education Services* (TMC Asser Press 2011)
Norris P, 'Representation and the Democratic Deficit' (1997) 32 European Journal of Political Research 273
Obradovic D, 'Civil Society and the Social Dialogue in European Governance' (2005) 24 YEL 261
—. 'Regulating Lobbying in the European Union' in Coen D and Richardson J (eds), *Lobbying the European Union: Institutions, Actors, and Issues* (OUP 2009)

O'Connor J, 'Policy Coordination, Social Indicators and the Social-Policy Agenda in the European Union' (2005) 15 JESP 345

Odudu O, 'The Meaning of Undertaking within 81 EC' (2005) 7 CYELS 209

—. *The Boundaries of EC Competition Law: The Scope of Article 81* (OUP 2006)

—. 'Economic Activity as a Limit to Community Law' in Barnard C and Odudu O (eds), *The Outer Limits of European Law* (Hart 2009)

—. 'Are State Owned Healthcare Providers that are Funded by General Taxation Undertakings Subject to Competition Law?' (2011) 32 ECLR 231

Offe C, 'The European Model of "Social" Capitalism: Can it Survive European Integration?' (2003) 11 The Journal of Political Philosophy 437

Office of Fair Trading, 'Exchange of Information on Future Fees by Certain Independent Fee-Paying Schools' (2006) <www.oft.gov.uk/shared_oft/ca98_public_register/decisions/schools.pdf> accessed 1st September 2015

O'Leary S, *The Evolving Concept of Community Citizenship: From the Free Movement of Persons to Union Citizenship* (Kluwer Law International 1996)

—. 'The Free Movement of Persons and Services' in Craig P and De Búrca G (eds), *The Evolution of EU Law* (1st edn, OUP 1999)

—. 'Free Movement of Persons and Services' in Craig P and De Búrca G (eds), *The Evolution of EU Law* (2nd edn, OUP 2011)

Olesen KN, 'Childcare and (Equal) Competition' [2012] EStAL 557

Osborne SP (ed), *The Third Sector in Europe: Prospects and Challenges* (Routledge 2008)

Outhwaite W, 'Who Needs Solidarity?' in Karagiannis N (ed), *European Solidarity* (Liverpool University Press 2007)

—. *Habermas: A Critical Introduction* (2nd edn, Polity Press 2009)

Papadopoulos Y, 'Implementing (and Radicalizing) Art. I-47.4 of the Constitution: Is the Addition of some (Semi-) Direct Democracy to the Nascent Consociational European Federation just Swiss Folklore?' (2005) 12 JEPP 448

—. and Benz A (eds), *Governance and Democracy: Comparing National, European and International Experiences* (Routledge 2006)

—. and Magnette P, 'On the Politicisation of the European Union: Lessons from Consociational National Polities' (2010) 33 West European Politics 711

Parks L, 'Improving Accountability in the European Union–The Potential Role of NGOs' in Gustavsson S, Karlsson C and Persson T (eds), *The Illusion of Accountability in the European Union* (Routledge 2009)

Pateman C, *Participation and Democratic Theory* (CUP 1970)

Peers S, 'From Maastricht to Laeken: The Political Agenda of Openness and Transparency in the European Union' in Deckmyn V (ed), *Increasing Transparency in the European Union* (European Institute of Public Administration 2002)

Pennings F, 'The Draft Patient Mobility Directive and the Coordination Regulations of Social Security' in van de Gronden JW, Szyszczak E, Neergaard U and Krajewski M (eds), *Health Care and EU Law* (TMC Asser Press 2011)

Pérez-Solórzano Borragán N and Smismans S, 'Representativeness: A Tool to Structure Interest Intermediation in the European Union?' (2012) 50 JCMS 403

Pernice I, 'Réferendum sur la Constitution pour l'Europe: Conditions, Risques et Implications' in Kaddous C and Auer A (eds), *Les Principes Fondamentaux de la Constitution Européenne* (Bruylant 2006)

Perri 6, 'European Competition Law and the Non-Profit Sector' (1992) 3 Voluntas 215

Persson T, 'Democratizing European Chemicals Policy: Do Consultations Favour Civil Society Participation?' (2007) 3 Journal of Civil Society 223

—. 'Civil Society Participation and Accountability' in Gustavsson S, Karlsson C and Persson T (eds), *The Illusion of Accountability in the European Union* (Routledge 2009)

Pestoff VA, *Beyond the Market and State: Social Enterprises and Civil Democracy in a Welfare Society* (Ashgate 1998)

—. 'Towards a Paradigm of Democratic Participation: Citizen Participation and Co-Production of Personal Social Services in Sweden' (2009) 80 Annals of Public and Cooperative Economics 197

Philipson TJ and Posner RA, 'Antitrust and the Not-for-Profit Sector' (2001) NBER Working Paper no. 8126 <www.nber.org/papers/w8126> accessed 1st September 2015

—. 'Antitrust in the Not-for-Profit Sector' (2006) NBER Working Paper no. 12132 <www.nber.org/papers/w12132> accessed 1st September 2015

Pichler JW (ed), *We Change Europe! The European Initiative, Art 8b(4) Treaty of Lisbon* (Intersentia 2008)

Pierson P and Leibfried S, 'Multitiered Institutions and the Making of Social Policy' in Leibfried S and Pierson P (eds), *European Social Policy: Between Fragmentation and Integration* (The Brookings Institution 1995)

Piewitt M, Rodekamp M and Steffek J, 'Civil Society in World Politics: How Accountable are Transnational CSOs?' (2010) 6 Journal of Civil Society 237

Piketty T, *Le Capital au* XXIe *siècle* (Seuil 2013)

Piris JC, *The Lisbon Treaty: A Legal and Political Analysis* (CUP 2010)

Pochet P, 'La Lutte contre la Pauvreté et l'Exclusion Sociale et la Méthode Ouverte de Coordination' [2002] Revue Belge de Sécurité Sociale 159

—. 'OMC: A Way to Democratise Europe or/and to Europeanise Social Rights?' (2003) paper prepared for the 8th EUSA conference, Nashville, Tennessee, 27th-30th March 2003

—. 'The Open Method of Co-Ordination and the Construction of Social Europe. A Historical Perspective' in Zeitlin J, Pochet P and Magnusson L (eds), *The Open Method of Co-Ordination in Action: The European Employment and Social Inclusion Strategies* (PIE-Peter Lang 2005)

—. 'What's Wrong with EU2020?' (2010) 45 Intereconomics 141

Pollack MA, 'Blairism in Brussels: the "Third Way" in Europe since Amsterdam' in Green Cowles M and Smith M (eds), *The State of the European Union: Risks, Reform, Resistance, and Revival* (vol 5, OUP 2000)

—. 'Theorizing EU Policy-Making' in Wallace H, Wallace W and Pollack MA (eds), *Policy-Making in the European Union* (5th edn, OUP 2005)

Powell WW (ed), *The Nonprofit Sector: A Research Handbook* (Yale University Press 1987)

Praesidium, 'Preliminary Draft Constitutional Treaty' (28 October 2002, CONV 2002, 369/02)

Prosser T, *The Limits of Competition Law: Markets and Public Services* (OUP 2005)

Public Policy and Management Institute, 'Evaluation of the Effectiveness and Impact of the Social OMC since 2006 – Suggestions for Improvement and Strengthening of the Effectiveness and Impact of the Social OMC' (2011)

Putnam RD, Leonardi R and Nanetti R, *Making Democracy Work: Civic Traditions in Modern Italy* (Princeton University Press 1993)

Quigley C, *European State Aid Law and Policy* (2nd edn, Hart 2009)

Quittkat C, 'The European Commission's Online Consultations: A Success Story?' (2011) 49 JCMS 653

—. 'New Instruments Serving Democracy - Do Online Consultations Benefit Civil Society?' in Kohler-Koch B and Quittkat C with Buth V and Altides C, *De-Mystification of Participatory Democracy: EU Governance and Civil Society* (OUP 2013)

—. 'Consultation in Daily Practice' in Kohler-Koch B and Quittkat C with Buth V and Altides C, *De-Mystification of Participatory Democracy: EU Governance and Civil Society* (OUP 2013)

—. and Finke B, 'The EU Commission Consultation Regime' in Kohler-Koch B, De Bièvre D and Maloney W (eds), *Opening EU-Governance to Civil Society - Gains and Challenges* (2008) CONNEX Report Series no. 5 <www.mzes.uni-mannheim.de/projekte/typo3/site/index.php?id=596> accessed 1st September 2015

—. and Kotzian P, 'Lobbying via Consultation - Territorial and Functional Interests in the Commission's Consultation Regime' (2011) 33 Journal of European Integration 401

Radaelli CM, 'The Open Method of Coordination: A New Governance Architecture for the European Union?' (2003) Sieps Report no. 1 <http://eucenter.wisc.edu/OMC/Papers/radaelli.pdf> accessed 1st September 2015

Radulova E, 'The OMC: An Opaque Method of Consideration or Deliberative Governance in Action?' (2007) 29 Journal of European Integration 363

Regent S, 'The Open Method of Coordination: A New Supranational Form of Governance' (2003) 9 ELJ 190

Richardson J (ed), *European Union: Power and Policy-Making* (3rd edn, Routledge 2006)

Risse-Kappen T, 'Exploring the Nature of the Beast: International Relations Theory and Comparative Policy Analysis Meet the European Union' (1996) 34 JCMS 53

Rodekamp M, 'Representing their Members? Civil Society Organizations and the EU's External Dimension' in Kröger S and Friedrich D (eds), *The Challenge of Democratic Representation in the European Union* (Palgrave Macmillan 2012)

Rodrigues MJ, 'The Open Method of Coordination as a New Governance Tool' (2001) 9–10 Journal Europa

—. and Xiarchogiannopoulou E (eds), *The Eurozone Crisis and the Transformation of EU Governance: Internal and External Implications* (Ashgate 2014, ebook)

Rodrigues S, 'Towards a General EC Framework Instrument related to SGEI? Political Considerations and Legal Constraints' in Krajewski M, Neergaard U and van de Gronden JW (eds), *The Changing Legal Framework for Services of General Interest in Europe: Between Competition and Solidarity* (TMC Asser Press 2009)

Rojanski V, 'L'Union Européenne et les Services d'Intérêt Général' [2002] RDUE 735

Rosenblum NL and Post RC (eds), *Civil Society and Government* (Princeton University Press 2002)

Ross M, 'Article 16 E.C. and Services of General Interest: from Derogation to Obligation?' (2000) 25 EL Rev 22

—. 'Promoting Solidarity: From Public Services to a European Model of Competition?' (2007) 44 CML Rev 1057

—. and Borgmann-Prebil Y (eds), *Promoting Solidarity in the European Union* (OUP 2010)
Rousseau JJ, *The Social Contract or Principles of Political Right* (first published 1762, Cole GDH tr, EP Dutton and Co 1913)
Ruzza C, *Europe and Civil Society* (Manchester University Press 2007)
Ruzza C and Della Sala V (eds), *Governance and Civil Society in the European Union: Normative Perspectives* (vol 1, Manchester University Press 2007)
Sabatakakis E, 'De Nouvelles Voies pour l'Europe Sociale: Réflexions autour des Services Sociaux d'Intérêt Général' [2010] RMUE 197
Sabel CF and Simon WH, 'Epilogue: Accountability without Sovereignty' in De Búrca G and Scott J (eds), *Law and New Governance in the EU and the US* (Hart 2006)
Sabel CF and Zeitlin J, 'Active Welfare, Experimental Governance, Pragmatic Constitutionalism: The New Transformation of Europe' (2003) draft prepared for the international conference of the Hellenic Presidency of the European Union, "The Modernisation of the European Social Model & EU Policies and Instruments", Ioannina, Greece, 21–22 May 2003
—. 'Learning from Difference: The New Architecture of Experimentalist Governance in the EU' (2008) 14 ELJ 271
Salamon LM and Anheier HK, 'Social Origins of Civil Society: Explaining the Nonprofit Sector Cross-Nationally' (1998) 9 Voluntas 213
Salamon LM, Sokolowski SW and List R, *Global Civil Society: An Overview* (Johns Hopkins Center for Civil Society Studies 2003)
Sánchez Salgado R, 'Giving a European Dimension to Civil Society Organizations' (2007) 3 Journal of Civil Society 253
—. 'Rebalancing EU Interest Representation? Associative Democracy and EU Funding of Civil Society Organizations' (2012) draft article
—. and Parthenay K, 'Fostering Regional Democracy Through Civic Organisations: Comparing EU Mechanisms in Europe and Central America' (2013) 35 Journal of European Integration 151
Saurugger S, 'The Professionalisation of Interest Representation: a Legitimacy Problem for Civil Society in the EU?' in Smismans S (ed), *Civil Society and Legitimate European Governance* (Edward Elgar 2006)
—. 'Interest Groups and Democracy in the European Union' in Beyers J, Eising R and Maloney W (eds), *Interest Group Politics in Europe: Lessons from EU Studies and Comparative Politics* (Routledge 2010)
Sauter W, *Competition Law and Industrial Policy in the EU* (Clarendon Press 1997)
—. 'Services of General Economic Interest and Universal Service in EU Law' (2008) 33 EL Rev 167
—. 'Harmonization in Health Care: The EU Patients' Rights Directive' in Cantillon B, Verschueren H and Ploscar P (eds), *Social Inclusion and Social Protection in the EU: Interactions between Law and Policy* (Intersentia 2012)
—. 'The Altmark Package Mark II: New Rules for State Aid and the Compensation of Services of General Economic Interest' (2012) 33 ECLR 307
—. and Schepel H, '"State" and "Market" in the Competition and Free Movement Case Law of the EU Courts' (2007) TILEC Discussion Paper no. 2007/24
—. and Schepel H, *State and Market in European Union Law: The Public and Private Spheres of the Internal Market before the EU Courts* (CUP 2009)

Scharpf FW, *Governing Europe: Effective and Democratic?* (OUP 1999)

—. 'The European Social Model: Coping with the Challenges of Diversity' (2002) 40 JCMS 645

—. 'Problem Solving Effectiveness and Democratic Accountability in the EU' (2006) Political Science Series no. 107, Institute for Advanced Studies, Vienna

—. 'Legitimacy in the Multi-level European Polity' in Dobner P and Loughlin M (eds), *The Twilight of Constitutionalism?* (OUP 2010)

—. 'The Asymmetry of European Integration, or Why the EU Cannot Be a "Social Market Economy"' (2010) 8 Socio-Economic Review 211

—. 'Monetary Union, Fiscal Crisis and the Pre-Emption of Democracy' (2011) 9 Zeitschrift für Staats- und Europawissenschaften 163

—. 'Political Legitimacy in a Non-Optimal Currency Area' (2013) MPlfG Discussion Paper 13/15

Schelkle W, 'EU Fiscal Governance: Hard Law in the Shadow of Soft Law' (2006–2007) 13 CJEL 705

Scheuerman W, 'Economic Globalization and the Rule of Law' (1999) 6 Constellations 3

—. 'Reflexive Law and the Challenges of Globalization' (2001) 9 The Journal of Political Philosophy 81

—. 'Democratic Experimentalism or Capitalist Synchronization? Critical Reflections on Directly Deliberative Polyarchy' (2004) 17 Can J L & Jurisprudence 101

Schiek D, 'Re-Embedding Economic and Social Constitutionalism: Normative Perspectives for the EU' in Schiek D, Liebert U and Schneider H (eds), *European Economic and Social Constitutionalism after the Treaty of Lisbon* (CUP 2011)

—. Liebert U and Schneider H (eds), *European Economic and Social Constitutionalism after the Treaty of Lisbon* (CUP 2011)

Schlesinger P and Kevin D, 'Can the European Union Become a Sphere of Publics' in Eriksen EO and Fossum JE (eds), *Democracy in the European Union: Integration through Deliberation?* (Routledge 2000)

Schmalz-Bruns R, 'The Euro-Polity in Perspective: Some Normative Lessons from Deliberative Democracy' in Kohler-Koch B and Rittberger B (eds), *Debating the Democratic Legitimacy of the European Union* (Rowman & Littlefield 2007)

Schmitter PC, 'Governance in the European Union: A Viable Mechanism for Future Legitimation?' in Papadopoulos Y and Benz A (eds), *Governance and Democracy: Comparing National, European and International Experiences* (Routledge 2006)

—. 'Revisiting some "Modest Proposals" for Making the European Union More Democratic' in Moury C and de Sousa L (eds), *Institutional Challenges in Post-Constitutional Europe: Governing Change* (Routledge 2009)

Scholte JA (ed), *Building Global Democracy? Civil Society and Accountable Global Governance* (CUP 2011)

Schoukens P and Smets JB, 'Fighting Social Exclusion under EU Horizon 2020: Enhancing the Legal Enforceability of the Social Inclusion Recommendations?' (2014) 16 EJSS 51

Schumpeter JA, *Capitalism, Socialism and Democracy* (5th edn, Allen and Unwin 1976)

Schweitzer H, 'Competition Law and Public Policy: Reconsidering an Uneasy Relationship: The Example of Art. 81' (2007) EUI Working Papers LAW 2007/30

<http://papers.ssrn.com/sol3/papers.cfm?abstract_id=1092883> accessed 1st September 2015

—. 'Services of General Economic Interest: European Law's Impact on the Role of Markets and of Member States' in Cremona M (ed), *Market Integration and Public Services in the European Union* (OUP 2011)

Scott J and Sturm S, 'Courts as Catalysts: Re-Thinking the Judicial Role in New Governance' (2006–2007) 13 CJEL 565

Scott J and Trubek DM, 'Mind the Gap: Law and New Approaches to Governance in the European Union' (2002) 8 ELJ 1

Semmelmann C, *Social Policy Goals in the Interpretation of Article 81 EC* (Nomos 2008)

Shapiro M, 'The Giving Reasons Requirement' [1992] U Chic Legal Forum 179

—. 'Codification of Administrative Law: The US and the Union' (1996) 2 ELJ 26

Shaw J (ed), *Social Law and Policy in an Evolving European Union* (Hart 2000)

Shuibhne NN, 'Case C-76/05 *Schwarz and Gootjes-Schwarz v. Finanzamt Bergisch Gladbach*, Judgment of the Grand Chamber of 11 September 2007, Not Yet Reported; Case C-318/05, *Commission v.Germany*, Judgment of the Grand Chamber of 11 September 2007, Not Yet Reported; Joined Cases C-11/06 & C-12/06 *Morgan v. Bezirksregierung Köln; Bucher v. Landrat Des Kreises Düren*Judgment of the Grand Chamber of 23 October 2007, Not Yet Reported' (2008) 45 CML Rev 771

Sintomer Y, *La Démocratie Participative* (La Documentation Française 2009)

Smismans S, 'European Civil Society: Shaped by Discourses and Institutional Interests' (2003) 9 ELJ 482

—. *Law, Legitimacy, and European Governance: Functional Participation in Social Regulation* (OUP 2004)

—. 'The Constitutional Labelling of "the Democratic Life of the EU": Representative and Participatory Democracy' in Dobson L and Follesdal A (eds), *Political Theory and the European Constitution* (Routledge 2004)

—. 'How to Be Fundamental with Soft Procedures? The Open Method of Coordination and Fundamental Social Rights' in de Búrca G and de Witte B (eds), *Social Rights in Europe* (OUP 2005)

—. 'Reflexive Law in Support of Directly Deliberative Polyarchy: Reflexive-Deliberative Polyarchy as a Normative Frame for the OMC' in De Schutter O and Deakin S (eds), *Social Rights and Market Forces: Is the Open Coordination of Employment and Social Policies the Future of Social Europe?* (Bruylant 2005)

—. 'Civil Society and European Governance: The Interdisciplinary Challenge of Reflexive Deliberative Polyarchy' in Smismans S (ed), *Civil Society and Legitimate European Governance* (Edward Elgar 2006)

—. (ed), *Civil Society and Legitimate European Governance* (Edward Elgar 2006)

—. 'New Governance - the Solution for Active European Citizenship, or the End of Citizenship?' (2007) 13 CJEL 595

—. 'New Modes of Governance and the Participatory Myth' (2008) 31 West European Politics 874

—. 'From Harmonization to Co-Ordination? EU Law in the Lisbon Governance Architecture' (2011) 18 JEPP 504

—. 'Interest Representation in the EU-Is There Any?' in Kröger S and Friedrich D (eds), *The Challenge of Democratic Representation in the European Union* (Palgrave Macmillan 2012)
Smith G, 'The European Citizens' Initiative: a New Institution for Empowering Europe's Citizens?' in Dougan M, Shuibhne NN and Spaventa E (eds), *Empowerment and Disempowerment of the European Citizen* (Hart 2012)
Snell J and Andenas M, 'Exploring the Outer Limits: Restrictions on the Free Movement of Goods and Services' in Andenas M and Roth W (eds), *Services and Free Movement in EU Law* (OUP 2002)
Sousa Ferro M, 'Popular Legislative Initiative in the EU: Alea Iacta Est' (2007) 26 YEL 355
Spaventa E, 'Public Services and European Law: Looking for Boundaries' (2003) 5 CYELS 271
—. *Free Movement of Persons in the European Union: Barriers to Movement in their Constitutional Context* (Kluwer Law International 2007)
—. and Dougan M (eds), *Social Welfare and EU Law* (Hart 2005)
SPC, 'Realising the European Union's Potential: Consolidating and Extending the Lisbon Strategy – Contribution of the European Commission to the Spring European Council, Stockholm, 23 and 24 March 2001' (Opinion) (2001) Doc 6455/01
—. 'Report on Indicators in the Field of Poverty and Social Exclusion' (2001) Doc 13509/01
—. 'The Lisbon Strategy – Making Change Happen' (Opinion) (2002) Doc 6644/02
—. 'Fight against Poverty and Social Exclusion: Common Objectives for the Second Round of National Action Plans– Endorsement' (2002) Doc 14164/02
—. 'Strengthening the Social Dimension of the Lisbon Strategy: Streamlining Open Coordination in the Field of Social Protection' (Opinion) (2003) Doc 12909/1/03
—. 'Common Outline for the 2003/2005 NAPs/Inclusion' (2003)
—. 'Report from the SPC Working Group on the Mutual Interaction between the Common Social Objectives and the Strategies for Growth and Jobs' (2007)
—. 'A Renewed Commitment to Social Europe: Reinforcing the Open Method of Coordination for Social Protection and Social Inclusion' (Opinion) (2008) Doc 15308/08
—. 'Operational Conclusions on the Application of Community Rules to SSGI' SPC (2008) 17 final
—. 'The Social Dimension of the Europe 2020 Strategy' (Opinion) (2010) SPC/2010/10/7 final
—. 'A Voluntary European Quality Framework for Social Services' (2010) SPC/2010/10/8 final
—. 'The European Platform against Poverty and Social Exclusion-Flagship Initiative of the Europe 2020 Strategy' (Opinion) (2011) Doc 6491/11
—. 'Reinvigorating the Social OMC in the Context of the Europe 2020 Strategy' (Opinion) (2011) Doc 10405/11
—. 'Preparation of the 2012 National Social Reports (NSR)' (Guidance Note) (2012) SPC/2012.2/4
—. 'Social Europe: Current Challenges and the Way Forward – Annual Report of the Social Protection Committee (2012)' (2013)

—. 'Social Policy Reforms for Growth and Cohesion: Review of Recent Structural Reforms 2013 – Report of the Social Protection Committee' (2013)
—. and EPC, 'Joint Opinion on the Communication "Working Together, Working Better"' (2006) Doc 6801/06
—. and EPC, 'Europe 2020 Strategy: Mid-term review, including the evaluation of the European Semester' (Joint Opinion) (2014) Doc 13809/14
SSGI Collective (ed), *Les Services Sociaux et de Santé d'Intérêt Général: Droits Fondamentaux versus Marché Intérieur?* (Bruylant 2006)
Steffek J and Ferretti MP, 'Accountability or "Good Decisions"? The Competing Goals of Civil Society Participation in International Governance' (2009) 23 Global Society 37
Steffek J, Kissling C and Nanz P (eds), *Civil Society Participation in European and Global Governance: A Cure for the Democratic Deficit?* (Palgrave Macmillan 2008)
Steffek J and Nanz P, 'Emergent Patterns of Civil Society Participation in Global and European Governance' in Steffek J, Kissling C and Nanz P (eds), *Civil Society Participation in European and Global Governance: A Cure for the Democratic Deficit?* (Palgrave Macmillan 2008)
Steinberg R, 'Nonprofit Organizations and the Market' in Powell WW (ed), *The Nonprofit Sector: A Research Handbook* (Yale University Press 1987)
Stevens S, 'Tax Aid and Non-profit Organizations' (2010) 19 EC Tax Rev 156
Stevenson A, *Oxford Dictionary of English* (3rd edn, OUP 2010)
Stiglitz JE, *Globalization and its Discontents* (Penguin 2002)
Stjerno S, *Solidarity in Europe: the History of an Idea* (CUP 2004)
Stoger K, 'The Freedom of Establishment and the Market Access of Hospital Operators' (2006) 17 EBLR 1545
Streeck W, 'Neo-Voluntarism: A New European Social Policy Regime?' in Marks G, Scharpf FW, Schmitter PC and Streeck W (eds), *Governance in the European Union* (Sage Publications 1996)
Sudbery I, 'Bridging the Legitimacy Gap in the EU: Can Civil Society Help to Bring the Union Closer to its Citizens?' (2003) 26 Collegium 75
Szyszczak E, 'The New Paradigm for Social Policy: a Virtuous Circle?' (2001) 38 CML Rev 1125
—. 'Experimental Governance: The Open Method of Coordination' (2006) 12 ELJ 486
—. *The Regulation of the State in Competitive Markets in the EU* (Hart 2007)
—. 'Modernising State Aid and the Financing of SGEI' (2012) 3 JECL&P 332
—. Davies J, Andenæs M and Bekkedal T (eds), *Developments in Services of General Interest* (TMC Asser Press 2011)
—. Neergaard U and van de Gronden JW, 'Conclusions' in Neergaard U, Szyszczak E, van de Gronden JW and Krajewski M (eds), *Social Services of General Interest in the EU* (TMC Asser Press 2013)
Tanasescu I, *The European Commission and Interest Groups: Towards a Deliberative Interpretation of Stakeholder Involvement in EU Policy-Making* (VUB Press 2009)
Taylor RCR and Hall PA, 'La Science Politique et les Trois Néo-Institutionnalismes' (1997) 47 Revue Française de Science Politique 469
Teubner G, 'Substantive and Reflexive Elements in Modern Law' (1983) 17 Law & Society Review 239

—. 'After Legal Instrumentalism? Strategic Models of Post-Regulatory Law' in Teubner G (ed), *Dilemmas of Law in the Welfare State* (De Gruyter 1986)
Thieffry P, 'Les Services Sociaux d'Intérêt Général sont-ils des Entreprises?' (2007) 63 AJDA Hebdo: L'Actualité Juridique. Droit Administratif 1331
Tholoniat L, 'The Career of the Open Method of Coordination: Lessons from a "Soft" EU Instrument' (2010) 33 West European Politics 93
Titmuss RM, 'What is Social Policy?' in Leibried S and Mau S (eds), *Welfare States: Construction, Deconstruction, Reconstruction* (Edward Elgar 2008)
Townley C, *Article 81 EC and Public Policy* (Hart 2009)
—. 'Which Goals Count in Article 101 TFEU? Public Policy and its Discontents: the OFT's Roundtable Discussion on Article 101 (3) of the Treaty on the Functioning of the European Union' (2011) 32 ECLR 441
Trenz HJ, 'A Transnational Space of Contention? Patterns of Europeanisation of Civil Society in Germany' in Ruzza C and Della Sala V (eds), *Governance and Civil Society in the European Union: Normative Perspectives* (vol 1, Manchester University Press 2007)
—. 'European Civil Society: Between Participation, Representation and Discourse' (2009) 28 Policy and Society 35
—. and Eder K, 'The Democratizing Dynamics of a European Public Sphere: Towards a Theory of Democratic Functionalism' (2004) 7 European Journal of Social Theory 5
Trubek DM and Trubek LG, 'The Open Method of Co-Ordination and the Debate Over "Hard" and "Soft" Law' in Zeitlin J, Pochet P and Magnusson L (eds), *The Open Method of Co-Ordination in Action: The European Employment and Social Inclusion Strategies* (PIE-Peter Lang 2005)
Tsakatika M, 'The Open Method of Co-Ordination in the European Convention: An Opportunity Lost?' in Dobson L and Follesdal A (eds), *Political Theory and the European Constitution* (Routledge 2004)
—. 'A Parliamentary Dimension for EU Soft Governance' (2007) 29 Journal of European Integration 549
—. 'Governance Vs. Politics: The European Union's Constitutive "Democratic Deficit"' (2007) 14 JEPP 867
van Apeldoorn B, Drahokoupil J and Horn L (eds), *Contradictions and Limits of Neoliberal European Governance: From Lisbon to Lisbon* (Palgrave MacMillan 2009)
van de Gronden JW, 'Social Services of General Interest and EU Law' in Szyszczak E, Davies J, Andenæs M and Bekkedal T (eds), *Developments in Services of General Interest* (TMC Asser Press 2011)
—. Szyszczak E, Neergaard U and Krajewski M (eds), *Health Care and EU Law* (TMC Asser Press 2011)
—. 'Free Movement of Services and the Right of Establishment: Does EU Internal Market Law Transform the Provision of SSGI?' in Neergaard U, Szyszczak E, van de Gronden JW and Krajewski M (eds), *Social Services of General Interest in the EU* (TMC Asser Press 2013)
Van den Abeele E, 'Les Services d'Intérêt Général. État du Débat Européen' (2005) 1901–1902 Courrier Hebdomadaire du CRISP 21

Van Der Mei AP, *Free Movement of Persons within the European Community: Cross-Border Access to Public Benefits* (Hart 2003)

—. 'EU Law and Education: Promotion of Student Mobility Versus Protection of Education Systems' in Spaventa E and Dougan M (eds), *Social Welfare and EU Law* (Hart 2005)

van Deth JW, 'The "Good European Citizen": Congruence and Consequences of Different Points of View' (2009) 8 European Political Science 175

—. Montero JR and Westholm A (eds), *Citizenship and Involvement in European Democracies: A Comparative Analysis* (Routledge 2006)

Vanhercke B, 'Delivering the Goods for Europe 2020? The Social OMC's Adequacy and Impact Re-Assessed' in Marlier E and Natali D (eds), *Europe 2020: Towards a More Social EU*? (PIE- Peter Lang 2010)

van Schendelen MP, *Machiavelli in Brussels: The Art of Lobbying the EU* (Amsterdam University Press 2002)

Verhoeven A, 'Democratic Life in the European Union, According to its Constitution' in Curtin D and Wessels W (eds), *Good Governance and the European Union: Reflections on Concepts, Institutions and Substance* (Intersentia 2005)

Verschueren H, 'Union Law and the Fight against Poverty: Which Legal Instruments?' in Cantillon B, Verschueren H and Ploscar P (eds), *Social Inclusion and Social Protection in the EU: Interactions between Law and Policy* (Intersentia 2012)

Vizcaino A, Jose M and Obradovic D, 'Good Governance Requirements Concerning the Participation of Interest Groups in EU Consultations' (2006) 43 CML Rev 1049

Voermans W and Schuurmans Y, 'Better Regulation by Appeal' (2011) 17 EPL 507

Von Bogdandy A, 'The European Lesson for International Democracy: the Significance of Articles 9–12 EU Treaty for International Organizations' (2012) 23 EJIL 315

Walker N and De Búrca G, 'Reconceiving Law and New Governance' (2006–2007) 13 CJEL 519

Walzer M, 'The Civil Society Argument' in Mouffe C (ed), *Dimensions of Radical Democracy* (Verso 1992)

Warleigh A, '"Europeanizing" Civil Society: NGOs as Agents of Political Socialization' (2001) 39 JCMS 619

—. 'Civil Society and Legitimate Governance in a Flexible Europe: Critical Deliberativism as a Way Forward' in Smismans S (ed), *Civil Society and Legitimate European Governance* (Edward Elgar 2006)

—. 'Making Citizens from the Market? NGOs and the Representation of Interests' in Bellamy R, Castiglione D and Shaw J (eds), *Making European Citizens: Civic Inclusion in a Transnational Context* (Palgrave Macmillan 2006)

—. 'On the Path to Legitimacy? A Critical Deliberativist Perspective on the Right to the Citizens' Initiative' in Ruzza C and Della Sala V (eds), *Governance and Civil Society in the European Union: Normative Perspectives* (vol 1, Manchester University Press 2007)

—. and Fairbrass J (eds), *Influence and Interests in the European Union: The New Politics of Persuasion and Advocacy* (Europa Publications 2002)

Warren ME, *Democracy and Association* (Princeton University Press 2001)

Watson P, *EU Social and Employment Law: Policy and Practice in an Enlarged Europe* (OUP 2009)

Weale A, *Democracy* (Macmillan Press 1999)
—. and Nentwich M (eds), *Political Theory and the European Union* (Routledge 1998)
Weiler JHH, *The Constitution of Europe: "Do the New Clothes Have an Emperor?" and Other Essays on European Integration* (CUP 1999)
Weisbrod BA, *The Nonprofit Economy* (Harvard University Press 1988)
Wendt I and Gideon A, 'Services of General Interest Provision through the Third Sector under EU Competition Law Constraints: The Example of Organising Healthcare in England, Wales and the Netherlands' in Schiek D, Liebert U and Schneider H (eds), *European Economic and Social Constitutionalism after the Treaty of Lisbon* (CUP 2011)
Wesseling R, 'The Commission White Paper on Modernisation of E.C. Antitrust Law: Unspoken Consequences and Incomplete Treatment of Alternative Options' (1999) 20 ECLR 420
—. *The Modernisation of EC Antitrust Law* (Hart 2000)
Whish R, *Competition Law* (6th edn, OUP 2008)
—. and Bailey D, *Competition Law* (7th edn, OUP 2012)
White R, *Workers, Establishment, and Services in the European Union* (OUP 2004)
Will C and Kendall J, 'A New Settlement for Europe: towards "Open, Transparent and Regular Dialogue with Representatives Associations and Civil Society"?' in Kendall J (ed), *Handbook on Third Sector Policy in Europe: Multi-Level Processes and Organized Civil Society* (Edward Elgar 2009)
Wincott D, 'Beyond Social Regulation? New Instruments and/or a New Agenda for Social Policy at Lisbon?' (2003) 81 Public Administration 533
Winterstein A, 'Nailing the Jellyfish: Social Security and Competition Law' (1999) 20 ECLR 324
Witt AC, 'Public Policy Goals under EU Competition Law–Now is the Time to Set the House in Order' (2012) 8 ECJ 443
Wolfe JD, 'A Defense of Participatory Democracy' (1985) 47 The Review of Politics 370
Wolff C, *Functional Representation and Democracy in the EU* (ECPR Press 2013)
Zeitlin J, 'The Open Method of Co-Ordination in Question' in Zeitlin J, Pochet P and Magnusson L (eds), *The Open Method of Co-Ordination in Action: The European Employment and Social Inclusion Strategies* (PIE-Peter Lang 2005)
—. 'The Open Method of Co-Ordination in Action: Theoretical Promise, Empirical Realities, Reform Strategy' in Zeitlin J, Pochet P and Magnusson L (eds), *The Open Method of Co-Ordination in Action: The European Employment and Social Inclusion Strategies* (PIE-Peter Lang 2005)
—. 'Social Europe and Experimentalist Governance: Towards a New Constitutional Compromise?' in De Búrca G (ed), *EU Law and the Welfare State: In Search of Solidarity* (OUP 2005)
—. 'The Open Method of Co-Ordination and the Governance of the Lisbon Strategy' (2008) 46 JCMS 436
—. 'The Open Method of Coordination and Reform of National Social and Employment Policies: Influences, Mechanisms, Effects' in Heidenreich M and Zeitlin J (eds), *Changing European Employment and Welfare Regimes: The Influence of the Open Method of Coordination on National Reforms* (Routledge 2009)

—. 'Towards a Stronger OMC in a More Social Europe 2020: A New Governance Architecture for EU Policy Coordination' in Marlier E and Natali D (eds), *Europe 2020: Towards a More Social EU*? (PIE- Peter Lang 2010)

—. 'Is the Open Method of Coordination an Alternative to the Community Method?' in Dehousse R (ed), *The "Community Method": Obstinate or Obsolete?* (Palgrave Macmillan 2011)

—. Pochet P and Magnusson L (eds), *The Open Method of Co-Ordination in Action: The European Employment and Social Inclusion Strategies* (PIE-Peter Lang 2005)

—. and Trubek DM (eds), *Governing Work and Welfare in a New Economy: European and American Experiments* (OUP 2003)

—. and Vanhercke B, 'Socializing the European Semester? Economic Governance and Social Policy Coordination in Europe 2020' (2014) SIEPS 2014:7

Zittel T, 'Participatory Engineering: Promises and Pitfalls' in Kohler-Koch B, De Bièvre D and Maloney W (eds), *Opening EU-Governance to Civil Society – Gains and Challenges* (2008) CONNEX Report Series no. 5 <www.mzes.uni-mannheim.de/projekte/typo3/site/index.php?id=596> accessed 1st September 2015

Zweifel TD, 'Who is Without Sin Cast the First Stone: The EU's Democratic Deficit in Comparison' (2002) 9 JEPP 812

www.ingramcontent.com/pod-product-compliance
Ingram Content Group UK Ltd.
Pitfield, Milton Keynes, MK11 3LW, UK
UKHW051041120926
8556IPUK00030B/497